An Introduction to Medical Sociology

An Introduction
to Medical Sociology

Edited by

David Tuckett

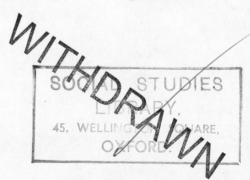

TAVISTOCK PUBLICATIONS

First published in 1976
by Tavistock Publications Limited
11 New Fetter Lane, London EC4P 4EE
Typeset by EWC Wilkins Ltd., London and Northampton
Printed in Great Britain by Fletcher & Son Ltd, Norwich

ISBN 0 422 74510 3 (hardback)
ISBN 0 422 74320 8 (paperback)

Contents

Acknowledgements

The publishers and authors would like to thank the following bodies for permission to repint material in the book:

Chapter 1: The Royal College of General Practitioners for *Tables 3, 4, 5, 6,* and *7* which appeared in *General Practice: Present State and Future Needs* (1973: 19—20). *The New England Journal of Medicine* for *Figure 1* which appeared in the article 'Reduction of Postoperative Pain by Encouragement and Instruction of Patients' by J.A. Egbert *et al.* (1964, 27: 826).

Chapter 4: Churchill Livingstone for *Figures 1 and 2* which appeared in *The Uses of Epidemiology* by J. Morris (1967: 57). *New Society* for *Table 4* which appeared in 'Workplace Inequality' by Dorothy Wedderburn (1970, 15: 593). Oxford University Press, Oxford for *Table 5* which appeared in *The Social Grading of Occupation: A New Approach and Scale* edited by John H. Goldthorpe and Keith Hope (1974: 134—43; © Oxford University Press). Routledge & Kegan Paul for *Table 6* which appeared in *Social Mobility in Britain* edited by David Glass (1954: 182). The Controller of Her Majesty's Stationery Office for *Table 6* which appeared in *Labour Mobility in Britain: 1953—63. An Enquiry Undertaken for the Ministry of Labour and National Service* (1966: 49). Routledge & Kegan Paul for *Table 7* which appeared in David Glass *op. cit.* (1954: 183). Routledge & Kegan Paul for pages 137—140 which appeared in *The Symmetrical Family* by Michael Young and Peter Willmott (1973: 43—5; 60—63). Cambridge University Press for *Table 8* which appeared in *The Affluent Worker in the Class Structure* by John H. Goldthorpe *et al.* (1969: 118—21).

Chapter 5: The American Medical Association for *Figure 2* which appeared in the article 'Health Behavior, Illness Behavior and Sick-Role Behavior' by S. Kasl and S. Cobb published in *Archives of Environmental Health* (1966, 12: 252, 258; © 1966 The American Medical Association). Routledge and Kegan Paul for *Table 1* which appeared in *Medicine Takers, Prescribers and Hoarders* by K. Dunnell and A. Cartwright (1972: 65).

Chapter 7: Aldine Publishing Company for *Figure 1* which appeared in *Hospitals and Patients* by W. Rosengren and E. Lefton (1969: 125).

Chapter 9: The American Academy of Pediatrics for *Table 1* which appeared in the article 'Streptococcal Infections in Families' by R.J. Meyer and R.J. Haggerty published in *Pediatrics* (1962), 29: 544). Pergamon Press for *Table 2* which appeared in the article 'Psychosocial Factors in the Epidemiology of Rheumatoid Arthritis' published in *Journal of Chronic Diseases (1958, 7: 468)*. Basic Books, Inc. for *Table 3* which appeared in *The Character of Danger* by D.C. Leighton *et al.* (1963: 331; © 1963 Alexander H. Leighton, Basic Books, Inc., Publishers, New York).

Chapter 10: Lois A. Monteiro for *Table 2* reproduced from *Social Factors Influencing the Outcome of Heart Attacks*, Ph.D. Dissertation, Brown University.

Chapter 11: Cassell & Collier Macmillan for *Figure 1* which appeared in the article 'Demography Culture and Economics and the Evolutionary Stages of Medicine' by W. McDermott, published in *Human Ecology and Public Health* edited by E.D. Kilbourne and W.G. Smillie (1969: 15). The British Association for the Advancement of Science for *Figure 2* which appeared in 'The Contribution of the Biological and Medical Sciences to Human Welfare', Presidential Address of the British Association for the Advancement of Science, Swansea Meeting, 1971.

Preface

This book is intended to fill what I have felt to to be a gap in the literature on medical sociology available to all those who work in the field of health and to sociologists. I hope that in it most of the issues that concern those working in the field are at least raised. Nonetheless it represents a personal choice of subjects and material and I would like to give some brief explanation of my purpose and of the way I hope the book will be used.

Above all it is not meant to be read religiously from one chapter to the next. Rather it is intended to serve as a resource — as a place to find some of the basic data and arguments and as a place to find opinions which can be challenged and discussed. I have made no attempt to disguise my prejudices and I have instructed the other authors to do the same. As a student and a teacher I have always hated textbooks and find it impossible to think and learn if all I am expected to do is to digest. The book is provocative enough to encourage thought. At the same time I hope it is sufficiently clearly written and argued to merit serious consideration and not to be put aside in indignation.

In the first chapter I have tried to suggest why I think sociology is now important for medical practice. I have also introduced some of the sociological concepts I find helpful (sociologists, who I hope will also read the book, can happily leave this out) before briefly reviewing what I take to be the scope of sociological contributions to medicine.

The book is then divided into three sections. There are three introductory chapters dealing with sociological methods, with theories of the family, and with social class and stratification. Although written with a medical bias those chapters are what might be expected in a general sociology text. They introduce basic sociological ideas and will I hope be useful to medical readers. Again they can be safely ignored by any sociologists. The main section of the book deals with various substantive areas of medical sociology — illness behaviour (Chapter 5); doctor-patient relationships (Chapter 6); the organization of hospitals (Chapter 7); the organization of the National Health Service (Chapter 8); social causes of disease (Chapter 9); and issues of labelling and stigma (Chapter 10). The final chapter tries to pull some of the threads together and presents some of my views on medicine and its future. But it is not a conclusion in any real sense.

I have used sections of individual chapters for teaching purposes as a background to present work, lectures, and discussion and this is how I hope the book will be used. Each chapter can, more or less, be used on its own and where necessary I have put in cross-references. Each chapter has its own bibliography, some of which are annotated and provide a guide to further reading as well as a chance to assess the evidence.

Producing the book has, for me, been hard labour and I would especially like to thank George Brown, Margaret Jefferys, and Alwyn Smith for their painstaking criticism and advice, without which the book would have been a great deal worse off. In addition many colleagues at the Social Research Unit (Bedford College) and at the Academic Department of Psychiatry (Middlesex Hospital Medical School), as well as others elsewhere, have given advice and support. I should particularly like to mention David Armstrong, John Ashley, Pamela Bull, Susannah Ginsberg, Uta Gerhadt, John Goldthorpe, Susan Harrow, John Hinton, Pearl King, Miller Mair, Juliet Mitchell, Marie Moyer, Adrian Munsey, Sue Pollock, Michael Shaw, Tae Willmott, and Sherry Zeffert. The writers of Chapter 8 would like to thank Tony Smart for advice.

I should also like to thank all my past students. The book is for them. Of course, the responsibility for the errors that remain and for the general tone and emphasis of the arguments, remain with me and the individual authors, all of whom bear responsibility only for their own chapters.

David Tuckett
March 1975

Part I

Introduction

Chapter I

David Tuckett

Introduction

It is now some years since the official bodies that control medical education in the UK recommended that all medical students should pursue studies of sociology (General Medical Council, 1967: 15; Royal Commission on Medical Education, 1968: 104—9). Over the last few years it has become commonplace for these students, as well as for many doctors with long experience in clinical work, to take some kind of sociology course. Yet to many of those required to follow sociology courses, and indeed to many of those who have required students to do sociology, the subject is something of an obscure mystery — often considered to have some relationship to socialism or to social work. In this chapter I want to consider some of the features of present-day medical practice that have led to the inclusion of sociology as a useful preparatory discipline and then go on to introduce some of the sociological concepts I consider salient to medical practitioners. Finally, I will review some of the issues in medical practice that I believe can be illuminated by sociology.

But first I should issue a warning: in some respects sociology may be frustrating to the would-be practitioner. Whereas the medical student, particularly at an early stage of his career, wants cut and dried answers, recommendations, and solutions, he will find that the sociologists writing in this book seem to provide only questions, complications, and ways of looking at medical practice. In this respect the sociologist's approach may be rather different from those he experiences in many other subjects. Nonetheless, I believe it to be profoundly useful. Through greater sociological understanding many clinical judgments may be made more rationally; much of the frustration in present-day practice may be overcome; the behaviour of patients, of colleagues, and of large organizations may be better appreciated; and the doctor may be able to exercise the therapeutic skills he has learnt in other parts of his training more effectively for the benefit of his patients. Wherever possible, the authors will try to indicate how we think sociology can be useful. But inevitably clinical practice consists of individual cases and each doctor has to learn how to use sociology to his own, and to his patients', advantage — just as he must decide how to apply the other knowledge he has gained in his training.

Some Changes in Medical Problems and Medical Practice

There are about 55,000 doctors employed in the National Health Service. About half of these doctors work in the community — the majority as general practitioners, but a few in the administration of the health, education, and social services, and a few more in industrial settings. About 11,000 doctors work as consultants providing specialist medical care in NHS hospitals, and about 19,000 others assist them as 'junior hospital doctors' in various stages of their apprenticeship (although not all such doctors ultimately become consultants) (Department of Health and Social Security, 1974a: 28).

Up to the present, regardless of the specialty or part of the health service that they will eventually work in, all doctors have a common undergraduate training. To a large extent this training concentrates on providing students with the basic scientific knowledge and clinical experience to diagnose quickly and accurately acute life-threatening disease. A student learns to recognize the signs and symptoms of those diseases for which medical science has an available treatment — the infectious diseases, acute appendicitis, trauma, some cancers, and so on. There is an obvious logic to this emphasis in training: when a student starts to practice without supervision the failure to recognize the appropriate signs and symptoms of acute, life-threatening disease would be immediately and unnecessarily fatal to his patients.

But an analysis of the types of conditions that doctors are now called upon to treat — whether in the hospital or as a general practitioner in the community — suggests that this kind of acute life-threatening illness, and the emphasis on speed and accurate diagnosis which it necessitates, is no longer a major part of most doctors' work. The very success of medical technology — notably the development of antibiotics, and the still more significant advances of preventative medicine — coupled with the rise in living standards, has dramatically reduced the significance of infectious disease. Smallpox, for example, was once the major killing disease. Now, in almost every country in the world, it is an unusual event and is seldom fatal. The present pattern of disease means that doctors are now mainly called upon to treat conditions that prevent individuals from performing self-supporting activities or from developing the intellectual and physical potentialities needed to achieve an inner sense of well-being — that is, conditions like chronic rheumatism and arthritis, chronic bronchitis, diabetes, epilepsy, anaemia, multiple sclerosis, and various forms of mental 'difficulties'. With these kinds of diseases the main danger is not that inadequate practice on the part of the doctor will lead to the patient's death, but that it will lead to unnecessary suffering, discontent, inconvenience, or humiliation. Furthermore, since modern medical techniques often keep alive a patient who in earlier times might have died, the doctor now has to help a patient react to and cope with the handicaps that the onset of a condition may impose.[1]

Table 1 Percentage of beds occupied in non-psychiatric hospitals in England by different age groups

age	all sexes	all sexes (excluding maternity cases)	males only	females only	females (excluding maternity cases)
0–4	0.5	4.9			
5–14	4.0	4.4			
15–19	3.3	2.4			
20–24	5.0	2.4			
25–34	8.4	5.0			
35–44	6.2	5.8			
45–64	20.9	22.9			
65–74	18.3 ⎱ 47.7	20.0 ⎱ 52.2	20.8 ⎱ 41.7	16.6 ⎱ 51.4	19.5 ⎱ 60.1
75+	29.4 ⎰	32.2 ⎰	20.9 ⎰	34.8 ⎰	40.6 ⎰

Source: Specially compiled by Dr John Ashley (of the London School of Hygiene) from information supplied by the DHSS in 1-patient enquiry (DHSS, 1974b). (See Klein and Ashley, 1972.)

An analysis of the usage of English hospital beds in 1972 gives some indication of the type of conditions doctors are now called upon to treat. *Table 1*, for example, shows how 30 per cent of all beds in non-psychiatric hospitals are taken up by individuals aged over seventy-five and that 50 per cent of all beds are taken up by individuals over sixty-five. If we look at female patients alone, and exclude those in hospital for maternity care, we find that nearly two thirds of all beds are taken up by individuals over sixty-five. The conditions that these older age groups suffer from are very largely of the degenerative chronic type — quite different to the acute, life-threatening disease of the past.

The department of Health's *Hospital In-Patient Enquiry* (1974b) provides details of a bed-census carried out in all English non-psychiatric hospitals in 1972. *Table 2* provides information on the most frequent diagnoses given on patients in hospital in 1972. The left-hand column gives a picture of the hospital population at any one moment — the individuals you could encounter in a walk around hospitals on an average day — and the right-hand column shows the number of discharges or deaths. Where there are differences these reflect the length of stay required for different conditions. From the table it can be seen that the major categories in terms of bed occupancy are: malignant neoplasus (7 per cent); strokes (9 per cent); arterial disease (3 per cent); childbirth (9 per cent); arthritis (4 per cent); and fractures (5 per cent). The great majority of these conditions are ones which have long-term implications for treatment and management. Infectious diseases, it will be noted, hardly figure at all.

All the figures reported above refer to non-psychiatric hospitals, which themselves account for about half of all hospital beds. The number of

Table 2   Bed occupancy and admissions in non-psychiatric hospitals in England 1972*
(All conditions over 1%)

disease classification (and ICD no.)	beds used % (rounded)	discharges % (rounded)
all Tuberculosis (A6—10)	1	0
all Malignant Neoplasms (A45—58)	7	7
of which Lung (A51)	(1)	(1)
Intestine (A48—9)	(1)	(1)
Breast (A54)	(1)	(1)
Multiple Sclerosis (A73)	1	0
Epilepsy (A74)	1	0
Diabetes Mellitis (A64)	2	1
Acute Myocardial Infarction (A83a)	2	2
other Ischaemic Heart Disease (A83b)	2	1
Hypertensive Disease (A82)	1	1
Varicose Veins (A88a)	1	1
Strokes (cerebrovascular) (A85)	9	2
Arterial (A80)	3	1
Venus Thrombosis (A87)	1	1
Acute Respiratory & Influenza (A89—90)	1	2
Pneumonia (A91—92)	2	2
Bronchitis and Emphysema (A93a)	2	1
Hypertrophy of Tonsils and Adenoids (A94)	1	3
Peptic Ulcer (A98)	1	1
Appendicitis (A100)	1	2
Hernia (A101a)	1	3
disease of Breast and Female Genitals excluding malignancies (A110, 111 (pt))	2	7
Pregnancy/childbirth (A112—118, Y60—61)	9	23
(no complications *at all* — not even minor) (A118)	(6)	(12)
Arthritis and Spondylitis (A121)	4	2
Fractures (AN138—142)	5	4
Accidental Poisoning (AN143—150 — excl. 150a)	2	9
total accounted for	62	76

(Source: DHSS, 1974b: Table 6)

* I am grateful to Dr John Ashley of the London School of Hygiene for help and advice in the preparation of this table.

psychiatric beds, therefore, is very large. The age distribution for psychiatric bed usage is very similar to that in non-psychiatric hospitals and the vast majority of psychiatric in-patients fall into the chronic category — patients whose conditions are treated and managed, in and out of hospital, over long periods of time. About one third of all psychiatric beds are taken up by patients who are mentally subnormal or mentally handicapped,

Table 3 Estimates of severity of disorders seen in general practice expressed as percentages of total consultations

	Backett et al. (1954)	Brotherston et al. (1959)	Eimerl (1960)	Forsyth and Logan (1962)*	Fry (1966)	Wright (1968)	Williams (1970)*
minor	54		75	53	68	56	54
serious	16		17	14	6	13	17
chronic	30		8	33	26	21	19

Source: Royal College of General Practitioners (1973: 19)

* adapted: recorded under physiological, trivial, acute serious, acute non-serious, chronic serious, and chronic non-serious

Table 4   Acute major illness (life-threatening)

illness	persons consulting per year
pneumonia and acute bronchitis	50
acute myocardial infarction	7
acute appendicitis	5
All new cancers	
lung	1—2 per year
breast	1 per year
large bowel	2 every 3 years
stomach	1 every 2 years
bladder	1 every 3 years
cervix	1 every 3 years
pancreas	1 every 4 years
ovary	1 every 5 years
oesophagus	1 every 7 years
brain	1 every 10 years
uterine body	1 every 12 years
lymphadenoma	1 every 15 years
thyroid	1 every 20 years
severe depression	12
suicide	1 every 4 years
attempted suicide	2 every year
acute glaucoma	1
acute strokes	5
killed in road accident	1 every 3 years

Source: Royal College of General Practitioners (1973: 30)

while the remaining two thirds are taken up by patients suffering from some form of 'mental' illness (DHSS, 1974a: 152 and 127).

The picture is even more clear in general practice. The average general practitioner with 2,500 patients on his list will spend between 6—17 per

Table 5 Minor illness (of short duration and
           minimal disability)

illness	persons consulting
upper respiratory infections	500
common gastro-intestinal 'infections and dyspepsias'	250
skin disorders	225
emotional disorders	200
acute otitis media	50
wax in external meatus	50
'acute back' symptoms	50
migraine	30
hay fever	25
acute urinary infections	50

Source: Royal College of General Practitioners (1973: 19)

Table 6 Chronic illnesses

illness	persons consulting
chronic rheumatism	100
rheumatoid arthritis	10
chronic mental illness	55
severe subnormality	5
educationally subnormal	3*
vulnerable adults	40
child guidance	4*
chronic bronchitis	50
anaemia	40
pernicious anaemia	2
hypertension	25
asthma	25
peptic ulcer	25
strokes	15
epilepsy	10
diabetes	10
Parkinsonism	3
multiple sclerosis	2
pulmonary tuberculosis	2
chronic pyelonephritis	1

Source: Royal College of General Practitioners (1973: 20)
* persons attending school or clinic

cent of his time dealing with acutely 'serious' disease of a life-threatening
variety. He will spend somewhere between 51/77 per cent of his time
treating 'minor' diseases and between 8—30 per cent of his time

managing 'chronic' complaints (Backett *et al.*, 1954; Brotherston *et al.*, 1959; Eimerl, 1960; Fry, 1966; Wright, 1968; Williams, 1970). The types of disease that the general practitioner sees in the various categories are set out in *Tables 3–6*.

From these tables it can be seen that the 'real' disease of medical school education is quite rare – a GP, for example, only sees a case of lung cancer, the second most common form of death in the UK, once or twice a year. Even acute myocardial infarction will only be encountered about seven times. To summarize, the great majority of the cases the GP sees are either 'trivial' or 'minor' in a medical sense and tend to be chronic either in their course or in their implications. Myocardial infarction, for example, although acute in its course, has long-term implications for the patient's life and medical management. As a result, therefore, of present patterns of health and disease or, more strictly, patterns of the demand of individuals for the doctor's help, today's practicing doctors, both in hospital and in general practice, are as often concerned with the long-term *management* as they are with the immediate *cure* of disease.

In modern conditions the management of disease is infrequently a matter of the individual treatment of a single patient by a single doctor. Hospitals are large, complex organizations in which teams of doctors, reliant on numerous basic support services, ranging from hospital porters and administrators to radiologists and bacteriologists, co-operate with teams of nurses, physiotherapists, occupational therapists, and others in a series of procedures. Once discharged from hospital, patients will often require continued management and the hospital 'team' will then have to co-operate with the community services to provide 'comprehensive care'. In the community there are medical services consisting of general practitioners, midwives, health visitors and district nurses, and social services staffed by social workers. The latter run special hostels, rehabilitation centres, and day centres, as well as providing case-work, home help, and access to a wide range of government sponsored benefits. Furthermore, the treatment of patients with chronic disease can last over many years, creating a need for constant monitoring and check-ups. If re-admission to a hospital – with its many emotional, economic, and social consequences for the patient – is to be avoided, all these arrangements (known collectively as 'comprehensive care') have to work effectively.

Just as the hospital doctor is often drawn into an involvement with the community from which the patient comes, so is the general practitioner. It is to the general practitioner that patients come prior to any hospital referral, and it is to him that the patient presents his complaints, many of which are as much related to aspects of the individual's social and emotional situation as to any traditional organic pathology. It is a matter of controversy as to how far a doctor should involve himself in those aspects of a patient's complaint that are not strictly concerned with organic pathology and to what extent he should leave this job to some other service or agency. However, whether or not a doctor involves himself in action designed to help an individual with non-organic problems — and many do — it is certain that a modern doctor will need to work in a team with those who have made it their business to act in this area. Patients do present non-organic problems to their doctors. The fine demarcation between what is organic and what is psychopathological or sociopathological is hardly appreciated by the mass of uninitiated patients whose physical lesions may only lead them to seek care because they are emotionally disturbed or socially embarrassed by them. In general, as the high proportion of complaints regarded as organically 'trivial' or 'minor' suggests, disease in general practice is inextricably linked to social and emotional problems.

The kinds of relationships that exist between the social environment and the causes and course of disease have been illustrated by doctors using epidemiological techniques. It is clear, for example, that behaviours that differ from one group to another, such as cigarette smoking, sugar consumption, or over-eating are partly responsible for such diseases as coronary heart disease and lung cancer — the two major causes of mortality in contemporary society. Similarly, the environment into which hospital patients are discharged is now recognized as being a significant determinant of the outcome of the treatment.

In short, changes in the types of disease doctors are now called upon to treat; changes in the organization of medical care and in the style and content of treatment procedures; the recognition of some of the factors that cause patients to seek help; and advances in medical research analysing the causes and outcomes of disease — all suggest that a doctor not only needs to understand and treat organic pathology but also needs to master some of the principles governing interpersonal relationships and organizational functioning, as well as to understand the forces influencing behaviour in social situations and the social environment from which his patients come. Many doctors who do not possess this knowledge have found their job more difficult and more frustrating than it need be.

Furthermore, research carried out by doctors and others in a number of medical situations indicates clearly that a large number of doctors practising today do not give sufficient attention and priority to the social, relational, and organizational aspects of their practices. For example, many studies have emphasized the inconvenience and unnecessary suffering experienced by patients as the result of inadequate communication between hospital specialists and general practitioners. Thus Brocklehurst and Shergold (1968), writing in the *Lancet*, followed up two hundred patients discharged from a geriatric unit and found that only a third of the patients had been seen by their general practitioner a month later; although in the authors' opinion contact with the general practitioner was essential if re-admission and relapse were to be avoided. In a second study sponsored by the King's fund (1970) it was found that no 'extra effort' was made by specialists in a general hospital when they discharged elderly patients. Less than 30 per cent of all patients of any age, were asked about their living situation and the percentage was no higher among older patients. Yet the authors argued that old patients almost always had problems at home that needed attention. In two further studies of elderly patients Hockey (1966, 1968) demonstrated that both hospital doctors and general practitioners made quite 'inadequate' use of the district nurse. More than a quarter of the patients were returning to the hospital for continuing nursing care that a district nurse could have provided with much less inconvenience to the patient (1968: XVI). General practitioners and hospital doctors were frequently found to be out of touch with one another and the general practitioners were highly dissatisfied with relationships (1968: 126–7).

I have chosen to discuss the treatment of elderly patients, although many other areas of medical practice could have been selected, because it is precisely in this type of practice that there is consensus among medical experts that 'comprehensive care' is essential and also good evidence that medical practice is not as it could be. The criticisms that doctors and others doing research on health care now make of their colleagues' practices does not relate to the failure to use appropriate life-saving techniques, but to the failure to attach sufficient importance and priority to the care of the patient in the community and also to the lack of knowledge of the community and the services within it. At the present time most doctors in the NHS are excellent at saving lives, but few doctors are as good at minimizing the discomfort, inconvenience, and physical or mental incapacity that are associated with the types of medical conditions (and their implications for the patient's activities and plans) that are now most frequently found in their surgeries and clinics. One aim of the application of sociology to medicine is to give doctors the ammunition, and the confidence, to deal as effectively with the patient's social and emotional needs as they now do with his physical ones.

Some Sociological Concepts

The particular sociological perspective that I think can be usefully applied in medicine is one that might be termed 'structural', the idea being that in any situation or in any interaction there are elements that are common to all situations of that type. In the second half of Chapter 6, for example, doctor–patient interaction is considered in structural terms: what sort of things commonly happen, what has to occur and what are the aims in the situation. By abstracting features of doctor–patient interaction that are common, it may be possible to create a model of what happens in order to understand more effectively what can go wrong or cause confusion. In the same way it is possible to analyse the work of being a doctor in terms of a structural approach that can be termed 'role theory'. Being a doctor involves doing certain things, having certain aims, facing certain problems that are common to all doctors, that is, people 'play' or 'act' the role of doctor. To say that doctors act out a role is not to say that they are not genuine. Rather, sociologists find it helpful to conceive of all social situations *as if* individuals are playing parts. This approach sensitizes us to the 'rules' involved in playing the role and to the common features of being a 'doctor', a 'patient', a 'wife', a 'son', and so on. By abstracting the common features of the role and leaving behind the peculiar or individual features, it is possible to clarify what is happening and thereby gain insight and understanding.

To take one example, looking at the common features of the role 'doctor' or of the role 'patient' sensitizes us to the way the same situation can look very different from the point of view of actors playing different roles within it. To a doctor it may seem regrettable but necessary that a patient undergo an examination by a student. To a patient, on the other hand, the presence of the student may seem an unwarranted intrusion. Similarly, looking at the common features of the role 'hospital consultant' or 'hospital administrator', 'hospital consultant' or 'general practitioner', and 'medical school teacher' or 'medical student' sensitizes us to the way in which playing different roles gives the participants different perspectives – often behaviour which seems sensible to one can appear inconceivably petty to another. For example, many hospital consultants consider hospital regulations an intolerable constraint on their freedom of action. Detailed analyses of the structure of roles and situations, as in Chapters Six and Seven, can generate more sophisticated insights into medical practice.

Basic to sociology is a concern with the implications of individuals living together in collectivities – for example, families, ethnic groups, schools, universities, regions, countries, and so on. Sociologists argue that certain aspects of the attitudes and behaviour of individuals cannot be understood without reference to this fact of collective existence.

The term 'social action' refers to behaviour that occurs in 'social situations', that is, where the individuals (conceptualized as *actors* to differentiate that part of their behaviour that derives from collective existence from that part of their behaviour that is idiosyncratic) orientate their behaviour to other people. These other people may in some senses be conceived of as existing inside the actor's mind. Individuals drive on the left side of the road because they are able to imagine what will happen if they do not; there may be someone else coming around the next bend or there may be someone else who will do or think something they would not like. Because actors can imagine the response of others, behaviour is not only orientated to people in the situation, but also to people remembered from the past or projected into the future.

Max Weber (1863–1920), a German whom many sociologists like to think of as a founding father of their discipline, once gave a neat example of what he meant by social action. If there were two bicyclists in accidental collision with one another, we could be confident that the behaviour of the bicyclists up to the time of the collision was not social action: by definition, they were not aware of each other. Afterwards, however, having been brought painfully to an awareness of an 'other' in the situation, and faced with having to relate to that 'other', the individuals' behaviour would be social action.

In medical practice, interactions between doctors and patients, patients and nurses, nurses and doctors, doctors and social workers are all, among other things, social action. The doctor–patient consultation, the ward round, the hospital board meeting, the medical school lecture are all, among other things, social situations. I shall argue that these interactions and these situations cannot be adequately understood without reference to the collective dimension of existence.

The main sociological concepts that I want to use to illuminate social situations are social factors. The sociologist who did most to emphasize the relevance of social factors to the understanding of social behaviour was the Frenchman, Emile Durkheim (1858–1917), who is also considered a founding father of sociology. Durkheim saw social factors as significant elements of behaviour and belief that are shared by the members of the group (i.e., a collectivity) and express 'the way in which the group conceives itself and its relations with the objects which affect it' (1901, trans. 1938: XLIX). What I think Durkheim meant by this was that the individuals in a group have, in the course of time, come to establish particular ways of thinking about things and people inside and outside the particular group, and they have also developed ways of acting towards each other and people outside. Although members of a group may not always think or act alike, they do share similar conceptions about appropriate attitudes and ways of behaving. These features of group life, common ways of doing and thinking, are what distinguish the individuals in the group from others. These are the products of collective life that interest sociologists.

Two significant social factors that are thought to govern social action are *values* and *norms.* Values refer to collective beliefs and are conceived of at a relatively abstract level. In a family there might be value placed on the family members' right to privacy, on the importance of marriage and chastity before it, on hard work, or on the idea that children owe their parents something for the love and attention they have received. In a social group such as a political party, there might be a belief in free enterprise, the right not to join a trade union, or in equality of access to medical services. Norms, on the other hand, although they are difficult to distinguish from values at a certain level of abstraction, are more concrete ways of feeling, thinking, and acting that reflect a set of beliefs. It may be considered right to behave in certain ways towards grown-ups or women, to treat patients with respect, to wear a white coat in the surgery, to speak only when spoken to, or it may be usual to save money for a rainy day, to invite friends to dinner at home, to stay at home and do the housework, or not to repeat to others what a patient says to oneself.

It is important to recognize that norms and behaviours are not identical. All the members of a social group may share common ideas about how they ought to behave, but they may not always behave in these ways. Norms, therefore, refer to the notions people have about 'right' behaviour; just because individuals do behave in some way, it does not follow that this is a norm. Put more simply, norms have an underlying moral force. They refer to behaviour conceived of as 'right' or 'natural' or 'normal'.

I do not suppose that it will be very provocative if I say that these notions that individuals have about 'rightness' and 'naturalness' and 'normalness', in other words the norms and values that exist in a group, are regarded by sociologists as very significant determinants of individual behaviour. In fact, social factors of this kind are regarded as realities of great force because, although they are internalized by any one individual, they exist independently of him within the other members of the group.

> 'When I fulfil my obligations, as brother, husband, or citizen, when I execute my contracts, I perform duties which are defined externally to myself and my acts, in law and custom. Even if they conform to my own sentiments and I feel their reality subjectively, such reality is objective, for I did not create them; I merely inherited them ... ' (Durkheim, 1901, trans. 1938: 1)

These are considered by sociologists to be the main determinants of social action. This is what Durkheim meant when he exhorted sociologists in a famous passage to 'consider social factors as things' (Durkheim, 1901, trans. 1938: 14).[2] Social factors influence individuals because they provide them with a particular way of seeing themselves and the world and of acting towards it. Although there are, in fact, many ways of organizing our lives and our society (or schools or families or universities), we have usually come to think of one or other way (or more probably one or other range of ways) as 'natural', 'right', and 'normal'. Other ways we often think of as 'unnatural', 'wrong', and 'strange'. For example, people brought up in a collectivity such as a family or a school that stresses the value of truth and honesty, will have some difficulty adapting to another group of people who regard falsehood and dishonesty as quite natural. Although most of the readers of this book will consider truth and honesty to be acceptable values, individuals in sixth-century Sparta or in street gangs in America or in Britain at other times, have not shared these beliefs. In such cultures lying and stealing were positively valued, and as a result, theft and deceit were endemic. This is still the case in many street gangs today. In this way norms and values determine behaviour. We often have an idea of what is right, and we do not even consider alternatives.

Norms and values, feelings of rightness and wrongness, of course, have to be learnt. In Freudian psychological theory, the young baby has to develop a 'sense of reality' which permits him to act in accordance with the demands of 'reality'. In other kinds of psychological theory, which do not emphasize the significance of an 'inner world' of phantasy, the child must learn which behaviours are rewarded and which punished. Whatever process, or combination of processes, is assumed in theory, 'reality' or 'the reward—punishment system' are very largely socially constructed. Different behaviours are rewarded and punished, or regarded as more or less appropriate, in different social groups. Masturbation, stealing, manners, dress, how and what to eat, the expression of emotion or sexuality, ways of relaxing or dealing with stress, to give but a few examples, are governed by different normative standards in different groups.

A growing child learns what behaviour is 'usual', 'right', or 'natural' according to the norms that exist in the group in which he grows. This process is known as *primary socialization* — a technical term denoting the process whereby norms and values are acquired (and, incidentally, has nothing to do with the nationalization of industry or going out to parties). Primary socialization may be informal, as when a child picks up from his parents or peers smoking habits, voting habits, ways of dealing with illness, and even ways of being ill (for example, a tendency to faint in a difficult situation or to get asthma instead of expressing anger); or it may be formal, as in a school where a child is taught the norms and values of those running the school. As Durkheim described it, education is 'a continuous effort to impose on the child ways of seeing, feeling and acting at which he would not have arrived spontaneously' (1901, trans. 1938: 6).

In addition to primary socialization, sociologists also conceive of a *secondary socialization* process which operates throughout a person's life. As a new member of a medical school or of a particular medical 'firm' (i.e., medical team), or as a visitor to his fiancee's parents, [3] an individual picks up and adapts to the new ambiance; he is sensitive to the particular norms and values that exist in the new situation. Again, an individual may be socialized formally (as when a new recruit to an undergraduate society undergoes an initiation ritual or when a new patient in hospital is formally admitted to the ward) or informally — by gradually attuning himself to the subtleties of meanings and actions in the new situation. The way in which recruits to occupations in medicine, the law, the army, sociology, or the administrative grades of the civil service are socialized so that they come to think, act as, and indeed 'are', doctors, barristers, officers, sociologists, or permanent secretaries, is a special form of secondary socialization termed *professionalization.*

The norms and values that exist within social groups are maintained by processes that sociologists conceive of as *social control.* Again, social control goes on informally as well as formally. Informal processes range from the simple fact that it is generally easier to get along in a social group if one acts according to the accepted norms and values, to more active processes such as gossip, ostracism, or ridicule, which all discourage deviance from norms. In what has been regarded as both a profound and a trivial demonstration, the American sociologist, Garfinckle, carried out some experiments with his students. In one experiment the students were asked to question any assumptions made in their next social interaction. The experiment revealed how many assumptions are involved in routine discourse. For example:

'(S) "How are you?"

(E)   "How am I in relation to what? My health, my finances, my school work, my peace of mind, my ... ?"

(S)   (Red in the face and suddenly out of control) "Look! I was just trying to be polite. Frankly, I don't give a damn how you are."

                                          or

My friend and I were talking about a man whose overbearing attitude annoyed us. My friend expressed his feeling.

(S)   "I'm sick of him."

(E)   "Would you explain what is wrong with you that you are sick?"

(S)   "Are you kidding me? You know what I mean."

(E)   "Please explain your ailment."

(S)   (He listened to me with a puzzled look) "What has come over you? We never talk this way, do we?" '

                                              (Garfinckle, 1967: 44)

I am sure that some readers will find these examples trivial, but they illustrate a point. If they seem silly to us, it is because we know what the subjects mean. We make the assumptions with them. Indeed, the great advantage of norms concerning language and behaviour is that they enable us to relate to each other without going through a long process of clarification. But can we always be sure that we are aware of the assumptions and that the other person in the interaction shares them?

However, before considering this question, I want to return to social control. In addition to the convenience of acting in 'normal' ways, there are usually social control pressures, from others in our social group, to conform. In the two examples quoted above the student experimenters who behaved in a deviant manner (by ignoring the assumptions of everyday discourse) were treated as 'odd' or 'ill' by the subjects, at least temporarily. Pressures of ridicule, gossip, ostracism, or stigmatization of this kind can be very powerful. The medical student who is *too* keen, or asks *too* many questions, or who tries to *prolong* a lecture is often hissed at or ridiculed by his peers. The peer group enforces the norms as to what constitutes a proper level of attention or diligence, how many questions should be asked, and how long a lecture should go on. And of course these standards can vary from school to school and year to year. Exactly the same kinds of pressures can be observed in political groups or trade unions. Because of the power of social control, individuals who deviate from norms will often do so in secret.

In addition to informal processes of social control there are also formal ones. Individuals also follow norms because they fear sanctions from those formally responsible for enforcing them — for example, the Dean, a disciplinary committee, the General Medical Council, or the police and the courts.

Norms and values are analysed by sociologists and regarded as *social factors* because they vary according to the social group under consideration. Different groups of university students have different standards, different families have different ideas about what a daughter may do with a boy-friend and when she should be home at night, different schools have different rules, and so on. Within societies the prevailing system of beliefs, norms, rules, and values is termed 'culture' — the sociological use of this word differing from the popular notion equating culture with 'the arts'.

Cultures tend to have different sets of meanings governing activities and different beliefs about the aims and content of appropriate behaviour. For example, there are differences between the French and the English, urban society and rural society. What is normal in one culture is often abnormal in another. To take an extreme example, homosexuality is highly valued in some cultures and a crime in others. Social anthropologists have documented these differences in great detail (see for example Benedict, 1934), and their work suggests that almost no aspect of behaviour may be held to be universally normal. As I hope will now be clear, we therefore have to be very careful when we make assumptions about 'normality'.

Just as there is cultural variation between societies, there is also variation within any given society. In a society there are 'sub-cultural groupings' where different norms and values are apparent. The Bloomsbury group, Pakistani immigrants in Bradford, Irish labourers in Liverpool, male rugby clubs, and 'women's groups' each have their own distinctive sub-culture, and appropriate actions and beliefs vary among them. They are different 'social worlds' — in each group there are different ground rules and assumptions about what is normal. It can therefore take some time for an outsider to comprehend what is happening in any group, whether it is an immigrant group or a school or a family.

A prime concern of the sociologist is to consider how an individual's membership of a social group — his particular social world or place in the *social structure* — influences his experience and behaviour. Influences from the social structure are much more powerful than is often realized. Chapter 3 is concerned with a particular form of such influence: the location of individuals in a hierarchical order of power and advantage termed 'social class'. Location in that order is influential in almost everything an individual is or does in modern industrial society. It plays a major part in determining life-chances and opportunities; it significantly influences aspirations and patterns of daily life; it helps to orientate individuals in their relationships with others (for example, by indicating how much deference and respect they must pay to or expect from others);

and it even influences the kinds of diseases individuals are likely to acquire and how they respond to them (below pp. 110–14).

Consider the opportunity to become employed in a highly socially-valued occupation (termed high status) such as being a doctor or lawyer. The most systematic published research project in the UK in this area showed that an individual's life-chances varied greatly according to the occupation of his father. The son of a docker or a dustman had virtually no chance of becoming a lawyer or top civil servant, whereas the son of a lawyer or top civil servant had about a four out of ten chance of entering such an occupational status level. The son of a bank clerk had about a one in a hundred chance (Glass, 1954: 177–188). In another study concerning access to selective secondary schools, the son of a non-manual worker was found to have a seven times better chance of admission to a grammar school than the son of a manual worker. Going to a university is even more influenced by paternal occupation: the son of a non-manual worker has a thirty times better chance than the son of a manual worker (Little and Westergaard, 1964). Research in many other countries demonstrates a similar pattern, and there are other factors such as race or sex which can have similar effects on opportunity.

It may be argued, of course, that these data are not the result of unequal opportunity but of the distribution of ability, that is, the cleverest people are in the top classes. However, there is considerable evidence to suggest that in absolute numbers there are as many people with a high IQ in the lowest class as in the top (Himmelwheit, 1954: 144–5); and in a study looking at the effect of class on education it was found that if IQ was controlled (the chances of entry to grammar school were compared for middle and lower class children of the same IQ) there was still a dramatic inequality of opportunity (Douglas, 1964: 123).

It is also well established that working-class psychotherapy patients and case-work clients drop out of treatment more readily than middle-class ones. Sociologists believe that some aspects of working-class attitudes to life, for example, the lack of a future-oriented perspective and an emphasis on present tangible goals, are responsible for this difference. The working-class patient's perspective contrasts with the long-term and rather nonspecific aims of psychotherapy, which is generally practised by therapists of middle-class origin for whom a future-oriented perspective is ingrained. Working-class patients are more likely not to comprehend what is happening in therapy and to drop out (Overall and Aronson, 1963; Mayer and Timmes, 1969). The psychotherapeutic session is in part a social situation. As such, it can be more adequately comprehended by taking account of the individual's social location. As we have seen, the customs, mores, values, and experiences of the group to which the participants belong, or aspire to (in this case the fact of the patient's location in the working class) can exert a dramatic influence on interaction.

We can observe many other relationships between aspects of social structure and different aspects of behaviour. For example, epidemiologists (doctors who study the distribution of disease in the population) have shown that coronary heart disease occurs more frequently in American-born than foreign-born Americans (Marks, 1967: 93–4); and, since this difference remains within different racial categories, it must mean that aspects of the life-style of contemporary American society are conducive to heart disease. In a classic study Durkheim (1897, trans. 1952: 178–202) showed that single, divorced, or widowed people commit suicide more often than married ones and a similar 'protective effect' of marriage, at least for men, was shown by Gove (1973: 65) when he studied mortality from a very wide range of diseases. In other areas of behaviour, to take but a few examples, it has been shown that industrial strikes occur more frequently in more isolated and socially integrated communities (Kerr and Siegel, 1954: 195); that the frequency with which patients visit their doctors varies with the patients' age, sex, and ethnic group (Mechanic, 1968: 117); and that middle-class individuals are more likely to vote Conservative than Labour (Butler and Stokes, 1974: 67 *et seq.*).

The kind of association described above, for example, the relationship between sex and patient consultation rates, is regarded by sociologists as a *social fact,* that is a fact that can be explained by social factors, in so far as the causal agent, in this case sex, can be understood as a product of collective existence. Hypothetically, if women visited the doctor more frequently because of something to do with the biological nature of sex differences – such as the fact that they bear children and need to visit the doctor in this connection – then an association would not be regarded as a social fact. If on the other hand, the association was something to do with the social experience of being a women – for example, if it was a norm that to be female meant you should appear ill and weak – then the association would be a social fact. The point is that social facts refer to observed regularities in human behaviour or experiences that derive from social location and the peculiarities that go with it. Social classes, ethnic groups, religious groups, and families are such locations in society because they provide certain experiences which are shared *as the result of collective existence.*

There is a tradition in sociology, which I accept, that social facts can only be explained adequately by taking into account social factors, that is, factors deriving from the particular collective experience. It was Emile Durkheim who first proposed this argument. In one classic study, he argued that suicide rates that vary between social groups must be explained by asking what it is about membership of the group that might produce these variations. He found, for example, that Protestants – whether living in Protestant or Catholic countries – usually have higher suicide rates than Catholics; that single or divorced people have higher rates than married people; and that countries with higher divorce rates have higher suicide rates. He suggested that Protestants, single and divorced individuals, all shared one characteristic: a low-level of integration into a social group. He then argued that suicide occurs more frequently in less well-integrated groups and societies because in such groups and societies there is less certainty about the meaning of life. He termed such groups and societies 'egoistic'. Thus the degree to which a society is egoistic, he argued, increases or diminishes the likelihood that those individuals with a psychological tendency to commit suicide will actually do so (1897, trans. 1952: 201–2).

To summarize, a sociological argument is that social action, social situations, and social facts can only be understood by taking into account distinctive aspects of the collective experience of individuals (i.e., social factors such as norms and values). But this does not mean that sociologists regard other perspectives, such as those of genetics or individual psychology as unimportant. In the case of psychotherapy drop-out rates, for example, a psychotherapist might think that a psychological variable, such as the patient's resistance to the therapist's interpretations, would be the factor that explains drop-out. Nonetheless, if the psychotherapist's theory were true then, given the fact that working-class patients do drop out more often than middle-class patients, resistance would have to be more common among working-class patients. An adequate explanation would therefore have to take into account what features of working-class life create more resistance. The psychological explanation would then be contained within the sociological, as an intervening or conditional variable (see Rosenberg, 1966: 54–83 and 105–30). A full understanding will often require compatible biological, psychological, and sociological theories.

The sociologist's perspective suggests, therefore, that if we are trying to understand the collective experience of human beings, we must not treat them as atomistic or isolated individuals. To do so would mean ignoring the distinctively human fact of culture: the set of learned beliefs, values, and symbols that individuals must to some extent share if any social life is to be viable. The patient coming into hospital or visiting his general practitioner brings with him the culture of his own social world.

There can be little question that assumptions about the 'naturalness' and 'rightness' of certain beliefs, thoughts, and actions (which individuals may not even be aware of making), that is, the social structure, are very significant in understanding why individuals behave as they do. I would argue that one of the most important contributions of sociological research has been its documentation of the naivety of 'common-sense' notions that people are 'free' to do what they want. We have seen, for example, that some people are much 'freer' than others to go to university. However, it must be recognized that in some senses social laws are not like other laws. I have already argued that norms and values are acquired. It follows that they can be changed, by individuals and by groups of individuals acting together. Norms and values are powerful because people believe in them. There is, therefore, a subjective element in all sociological thinking.

Consider an individual suffering from the onset of cancer symptoms; as far as we know, whether he is aware of it or not, the physiological process operates. However, if he is to have anything done about it, i.e., if he is to go to the doctor and ask for help, he must recognize the symptoms as a problem that requires help. Otherwise, how could he do anything? The ways in which a person reacts to symptoms, termed *illness behaviour*, is influenced by the beliefs he has concerning the symptoms and what he should do about them. There are norms and values surrounding the definition of illness and the meaning attached to a visit to the doctor. A visit to the doctor is a piece of social action, and as such, must be comprehended in terms of social influences.

Looked at from the point of view of the actor, a visit to the doctor could have many different meanings, so could his symptoms. Much research has shown how different social groups vary in the way they interpret the signs and symptoms that scientifically trained doctors would regard as serious indicators of disease (for example Suchman and Phillips, 1958). Other research has suggested that individuals do not necessarily go to the doctor primarily to seek help with their symptoms (Zola, 1963). To the actor the meaning of his symptoms and of a visit to the doctor may vary, both idiosyncratically or in socially patterned ways, and it is unlikely, therefore, that we will manage to understand why people go to doctors, or, as is statistically more frequent, do not go, without taking the actor's subjective perspective into account. A sufficient explanation of any social behaviour must take into account the fact that it is individuals who take decisions to behave in a particular way. Research on 'illness behaviour', which is reviewed in Chapter 5, shows that a sociological approach to help-seeking, taking account of the subjective element in social action, can greatly widen our understanding of what patients want from doctors.

One of the main tasks of the sociologist, therefore, is to grapple with the complexities of subjective meaning in any social situation. However, this emphasis on individual subjective meaning does not imply that there can be no scientific generalization about social behaviour. As I have discussed earlier, socialization results in individual meanings being patterned according to social groups. That is individuals with a common collective experience tend to share common subjective definitions of the situation. The study of social structure attempts to discover such patterns. To a sociologist studying the social structure of different social groups it is especially interesting that each society or sub-cultural grouping (such as a group of students, an occupational group, or a family) tends to regard its culture, its beliefs, and its ways of doing things, as legitimate and absolute, and rarely hesitates to control divergence. Each group selects from the whole range of conceivable behaviour and presents its selection as 'right'. As suggested, the members of the group usually then act to a great extent in accordance with these constraints. From within a culture choices seem highly constrained. But it is important to re-emphasize that, from the standpoint of an observer, this apparent constraint results not from the essential 'rightness' of the norms and values of the culture, but from enough people believing in them. This allows them both to follow the norms themselves, and to successfully apply (or allow to be applied) sanctions of differing degrees to those who do not. Therefore, as I have suggested, norms and values are somewhat different types of constraint on action than biological laws, such as man's inability to fly, even if he wants to, without aeronautical aids. The constraints on behaviour that derive from social location are of human making. With enough power and support individuals can alter the social structure at will. If enough people believe in a new set of norms, then they will become *the* norms.

Because social constraints ultimately derive from subjective belief it is important to recognize that the sanctions which are used to back-up norms and values are effective because the enforcers are allowed the 'power' to utilize them. This power derives from each individual's implicit agreement not only with the norms and values but also with the consequences of breaking them, and from the willingness of enough people, ultimately with the support of the police or the army, to back up those applying sanctions. A society has no metaphysical existence. The policeman does not exercize his power by divine right but through the fact that he has been delegated the legitimate right to use force.

Of course, not every member of a society has equal influence on the creation and maintenance of norms and values. Such influence will tend to vary according to the amount of power an individual has, that is according to his position in the social structure. In British society and in most others power is very unequally distributed (pp. 127–40).

Sociology, then, is concerned with understanding social action and social facts regarding the various factors deriving from the collective experience of human beings. In any situation the sociologist will be asking questions: what regularities in experience and behaviour do we find? what accounts for them? what are people trying to do with each other? what are their relationships to one another? how are their relationships organized in institutions? what do they expect of themselves and each other? how do they define the situation? what features of their own social worlds are they bringing to the situation? in what way does their social location determine their experience, attitudes, and behaviour?

Sociology in Medicine

One area of medical practice to which sociology can contribute is the study of the way in which individuals seek help from doctors (discussed in Chapter 5). It can be argued that a sociological approach to help-seeking provides us with much more systematic knowledge than we have had previously. However, research work is only beginning to make real progress.

Many surveys, mostly carried out by doctors, have shown that there is a large amount of untreated disease within any population. Although some of this disease is trivial, in the sense that it is self-limiting and not life-threatening or severely incapacitating, it is also clear that a number of people with symptoms such as those of haemotopsis which most members of the medical profession would consider 'major', go untreated (Butterfield, 1968: 15). At the same time it is known that sufferers from major diseases, such as cancer, 'put off' consulting a doctor for a considerable time (Kutner *et al.*, 1958). The number of relatively serious diseases that exist undiagnosed in an average general practice of 2,500 is estimated in *Table 7*.

Table 7   Undiagnosed disease

disease	persons
high blood pressure (only 15 will have complications)	250
anaemia	200 (almost all are women)
chronic bronchitis	150
bacteriuria	100
obesity	60
diabetes	10
cancer of cervix – with positive smears	3
pulmonary tuberculosis	1
glaucoma	1
cancer of lung – MMR pick-up	1 every 2 years
phenylketonuria	1 case every 200 years

Source: Royal College of General Practitioners (1973: 20)

It is only very recently that the kind of sociological perspective discussed above has been applied to help-seeking, and a review of the evidence (pp. 170–1) suggests that until now very little progress has been made. Investigators have usually tried to understand the 'failure' of individuals to seek help quickly, or at all, in terms of a series of variables (social class, ethnic groups, age, education, religion) in attempting to explain why people did not take the 'rational' course of going to their doctor. This work has produced many interesting associations such as the fact that the uneducated, the lower class, and the non-European minorities in the United States are (even allowing for the disincentive created by the high cost of medical care) somewhat lower utilizers. However, none of these factors begin to explain the variability – who goes and who doesn't.

As I indicated earlier, a sociological approach to illness behaviour would concentrate on the meaning of the symptom to an actor and on the norms and values surrounding disease and the appropriate action to be taken. Above all, it would not *assume* that the patient comes to the doctor for *any particular reason* (be it to get rid of his symptoms, to complain about his grandmother, or both), nor would it assume that to seek medical aid for a symptom was necessarily a 'rational' action. As an individual I would have my own views on these matters. However, as a sociologist, I would try not to make any assumptions. I would ask what people in different social groups usually do about their health and any symptoms they experience; I would try to get some idea of their motives for consulting a doctor; and I would compare individuals in the community who do take their symptoms to the doctor to those who do not.

On the basis of the evidence discussed in Chapter 5, it is reasonable to say that we are now getting some idea about the answers to such sociological questions. It seems that individuals have symptoms much of the time and that dealing with them, particularly by self-medication, is a day-to-day activity; that individuals visit the doctor on average for only one of about ten symptoms that they suffer; that when they do go, these symptoms have not necessarily got worse; that their motives for going, and what they want from the doctor, may often have more to do with some change in their social circumstances than with any change in their symptoms. If this kind of research work is continued and confirmed, there can be little doubt that a contribution will have been made to medical practice: to think sociologically about help-seeking will enable doctors to meet the needs of their patients much more adequately; it will help us to understand what it is that a patient brings to the doctor, and to prevent us from too readily assuming we know the answer.

A second contribution sociology can make is in the analysis of the doctor–patient relationship and the doctor's role. In Chapter 6 it is argued that the role of 'doctor' involves a whole series of potential conflicts, such as that between the interests of one patient and those of another or between the interests of a patient and those of his relatives. Research work indicates that the way many doctors behave suggests they do not acknowledge these conflicts or the coping devices they have developed to deal with them. The characteristic emphasis on clinical freedom and autonomy, for example, is a coping device because it protects doctors from the harsh judgments of lay individuals who do not have to experience, and arbitrate, the conflicts. It is also argued that certain problems observed in some doctors' treatment of patients, such as insensitivity to the patient's social and emotional needs or the belief that those needs are trivial, result from the fact that the doctor's own need, to 'successfully' cure patients, conflicts with his ability to do so. Such coping devices can prevent doctors and others from recognizing what is happening and from engaging in constructive criticism and discussion, which is not only dysfunctional to good quality medical care, but is also likely to lead to frustration among doctors. I would suggest that a greater understanding of the doctor's own social role could help to reduce some of these problems.

Figure 1   *Post-operative treatment with narcotics (means for each day ± standard error of the mean)*

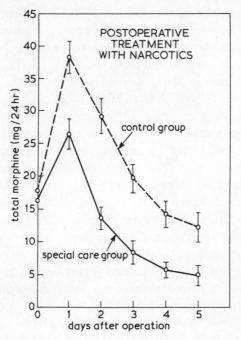

Source: Egbert *et al.* (1964: 826)

In Chapter 6 evidence is also presented to show that the way in which the doctor—patient relationship is handled can significantly influence the outcome of treatment. There is much exciting work in this area, but I want to mention, as an example, a study showing how a deliberate attempt by doctors to take account of patients' anxiety and powerlessness can be crucial to what happens. The study was conducted by Egbert and his colleagues (1964) in a large American hospital and involved an examination of the effects of warning pre-operative patients what to expect. Ninety-seven patients undergoing elective intra-abdominal operations were included in the study, but fifty-one and forty-six, respectively, were assigned to two groups according to the classic principles of double-blind experimental design. Fifty-one patients (the control group) were treated as usual. The second group of forty-six patients was seen by the anaesthetist (for a much longer time) prior to the operation and was told what sort of pain to expect and how to cope with it after coming round. Nurses, surgeons, and the remainder of the operating and ward staff did not know about the experiment and therefore could not behave differently with the patients in the different groups. The study found that the patients in the experimental group (given the extra information) needed a lower dosage of pain-relieving drugs after the operation (see *Figure 1*) and, furthermore, left hospital on average two and seven-tenths days earlier. Because the only difference between the control group and the experimental group was the special treatment the latter received, it is clear that the anaesthetist's recognition of the patients' anxiety and powerlessness, and their willingness to take deliberate steps to inform the patients of what was happening, were very important in the treatment process.

Up to this point I have argued that a concern with an individual's collective existence, with social factors, and with the meaning individuals give to actions, can help to add to our understanding of the ways of seeking medical attention and to the kinds of interaction that occur between doctors and patients. Given that treatment has a chance of altering the disease process, the fact that an individual visits a doctor is one important determinant of the outcome of disease. Similarly, the kind of deliberate attention given to the doctor–patient relationship, illustrated in Egbert's experiment above, can also affect outcome. However, these are not the only ways in which collective existence is important. Social factors can also affect outcome because of their influence on the treatment setting and because an individual's background places severe limitations on the scope for 'successful' treatment. Finally, social factors can also influence what our concept of 'success' is in the first place.

In an intriguing study in the United States, Imboden (1961a) and his colleagues have shown how the disease known as chronic brucellosis — a possible sequel to an acute brucellosis infection — has to be understood in terms of the patient's social and emotional background. The study made use of a chance occurrence that created the conditions for an experimental design: twenty-four workers in a bacteriological laboratory became ill with brucellosis over a relatively short period of time. Eight of these recovered, in the sense that they had no trace of the brucellosis virus or symptoms, within two to three months (on average) after onset, and the remaining sixteen were regarded as having 'chronic brucellosis'. Intensive medical and laboratory examinations were made to find evidence that would differentiate the two groups in terms of clinical data, but none could be found. Rather, differences emerged only after interviews with patients in each group had revealed information about the patient's life situations and emotional difficulties. For example, eleven of the sixteen chronic patients, but none of the acute patients, displayed evidence of 'disturbed or troubled life situations existing at the time of the acute infection or within a year before or after the infection'. In eleven of the 'chronic' patients and only two of the 'acute' patients, there was evidence of 'gross traumatic events or circumstances' in their early life. One of the cases cited by the authors as representative of the chronic-symptomatic group gives an idea of the complex interplay of present and past socio-emotional factors:

'This 34-year old chemical engineer in the chronic-symptomatic group developed brucellosis in 1952. His initial symptoms consisted principally of severe headache, fever, and fatigue. The latter persisted after hospitalization and treatment with antibiotics for about a year, after which the patient gradually improved. The main symptom that continued was weakness.

This patient was reared in an emotionally cold, strict, and poverty-stricken home. He had always been a socially isolated person who preferred various intellectual activities which did not require the company of others. He was shy, inhibited, and self-conscious about his appearance.

Prior to and during his illness the patient considered himself to be in an extraordinarily troublesome situation in which he felt rejected and deprecated by certain members of his family and indeed, wondered if he had a friend in the world. In this setting, he contracted brucellosis and accepted the diagnosis with a conscious sense of vindication and relief. It was of interest that the patient's symptomatic improvement paralleled partial resolution of his complicated family problem and that his remaining symptom was similar to that with which an aged relative, for whom he felt considerable responsiblity, was afflicted.' (Imboden *et al.*, 1961a: 46)

In other studies (Imboden *et al.*, 1961b: Eifrig *et al.*, 1961) Imboden and his colleagues describe how they later reached similar conclusions when studying patients recovering from Asian influenza and from constrictive pericarditis.

In another study, Querido and his colleagues (1959) found that knowledge of an individual's social and emotional background was a very important factor in determining recovery from a wide range of disorders in a general hospital; it could therefore be said that social and emotional background influenced outcome. Altogether more than 2,000 patients admitted to the surgical, medical, and psychiatric wards of the Weesperlein Ziekehuis municipal hospital in Amsterdam were studied. Estimates of prognosis were made on the basis of the usual clinical information alone, and then, independently, on the basis of a full psycho-social history taken in a special interview. It was found that 1,128 cases were judged to have a favourable prognosis on the basis of clinical data and 871 on the basis of the psycho-social assessment. On follow up, 58 per cent (660) of those cases estimated to have a favourable prognosis on clinical criteria actually had a favourable outcome, and 69 per cent (592) of these judged to have a satisfactory psycho-social prognosis actually had a successful recovery. Of the 759 patients judged to have a distressed psycho-social background, only 30 per cent (225) managed a favourable recovery. This latter figure compared with 68 per cent (597) of those with a satisfactory psycho-social background who managed a favourable recovery. A distressed psycho-social background was defined as one where the patient was unable to cope with particular problems in his life situation — within his marital relationship, with his children, with his work, with housing and so on. In summary, those with psycho-social distress did half as well as those without it. The study thus demonstrates that a patient's psycho-social background places powerful constraints on the effectivness of treatment even when, on purely clinical grounds, the prognosis is optimistic.

It remains for research to spell out more precisely what aspects of the individual's life situation contribute to poor outcome in specific disease conditions. Some progress in this direction was made in another study where Brown, Birley, and Wing (1972) showed how the quality of the emotional relationships within an individual's home situation was a good predictor of his chance of relapse with further schizophrenic symptoms following discharge from hospital. A measure of the extent of expressed emotion in the home predicted relapse independently of other factors such as length of the history, type of symptoms, or severity of previous disturbance. Three and a half times the number of patients (58 per cent as compared with 16 per cent) in the high emotional involvement group relapsed. More precisely, it was found that in homes where key relatives were critical of the patient (some of the techniques used to measure their concept are described below, pp. 56–7), or where there was, in the judgment of the investigators, a surfeit of emotional involvement in the patient's life on the part of key relatives, patients were much more likely to relapse. Criticism was found in three and a half times more homes where a patient later relapsed and emotional over-involvement was found in twice the number of homes. These results are now being used to advise discharged schizophrenic patients about where to go on leaving hospital.

Such studies as those by Imboden, Querido, Brown, and their colleagues illustrate the great significance of the relationships and situations obtaining outside the treatment setting for determining the outcome of intervention. There are also other ways in which social factors can influence outcome. Particular norms and values can affect the way doctors and patients think about 'outcome' and the kinds of emphasis they place on different dimensions of outcome when deciding whether or not it has been successful (for example, is an outcome 'successful' if a patient can no longer work?). The hypothetical case of a man who has had a leg amputation for cancer illustrates some different dimensions that are conceivable six months afterwards.

The five alternatives[4] in *Figure 2* represent only a few of the many different possibilities (the amputee may also have had to cancel his holidays, may be seeing less of his friends, may have his routine totally altered because of frequent hospital visits, may be depressed, etc.). At times, as is discussed in Chapter 6, some of these outcomes may conflict. For example, the wish to get a patient out of hospital quickly and the desirability of doing so (from the point of view of scarce hospital beds or the fact the patient hates institutions) may conflict with the disadvantages of keeping him at home (the inconvenience to medical staff and relatives, the extra risks, etc.). The main point to emphasize is that 'outcome' is a multidimensional concept defined by social values. What is an 'adequate' outcome may be quite different depending on one's role (think of the famous

Figure 2   *Possible outcomes*

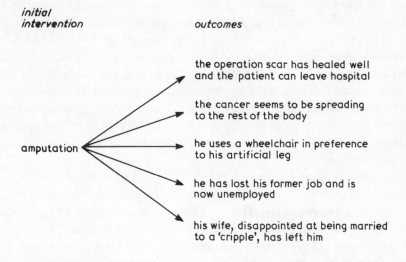

*initial
intervention*

outcomes

amputation

the operation scar has healed well
and the patient can leave hospital

the cancer seems to be spreading
to the rest of the body

he uses a wheelchair in preference
to his artificial leg

he has lost his former job and is
now unemployed

his wife, disappointed at being married
to a 'cripple', has left him

joke 'the operation was successful but the patient died'). Decisions have to be made about those aspects of outcome which are to be regarded as priorities (medical, social, psychological, economic) and therefore about the criteria that will be used to assess treatment. Apart from some work suggesting that 'harder' measures of outcome (like costs, number of days in hospital, and so on) are easier to measure and therefore more frequently used to assess success, with a consequent bias against 'softer' criteria (for example, the patient's 'happiness'), little work has been done in this area. In the absence of research a sociological approach can at least emphasize the fact that there are choices to be made and that different values (desirable or otherwise, depending on one's point of view) determine them. Chapter 11 considers some of the possible priorities of health care.

Assuming that we have a clear idea of the outcomes we are trying to effect, another set of studies suggests that the influence of the treatment setting can often be just as important in bringing about the desired results as the treatment itself; indeed in the treatment of some psychiatric patients the idea of the therapeutic community is to use the treatment setting as *the treatment* (Main, 1946).

One aspect of the treatment setting already discussed is the relationship created by doctors with patients. Much work, such as the experiment done by Egbert, indicates the significance of this relationship. In another study Skipper and Leonard (1968) focused on the fact that, independent of the anxiety produced by illness the social environment of the hospital may increase stress for children undergoing surgery and also for their mothers. Skipper and Leonard could usually observe raised blood pressure, post operative enuresis, disturbed sleep and 'a longer than necessary' period of post-operative recovery in the children they studied. They arranged in an experimental study for hospital personnel to provide information and emotional support to the mothers. By reducing the mother's stress (by giving her information) and thus changing her definition of the situation they found they could reduce the level of stress on the child and improve his psychological and physiological reaction to the hospitalization and surgery. The length of stay in hospital could be reduced. A great deal of other work suggests similar possibilities (for example, Friedman *et al.*, 1963; Davis, 1963) and the implications seem reasonably clear: taking account of social factors and the issues raised earlier (in the discussion of illness behaviour and the relationship between doctors and patients), will lead to a more complex view of the aims and results of treatment, and will, almost certainly, increase our ability to intervene effectively.

Other studies show how the organization of the hospital ward can influence the patients' symptoms and recovery process. For example, in a classic set of observations Goffman (1968) drew attention to the dangers of institutionalization among American mental patients. In this country Wing and Brown (1970) have demonstrated, in a very precise way, that factors such as the amount of time a patient spends doing nothing on a ward or his degree of social isolation, influence his symptoms and recovery, independent of his previous history, mental state, and so on.

Chapter 7 is specifically concerned with the influence of the hospital setting on the treatment of patients and it attempts to indicate how the sociology of complex organizations can aid our understanding. Two different but complementary approaches are outlined: one concerning the organization of work and the other the performance of work. In the first approach the emphasis is on the hospital or institution in terms of its organization for work and its formal decision-making structure. With the many different occupational roles of specialists to be co-ordinated, clear paths of command have to be set up for taking decisions and facilitating co-ordination. In the second approach, the emphasis is on the way in which those in the formal positions of the organization interpret their roles and interact with each other. There is an organizational problem concerning the ways in which decisions taken at the top of the organization are delegated downwards. General goals are specified in the form of sub-goals and these sub-goals are then delegated to particular individuals or departments. In such cases it should be emphasized that what is delegated as a goal or end for one department, is, for the organization, only a means of attaining a more general objective. However, sub-goals can often be followed to such an extent that they subvert the overall goals. This process is known as goal displacement. For example, one of the goals for nurses in a hospital is to maximize efficiency by ensuring that scarce beds are used as fully as possible. Such a goal is only a sub-goal for the hospital as a whole, but on occasions it can tend to dominate practice. Research has drawn attention to some horrifying examples. For example, Sudnow (1967) found that nurses would often leave patients whom they thought were about to die lying on a trolley in the ward corridor. In this way, should they die before the end of the shift, the nurses would be spared the trouble of re-making the bed and cleaning the sheets. Time would be saved, and the next patient could be admitted more quickly. The pursuit of a sub-goal led to the overall goal, the maximum welfare of each individual patient, being subverted.

The many problems that arise in large organizations encourage us to focus on the institution from a different perspective: the performance of work. The goals and tasks of the organization have to be interpreted by the individuals who work in it. These interpretations can be different; the interests of particular individuals in the organization are not necessarily the same, and the interests of the workers may not be the same as those of the clients. All sorts of complications follow from this potential conflict. In analysing organizations, Chapter 7 suggests a focus on 'compliance' — how members of the organization control each other's behaviour and that of their clients. It is argued that socialization and training, monitoring and surveillance, and the setting of tasks and rewards are important if an organization is to fulfil its aims.

A fifth area in which sociology can contribute concerns the coordination and organization of the medical care system as a whole. The medical care system in Great Britain, the National Health Service, is discussed in Chapter 8 with particular emphasis on its recent re-organization. The authors argue that the changing nature of disease and medical practice has implications for the health care system (such as the need for more preventative work, for greater scepticism concerning the value of new medical technology, for greater recognition of the requirements of chronically ill patients, and for the development of the 'health-team' approach), and they suggest that future advance and innovation in the health service may come from flexible experimentation with health care organization. They suggest that if this argument is accepted, the highly-centralized administration, which they believe the re-organization imposes, may be a disadvantage.

A sociological analysis of the health care system provides insights into the working of the political system and into the way change is dependent on powerful vested interests, each of which may have different ideas about the optimal solution. After encountering this kind of analysis of the National Health Service, it may be easier for those who work in it to understand some of the rules and regulations to which they are subject.

The sixth, and perhaps the most exciting, way in which sociology can contribute is through the study of social factors in the aetiology of disease. From the review of developments in Chapter 9, it is clear that social factors are of crucial significance in causing a wide range of diseases. Such findings clearly contribute to medical research. To take one example, some recent work on depression, by the author of Chapter 9 (Brown, 1973; Brown, Ní Bhrólcháin, and Harris 1975), concentrates on fairly simple aspects of an individual's immediate social environment — life crises such as bereavements, job losses, marital separations, moving house, and so on. The study was limited to women between the ages of eighteen and sixty-five and tried to link life crises to the onset of depressive symptoms. Detailed attention was given to clinical issues, particularly the history of changes in symptoms, and also to methodological issues in the collection of data on life crises.

Careful attention to methodology (see pp. 314–16) produced an important result: patients with a recent onset of depressive symptoms had, on average, approximately three and a half times as many 'major' crises in the last forty-eight weeks as did members of a control group in the general population. But how important are these life-crises? Are they not simply triggers: the last straw that produces symptoms in a predisposed person? Brown and his colleagues found that the particular life-crises that provoke depression are relatively rare in people's lives (such as the loss of a job, the end of an affair, the death of a wife) and calculated that the crises could be seen as important because, without them, individuals would have remained well for several years or perhaps forever (pp. 318–20). They also found that long-term difficulties (such as bad housing or severe economic deprivation which had continued for at least two years) could cause depressive symptoms. Furthermore, the wives of semi-skilled and unskilled workers had twice the rate of symptoms of other wives (26 per cent as opposed to 13 per cent). In their recent paper Brown, Ní Bhrólcháin, and Harris (1975) argue that a combination of life-crises, difficulties, and other aspects of an individual's life situation (such as whether a woman works outside the home) explain most of the depressive onsets discovered. The results of other investigators suggest that life-crises may be important in a wide range of diseases such as heart disease, cancer, stroke, rheumatoid arthritis, streptococcal infection (Rahe, 1969; Gove, 1973; Cobb, 1973; Meyer and Haggerty, 1962). These studies are discussed in Chapter 9.

One last area where sociology can contribute to medical practice is discussed in Chapter 10 and concerns the fact that illness and disability are social facts as well as simply medical ones. The terms 'illness' and 'disease' can be used to make a helpful distinction. 'Illness' refers to a subjective feeling of discontent experienced by an individual; 'disease' refers to the signs, symptoms, and behaviours regarded by doctors as pathologically abnormal. Of course illness, which is usually what patients complain about, and disease, which is part of a vocabulary that helps to apply systematic procedures to treatment, do not necessarily coincide and there tends to be conflict between the concepts. This conflict is best expressed in situations where patients claim they are ill while doctors say they are not diseased (for example 'malingerers') and where doctors say patients are diseased while patients insist that they are not ill (for example, where someone is compulsorily admitted to a mental hospital).

As I argue in Chapter 5, when discussing illness behaviour, the subjective feelings of discontent which people experience are mediated by norms and values, so that behaviours, symptoms, and pain are (or are not) perceived as 'illness' by individuals in different cultures. Similarly, accepted ideas about disease which are held by doctors and others may vary from culture to culture so that similar physiological or behavioural facts are differently regarded as symptoms of pathology. In this country abnormally low blood pressure is not treated and is in fact an asset when applying for life insurance, whereas in Germany it would be treated by doctors (Jarman, personal communication; Gerhadt, personal communication). Similarly a study recently conducted by the World Health Organisation showed how psychiatric diagnosis varied dramatically across cultures – different clusters of behaviour were interprcted as symptoms of 'schizophrenia' in places such as the USSR, Nigeria, and Britain (Wing, personal communication). The categories of 'illness' and 'disease' because they both imply differentiation from the normal, are necessarily influenced by the typical ideas that exist within a culture. In this sense 'illness' and 'disease' are culturally defined and are therefore social facts. What is illness or disease in one place may not be in another. From this perspective, who is defined as 'ill' or 'healthy', and how he or she came to be labelled in this way, are interesting sociological questions.

To the extent that illness is defined as an abnormal state by a society or a social group then it is, by definition, a deviant attribute, and the sociology of deviant behaviour – typically dealing with more obvious deviants like pickpockets, thieves, drug addicts, and homosexuals – can provide a relevant perspective for analysis. One interesting notion taken from the sociology of deviance is the idea of labelling (see Lemert, 1967), which focuses on the way in which someone who possesses a deviant attribute (in medicine the signs and symptoms of 'disease') comes to be formally recognized as 'deviant'; for our purpose, how a person who is ill becomes defined as a patient. It can be argued that most individuals almost every day do things which are 'officially' considered deviant in their society. For example, they tell lies or half-truths, exceed the speed limit, or cross the road other than at a pedestrian crossing. However, only some people are officially regarded (labelled) as deviant. The labelling perspective is not concerned with the reasons why someone possessed the deviant attribute (symptoms) in the first place, but with the effect of the attribute being formally and publically recognized. From work involving criminals and drug addicts (for example, Rubington and Weinberg, 1968: 389–463) it is clear that the process of being labelled and the effects of public recognition can be very important in the person's future life. Thus, in connection with medical situations, it may be instructive to ask what effects the provision of a diagnosis, either by word of mouth or by an entry on medical records, has on the person so defined.

One danger of any diagnosis (and this has been eloquently treated by Erving Goffman, 1968) is that it can stigmatize or 'spoil' the identity of . the person to whom it is given. The public recognition of a deviant attribute can lead to a person being perceived by others primarily in terms of that attribute rather than by all the many others that the person may possess as a human being. In such a situation there is a danger of the person's whole identity becoming bound up with his 'stigma' for the rest of his life. It is argued that criminals can become habitual offenders, drug experimenters can become drug addicts, and patients can become chronic cases, due to labelling. The effects of labelling and the individual's reaction to his official recognition as a deviant are analysed as 'secondary deviance' to distinguish it from the factors that caused the person to possess the deviant attribute in the first place (known as primary deviance; Lemert, 1967). Because the attachment of a label (such as a diagnosis) can have such significant negative effects, it is clear that any diagnosis must be given with great caution and with careful consideration of the costs and benefits to the patient.

A second interesting notion taken from the sociology of deviance is the idea of 'social control', referred to earlier in this chapter. This notion is concerned with the fact that in most societies there are institutions and individuals that deal with deviation from norms and thus help to maintain the norms and the existing social structure — the most obvious examples being the police, the courts, and the penal institutions. However, illness of any sort, by definition, can be viewed as a disruption to the orderly working of society and thus the way it is defined and handled is an important aspect of social control.

Medical intervention is a significant feature of social control in two ways: it acts to define and legitimate what is illness and what is not, and it has the task of managing and returning to their former 'healthy' status those who become defined as 'ill'. Thus doctors issue sickness certificates, offer courts advice about a person's sanity, and permit people to avoid the draft where there is military conscription. They try to make 'well' those who are 'sick' and thus reinforce notions of 'health' and 'sickness'.

Whether particular problems should be defined as medical has been fiercely debated, particularly with reference to psychiatry. Writers like Thomas Szasz (1960) and R.D. Laing (1967) have tried to demonstrate that in many cases of what we call 'mental illness', the label 'illness' may in fact be mistaken. Szasz argues that many of the problems defined as 'illness' are merely 'problems of living' and that to label them as 'illness' diverts attention from very real social problems that need to be faced up to rather than seen as illness and swept under the carpet by 'treatment'. In the same way Laing has argued that many supposedly crazy acts are not crazy at all when considered from the point of view of the actor. They are attempts to communicate a predicament, and it is this communication rather than the crazy acts, called symptoms, that should be considered. That the truth or falsity of these arguments has not been demonstrated may not be important. The arguments warn doctors that they should at least consider whether the label 'disease' describes a situation better than some other, and that they should recognize the potentially dangerous implications of such a label, both to the individual and to society.

Concluding Remarks

I have argued that sociology can make a number of contributions to the understanding of medicine and medical situations, and I shall argue in the next chapter that they can be based on scientifically reliable procedures. In the remainder of the book these contributions will be explored further. However, doctors sometimes ask a rather special set of questions about the usefulness of sociological work. Is not sociology a matter of generalization? Are not its findings based on aggregates? What use can such information be to medicine, which is concerned to treat individuals?

I must make it clear that I believe these questions are misguided. Although it is true that sociological statements, because they are based on aggregates, are probability statements, they are, in this respect, no different from the majority of statements made in other basic medical sciences. Consider, for instance, the relationship between rubella in a pregnant woman and blindness in her future child. It is known that the acquisition of rubella at a certain time in pregnancy is *likely* in a known number of cases to produce blindness in the child. In the same way, smoking has a *probability* relationship to lung cancer, heart disease, and to various difficulties in pregnancy and its outcome for mother and child. Similarly, the presence of particular bacteria or of particular genetic traits confers a *probability* of particular diseases. Again, the results of most diagnostic tests do no more than suggest a probable presence of disease process. There are always false negatives and positives. Finally, most medical treatments and many surgical operations carry a *probability* of 'success' — usually much less than 100 per cent and sometimes no more than chance (see Chapter 11). Despite the absence of one-to-one relationships in medicine, most doctors would agree, I think, that known probabilities are better than no knowledge at all. In this sense sociological statements (such as the fact that about 60 per cent of depressive onsets in women result from the interaction of life-crises with the individual's ongoing social situation) can be treated in exactly the same way as the other basic scientific information that medicine utilizes. Sociological statements can guide the doctor towards a possible understanding or course of action.

Sociological information is, therefore, neither 'softer' nor 'harder' than most other scientific information utilized by doctors, and is subject to the same strengths and weaknesses in application. A doctor applying any of the medical sciences to treatment and diagnosis always takes a risk that the particular case will be an exception (see below, pp. 215–16).

Unfortunately, it must be admitted that much sociological work is not yet able to make probability statements about disease, treatment, outcome, and so on. Therefore, although sociology is often unable to make precise recommendations, it can make an important contribution to medical practice by providing a new way of looking at things — a further perspective.

In particular, sociology sensitizes us to the weakness of the implicit 'national' perspective that has caused great problems and frustrations in medicine. It helps us to acknowledge that other people have different values and different ways of doing things from ourselves, and that our way of seeing or doing things is not the only way. We may still choose to do and think as we have always done, but we will be that much more aware of our own role, of the potential effects of our actions, of the needs of patients, and of the functioning of the institutions in which we work.

Notes

1. These and other arguments are developed in various papers by Margaret Jefferys (1969, 1970, 1971a and b, 1974).
2. I am following Lukes in substituting 'social factors' for the less meaningful 'social facts' that appears in many translations of Durkheim (Lukes, 1973: 9).
3. Female medical students may wish to note here how writers of medical sociology textbooks — in their choice of examples, pronouns, and so on — can be influenced by the norms of a predominantly male establishment. It would be very 'inconvenient' to use him and her/he and she, etc. throughout a text.
4. I am grateful to David Armstrong for ideas and arguments covering this issue.

References

Backett, E.H., Heady, J.A., and Evans, J.C.G. (1954) Studies of General Practice. The Doctor's Job in an Urban Area. *British Medical Journal* 1: 109—115.

Balint, M. (1957) *The Doctor, His Patient, and the Illness.* New York: International Universities Press.
 A fascinating account by Balint (a psychoanalyst) about his work with a group of general practitioners. Balint makes the point that many visits to the doctor are concerned with psycho-social problems presented under the guise of illness and examines the role of the doctor in such circumstances. The account is, however, largely anecdotal.

Benedict, R. (1934) *Patterns of Culture.* Boston: Houghton-Mifflin.
 An early anthropological classic which explores the variations in norms and values amongst different 'primitive' tribes.

Brocklehurst, J.C. and Shergold, M. (1968) What Happens when Geriatric Patients leave Hospital? *Lancet* 2: 1133.

Brotherston, J.H.F., Cartwright, A., Cowan, J.L., Baldwin, J.T., Douglas, E.C.K., and Steele, G.A. (1958) Night Calls: their Frequency and Nature in one General Practice. *British Medical Journal* 4: 797—99.

Brown, G.W., Ni Bhrólcháin, M., and Harris, T. (1975) Social Class and Psychiatric Disturbance among Women in an Urban Population. *Sociology* 9 (2): 225—54.

Brown, G.W., Birley, J., and Wing, J.K. (1972) Influence of Family Life on the Course of Schizophrenic Disorders: a Replication, *British Journal of Psychiatry* 121: 241—58.

Brown, G.W., Sklair, F., Harris, T.O., and Birley, J.L.T. (1973) Life Events and Psychiatric Disorders. Part 1: Some Methodological Issues. *Psychological Medicine* 3 (1). 74—87.

Butler, D. and Stokes, D. (1974) *Political Change in Britain* (2nd edition). London and Basingstoke: Macmillian and Co.

An analysis of trends in voting.

Butterfield, W.J.H. (1968) *Priorities in Medicine.* London: Nuffield Provincial Hospitals Trust.

Cobb, S., Schull, W.J., Harburg, E., and Kasl, S.V. (1973) The Intra-familial Transmission of Rheumatoid Arthritis: Summary of Findings. *Journal of Chronic Disease* 22: 295—96.

The whole issue of this journal is devoted to the important research which suggests that the way in which a family handles aggression can be an important aetiological factor in an individual's later development of rheumatoid arthritis. See chapter 9.

Davis, F. (1963) *Passage through Crisis.* Indiannapolis: Bobbs—Merrill.

A detailed account of the way in which families recognized, reacted to, and dealt with the onset and treatment of poliomyletis in one of the children.

Department of Health and Social Security (1974a) *Health and Personal Social Service Statistics.* London: HMSO.

— (1974b) *Report on Hospital In-patient Enquiry for the Year 1972.* Part I, Tables. London: HMSO.

Douglas, J.W.B. (1964) *The Home and the School.* London: McGibbon and Kee.

A study of a large sample of children born in March 1946 and their subsequent development. This report (one of a series) describes the experience of the children at the time when they were allocated to the various types of secondary schools. The study looks at the effects of family background, social situation, and IQ on their achievement and selection.

Durkheim, E. (1897 trans. 1952) *Suicide.* Translated by G. Simpson. London: Routledge & Kegan Paul. Originally published in France.

In an analysis of suicide rates and the way they vary between countries and social groups Durkheim made a powerful case for the importance of the social context in which a suicide takes place. The book is a methodological classic demonstrating the possibilities for sociological analysis.

(1901, trans. 1938) *The Rules of Sociological Method.* Translated by Sarah Solovay and John Mueller. New York: The Free Press.

Durkheim's classic exposition of his view of the aim and task of sociology. Originally published in France.

Egbert, J.A., Battit, G.E., Welch, C.E., and Bartlett, M.K. (1964) Reduction of Post-operative Pain by Encouragement and Instruction of Patients. *New England Journal of Medicine* 270: 825—27.

Eifrig, D.E., Imboden, J.B., Mckusick, V.A., Canter, A.D. (1961) Constrictive

Pericarditis: Psychological Aspects of Convalescence following Pericardectomy. *Journal of Chronic Disease* **13**: 52–8.

Eimerl, T.S. (1960) Aspects of General Practice 1949–1960. MD thesis, University of Liverpool.

Friedman, S.B., Chodoff, P., Mason, J.W., and Hamburg, D.A. (1963) Behavioural Observations on Parents Anticipating the Death of a Sick Child. *Pediatrics* **32**: 610–25.

The authors describe the results of a study where they recorded the behaviour and physical and emotional reactions of parents who were waiting for their child to die of leukemia. The grief reaction is related to the way in which parents dealt with the anticipatory period.

Fry, J. (1966) *Profiles of Disease.* London: E. & S. Livingston.

Garfinkle, H.D. (1967) *Studies in Ethnomethodology.* Englewood Cliffs, New Jersey: Prentice Hall.

General Medical Council (1967) *Recommendations as to Basic Medical Education.* London: GMC.

Gerhadt, U. Personal Communication.

Goffman, E. (1968) *Asylums.* Hardmondsworth: Penguin.

A brilliant but anecdotal account of participant observation in American mental hospitals.

Gove, W.R. (1973) Sex, Marital Status and Mortality. *American Journal of Sociology* **79**: 45–67.

Suggests that marital life, under certain conditions, may afford protection to a whole range of diseases. See chapter 9.

Glass, D. (1954) *Social Mobility in Britain.* London: Routledge & Kegan Paul.

Himmelwheit, H.T. (1954) Social status and secondary education since the 1944 Act: some data for London. *Social Mobility in Britain*, 141–159. London: Routledge & Kegan Paul. In D. Glass (ed.)

Hockey, L. (1966) *Feeling the Pulse: A Survey of District Nursing in Six Areas.* London: Queens Institute of District Nursing.

– (1968) *Care in the Balance: A Study of Collaboration between Hospital and Community Services.* London: Queens Institute of District Nursing.

Imboden, J.B., Canter, A.B., Cluff, L.E., Trevor, R.W. (1961a) Symptomatic Recovery from Medical Disorders. *Journal of the American Medical Association* **178**: 1182–84.

Suggests that an individual's social background and emotional state will affect the speed and extent of recovery with reference to Brucellosis and Influenza.

– (1961b) Brucellosis: III. Psychological Aspects of Delayed Convalescence. *American Medical Association Archives of Internal Medicine* **103**: 408–14.

Jarman, B. Personal communication

Jefferys, M. (1969) Sociology and Medicine: Separation or Symbiosis? *The Lancet* **i**: 1111–16.

– (1970) The Doctor's Dilemma – A Sociological Viewpoint. Social and Economic Administration 4: 37–44.

– (1971a) What is the Purpose of Teaching Behavioural Sciences in Medical Education. *Acta Socio-Medica Scandinavica* **3**: 157–60.

– (1971b) The Relationship of Sociology to Medicine. *British Journal of Hospital Medicine*, January: 8–11.

– (1974) Does Medicine need Sociology? A Defence of the Todd Commission Proposals for Broadening the Base of Medical Education. *University of London Bulletin* (16) March: 7—9.

Kerr, E. and Siegel, M. (1954) The Inter-Industry Propensity to Strike. In A. Kornhasuer, R. Dubin, and A. Ross (eds.), *Industrial Conflict*. New York: McGraw-Hill.
A classic sociological paper where it is shown that strike rates vary according to factors such as the type of industry and that features of the collective experience of workers in such situations (for example, their isolation) causes more solidarity and militancy.

King Edwards Fund (1970) *Elderly People: Home from Hospital*. London.

Klein, R. and Ashley, J. (1972) Old-Age Health. *New Society*. January 6: 13—15.

Kutner, B., Malcover, H.B., and Oppenheim, A. (1958) Delay in The Diagnosis and Treatment of Cancer. *Journal of Chronic Disease* 7: 95—120.

Laing, R.D. (1967) *The Politics of Experience*. Harmondsworth: Penguin.
A provocative and stimulating analysis of the nature of sanity and madness in Western societies. Laing suggests that just as many apparently insane acts by 'sane' people such as Presidents and Prime Ministers may take on meaning when viewed in context, so the acts of those called 'schizophrenic' can also be understood within their familiar background. Neither Laing, nor his critics, have yet demonstrated how far, 'schizophrenia' is intelligible and how far the comments and delusions of 'schizophrenics' make 'sense'.

Lemert, E. (1967) The Concept of Secondary Deviance. In E. Lemert (ed.), *Human deviance, Social Problems and Social Control*. Englewood Cliffs, New Jersey: Prentice Hall.
Perhaps the key statement of 'labelling' theory.

Little, A. and Westergaard, J. (1964) The Trend of Class Differentials in England and Wales. *British Journal of Sociology* 15: 4.

Lukes, S. (1973) *Emile Durkheim and His Work*. London: Allen Lane.

Main, T. (1946) The Hospital as a Therapeutic Institution. *Bulletin of the Menninger Clinic* 10: 66—70.

Marks, R.U. (1967) Factors involving Social and Demographic Characteristics: A Review of Empirical Findings. *Millbank Memorial Fund Quarterly* 45 (2): 51—108.
A summary of the state of epidemiological research into Coronary Heart Disease. A large number of social factors have been isolated but no developed theory relating them together has been outlined. For a critique of this work see Suchman in the same issue of the journal.

Mayer, J.E. and Timms, N. (1969) Clash in Perspective between Worker and Client. *Social Casework*, January: 32—40.

Mechanic, D. (1968) *Medical Sociology: A Selective View*. New York: The Free Press.
Chapter 4 provides an excellent review of research findings concerning patient consultation rates.

Meyer, R.J. and Haggerty, R.J. (1962) Streptococcal Infections in Families. *Pediatrics* 29: 239—49.
Suggests that Streptococcal infections are caused by stress. See Chapter 9.

Moran, L.J., Fairweather, G.W., and Morton, R.B. (1956) Some Determinants of Successful and Unsuccessful Adaptation to Hospital Treatment of Tuberculosis. *Journal of Consulting Psychology* 20: 125—131.

Overall, B. and Aronson, M. (1963) Expectations of Psychotherapy in Patients of Lower Socio-Economic Class. *American Journal of Orthopsychiatry* 43: 41.

Querido, A. (1959) An Investigation into the Clinical, Social and Mental Factors

Determining the Results of Hospital Treatment. *British Journal of Preventive and Social Medicine* 13: 33—49.

Rahe, R.H. (1969) Life Crisis and Health Change. In P. May and J. Witterborn (eds.), *Psychotropic Drug Response: Advances in Prediction.* Springfield (USA): Charles Thomas Publications.

Rosenberg, B. (1966) *The Logic of Survey Analysis.* New York: Basic Books.

Royal College of General Practitioners (1973) *General Practice: Present State and Future Needs.* London.

Royal Commission on Medical Education (1968) *Report.* London: HMSO.
Sets out the rationale for the revised medical curriculum.

Rubington, E.S. and Weinberg, M.S. (eds.) (1968) *Deviance: the Interactionist Perspective.* New York: Macmillan.
A basic text in labelling theory.

Skipper, J. and Leonard, R. (1968) Children, Stress and Hospitalisation: A Field Experiment. *Journal of Health and Social Behaviour* 9: 275—86.

Suchman, E. and Phillips. B. (1958) An Analysis of the Validity of Health Questionnaires. *Social Forces* 26: 223—32.

Sudnow, D. (1967) *Passing On: The Social Organisation of Dying.* New York: Prentice Hall.
A fascinating account of death and dying in two different types of hospital in the USA — one fee-paying and the other state owned.

Szasz , T.S. (1960) The Myth of Mental Illness. *American Psychologist* 15: 113—18.

Williams, W.O. (1970) A Study of General Practitioners' Work Loads in South Wales, 1965—66. *Royal College of General Practitioners, Reports from General Practice.* no. XII.

Wing, J.K. Personal communication concerning data from the World Health Organisation study of schizophrenia.

Wing, J.K. and Brown, G.W. (1970) *Institutionalism and Schizophrenia: A Comparative Study of three Mental Hospitals 1960—1968.* Cambridge: Cambridge University Press.
A longitudinal study relating measures of the ward environment (and changes in it) to the improvement and decline of patients' symptoms.

Wright, I.K. (Recorder) (1968) *General Practice in South-West England.* London: Royal College of General Practitioners.

Zola, I.K. (1963) Problems of Communication, Diagnosis, and Patient Care. *Journal of Medical Education* 38: 829—38.

Part II

Background

Chapter 2

David Tuckett

Sociology as a Science

'. . . from time to time, the argument is advanced that surveys only put into complicated form observations which are already obvious to everyone.

Understanding the origin of this point of view is of importance far beyond the limits of the present discussion. The reader may be helped in recognising this attitude if he looks over a few statements which are typical of many survey findings and carefully observes his own reactions. A short list of these, with brief interpretative comments, will be given here in order to bring into sharper focus probable reactions of many readers. [The reader is strongly advised to consider these findings carefully.]

1. Better educated men showed more psycho-neurotic symptoms than those with less education. (The mental instability of the intellectual as compared to the more impassive psychology of the man-in-the-street has often been commented on.)
2. Men from rural background were usually in better spirits during their Army life than soldiers from city background. (After all they are more accustomed to hardships.)
3. Southern soldiers were better able to stand the climate in the hot South Sea Islands than Northern soldiers. (Of course, Southerners are more accustomed to hot weather.)
4. White privates were more eager to become non-coms than Negroes. (The lack of ambition among Negroes is almost proverbial.)
5. Southern Negroes preferred Southern to Northern white officers. (Isn't it well known that Southern whites have a more fatherly attitude towards their "darkies"?)
6. As long as the fighting continued, men were more eager to be returned to the States than they were after the German surrender. (You cannot blame people for not wanting to be killed.)

We have in these examples a sample list of the simplest type of interrelationships which provide the "bricks" from which our empirical social science is being built. But why, since they are so obvious, is so much money and energy given to establish such findings? Would it not be wiser to take them for granted and proceed directly to a more sophisticated type of analysis? This might be so except for one interesting point about the list. *Every one of these statements is the direct opposite of what actually was found.* Poorly educated soldiers were more neurotic than those with high education; Southerners showed no greater ability than Northerners to adjust to a tropical climate; Negroes were more eager for promotion than whites, and so on.

If we had mentioned the actual results of the investigation first, the reader would have labelled these 'obvious' also. Obviously something is wrong with the entire argument of "obviousness". It should really be turned on its head. Since every kind of human reaction is conceivable, it is of great importance to know which reactions actually occur most frequently and under what conditions; only then will a more advanced social science develop.' (Lazarsfeld, 1949: 379–80).

As human beings we are endlessly involved in our daily lives in making inferences and drawing conclusions (what does he do? is that a space for my car? does he want me? is that man's expression warm?). We have to. Life demands that we make judgements and act on them. Indeed, much of the time the process is so automatic that we hardly realize it is happening (that empty space is a space for my car; that man is behaving strangely etc.). We use what we consider 'common sense', believing things to be obvious. Certain things go together; certain actions lead to other actions; certain situations lead to other situations. Nonetheless, the previous chapter illustrated some examples of how the usual assumptions that individuals make in a wide range of activities can vary; how 'common sense' is different in different social groups.

In both scientific experiments and day-to-day activity the individuals involved draw inferences from their observations. The difference between the two activities is that in scientific activity the onus is on the investigator to draw conclusions explicitly; that is the logic of his reasoning should be clear for all to see. There should be a clear statement of the evidence for conclusions because the objective of science is to make inferences in which we can have confidence, that is inferences we can believe to be 'true'.

In the laboratory sciences, which form the bulk of the basic medical sciences, a large number of conventions have been developed to permit investigators to confidently assert that their findings are 'correct' — in the sense that other possible explanations of the findings (such as investigator bias or error) can be discounted. Workers have established methods of designing and conducting experiments; of making observations; and of analysing results. In the laboratory sciences these methods have often been tried and tested in many different laboratories in many different parts of the world and are a part of the day-to-day vocabulary of the research scientist. So much so in fact that research reports often take it for granted that the reader will understand the logic of the method employed (that is, the reasons underlying a particular set of procedures). The following quotation was taken at random from the *Lancet* and illustrates the point well:

'*Enzyme Assays*
A.D.A. activity in R.B.C. haemolysates was determined by a linked assay at 37°C (method 1) using 0.4 mg. adenosine per ml. 0.05 M phosphate buffer pH 7.5 as substrate. In the presence of endogenous nucleoside phosphorylase and exogenous xanthine oxidase (0.2 units per ml.), uric acid is produced and measured at 293 nmo. A modification of this method (method 2) was also used. The two methods showed a correlation coefficient of 0.93. Values for R.B.C. activity were expressed as nmol per mg. Hb per hour. A log transformation of all values was performed because of a skewed distribution towards higher A.D.A. values. R.B.C.S. were also typed for the genetically determined polymorphism demonstrated by R.B.C.–A.D.A. ...' (Hirschorn *et al.*, 1975: 73–4).

I am not qualified to judge this research report and am not familiar with the procedures, but those who are will immediately know, on reading it, which measurement biases have been excluded. As a result, if these are the biases they consider significant, they will be able to take the conclusions of Hirschorn and his colleagues seriously. The logic of scientific method is to permit precisely this evaluation.

As will become clear in this chapter, and the remainder of the book, sociological research has not reached nearly this level of sophistication, certainty, and conventionality in its methods. Nonetheless, exactly the same kind of scientific logic can be applied to sociological study.

In my view sociological statements may be taken seriously and they represent ideas about the social world that merit special attention (over and above that given to those of any person in the street), insofar as they rest on a series of systematically derived observations and inferences, where the procedures involved are open and at least potentially repeatable. Sociologists, like other 'experts' have no automatic access to wisdom, and care should always be taken to distinguish between systematically derived conclusions and mere assertions. All too often scientific 'experts' (and doctors are as much to blame here as economists, drug company executives, sociologists, or psychologists) have given wholly unjustifiable advice based on pseudo-scientific assertion. We need to protect ourselves from advice of this kind and it is for this reason that understanding scientific methodology is important. However, before trying to provide the reader with guidelines for evaluating sociological research, I want to spell out the logic implicit in scientific activity more clearly. I hope this will allow the reader to understand the similarity in the sociologist's approach to research — despite the obvious differences. Since the ideas apply to science in general, they may also help to suggest principles for a more general evaluation of the evidence offered us as students in many different subjects.

Alternate hypotheses

For me, the aim of scientific research is to try to make choices between explanations on a systematic basis. The approach to scientific logic, which I intend to outline and which I believe to be most helpful, relies very heavily on the arguments of Karl Popper. It is not, however, the only possible approach. In Popper's 'third view' the scientist aims at a 'true' explanation of observable facts; but, although this remains the aim of the scientist, he can never know for certain whether his findings are true. He has to content himself with sometimes establishing with reasonable certainty that a particular theory is false (Popper, 1972: 114–5). In this model our knowledge of the world is based on conjectures which we submit to tests. In general, advances in knowledge are made by choosing between rival explanations of the same phenomena. In the previous chapter (pp. 18) I have already illustrated one example of this approach when I considered the possibility that the significant determinant of an individual's entry to a selective secondary school was not his father's occupation but his own I.Q. By analysing the relationship between father's occupation and entry to a selective school, for each level of I.Q., it was possible to show that the father's occupation did have a significant effect — the sons of non-manual workers continue to have a seven times better chance of entry to a grammar school than do the sons of manual workers. As a result of this analysis it is possible to be more confident that the father's occupation does exert influence on entry to a grammar school.

In the laboratory sciences the choice between explanations is generally made by using the experimental method. The logic in this approach is that, by controlling *when* something (X) happens, *how* it happens, and to *whom* or *what* (Y) it happens, it is possible to determine whether X produces an effect on Y. Typically, two (or more) matched situations are created and then the experimental variable X (a particular drug, bacteria, chemical, etc.) is applied to one situation (Y) but not to others. Subjects (or guinea pigs or bone marrow cells or whatever) may be matched according to given characteristics or may be randomly allocated to experimental and control groups. The effect of the introduction of X is then compared to an assumed identical situation where X is not introduced. The experiment is then repeated (replicated) many times. Statistical techniques are used to help estimate whether any different results observed between the experimental and control groups are greater than might have been expected by chance and, consequently, may therefore be taken seriously. An inference is then made that any change in Y, that can be observed in the experimental but not in the control group, must be due to the introduction of X. This explanation rather than some other is therefore confirmed.

The underlying logic is that the particular causal explanation depends on (1) a correlation between the two variables (X and Y) such that when one varies, so does the other; (2) the assumption that because it has been arranged that X occurred before Y, it is reasonable to assume that X caused Y and not vice versa, and (3) the assumption that since the *only* difference between experimental and control situations is the introduction of X, then it must be X and not some other factor that causes Y to change. The method therefore establishes co-variation and time-order and also rules out alternative explanations that something other than X influenced Y. It thus permits systematic choice.

In sociological research and in much medical (and other) research, which involves observation of individuals engaged in their daily lives (for example, studies of what aspects of an individual's life-style cause depression or heart disease), it is usually impossible, for practical or ethical reasons, for an experiment to be performed. Although, regrettably, it is not unknown, scientists are not in the habit of randomly infecting individuals or of forcing them to live their lives in prescribed ways.

Because they do not have control over *who* gets *what, when,* sociologists and others working in non-experimental situations have had to devise other methods for testing for co-variation and time-order and for ruling out alternative hypotheses — thus permitting choice between rival explanations.

Figure 1   *Possible sources of error when inferring causal relationships*

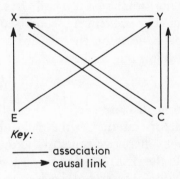

Figure 1 illustrates some of the rival explanations that are possible when an investigator is attempting to establish a causal relationship between X and Y. I will take the sources of difficulty in turn.

'E' type error occurs where a third variable (termed extraneous or spurious) is regarded as causing the observed co-variation between X and Y. In a study, for example, investigating the influence that an individual's experience of life-crises can have on his subsequent health, measures of an individual's experience of life-crises (how many, how serious, etc.) might be made and might be related to records of medical examinations of the individual. In such a case it is possible that if medical examinations reveal more ill health among individuals with more serious life-crises, then we might want to infer that life-crises actually cause illness. On the other hand, we might equally suspect that some other explanation — a third factor — caused this apparent relationship. Individuals who are more anxious than others, for instance, might be more likely both to get ill and to report life-crises as more threatening. An extraneous variable could be causing an apparent relationship between X and Y whereas in fact X might not actually cause Y at all. In experimental method this difficulty can be ruled out by the assumption that all 'third factors' are ruled out by direct control — for example, matching or randomization.

'C' type error occurs where a third variable *contaminates* the relationship between X and Y. This difficulty is well known in experimental work: the knowledge of a research hypothesis (i.e., knowledge of Y) may influence the investigator's measurement of the experimental variable (X). Any relationship between X and Y would therefore be caused by the experimenter rather than by the fact that X actually causes Y. Cordaro and Ison (1963), to quote but one example, have shown how laboratory experiments on planarium can suffer from this difficulty. In fact, experimental and non-experimental research are both equally at risk for this type of error.

'J' type error occurs where some unknown variable, other than X, influences Y and the change in Y is then falsely thought to result from the introduction of X. This kind of error can normally be excluded in experiments by randomization or matching, but this need not be the case. Campbell and Stanley (1966), for instance, have given examples of how the way the experimental situation is treated, after matching or randomization, but before final measurement, can create 'J' type error. For example, one group of subjects on the way to an experiment, but not another may be involved in a bus crash.

Validity

The choice of an erroneous inference in research can result from two different sources — factors internal to the particular experimental study and factors external to it. These two types of factors are known as internal and external validity. In the first type we must ask whether the techniques of study (experimentation, observation, measurement, analysis) make a difference in this specific study (did bias arise from the investigator knowing the hypothesis being investigated; did the investigator measure what he said he did; etc.). In the second type we ask, assuming the study is internally valid, to what populations, settings, treatment variables, and measurement variables can it be generalized.

Precise measurement, which obviously contributes to internal validity, and precise control over the variables in a situation, which will also rule out internal error, can often decrease external validity. A key factor in this connection is the obtrusiveness of the study. Are the specific answers given to interview questions the products of the fact that someone is being asked questions? Is behaviour in experimental situations the same as 'usual' behaviour?

Evidence concerning many types of laboratory experiments suggests that results cannot be assumed to apply to behaviour in non-experimental situations (see, for example, Friedman, 1969; Orne, 1959). A crucial question is whether the research situation produces expectations in the subject which in themselves produce the results. In a number of experiments by Beecher and his colleagues, the effect of large doses of morphine (15 mg), for example, and a 1 ml dose of saline solution could not be distinguished by way of their ability to relieve experimentally induced pain. This deviation from normal pharmacological reactions was explained by the fact that subjects in an experiment do not expect that the experimenters will 'really' hurt them (Beecher, 1965: 115–6). Other work on the importance of the situation in which a potentially pain-producing stimulus is given confirms that such a result would not be surprising (pp. 165, 167–8). In the same way, it has proved difficult to induce boredom in the laboratory (Orne, 1962).

With the types of error and invalidity so far discussed in mind, I now want to consider the ways sociologists set about trying to overcome them. I will discuss the different techniques under the headings of research design, observation and measurement, and methods of analysis. Although I am using these different headings for the purpose of exposition, it is my belief that actual research and the evaluation of research involves a great deal of interplay between the headings.

Research Design

The purpose of research design is to permit the investigator to choose between rival explanations that he considers relevant. The first thing to be recognized, therefore, is that the investigator's ability to imagine alternative interpretations and devise ways of testing them, is a key determinant of success. We will be as confident in his results as he can make us by demonstrating that the objections we raise do not fit the facts. Some progress towards this aim can be made by the use of appropriate research design.

If an investigator is trying to establish co-variation, that is that X and Y vary together, the first thing he will have to do is show that for different values of X there are different values of Y. As in the experimental method, the critical idea here is the notion of a comparison rate or base rate. If I want to know whether bereavement leads to an increased rate of mental and physical impairment over a given period, I will need to know how much impairment I could expect without bereavement over this period of time. If I do not have this information, then when I actually find bereavement, I will have no idea whether there has been an increase in impairment or not.

A comparison rate is generally obtained by designing research so that it is possible to get information not only about the study group (for example, the bereaved) but also from a comparison or control group made up of 'typical', comparable individuals who do not have the study group characteristic — in this case, are not bereaved. Two approaches are used to obtain a comparison group: study group individuals may be matched on relevant characteristics or a random sample may be taken from a relevant population. The disadvantage of 'matching', which is a great deal more common in medico-social research than in sociology, is that it can often control out variation that might be relevant. For example, the effect of X on Y may be dependent on the presence of a further (conditional) variable Z. If Z is controlled, a relationship between X and Y may appear stronger or weaker than it is, or even appear not to exist at all. In general, matching in social research is both inefficient (some of the information that is obtained is not used as a result) because it reduces the comparisons that can be made, and it is dangerous in terms of external validity — one can never be sure to what situation results can be generalized. An investigator should certainly never match until he is aware of the relationship between the matched variable and the dependent variable.

In a study investigating the influence of life events on psychiatric disorder, for example, a group of female psychiatric in-patients (study group) were compared in their experience of recent life-events to a randomly selected comparison group of women of similar age drawn from the same area as those in hospital. For what I assume will seem obvious reasons, psychiatrically disturbed women randomly encountered in the population were excluded from this comparison group. The selection of a random sample in this way had the advantage that the investigator could not only analyse the different life-events experienced by the study and comparison groups but could also consider the way in which the distribution of background variables, which might often be controlled by matching (such as position in the life-cycle, marital status or social class), were different in the two populations. This is a more efficient use of resources. In fact some of the most interesting results demonstrated the interaction between background variables, independent variables, and dependent variables. As we shall see 'matching' can be achieved statistically with far fewer difficulties.

The second thing an investigator will wish to do is to design his research in order to rule out the possibility that it is Y that causes X and not vice versa. The way this is achieved through research design is by making certain that measurement of any postulated independent variable takes place prior to the measurement (and occurrence) of the postulated dependent variable. This type of study is known as a longitudinal or prospective study. Doll and Hill's (1964) study of the effect of smoking on lung cancer or Hammond's study of coronary heart disease (1966) are two examples — in both, questioning (and measurement) concerning assumed aetiological agents (X) took place prior to the onset of disease (Y). The two studies therefore reduce the danger of 'C' type error, i.e. the possibility that knowledge of the hypothesis (e.g. the fact of having cancer) would lead to a bias in reporting (by the 'victim' of smoking habits) or recording (by the investigator) of X.

A study that failed to take account of this particular difficulty is one by Mechanic and Volkart who tried to explain individual variation in attendance at a university health centre. Mechanic and Volkart (1961) looked at the relationship between the tendency to adopt the sick role, as measured by answers to three hypothetical questions,[1] and the illness behaviour of the respondents, as measured by their utilization of a medical clinic. Illness was assumed to be evenly distributed through groups with either a high or low tendency to adopt the sick role. In this way the 'need' to visit the doctor would be the same. Using these measures Mechanic and Volkart were able to show a small but statistically significant relationship between the tendency to adopt the sick role and illness behaviour. However, the information they obtained on people's use of services was obtained *before* their information on individual's tendencies to adopt the sick role. In other words, it is possible that the information which Mechanic and Volkart used to measure the tendency to adopt the sick role was a rationalized response of those who had used medical services in a particular way during the previous year. In short, it could be the case that instead of a tendency to adopt the sick role — as measured by Mechanic and Volkart — causing a particular type of medical clinic utilization, the direction of causation was the other way round; that is, the pattern of utilization determined the responses to the questions that Mechanic and Volkart claimed measured tendency to adopt the sick role. There is a 'C' type error where knowledge of Y can lead to contaminated measurement of X.

Once an investigator feels he has reasonably established co-variation and time-order he will need to design his study to attempt to discredit further alternative explanations of variation in Y. One study that fails to consider an alternative explanation, which many people would consider likely, is that of compulsory committal to mental hospitals, done in the USA by Wilde (1968). From observations and measurements made during the legal assessment of patients (when it was decided whether the relatives' request for committal would be granted), Wilde argued that the key determinant of patient committal was the relatives' behaviour and, in particular, the amount of fuss they made in front of the judge. He concluded that such social pressures were the most important factors in determining the outcome of the legal assessment. An alternative interpretation, however, could be that the relatives who complained most were those with the most severely disturbed patients. If this were the case, the social pressures would not really be as critical as clinical factors. Co-variation could have been produced by 'E' type error. This alternative situation is expressed diagrammatically in *Figure 2*. This difficulty could have been overcome by designing the study in order to allow independent measurement of patient

Figure 2   *'E' type error in a study of committal to mental hospital*

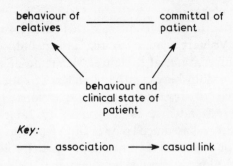

behaviour at home -- although this might have been a complicated task. Certainly, without this additional information we are in no position to feel confident about the hypothesis.

In the evaluation of pharmaceutical products, it is now recognized that any procedure can have both a pharmacological and a placebo (psychological) effect. In other words 'J' type error may lead to an incorrect inference that a drug is successful. The administration of a particular drug (particularly because of cost and possible side effects) has therefore to be justified by showing that it really has a beneficial pharmacological result. The key procedure here is a research design using an adequate comparison group. If those given the drug do significantly better than a similar group who are not given it, then we have faith in the drug. But there is still the possibility that the psychological effect of a particular coloured pill, or the faith that the patient has in the doctor who is giving the pill, has actually caused the improvement. To exclude these alternative hypotheses we need to ensure that the comparison group are given a similar looking pill 'double-blind'; that is, that neither the patient nor the doctor know which treatment is being used. We also need to ensure that the patients taking both kinds of pills are treated by the same doctor or doctors. If differences are still obtained under these strict circumstances, we can have much more confidence in the inference that it is the drug itself that is making people better, rather than the psychological effect of its administration. A similar design was used by Egbert and his colleagues in their study of the influence of patient expectations on post-operative pain (above pp. 25–6).

Observation and Measurement

Just as an appropriate research design can help us to have more confidence in the results of a piece of research so accurate and imaginative observation and measurement can be a great help.

At various times scientific debates have been characterized by fierce controversy, and various kinds of logic and procedure have been submitted to sustained and piercing criticism. One idea, which has come under much criticism, is the idea that science is in some way an 'objective' discipline and that 'facts' somehow speak for themselves. The scientist merely has to observe these facts to develop theory and understanding. However, such a position is ultimately untenable, not only in the behavioural sciences but also in the physical ones. Fundamentally, it is never possible to be sure that one has observed all relevant data.

Observation necessarily implies a focus of attention and thus a reduction of possible input from the outer world. For example, there were probably people before Alexander Fleming who had seen the same thing he saw when he discovered penicillin. However, it took his particular way of seeing to 'invent' it. It does not matter if one is a nuclear physicist attempting to observe sub-molecular particles, a biologist studying the response of planaria under different conditions, an ethologist studying the behaviour of rhesus monkeys when their mother is taken away, or a sociologist observing interaction between nurses and patients in a hospital ward. In each case, observation is essentially a subjective affair. On the basis of more or less well-defined theoretical ideas the scientist decides on what to focus. His very choice of perspective, his conceptions, may prevent him from seeing all that is happening. Moreover, the fact that he is observing may influence what is observed.

What the scientist can do, however, is to consider the likely difficulties and record his way of tackling them by specifying the rules he is following in his observations and experiments. He can develop precise methods for recording what he sees and for systematically analysing these results. Although scientific observation can never be 'truly' objective — no observations are independent of observers — the scientist can at least try to make clear his subjective frame of reference. He and his audience will then be able to consider why his experiments and observations, his conceptions, or his method of analysis may be faulty.

Levels of measurement

Most scientific research consists of relating sets of observations to one another, and, to make accurate observations the first thing a scientist must do is to decide exactly what it is he is trying to observe. This involves the development and specification of concepts, and of indicators with which to measure them. Suppose that one is trying to relate one's observations (indicators) or people's life-styles (a concept) to observations (indicators) of whether or not they have anaemia (another concept). One of the first things to do is to decide what is meant by the concept 'anaemia', that is, to make a precise definition of it. Knowing what you are observing is the first step towards doing it accurately, and it will also permit relatively unequivocal interpretation of the results. Too often one set of research findings may be incompatible with another simply because the two investigators have employed different concepts — for example, different ways of defining anaemia or life style — and consequently different indicators of their presence or quality. They simply have not investigated the same thing. To interpret any set of results one must know what has been measured; to make measurements, one must decide what to measure.

This sort of difficulty is endemic in much research. Take for example some of the research that has gone into the relationship between social class as defined by the Registrar General and a whole series of diseases (see for example, Morris, 1964). These studies appear to have established a clear relationship between social class membership and the likelihood of death from certain diseases. However, to understand this relationship, that is, to know what it is about social class that produces these effects and thus to have a precise idea what to do about it, we need to know how the Registrar defines social class, and herein lies the difficulty. The Registrar General's five-fold classification of class is based on an occupational classification. In the 1966 census, 50 per cent of the occupied male population were categorized as Social Class III, a class that included most skilled workers and also most junior or routine non-manual workers (Central Statistical Office, 1972: Table 16). Now we know very well that there are many differences in the work and life-styles of manual workers and non-manual workers. How then should we interpret a finding that Social Class III males (or females married to Social Class III males, for that matter) are less likely to die from Ischaemic heart disease than men in Social Class I or the equivalents? To be useful the social-class categories would have to be broken down to homogenous equivalence classes. Only then could we determine the meaning of results. The important point to note is that there is no predetermined 'right' way of classifying occupations or any other class of activities or events; what we are doing must be determined by our theoretical needs and spelled out precisely so that we can interpret the results we obtain. Classifications, such as the Registrar-General's five-fold social-class categorization, that can be interpreted in many different ways simply confuse the issue.

Having decided what it is we want to observe — that is, having established concepts and indicators with which to measure them — we can make observations in a more precise or less precise way, depending on the questions we want to answer. Most basically, for example, we may want to know whether something is present or not. We are more likely, however, to want to know whether it is present in greater or smaller amounts. And then we might want to know how much more or less it is present in one situation than another.

Making an observation of something is a way of measuring it. Measurement proceeds by categorizing observations. The observations that something is present, that it is more present in one situation than another, and that it is more present to a certain degree in such a situation, correspond to three levels of measurement recognized in mathematics:

nominal scale, ordinal scale, and interval scale measurements. Nominal scale measurement involves the division of observations into any number of like and unlike categories or dichotomies; ordinal scale measurement involves the further step of ordering hierarchically the different categories so created; and interval scale measurement involves, in addition, the specification of the distances between the categories. Classification and categorization are central to science, and they are the basis of measurement.

The level of measurement used depends on the theoretical conceptualizations adopted about the phenomena being observed (Galtung, 1967: 72–79). In the laboratory sciences measurements of temperature, numbers of blood cells, height or weight are all susceptible to interval scale assumptions — with the great advantage that the most powerful statistical techniques can then be applied. In the social sciences, however, investigators are usually willing to assume that they can divide observations into dichotomies (ill/not ill; have an event/do not have an event; married/not married; and so on) and even order their observations (high/medium/low warmth or stress or happiness or social class), but they are much more dubious, in the case of social science data, about interval scale measurement. Can one say, for example, that the loss of one's mother is equivalent to three times the loss of one's cat? The majority of social scientists believe that most of the observations they make do not make sense at this interval level of measurement and it is therefore infrequently used, compared to measurement at nominal or ordinal levels. [3]

Again, in the laboratory sciences, measurement instruments (indicators or concepts) — the classic examples being the thermometer and barometer which indicate the concepts temperature and pressure — are often to hand. Indicators such as the thermometer or the meter rule have been developed by many workers over many years. For the social scientist, as for many laboratory scientists in new research areas, his task is to develop indicators that tell him in which category the observed phenomenon is to be placed. To establish the presence of certain types of anaemia (concept), for example, one counts the number of red blood cells (indicator) and then places individuals within the category, anaemic or not anaemic (the level of cells indicating the presence of anaemia having been previously determined). Much measurement, like counting blood cells, assessing blood pressure, or judging the warmth expressed by a mother towards a child, involves the creation of precise cut-off points (when is a blood cell a cell; when is warmth not warmth etc.). Without these, it is impossible to allocate observations to categories reliably. However, most cut-off points tend to be arbitrary. Most phenomena actually exist on a continuum. Thus, for example, it is customary to divide the spectrum of light into distinct colours based on arbitrary conventions. The validity of the exercise will depend on theoretical considerations (is measurement good enough for the purpose intended) and the usefulness of the whole operation and cannot be judged independently. Categorization for itself is a meaningless and often dangerous activity, as is the use of categories developed for one purpose in a different situation.

Often, in order to place phenomena into categories, one needs more than one indicator. For example, in order to establish that someone has a 'strep' throat, one needs to find streptococci (indicator) and an inflamed larynx (indicator). Either may be present without the other. In the same way, some measures of social class depend upon information about the individual's education and income, as well as his or her occupation.

To summarize so far, measurement involves: first, the conceptualization and development of ideas about precisely what to measure; and, second, the creation of indicators (the choice of precise examples of what will be counted as indicators of the concept). The more this process is spelled out in any research, the easier it is to determine what the results actually mean.

A research example

At this point an example of what is meant by the development of concepts, and of indicators to measure them, may be useful. Brown and Rutter (1966) were interested in trying to relate the emotional involvement of relatives of patients diagnosed schizophrenic to the patients' relapse. Both emotional involvement and relapse were concepts for which indicators had to be developed. The first problem for the investigators was to decide what they meant by emotional involvement, and then to work out ways of placing the families on a scale of high/low involvement.

They found that they had three main things in mind when they thought of the emotional involvement of relatives with patients: the amount of warmth expressed towards the patient (which they perceived as positive); the amount of criticism of the patient (which they defined as negative); and the amount of over-involvement (which they perceived as unrealistic or inappropriate anxiety and concern about the patient). They decided to measure each of these dimensions of emotional involvement separately. At this point, then, the investigators had established their concepts, and decided what it was they wanted to observe.

The next step was to set out ways of measuring these concepts, that is, ways of placing families unambiguously on a point on an ordinal scale for each of the dimensions of emotional involvement. The measure of criticism was to be based on observation of the relatives' behaviour in a long (three to five hour) interview. Most emphasis was to be placed on the way something was said rather than what was said, the tone of voice being regarded as particularly significant. Many questions were to be asked about routine family activities (doing the washing-up, looking after the children, going out shopping, etc.), since it was known from previous developmental work (which had lasted eighteen months) that in the course of such questioning relatives would make spontaneous comments, critical or otherwise, about the patient. Defining in advance what they meant by a critical comment, the investigators proceeded to measure criticism by counting the number of such comments made about the patient during the interview. Considerable weight was placed on the 'tone of voice' in which a comment was made. Families were then placed on a scale measuring 'criticism' by comparing them according to the number of such comments. Thus, in this case, critical comments, carefully defined, were indicators of negative emotional involvement.

In evaluating this or any other research result, there are certain questions that need to be asked and certain tests that can be applied. One important test of any observation is its reliability: would several observers looking at the same phenomenon come up with the same result? With the criticism scale, the crucial test is whether several observers witnessing the same phenomena, and one observer classifying the same phenomena at different times, would get the same answer; in other words, would all the resulting observations place the family on the same scale point? In evaluating a research report, it is always worth asking whether or not the researchers have tested the reliability of their methods. In the study of family relationships just described the agreement between raters was usually better than .80.

A second test of observation concerns its validity. Does the indicator measure what it purports to be measuring? This is not, of course, a simple question, and there are various ways of considering an indicator's validity. We can ask first, for example, whether the investigators have made out a logical case for the relationship between the concept and their way of measuring it, the indicator. This is called 'face' validity by some methodologists, logical validity by others. In the study just described the relationship of 'critical comments' to 'criticism' is reasonably clear.

Another type of validity is called 'concurrent'[4] validity. This can be established in three ways. For example, in the research discussed above we can find a family which we can infer — from the observations by other researchers on other criteria (for example research psychiatrists) — has emotionally negative feelings, and then see whether the particular measure we use also places them high on negative feelings. This would be called 'convergent' validity. Alternatively, or as a supplement, we can find a family that we know is not high on criticism, and make sure that the measure gives us the right result. This is known as 'discriminant validity', [4] and is really a mirror image of the convergent approach.

In every case of measurement, the procedure stands or falls, first, on the ability of many observers to get the same results (called reliability); and, second, on whether or not the results stand up according to other measures of the same concept (validity). In other words, a case must be made as to why this measure, in this circumstance, is both reliable and valid. If the procedures pursued are open, each reader can decide for himself how much faith to put in the results and their interpretation. Conclusions can never be more definite than that.

Measurement and the establishment of time-order

The establishment of valid and reliable measures, of course, gives confidence in research inferences because it helps to rule out the interpretation that results are the product of unknown investigator bias and error. But measurement can also help to answer questions about time-order, that is the possible interpretation that instead of X causing Y, Y actually causes X. Since the prospective research design solution, mentioned earlier, is very expensive and time-consuming (and often impractical since some causal agents may occur ten or more years before what they cause) any help that measurement techniques can give to confidence concerning time-order would clearly be very helpful.

The measurement approach to time-order is based on the fact that just because the investigator is interested in events at different points in time it does not follow he has to make direct observations at these points of time: in an interview situation, for example, it is quite possible to ask not only about the present but also about the past. *Insofar as* it is possible to obtain valid data in this way, and I shall return to this, a single interview at one point in time may be enough.

In the study of life-events and psychiatric disorder already referred to (above pp. 32 and below pp. 311–16), for example, it was necessary to establish that more events occurred with individuals who suffered an onset of psychiatric disorder. Individuals with an onset were asked about events in the previous year and they were then compared with randomly selected individuals (without psychiatric disorder) who were also asked about events in the year prior to interview. The rate of events in the year prior to onset (patients) or interview (comparison group) were compared and it was found that three and a half times as many events had occurred with the patients as to those in the comparison group.

At least two types of error, both 'C' type, could be anticipated in this study of life-events (and in any case where measurement is retrospective). First, it is possible that patients would 'remember' more events, or class 'less severe' events as 'severe', than would the comparison group — patients, after all, might be trying to give 'meaning' to their onset whereas the comparison group would not have a reason to do this. Thus there would be 'C' type error: knowledge of Y (psychiatric disorder) is influencing the measurement of X. The bias might affect either the respondents' reporting or the investigators' recording. Second, it is possible that the surreptitious onset of the disorder 'caused' patients to have events. In this case the 'true' causal relationship is that Y causes X and not vice versa. There is, therefore, a potentially false inference about time-order.

Techniques for dealing with these, and other, difficulties are described by Brown and his colleagues (1973 and below pp. 314–16). Essentially a great deal of effort had to be put into measurement. To solve the first problem all events that would be considered as events were defined in advance (what was an event, to whom did it have to happen, and so on).

Interviewing was intensive and exhaustive efforts were made to ensure that every relevant event that occurred to patient and comparison groups was recorded. Checks were made with relatives, employers, hospitals, police, newspapers, and so on with the result that a very high agreement could be demonstrated between the respondents' accounts and those from other sources. A rating of the seriousness of the event was made by a team who did not know whether the respondent being discussed was a patient or came from the comparison group. These measures reduced the possibility that patients would falsely report more serious events. The second difficulty was overcome by means of a conception of independence. Events could be classed as 'independent' on logical grounds. Some events such as the loss of a job when a whole factory had shut down, just could not be regarded as the product of a surreptitious onset of the disorder. A separate analysis of events classified as 'independent' and not independent revealed that patients still had three and a half times as many events as comparison group members. The second source of difficulty, that the disorders produced the events, was therefore discredited. Other studies, however, have not overcome these kinds of problems (see below pp. 311—14).

Methods of data-collection

In scientific research the measurements made in order to investigate relationships and draw inferences are of various kinds, and there are different ways of obtaining and recording data. For example, current behaviour can be recorded by an observer either while it is occurring or immediately afterwards; the observer of social events may be a participant in the activities he records or he may be outside them — if the former, his data recording method will be called participant observation; if the latter, direct or non-participant observation. Most data obtained in the natural sciences or in the laboratory are obtained in this way.

But most of the data obtained in sociological research refer to things that are not directly observable; that is, to past events or to feelings and attitudes. If the data are to be obtained from living respondents, they can be obtained either by interview or by asking them to write down their information. If interviewing is employed, it can be done in a number of ways: a tape-recorder can be used to provide a verbatim account, and various measurements can be recorded afterwards, or measurements can be recorded at the time (by noting answers to questions, tone of voice, and so on). The interviewer can ask standard pre-prepared questions of all his respondents in a certain order, or he can make sure he obtains the relevant data by less direct questioning, allowing the respondent to bring up the information more spontaneously. Alternatively, the respondent can be asked to record his answers to certain questions. These questions, like those in an interview, may be ones that allow the investigator to restrict the possible answers to those falling in certain categories (i.e. pre-coded or closed-ended questions), or ones that elicit the fullest information from the respondent in the respondent's own terms (i.e. open-ended questions).

Yet another form of data is that obtained from records of past events. The historian is of course obliged to use such data in his reconstruction of the past, but the sociologist often uses such data too. He does so when he makes use of statistical or other information compiled on behalf of governments or other bodies, or by individuals, for purposes which may be very different from those of the researcher. Such data are known as secondary data in contrast to the primary data obtained by the investigator through direct observation or interviewing. The use of secondary data, which has often produced some of the most impressive empirical work in sociology, raises particular problems associated with the need, if we are to be sure of the meaning of our results, to take account of the process by which the data was compiled. Official statistics, for instance, may be compiled from officially required forms (such as tax assessment forms or employment details), and the context in which these were compiled may be important. For example, in the official statistics only about 10 per cent of all skilled manual workers are women, whereas women form a much larger part of the total manual labour force. It has been argued that this figure reflects not a great disparity in the degree of skill exercised by men and women in manual jobs, but the fact that women doing the same job as men may be classified as semi-skilled in order to pay them less.

A classic example of the problem of interpreting results of secondary data occurs in Durkheim's (1897 trans. 1951) famous analysis of suicide rates. His finding that suicide rates in Catholic countries and Catholic areas of Protestant countries were lower than those in Protestant countries and Protestant areas of Catholic countries could reflect reality or, on the other hand, the differential practice of death certification by coroners or their functional equivalents in Catholic and Protestant areas. For Catholics, suicide means that burial cannot take place in sanctified ground with the rites of the Church. It is therefore possible that relatives will try to disguise the circumstances of death and persuade those responsible for recording it to place 'accidental death' on the certificate. While suicide has also been regarded as stigmatizing for suiciders' surviving associates in Protestant countries, and while it may indeed result in an inability to collect life insurance, there is evidence to suggest that it does not have the same emotional and religious significance amongst Protestants (Douglas, 1967).

These sorts of difficulties should be carefully borne in mind in analysing secondary data, such as referral letters from doctors to psychiatrists or hospital records. However, in evaluating a study based on secondary data, the critic needs to consider whether there are ways of showing if an alternative interpretation is equally plausible. In the case of Durkheim's work, for example, Barraclough (1970) found that even when accidental deaths (by drowning, overdose, and so on) were added to suicides, the differences in suicide rates in different areas persisted. Therefore, Durkheim's method is not, in this case, a significant barrier to the acceptance of his theory. This example is given to suggest that criticism can be constructive rather than a mere debating point.

Ways of interviewing

The basic problem in collecting primary data is ensuring that each observation is of the same phenomenon. If this is done, it can be argued that the differences in responses reflect real differences in the nature of the phenomenon being measured and not differences in measurement procedures. This implies an obligation on the part of the researcher to consider carefully his measurement procedures and his data-collection techniques.

Some sociologists have taken the requirement of controlling for the possible effect of measurement and data collecting techniques to the point where they have argued that, if different respondents are given different stimuli, their responses cannot be compared. The result has been the development of a strict schedule-type interview (for example, Office of Population Census and Surveys, 1973) where, to avoid variation in the interviewer, each question has to be phrased identically to each respondent and no change in the order of questions is permitted. In recent years this approach has been criticized (for example, Cicourel, 1964; Richardson *et al.*, 1965). It is argued that the same questions and the same ordering of questioning can result, paradoxically, in providing different people with a different stimulus, since the same words can have different meanings for different people. In research involving questioning across sub-cultures, where the meaning of words and actions may vary, or in research involving intimate detail, where there can be tremendous individual variation in meaning, the tightly-controlled questionnaire approach may not lead to standardization at all. The answers are difficult to interpret and are open to numerous response sets and misunderstandings which are out of the control of the investigator.

An alternative approach involving more flexibility is one where the responsibility for insuring that the responses of different respondents relate to the same phenomena rests with the interviewer (Richardson, 1965; Brown *et al.*, 1973). Typically, the interviewer has a list of topics to cover and a list of questions to himself that he sets out to answer. While avoiding questions that may lead the respondent to feel that he should respond in a certain way, the interviewer is told to question as he sees fit until he is satisfied that the respondent has fully understood what information he has been asked for, and that he, the interviewer, has fully understood the answers. Such interviews are often time-consuming, and they require highly-trained interviewers capable of eliciting and recording information that has not been influenced at all by their own presence. However, accurate, valid, and reliable data can be obtained in this way. In a number of areas, particularly those where it is possible that strong emotions or strong normative beliefs about appropriate roles can influence answers (for example in investigation of sex roles or work satisfaction), there is increasing evidence that this standardized non-schedule procedure produces more easily interpretable data and, therefore, information that is more valid and reliable. In comparison, general and even specific direct questions, which would be possible on a schedule, tend to pick up general emotional and normative responses, rather than the specific information required (unless, as is possible in the non-schedule approach, there is a chance for the interviewer to cross-question the respondent in a precise way). The elimination of 'C' type error in the study of psychiatric disorder discussed above (pp. 58–9) would not have been possible, for example, if interviewers had not been permitted to cross-question respondents about events.

The powerful influence of feelings in causing biased answers to questions about activity was demonstrated in the Brown and Rutter (1966: 255) study, where the difference between the husband's and wife's independent accounts of who did the washing-up, took the children to school, etc., was shown to be related to the wife's dissatisfaction with the husband's participation in child care and household tasks; that is, dissatisfied wives tended to report less participation than their husbands reported, while satisfied wives tended to report much the same or a little more participation. Only very careful interviewing of the type not possible in a schedule approach could establish accurate data about activities in this area.

Similarly Oakley (1974: 204), in a study of women's attitudes to housework, showed how answers to a direct question about liking or disliking housework were quite different from results obtained after more detailed interviewing. In another study the answers to direct questions aimed at determining what people would do in hypothetical illness situations proved, on the basis of further interviewing, to be misleading (Tuckett, forthcoming). Such work suggests that the faith that many sociologists have placed in direct questions may well be misplaced, and the answers to such questions should be interpreted very carefully indeed. For some purposes, therefore, it would seem that data obtained through a standardized non-schedule approach are more satisfactory than those obtained in the more traditional way employed by many survey organizations wanting to cover considerable numbers. The non-schedule interview offers much more scope for utilizing the human qualities of the interviewer in communication and is thus more satisfying to the interviewer and the respondent. It is perhaps particularly appropriate when the measures relate to subjects of high emotional content where the respondents may have anxiety in expressing their feelings or in providing information about behaviour that is often concealed within a small group.

Nonetheless, it should be reasonably obvious that the non-schedule technique, if used reliably, requires a great amount of preparatory work and training of interviewers — only then can interviewing styles be controlled and adequate inter-interviewer agreement be assured. In many areas of social research this kind of approach, therefore, which is extremely expensive in time and resources, is quite unnecessary. The various studies carried out by Ann Cartwright (1964; 1967; 1970; Dunnell and Cartwright, 1972; Cartwright, Hockey and Anderson, 1973) and her team, for example, will be referred to frequently in this book and provide exciting and useful basic data describing medical care and issues related to it. Yet in all the studies a strict schedule approach to interviewing predominated. It would have been quite impossible to cover the amount of ground described in these studies without it.

The relative merits of different styles of interviewing need to be assessed in terms of the problem under investigation. Wherever possible the simplest method that will permit confident inferences should be used. The task of an investigator is to demonstrate how far the difficulties that attach to the different methods he employs (for instance in the case of the non-schedule interview, inter-interviewer reliability and the control of investigator bias; in the case of the schedule interview, the control of meaning and of response sets) have been tested and difficulties overcome. One way of doing this is to use both methods in a pilot study and to compare their results.

Methods of Analysis

In the laboratory sciences the analysis of results is often confined to testing them against chance. Although this is important in the social sciences a sociological analysis can also be used to 'control' variables (statistically) and thus examine relationships under different conditions. In this way it is possible to produce further evidence with which to choose between explanations. The use of analysis for this purpose constitutes, I believe, a major contribution of the social sciences to scientific enquiry and is relevant to medicine wherever research is carried out in the general population and 'true' experimental conditions do not prevail.

Statistical tests

However, the first thing to establish in the analysis of results is the fact of co-variation. In how many cases does a change in X bring about a change in Y and is this more frequent than we should expect by mere chance association (the fact that when I last knocked over an electric fire the lights went out — not because, as I later discovered, a fuse had blown but because the electricity I had paid for with my last shilling had run out — was pure chance).

Two sets of statistical techniques are useful in this regard: tests of significance and measures of association (Blalock, 1960). They are quite different and should not be confused.

A test of significance (such as chi-square or students 'T') is used in both the laboratory and social sciences to rule out the possibility that 'chance' is responsible for observed co-variation. Whenever we sample (or carry out a series of experiments) there is always the risk that we will be unlucky, that is to say, that if we had drawn further samples or completed further experiments, we would have obtained different results. We can never be sure that the sample of individuals or experiments we are observing are representative of the population of individuals or situations to which we wish to generalize: we can never be sure we have achieved external validity.

Given the size of the sample (or number of experiments) and making certain other, usually testable, assumptions, we can estimate the generalizability of our results by assessing the likelihood that we have been unlucky in the selection of our sample. 'Tests of significance' are useful only for this purpose. They tell us nothing except the probability with which we can generalize any finding. They assume that the sample of individuals or experiments is random, and this is why most researchers select their samples in that way.

When reading a research report, one should find the evidence for generalizability at the bottom of any table. P greater than 0.05, for example, means that in no more than five out of a hundred cases would there be a chance that the finding is the result of exceptional luck. The chance of 'exceptional luck' in the selection of a sample is therefore small. P less than 0.05 means that in more than five out of a hundred cases there would be a chance of 'exceptional luck'. It would be unsafe to generalize at this level of probability. The level of significance acceptable will depend on the risks the investigator is willing to take.

Unfortunately all tests of significance are influenced by the number of experiments performed or by the number of individuals in the sample — this is perfectly sensible since the bigger the sample the more likely that exceptional luck will not prevail. However, what this means is that whereas with small samples even big differences (say 20 per cent) in the effect of X on Y may not be statistically significant (*and* have occurred by chance), in large samples even small differences (say 4 per cent) can be statistically significant. This is true of all significance tests but I will take an example from the case of chi-square (Blalock, 1960: 225–234).

Supposing we have the following hypothetical data from a survey attempting to relate a psychiatrist's independent assessment of personality at one time to the onset of psychiatric disorder two years later. We can see from *Table 1* that in a survey of 100 women we arrived at small differences (52 per cent of the women with an immature personality had an onset compared to 48 per cent with a 'normal' personality) which are not statistically significant ($X = 0.16$). In another hypothetical study with much greater resources 10,000 women were investigated, as shown in *Table 2*. In this second study the proportion of women with immature personalities who became depressed were identical (52 per cent as

Table 1 Immature personality adjustment and getting depressed in a hypothetical survey of 100 women.

	immature personality	'normal' personality
depressed	26 (52%)	24 (48%)
not depressed	24	26

$\chi^2 = 0.16$ n.s.

Table 2 Immature personality adjustment and getting depressed in a hypothetical survey of 10,000 women.

	immature personality	'normal' personality
depressed	2,600	2,400
not depressed	2,400	2,600

$\chi^2 = 16$ $p < 0.001$ (1 df)

compared to 48 per cent) but this time the result is significant at the 0.001 level (i.e. the result would be repeated in at least 999 out of a thousand studies).

The fact that a relationship is statistically significant therefore does not tell us that we should treat it as *theoretically* significant or important. To establish theoretical significance there are other sets of statistical tests called *measures of association* which, roughly speaking, tell us how far knowledge of one variable X will enable us to predict another variable Y. This is known as the degree of variance explained. There are a number of tests of this kind such as gamma, Kendall's Q, Spearman's Rho, and the product-moment correlation coefficient (R^2) (see Galtung, 1967; Blalock, 1960). Actually, a good deal can be achieved by simply looking at percentage differences. In the example above the 4 per cent difference is obviously trivial whereas when I reported that life-crises were three and a half times as common among psychiatrically disturbed patients as compared to members of a comparison group, it is clear that the difference must be taken seriously.

The method of sub-group classification
The usual way in which sociologists set about trying to choose between explanations, at the stage of analysis, is by postulating the hypothesis that a particular factor is influencing the apparent relationship between X and Y and then statistically controlling the data to determine if this is true.

Obviously everything done at this stage depends on the accuracy of the original measurement. For the purpose of clearer exposition I am going to concentrate on the way in which a third variable might influence the apparent relationship between X and Y but the same logic could be applied to the way several variables interact.

Suppose we were interested in the possible effect of an individual's sex on their visits to the doctor. A survey of 100 men and 100 women selected at random from the population of London might show, on the face of it, that women were more likely to visit than men (see *Table 3*).

Table 3   Respondent's sex and visiting the doctor (hypothetical)

		female	*male*	
visits to	high	60	40	
the doctor	low	40	60	
	total	100	100	200

However, we might feel that the amount of disease an individual experienced in a given year could influence this result. Women may get ill more frequently and be more likely to visit the doctor. Our earlier inference would therefore result from an 'E' type error. In this case, were this alternative explanation correct, we would expect both X and Y to be correlated to the 'amount of illness experienced by an individual over the year' (T) and would expect the relationship between X and Y to disappear when we control for T. *Table 4* shows what could happen when we compare men and women with different amounts of illness (there are only two illness categories to facilitate exposition). However, in order to see what happens more clearly I have percentaged the results in *Table 4* and they appear in *Table 5*.

Table 4   Respondent's sex and visiting the doctor according to the amount of 'illness' in the year

		'more' illness		*'less' illness*		
		F	M	F	M	
visits to	high	20	6	40	34	
the doctor	low	13	10	27	50	
	total	33	16	67	84	200

Looking at *Table 5* we can see that the introduction of T, the amount of illness, has not reduced the relationship between X and Y. There is still a 50 per cent excess of women over men who visit the doctor. It is therefore possible to deduce, on the evidence considered, that in this hypothetical example women differ in their use of the doctor from men. Note that this is true despite the fact that women also are more 'ill' (more than

Table 5 Percent of male and female respondents visiting the doctor according to the amount of 'illness' in the year

	'more' illness		'less' illness	
	F	M	F	M
high	60	40	60	40
low	40	60	40	60
i.e. no change				

twice as many appearing in the 'more ill' category). Through the method of sub-group classification, therefore, we have been able to choose between two alternative explanations of a relationship (the method and the logic underlying it are fully described by Rosenberg, 1966).

Epidemiologists (who are concerned with the distribution of disease in the population) use a technique called *standardization,* which is logically similar to that described above. One factor for which they frequently standardize is age. The logic here is simple. In comparing two groups, for example an urban and a rural population, it is possible that different death rates reflect not just different qualities arising from urban and rural living, but different things about the population. Similar overall death rates in two populations may mask the fact that death rates at all ages may be higher in the city than in the country – the overall death rates in the country, for example, may simply reflect a preponderance of older people resulting from the migration of young people to the towns. By comparing populations after making adjustments for varying age-structure it is possible to test which explanation is the more likely.

However, Rosenberg (1966: 39) states a point: '... before one introduces a control variable one must have some idea of the relationship of the test factor to the independent and dependent variables ...' or 'one must consider whether the control variable is *relevant* or is otherwise implicated in the result. This is a logical, not a statistical operation.' In short, the introduction of a test factor or standardization must not be done mindlessly – it is essential to know for what effect one is controlling. To return to 'age' as a variable it must be clear what the measure 'age' is supposed to indicate and what effect it is supposed to have. 'Age' could be considered as a mere biological concept indicating the years a person has been living and hence, presumably, giving some idea of his biological state. It could well be used, however, to distinguish a particular cohort or generation of individuals, that is, as an indicator of particular life experiences. Males aged between forty-three and seventy-four in 1974, for example, are more likely to have seen active service in the Second World War than subsequent or previous age cohorts. In this instance age is used as an indicator of generational experience, and we might be controlling out the variable we seem to explain by standardizing on the age structure of the population. There might be something important about people who had seen active service.

A great deal can be achieved by the imaginative use of standardization or sub-group classification and the practice of examining the relationship between two variables (in this case urban and rural living and death) whilst controlling for a third, or for that matter a fourth, or sixth, or ninth variable, is a very useful technique for choosing between alternative explanations.

So far I have concentrated on the use of the technique for ruling out alternative interpretations but it can also be used to show how a number of variables relate to one another; that is, it can help to elucidate and specify a complex relationship. In the early days of medical and sociological research there was a tendency to search for simple causal relationships; for instance, to search for *the* cause of cancer in a single uncomplicated chemical phenomenon or for *the* cause of crime in a simplistic sociological construct such as the broken home. But, although some research work in both the biological and social sciences is still naively mono-causal in its approach, most researchers are aware that the relationship between any two variables, for example, exercise and death, is an extremely complex one and that there are many possible ways in which they may be related to one another.

The simultaneous study of all the phenomena that may be related directly and indirectly to a behaviour or trait that we want to examine (for example, the psychiatric disorders we have already discussed) is a council of perfection. It is seldom possible to approximate to the ideal. But it is possible to design a study that can show for a limited number of variables the nature of their relationships to one another, and the relationships can be of many kinds.

For example, it may be that a third variable is indeed entirely responsible for an apparent relationship between two others; or a third factor may enable us to refine one of the variables so that we are able to see what is or is not important about a concept; or a third variable may suppress the real effect of one variable on another as in the urban—rural relationship just discussed; or a third variable may act as a mediator or intervening influence on the relationship between the other two; or yet again, a third factor may distort the relationhip of the other two to such an extent that it appears to be the opposite to what it actually is. A third factor may also operate independently in a complex theoretical model. (See Rosenberg, 1966 for a discussion of the way the sub-group classification method can be applied to elucidate all these situations. Blalock (1964) discusses other more complex mathematical techniques.)

Conclusions

I have tried in this chapter to give an idea of how behaviour in some situations can be systematically and reliably investigated so that it is possible to make statements about it that are demonstrably 'superior' to alternate explanations. I have also tried to show how the essential logic of sociological research is not that different from the logic used in the laboratory sciences. Unfortunately, much of what passes as sociological research — and, of course, other kinds of scientific research — does not come up to the standards that have been outlined in this chapter. This is perhaps not surprising. Research is not an easy exercise; it is not just commonsense. It requires not only a knowledge of the phenomena being measured, but also the capacity to think originally about the nature of inference and the process of conceptualization.

However, I hope I have said enough to justify my belief that social action and social situations can be studied in a scientific way. I also hope that I have sufficiently emphasized the critical significance of the observer or investigator in the scientific process. At each stage decisions and arguments rest not on the uncritical or automatic use of established techniques but on a set of logical decisions which must be taken on theoretical grounds with a full consciousness of what is being done. Thus the observer must decide what to observe, which indicators to choose, how to conceptualize his variables, which alternative interpretations to take seriously and try to exclude, what his measures mean, which level of significance to accept, etc. In this connection, the recent fascination of sociologists for what has been termed the 'ethnomethodological approach' is important. Although ethnomethodologists have made many criticisms that are exaggerated and probably at least implicit in much earlier sociological work (for an introduction to ethnomethodology see Dreitzel, 1970, and for a recent evaluation of the approach see Goldthorpe, 1973), they have emphasized the fact that the scientific process is as much a social and cultural process as any other and, far from being objective, is only one set of views about the world. The type of approach to scientific enquiry outlined in this chapter cannot suggest what decisions an investigator should take, but what it can do (and it is in this area that methodology is important) is suggest some of the questions that should be asked and some of the techniques that can be used to permit a choice between interpretations.

Thus the scientific approach involves the setting out of procedures, the assessment of evidence, and the consideration of alternative interpretations. It offers some possibility of arbitrating in disputes between alternative explanations, of deciding that one explanation is more plausible than another. But in the end, every scientific explanation is valid only in so far as the investigator can provide a rationale for what he has done. No procedure is in itself valid, and the seriousness with which we regard any one explanation depends on the imaginative foresight of the investigator, that is, on his ability to anticipate and exclude alternative explanations. It is with this view in mind that I hope readers will evaluate scientific studies.

Notes

1. e.g. During the past school year would you have reported to the University health service in the following hypothetical situations?
   (a) You have been feeling poorly for a few days
       0 = certainly; 1 = probably; 2 = not very likely; 3 = very unlikely.
   (b) You felt you had a temperature of about 100
       0 = certainly; 1 = probably; 2 = not very likely; 3 = very unlikely.
   (c) You felt you had a temperature of about 101
       0 = certainly; 1 = probably; 2 = not very likely; 3 = very unlikely.
2. Quite often, of course, the urgency of a problem requires us to try out solutions before we fully understand it. Many medical procedures are based on less than a full understanding and are used simply because they seem to work. In this connection, however, it is instructive to look at the attempts of the public health movement to control cholera in the nineteenth century. Pioneered by people like Owen Chadwick and Sir John Simon, the movement was one of the chief causes of reduced rates of the disease. Using the later-disproved 'vapours' theory, public health officials set out to remove the rubbish from city streets, often with successful results. However, because the 'vapours' theory concentrated on the idea that the disease was air-born, the officials would dump the rubbish at the most convenient place in a nearby river. Sometimes they dumped the rubbish up-stream of the city, with quite disastrous results; on other occasions when it was more convenient to dump rubbish down-stream, the action was successful. What the officials did not know was that cholera is in fact water-born. Their experience suggests why ideas which merely 'get results' may be dangerous if they are not firmly based in empirically tested theory. In order to avoid the danger of successful prediction without understanding, it is necessary to specify the theory underlying a relationship as precisely as possible.
3. Even a concept like 'income' which may appear to be easily treated in an interval manner (£1,000 is half £2,000) presents difficulties. Is the difference between £3,000 and £6,000 really the same as that between £10,000 and £13,000?
4. The terms used to describe kinds of validity (concurrent, logical, discriminant, etc.) do vary between different writers on this subject. The reader is therefore advised to grasp the underlying logic being considered under the different headings.

References

Barraclough, B. (1970) The Effect that Coroners have on the Suicide Rate and the Open Verdict Rate. In G.H. Hare and J.K. Wing (eds.), *Psychiatric Epidemiology*. London: Oxford University Press.

Beecher, H.K. (1965) The Quantification of the Subjective Pain Experience. In P.H. Hoch and J. Zubin, (eds.), *Psychopathology of Perception*. New York: Grune and Stratton.
This is a fascinating paper dealing with the complexities of the pain reaction. Reviews a number of laboratory experiments trying to measure subjective pain.

Blalock, H.M. (1960) *Social Statistics*. London: McGraw Hill.
A useful statistics text.

— (1964) *Causal Inference in Non-Experimental Research.* Chapel Hill: University of North Carolina Press.

An advanced level textbook of research methods.

Brown, G.W. and Rutter, M. (1966) The Measurement of Family Activities and Relationships. A Methodological Study. *Human Relations* 19: 241—63.

An important paper describing an interview and rating technique for making reliable measurements of family activities (doing the washing-up, taking the children to school, etc.). Demonstrates that accurate measurement is possible provided sufficient care and attention are taken.

Brown, G., Birley, J., and Wing, J.K. (1972) Influence of Family Life on the Course of Schizophrenic Disorders: A Replication. *British Journal of Psychiatry* 3 (1): 74—87.

Presents the results of a study designed to measure the effects of different family backgrounds on the relapse of discharged schizophrenic patients. The study used the measure of family activities described in the paper above.

Brown, G., Birley, J., Harris, T., and Sklair, F. (1973) Life events and Psychiatric Disorder: Part One, Some Methodological Issues. *Psychological Medicine* 3 (1): 74—87.

Discusses some of the methodological safeguards that are required to investigate the role of life-events in the aetiology of psychiatric disorders. Suggests an important but differing role for such events in schizophrenic and depressive conditions.

Campbell, D.T. and Fiske, D. (1959) Convergent and Discriminant Validation by the Multitrait-multimethod Matrix. *Psychological Bulletin* 56: 81—105.

Two psychologists discuss methods of validating measures and present the case for measures that produce 'expected' results on similar and dissimilar subjects using different methods.

Campbell, D. and Stanley, J. (1966) Experimental and Quasi-experimental Designs for Research. In N.L. Gage (ed.), *Handbook of Research on Teaching.* Chicago: Rand-McNally.

Compares and analyses different types of research designs in terms of their logical structure. An excellent summary of the basic experimental model.

Cartwright, A. (1964) *Human Relations and Hospital Care.* London: Routledge & Kegan Paul.

— (1967) *Patients and Their Doctors.* London: Routledge & Kegan Paul.

— (1970) *Parents and Family Planning Series.* London: Routledge & Kegan Paul.

Cartwright, A., Hockey, L. and Anderson, J. (1973) *Life Before Death.* London: Routledge & Kegan Paul.

Central Statistical Office (1972) *Social Trends* No. 3. Table 16: 71. London: HMSO.

This is a government publication summarizing many useful statistics referring to the social and economic fabric of the UK. Includes data on population, employment, income, health issues, etc. Table 16 refers to the distribution of the population by social class.

Cicourel, A.V. (1964) *Method and Measurement in Sociology.* New York: Free Press.

An important, if polemical, statement of the ethnomethodological position in relation to sociological research. Criticizes many sociologists for failing to recognize that sociological research, like the subject matter it studies, is culturally and socially located. The discussion of the survey, interviewing, and the questionnaire is particularly incisive.

Cordaro, L. and Ison, J. (1963) Psychology of the Scientist X. Observer bias in classical conditioning of the Planarium. *Psychological Reports* 13, 787—9.

Doll, R. and Hill, A.B. (1964) Mortality in Relation to Ten Years' Observation of British Doctors. *British Medical Journal* 1: 1399 and 1460.

Douglas, J.D. (1967) *Social Meanings of Suicide.* Princeton: Princeton University Press.

Dreitzel, H.P. (ed.) (1970) *Patterns of Communicative Behaviour.* Recent Sociology No. 2. New York: Macmillan.

A book of readings dealing with the ethnomethodological approach to social phenomena. The chapters by Dreitzel and Cicourel provide a good introduction to this perspective.

Dunnell, K. and Cartwright, A. (1972) *Medicine Takers, Prescribers and Hoarders.* London: Routledge & Kegan Paul.

Durkheim, E. (1897, trans. 1951) *Suicide.* Translated by G. Simpson. London: Routledge & Kegan Paul.

One of the great sociological classics and a brilliant example of the possibilities of secondary analysis. Durkheim argues that since suicide rates vary from society to society the causes of this should be sought in different aspects of these societies' social structures. Suicide statistics are manipulated with great effect to investigate various hypotheses and exclude others. The book was originally published in France.

Friedman, N. (1969) *The Social Nature of Psychological Research.* New York: Basic Books.

A polemical critique of the value of laboratory experiments in psychology.

Galtung, J. (1967) *Theory and Methods of Social Research.* London: George Allen and Unwin.

A good, but difficult, textbook of research methods in sociology.

Goldthorpe, John H. (1973) A Revolution in Sociology? *Sociology* 7: 449–62.

A critical review of the ethnomethodological contribution to sociology.

Hammond, E.C. (1966) Smoking in Relation to the Death Rates of One Million Men and Women. *National Cancer Institute Monograph.* 19: 127.

Hirschhorn, R., Beratis, N., Rosen, F., Parkman, R., Stern, R., and Polmar, S. (1975) Adenonine-diaminase Deficiency in a Child Diagnosed Prenatally. *The Lancet* i: 73–5.

Lazarsfeld, P. (1941) Expository Review of the 'American Soldier'. *Public Opinion Quarterly* 3: 337–404.

Lazarsfeld, who has been a principal figure in the development of modern sociology, provides an excellent statement of some of the things sociological research can, and cannot, be expected to achieve.

Mechanic, D. and Volkart, E.H. (1961) Stress, Illness and the Sick-Role. *American Sociological Review* 26: 51–8.

Morris, J. (1959) Health and Social Class. *The Lancet* i: 303–5.

— (1964) *Uses of Epidemiology.* London: Livingstone.

A standard epidemiological text.

Oakley, A. (1974) *The Sociology of Housework.* London: Martin Robertson.

An account of a study of women's attitudes to housework.

Office of Population Census and Surveys (1973) *The General Household Survey: An Introductory Report.* Appendix A. London: HMSO.

Orne, M.T. (1959) The Nature of Hypnosis: Artefact and Essense. *Journal of Abnormal and Social Psychology* 58: 277–99.

A fascinating study comparing a group of hypnotized subjects with a group of controls who thought they had been hypnotized.

— (1962) On the Social Psychology of the Psychological Experiment. *American Psychologist* 17: 776–83.

Another fascinating laboratory experiment where the investigators finally gave up trying to make subjects bored. They argued the situation itself gave meaning to otherwise boring activities (adding columns of figures and then tearing them up!).

Popper, K. (1972) *Conjectures and Refutations* (revised edition). London: Routledge & Kegan Paul.

Richardson, S.A., Dohrenwend, B.S., and Klein, D. (1965) *Interviewing: Its Form and Functions.* New York: Basic Books.

An extremely detailed and readable account of research interviewing and the many techniques that can be utilized to provide reliable and valid data. Includes the distinction between schedule and non-schedule attempts to collect systematic information.

Rosenberg, B. (1966) *The Logic of Survey Analysis.* New York: Basic Books.

The best written account of the technique of introducing a third variable in order to elucidate the relationship between two others. Particularly useful is an arithmetical appendix demonstrating the underlying structure of what happens to a table with two variables when a third is introduced.

Selltiz, C. (1965) *Research Methods in Social Relations* (2nd revised edition). London: Methuen.

The best elementary introduction, but suffers from being psychologically orientated (if used for sociological purposes).

Senter, R.J. (1969) *Analysis of Data.* Illinois: Scott Foresman and Co.

An elementary statistical introduction.

Suchman, E.A. (1967) Appraisal and Implications for Theoretical Development. *Millbank Memorial Fund Quarterly* **45**: 109–13.

Discusses the theoretical weakness of much epidemiological work in Ischaemic Heart Disease.

Tuckett, D.A. (forthcoming) Account of project investigating the experience of psychiatric outpatients following a referral by their general practitioner.

Wilde, W.A. (1968) Decision-Making in a Psychiatric Screening Agency. *Journal of Health and Social Behaviour* **9**: 215–21.

Chapter 3

Ann Oakley

The Family, Marriage, and Its Relationship to Illness

One of the distinguishing features of the family as a subject of social discourse is that it is easy to define: everybody knows what 'the family' is. This universal understanding is attributable to the fact that the vast majority of people come from, and are members of, families. In other words, it is due to the importance of the family as a basic unit of social life.

For sociologists, the family is not simply a biological grouping. It is a system of social relationships. A family that consists of a married couple and their adopted children illustrates this point. A group of this kind *acts* like a family, feels itself to *be* a family, and is perceived by other people *as* a family. If one considers, on the other hand, the case of a woman on her own without a man but with children, it is less clear that this is a 'family' situation. Terms such as 'fatherless' family or 'single-parent' family are used to differentiate this situation from others — to point out what it lacks. In practice, the woman-and-her-children are far less able to act and feel like a family than are the man-woman-and-their-adopted-children; the community does not treat them like an 'ordinary' family (Marsden, 1969: 105–9).

The contrast between the two examples outlines the sociologist's approach to the family and marriage. Approaching the family as a social unit, the sociologist considers what is characteristic of families in general, rather than what is specific to individual families. Before going on to look at some of the ways in which the family may influence illness, and some of the reactions the family may have to the illness of one of its members, I want to enlarge on the sociological approach to the family: what is the place of the family in society as a whole, and what is the place of men, women, and children within the family?

The Sociological Perspective on the Family

A common method of defining the family is to look at the functions it performs: this is known as the 'functionalist' approach. In modern society, the family's functions are usually said to be (1) the satisfaction of adult sexual needs, and (2) the procreation and rearing of children (Bell and Vogel, 1968a). These are 'minimal' or 'residual' functions. The family may have other functions: in the past — and still in other cultures today — the family's frame of reference has been much wider than this. Before industrialization in the West, for instance, it functioned as an economically productive unit, with mother, father, and children working together, producing goods for their own use, for sale, or exchange, sharing economic capital and the monetary return for their labour. In the era before the introduction of a universal school system, it also functioned as the context for any formal education children received. The disappearance of these functions of the family has, together with other changes, led to a description of the family in terms of the functions it has lost, rather than in terms of any it has gained. In turn, this has produced an image of the family as an adaptive unit, flexible and responsive to the demands made on it by economy and society. It is argued that the modern demand for mobile labour power has brought about a diminution in the size of the family: families today are typically 'nuclear' rather than 'extended' (Vincent, 1969). That is, the 'nucleus' of an adult couple and their dependent children tends to form a separate domestic unit, and other relatives — grandparents, aunts, uncles, and so on — live elsewhere.

This view of the family as an institution which passively adapts in response to changes in the economy and society is clearly one-sided. If the family is as important a social unit as is supposed, it would obviously be expected to have some independent influence on economic and social life itself (Parker *et al.*, 1967: 46–50). However, the 'functionalist' approach draws attention to the crucial fact that historical changes have rendered the family a more specialized agency.

According to the American sociological theorist, Talcott Parsons:

'The functions of the family ... are not to be interpreted as functions directly on behalf of the society, but on behalf of personality ... It is because the *human* personality is not "born" but must be "made" through the socialization process that in the first instance families are necessary. They are "factories" which produce human personalities.'
(Parsons, 1956: 16)

The functionalist school of sociologists argues that families produce people in two ways. First, there is the upbringing of children to perform adult roles of the kind accepted and expected by the social group they live in. Second, the family acts to stabilize *adult* personalities in the socially stereotyped roles of husband and wife. In their roles as wives and mothers, women's main occupations are domestic ones; their interests are home-centred, and the emotional well-being of the family is their concern. Men, on the other hand, have as their primary duty the earning of money to support the family; their activities and interests are much more concerned with the world outside family life. Thus it could be said that belonging to a family pressures people to behave in traditionally feminine and masculine ways.

Although the contraceptive advances of this century have contributed to a reduction in the size of families, other changes have effectively amplified the family's childrearing function. Children are now more important. The development of child psychology as a separate scientific discipline, and the emergence of psychoanalysis in the first decades of this century, have attached a new significance to childhood. As the anthropologist Margaret Mead has said of modern American society:

'Parenthood is a responsible, anxious matter, in which the mother must keep herself continually up to date with changing standards of childcare. Within this family, children are given an extraordinary amount of attention, when judged by the standards of most other societies. Their needs, their wishes and their performances are regarded as central and worthy of adult attention.' (Mead, 1952: 5–6)

Child care has become a subject of scientific interest. Until late in Western history the only experts in child care outside the family were the midwife and the teacher. Now the world is full of experts. Structures for the dissemination to families of knowledge about child care include antenatal and child welfare clinics, television, and the mass media generally. The general tone of much of the advice thus given and received is that parents cannot know how best to bring up children unless they are guided. This adage has obvious disadvantages in the erosion of parental confidence, as recognized by Spock in his advice to new parents in the first chapter of the world-famous *Baby and Child Care*:

'You know more than you think you do ... you have been listening more carefully to your friends and relatives when they talk about bringing up a child. You've begun to read articles by experts in the magazines and newspapers. After the baby is born, the doctors and nurses will begin to give you instructions too. Sometimes it sounds like a very complicated business ... Don't take too seriously all that the neighbours say. Don't be overawed by what the experts say. Don't be afraid to trust you own commonsense.' (Spock, 1957: 3)

These admonitions are followed by 594 pages of advice.

Another way the family's childrearing function has been enlarged is through the increased emphasis of societal institutions on the family. 'Familism', the sociological name for this family-orientation, entails a style of living centred on the small family of two parents and children: a major emotional investment in family relationships which constitute, for all family members, their chief source of social and psychological support. If work has become for many people less satisfying, because it is increasingly specialized and monotonous, an alternative orientation is to home and family (Goldthorpe *et al.*, 1968). Sociologists themselves have followed this orientation, and much of the research done in the last two decades reflects a concern with the importance of family background as a determinant of the individual's behaviour.

The family socializes* children for the roles* expected of them in adult life. It teaches them the norms of conduct they should follow — for instance that they should act responsibly, with kindness and consideration for other people, that they should not break the laws of the country, and so on. Children's learning of future adult roles within the family also embraces the differential learning of sex roles. These are better described as 'gender' roles, since feminine and masculine behaviour, as Western culture defines them, are complexes of behavioural and personality attributes based on, but not in any way tied to, the criterion of biological sex status — male or female (Oakley, 1972a). The rearing of a girl for her feminine role generally implies an emphasis on exterior attractiveness, a curtailment of 'tomboy' activities, a reduction of her 'natural' assertiveness, and the inculcation of marriage as an ideal life-goal. The rearing of a boy usually involves the encouragement of his independence and his active interests in the world outside himself; an emphasis on self-confidence, self-sufficiency, and inherent self-worth. Girls are usually socialized for domesticity and motherhood, boys for a job or career. The growth of sex equality in the fields of education and employment has reduced this differentiation of gender role to some extent. But studies of the way gender roles are taught to small children have revealed the persistence of long-standing ideas about the roles of men and women (Oakley, 1972a: 173–88).

Gender is not only important in the socialization of children. The family can be seen as a system of interlocking roles. The roles of husband and wife, mother and father, parent and child, are interrelated and cannot be defined in isolation from each other. Differentiation between age and gender roles is the axis of the family's structure. This is particularly so with gender. The following linguistic couplets are useful clues: 'husband and wife', 'mother and father', 'man and wife'. In each case the order is the conventional one. 'Husband' takes precedence over 'wife', but 'mother' comes before 'father'. The explanation is not that adult feminine and masculine roles in the family are simply different but equal; the distinctions between them are fundamental ones. This is borne out by the implications of the third couplet, 'man and wife', which are neatly summarized by the old Russian proverb: 'I thought I saw two people, but it was only a man and his wife' (Rowbotham, 1973: 134).

The role of women in the family is quite different from the role of men and in many ways it is in direct contrast to it. In the later discussion of the relationship between illness and the family this statement will gather

* See Introduction (pp. 14–15 and pp. 11–13) for discussion on socialization and roles.

significance. Women as family members are (1) housewives, (2) wives, and (3) mothers. Their role as housewives is not paralleled by an equivalent masculine role. In concrete terms, and according to recent figures, what this means is that some 85 per cent of all women aged between sixteen and sixty-four years in Britain today carry the responsibility for running a household (Hunt, 1968: II, 4). However much their husbands participate in daily household tasks, all the indicators point to the fact that it is women as housewives who retain the responsibility for housework performance. They also spend a substantial amount of time engaged in housework activities. A range of studies suggests that weekly hours spent in housework average over seventy hours, varying from between twenty and forty hours (childless housewives who are employed outside the home) to sometimes over a hundred hours (non-employed housewives with two or more children) (Oakley, 1974: 92–5).

The housewife-houseworker role as a feminine role in the family over-laps with the role of wife. As a wife, a woman is usually expected to take care of her husband's routine physical needs: the provision of meals, clean clothing, and so on. *He* is not expected to do these tasks for *her*. Similarly, housewifery and mothering have some degree of continuity. The routine physical care of children is a mother's responsibility. Sociological research studies of family role-behaviour have shown a tendency for fathers to undertake some child care tasks which they would probably not have done fifty or a hundred years ago (Newson and Newson 1965; 1970). However, such studies do not indicate any pronounced tendency for men to share equally with mothers the routine physical aspects of child care – feeding, dressing, nappy changing, and so forth (Oakley, 1972b). For the husband–father, it seems that the counterpart of these family-care and home-care roles is the role of breadwinner.

The greater prominence of feminine over masculine roles in the family has an interesting linguistic tag: for the phrase 'a family man' there is no equivalent 'a family woman', because, in one sense, women *are* the family. Our cultural ideals assign the key family role of childrearer to women, who also in their roles as housewives and wives are expected to subvert their own interests and goals to the interests of the family as a group. The woman–housewife–wife–mother is a cultural ideal. For women themselves this combination of roles represents the modal pattern of feminine adjustment (Janeway, 1971).

In many cases, sociologists have tended to reflect, rather than detach themselves from, these values. Our information about what actually goes on in families is, as a result, much less than complete. Much sociological research on the family is based exclusively on the observations or inform-ation of wives and mothers. Research into childrearing attitudes and techniques suffers particularly from this bias, which is usually concealed through the use of gender-neutral titles such as *Patterns of Childrearing* (Sears, Maccoby and Levin, 1957), *The Changing American Parent* (Miller and Swanson, 1958), *Patterns of Infant Care in an Urban Community* (Newson and Newson, 1965).[1] Husbands and fathers are heavily under-represented, not only because they are less available for study (being at work all day) but also because it is assumed that their place in the family is, and ought to be, a marginal one (Tavuchis, 1970).

The approach to the family as a role-system is a useful one in the study of the relationship between the family and illness. Studies of the relationship between physical and mental illness and the family and marriage fall into two broad categories: those in which the family is conceptualized as the *context* of illness, and those in which the family is identified more specifically as playing a *causative* role in the disease process. Research in the first category has produced insights to which, generally speaking, higher confidence can be attached than in the case of research in the second category. The family's causative role in illness is an area to which inadequate research attention has been given. As a result much of existing research is strictly speculative.

The Family as the Context of Illness

Davis's study of fourteen child victims of spinal paralytic poliomyelitis is a study of family action and reaction in an illness crisis; of the family as the context in which a person becomes ill, is hospitalized, then rehabilitated to a family situation (Davis, 1963). Though polio has now ceased to be the illness of major importance it was when Davis conducted his study, his insights are of lasting relevance to the following questions: how do families accept — or not accept — the diagnosis of a potentially disabling illness? Does their differential acceptance of the medical situation affect the patient's progress? What changes occur in the child's family role as a result of the illness process? How do particular family reactions help to bring about these different consequences?

The parents of the fourteen children in Davis's study were seen by the research team shortly before the admission of the children to hospital, and then at intervals until fifteen months after their discharge from a convalescent institution. At the beginning of the illness all parents applied a 'commonplace explanatory framework' to the child's first symptoms (he's got a cold/stomach upset, he's overtired/out-of-sorts). But families differed in the cues that alerted them to the possibility of a more serious illness. For one father it was the sight of his three year old winning a fight with the six year old that warned him that the six year old's symptoms were more than commonplace and medically trivial. Other parents had considered polio as a possibility from the beginning of the illness, and were on the alert for appropriate symptoms. This differential perception of physiological cues had an influence on the stage at which medical help was sought.

Parents' abilities to accept the diagnosis of polio also varied a great deal.

As Davis points out, acceptance of the polio diagnosis and the possible consequences of the illness forges a dramatic change in basic family perspectives, and will often be resisted for this reason. Davis draws attention to the manner in which the diagnosis of polio was presented to the families concerned. In every case the family doctor who visited the child at home did not definitely diagnose the illness as polio; rather, doctors evaded the issue and either mentioned polio as one of several possible diseases — e.g. meningitis unspecified, spinal meningitis — or did not mention polio at all. The object of this evasive tactic was presumably a desire not to be proved wrong, combined with a protective attitude on the doctor's part towards his future role as physician to that family. However, its consequences were unexpected: many parents persistently maintained their own doctor's lack of certainty about the polio diagnosis in the later hospital situation.

One possible family reaction to an illness crisis is an affirmation of its solidarity as a social-emotional unit. In Davis's study, this was the response of a number of families, with parents openly stating the view that a child's polio represented a 'test' of the family's strength. Although in the stage *before* the final diagnosis was made, fathers acted as 'comforters' to their wives — an action congruent with the masculine family role generally — *after* the parents had accepted the diagnosis, fathers as well as mothers commonly broke down and wept. Overtly dismissed by the men as a temporary loss of control, this departure from their usual emotional role in the family was to their wives a much welcomed sign of the men's intense involvement in the family illness crisis.

Illness, particularly if it is serious, sets up an out-of-the-ordinary situation. The daily routines of family life are disturbed: nothing can be taken for granted any more. Emotions, usually hidden in everyday life, are laid bare. For this reason, the experience of families in an illness crisis has something to tell us about 'normal' families — that is, about the family and marriage as institutions. Although theoretically founded on love or romantic attachment, the experience of being in a family is often directly antithetical to the communication of positive feelings. One main reason for this is the differentiation of gender roles — the separation between the worlds of the man and the woman in marriage — that marriage entails. This point is returned to later.

The family's reaction to illness may influence the stage at which medical help is brought in and its attitudes towards the convalescent patient are also of crucial importance. Davis lists three stratagems that are available for the handicapped person in his subsequent adjustment to life in the community: (1) 'passing', when the handicap is simply disguised, so far as is possible; (2) 'normalization', in which the handicap is dismissed as unimportant; (3) 'disassociation', which alone of the three stratagems requires some abdication of the normal standard. For many people this last consists of cutting down involvement with other people in the community, so as to avoid a possible confrontation with the fact of handicap. In the case of child patients it is largely up to the family as to which of these stratagems is employed. The child himself may not realize his difference from others. Nine of Davis's fourteen polio victims emerged from the illness with a moderate or severe degree of handicap. 'Normalization' evolved as a stratagem in the four families with moderately handicapped children, and two of those with severely handicapped children. The three remaining children all had severe handicaps and their families chose 'disassociation' as a technique of coping with the disability.

Davis is unable to provide a complete explanation as to why different stratagems are adopted by different families. But he lists four variables as correlated with the differential choice of 'normalization' or 'disassociation': the child's degree of handicap, the age of the child at discharge, sibling constellation, and style of family functioning. The relevance of the first is obvious. The child's age is apparently influential in the sense that families feel that the abnormal physical appearance of older children is more difficult to normalize — all the families who favoured disassociation had affected children in the nine to twelve year old age group. Sibling constellation affects the likelihood of equal treatment for the handicapped child, since when there are other children close in age it is more difficult for the parents to treat the handicapped child differently from the others. Lastly, Davis suggests that the family's life-style — the flexibility of roles in an egalitarian family, the relative rigidity of roles in a traditional family — is also a factor influencing the manner in which the handicapped child is rehabilitated to family and social life. In particular, it appears that 'normalization' is more likely in an egalitarian than in a traditional family.

Two aspects of a patient's family background would appear to be of specific relevance to the question of his illness. First, there is the internal structure of roles, which makes up one patient's family, a structure that is essentially the same in all 'normal' families. Second, there is the particular constellation of personality types and events associated with each particular family. Friedman's investigation of forty six parents anticipating the death of a child from cancer emphasizes the need for physicians to take into account the particular characteristics of individual families (Friedman *et al.*, 1963). Assumptions about a 'normal' way of behaving are not necessarily relevant, and may be misleading.

In this study it was the parents of the ill children who were the 'patients', and what is at issue is the effect of a fatal illness on family life. Friedman found that two approaches on the part of physicians were particularly helpful: (1) an attitude of flexibility towards the involvement or non-involvement of parents in the care of their dying child; (2) an attempt to make the parents view the child's illness realistically. To some extent, 'coping behaviour' is a personal business: that is, there are recognizably different coping styles of which physicians should be aware.

Although the parents in Friedman's study were all able to participate in their child's care, only some chose to do so. The parents' decision was dependent on the course of action they felt would facilitate their own coping behaviour. Generally, Friedman found that a nursing role was chosen more by mothers than fathers, and he suggests this is because it is more congruent with their previous self-image.

A realistic assessment of the prognosis on the part of parents is a condition of 'anticipatory mourning' or 'grief-work'. It is now well established that the working-through of a person's approaching death is helpful to the survivor of the relationship[2] — the parents, in Friedman's study. The consequences of grief-work among these parents of leukaemic children were not a lessening of love or the ability to care for the dying child, but a superior ability to survive the emotional trauma of its death.

The presentation of medical data on the patient's condition facilitated this realistic approach, although Friedman felt that it could go too far. He believed that 'requests for detailed medical information, such as the daily laboratory findings, should be discouraged and evaluated in terms of what underlying needs the parents are attempting to fulfill' (Friedman, 1963: 623).

One unexpected finding of this study was that other family members — particularly grandparents — did not aid this process of adjustment, largely because they challenged the seriousness of the illness situation as doctors and parents presented it. Therefore, paradoxically, parents found themselves playing a supportive role to the child's grandparents. A partial explanation of this paradox is an inherent contradiction in social attitudes to the families of seriously ill people, who are expected to be thoroughly grief-stricken, but at the same time to remain persistently hopeful. The social interpretation of illness is a factor with which families have to contend.

The need for families to confront possibly critical and 'irrational' social attitudes is especially evident in the case of mental illness, to which a continuing social stigma attaches. A look at the impact of mental illness on family life is the converse of the more popular approach, in which the family is viewed as a cause of mental illness, but it has much to tell us about the way in which families are socially implicated in illness. Like Davis's study of polio crises, an analysis of family responses to mental illness also tells us something about the normal role of the family in social life.

A study by Yarrow of the wives of mental patients focuses on the expectations family members have about social reactions to mental illness, and on the patterns of communication manifested between the patient's family and the outside world (Yarrow, 1955). The predominant expectation among these wives was that the family would be stigmatized. Overt protestations of sympathy were discounted on the grounds that the person might actually be thinking something quite different. Ascribing to others the image of the mentally ill person as 'crazy', these women also talked about a fundamental disturbance in the stability of their family worlds: 'The "reputation of the social front" of the family as a congenial, happy group seems shattered. The marriage may be seen as a failure. As one wife describes this: "It's hard to admit you can't manage on your own". (Yarrow, 1955: 35).

The stigma of mental illness is a matter of the 'family name' being at stake. Marriage and the family as modern social institutions are governed by an ethic of privacy. Husband and wife 'keep themselves to themselves'; so do families. As long as a family is seen by others to be a self-sufficient, closed grouping, its actual intimacy and success is rarely called into question. Mental illness ruptures the family's appearance of normality. It arouses suspicions about what goes on in *that* family, about what the people in it do to each other, and about the sanity of its other members. The fact that these suspicions are rarely articulated adds to their weight.

For the wives in Yarrow's sample, the basic problem was a conflict between needing help with a stressful situation, and not feeling able to share thoughts and feelings about the husband's illness with other people. Predictably, adolescent or adult children were the wives' closest confidants. No breach of the family's privacy was entailed by this pattern of communication; instead the solidarity of the family as a unit was affirmed. So far as outsiders were concerned, a major communication pattern was 'concealment' — a pattern involving minimal contacts, designed to avoid any situation in which the husband's illness had to be acknowledged.

Yet outsiders — comparative strangers to the wife — were more likely than relatives or friends to receive the most intimate communications on the subject of the husband's illness. Yarrow distinguishes two kinds of communication: (1) the communication of facts, and (2) the communication of emotional experiences. While friends and relatives received the former kind of communication, the latter was withheld from them, because of the judgmental position in which they would, as a consequence, be placed. Their intimacy with the family was felt to provide a basis for possibly critical observations about the wife's or the husband's past errors. The wife's desire to maintain the social front of the family entailed an avoidance of any situation in which criticisms of her role-performance were likely.

This refusal to share the communication of emotional experience was particularly acute in the case of the married couple's parents. In their dealings with in-laws, more than half the wives either expressed or experienced hostility. Wives blamed mothers-in-law for causing the husband's illness through faulty upbringing; mothers-in-law blamed wives for driving their sons to mental hospitals. In eighteen out of twenty-nine cases with living relatives, the husband's family was made to assume some responsibility during the period of his illness — this compared with three cases in which the wife's family took the same responsibility.

These difficulties express, in part, the structural problems of family and marriage relationships in modern society. Reared in their separate families, a man and a woman come together to form a new family of their own. The division of loyalties must be finely balanced. Social norms validate the priority of place the couple's own marriage and children assume, but prescribe at the same time the continuation of filial responsibilities towards their families of origin. The husband's mental illness disturbs the normal structural equilibrium and both reflects, and impinges on, the interconnections between the related families. To the wife, the husband becomes what he once was — the child of his parents. The wife herself may re-assume the dependent daughter-role in her own family of origin. In Yarrow's study this tended to happen especially during the period of the husband's hospitalization. The wife may be helped by her parents financially; she may move in with them or send her children to live with them. Ties of dependence, severed by marriage, and not regarded as normally compatible with the self-sufficiency of the nuclear family unit, are re-established.[3]

These findings raise the recurrent sociological issue of how 'nuclear' the nuclear family is. Do people really live out their emotional lives in these closed two parent - 2.3 child families as conventional sociological theory supposes they do? Or are close relationships with other kin maintained after marriage and the setting up of a new family? Has the family really been reduced in size by industrialization, or is this view simply the projection of 'certain middle-class hopes and ideals onto a refractory reality?' (Moore, 1969: 456).

The position of old people — who are, of course, not necessarily ill — is one social issue on which this theoretical discussion can safely be grounded. Townsend's work on the social contacts of the elderly has shown that relationships with adult children are more common than the stereotyped image of the isolated old person would suggest. In his Bethnal Green survey of 203 old people, Townsend found that nearly one half actually shared a household with relatives other than a husband or wife, that between them they had 2,700 relatives living within a mile, and that only 4 per cent did not see at least one of their children once a week (Townsend, 1963: 33, 43, 49). In the event of sudden or chronic illness, the existence of willing relatives can make all the difference. Two thirds of Townsend's sample counted near relatives as sources of help in an illness crisis. The remaining third had no reserves of help; these were chiefly single or childless people, and people with sons but without daughters (Townsend, 1963: 66). Other medical studies have shown how it is very rare for the family not to care for those of its members who are old and ill (Isaacs, 1971). In a comparative survey of old people in the United States, Britain, and Denmark, between a quarter and a third of the elderly in all three countries had been ill in the year previous to interview; for those without spouses, children had been the single most important source of help with shopping, cleaning, and the provision of meals. In the

British sample, 77 per cent had received help with housework from their families, 80 per cent with shopping, and 82 per cent with meals and personal toilet (Townsend, 1968a).

Townsend's work shows that not only does the care of old people depend on whether they have children; it depends on the sex of their children. About a third of old people in Britain have no children or only male children. According to Townsend, these individuals make up a single category with respect to their isolation from the system of family care (Townsend, 1968a).[4] The consequences of such isolation vary from housekeeping difficulties to extreme physical neglect resulting in death. To some extent, a higher incidence of morbidity and mortality among old people is a symptom of the general finding that the incidence of both these is raised in populations of socially isolated people. Mortality is higher than would be expected among individuals whose spouses have recently died (Parkes, Benjamin, and Fitzgerald, 1969: 741). In general, mortality is also higher among those who have never married and among those whose marriages have been terminated. There are several categories of disease in which the unmarried or no longer married have very much higher mortality rates than married persons, including influenza, pneumonia, syphilis, and cirrhosis of the liver (Chen and Cobb, 1960).

Although many old and ill people are cared for by their families, this is not done without difficulty. For example, one study of geriatric admissions in Glasgow in 1971 showed that a major reason for admission was because relatives were suffering 'undue strain' in caring for the old person (Isaacs, 1971). The care of old people is not a key function of the nuclear family in modern society. Wider kin networks may often be involved in the care of the elderly, and the nuclear family may be generally supportive, but the absorption of one or more old persons into the interior of the nuclear family challenges the actual and idealized privacy of the nuclear unit. Solving the 'problem' of the isolated old person, it may set up further difficulties for the family as a whole.

Clark and Sommers's study of the family backgrounds of maladjusted children pinpoints some of the disturbances in family life consequent on the admission to it of one or more other adults (Clark and Sommers, 1961). An unsatisfactory relationship between a child's parent and the 'extra' adult was, in this study, found to be associated with maladjusted behaviour of the child at home and at school — with such symptoms as tics, stammering, enuresis, failures at school work, and so on. 'Unsatisfactory' here covers the typical situation of a mother's emotional dependence on her own mother, a common source of strain in the marital relationship. A frequent reaction to the mother–grandmother dependence syndrome was the husband–father's withdrawal from participation in family activities, especially from the area of child care. The father's reduced family role was associated with maladjusted behaviour in the child. Mother and grandmother fought a battle for the child's allegiance, establishing a situation of contradictory demands for the child.

Studies such as these, of what actually goes on in the interior of the family, show that family life is not an unmixed blessing. The ethic of privacy may lead to the concealment of negative emotions, and adherence to the idealized model of the family as a place where people are happy and fulfill themselves may conceal a wide range of failures and dysfunctional elements in family life. As one outspoken critic, David Cooper, puts it in *Psychiatry and Anti-Psychiatry*: 'Some of the "closest" families and the "happiest" marriages are those in which relations are the most estranged' (Cooper, 1970: 51).

One particular area of family life — emotional involvement — has been studied by Brown and others in relation to the course of schizophrenic illness. In an exploratory study of discharged, long-stay male patients, Brown and his colleagues found that, contrary to expectations, close emotional ties with parents or wives indicated a poor prognosis (Brown, 1959). A second study demonstrated that patients returning home to live with relatives who were highly emotionally involved with them (the degree of involvement being judged by ratings of the relatives' behaviour) were more likely to experience a relapse (Brown *et al.*, 1962). Further investigation of the key variable — emotional involvement — showed that it could be more precisely defined as 'expressed emotion', and that in the main the emotions expressed by family members were negative ones (Brown *et al.*, 1972). This finding directly relates to the question of drug treatment. Brown *et al.* show that drugs appear to have no effect on the outcome (relapse or no relapse) for patients living with relatives rated low on expressed emotion, so that medication may be a necessary method of protecting patients who return to high expressed emotion homes (Brown *et al.*, 1972).

Brown concludes that a schizophrenic's close emotional ties with family members may be a hindrance rather than an aid to the maintenance of a symptomless state. Indeed, there is a direct relationship between the chances of relapse and the amount of time a patient spends in face-to-face contact with adults in the home, in the case of high expressed emotion households (Brown *et al.*, 1972). The optimal situation for the schizophrenic patient could thus be described as a non-stimulating social environment; one in which warmth is expressed; without criticism of the patient's behaviour, and without emotional over-involvement on the part of other family members. However, the practice of returning mentally ill people to their homes has developed well in advance of knowledge about the effect of this practice on the patient's welfare (and on that of his family).

The Family as a Cause of Illness

The work by Brown and his colleagues is a careful investigation of the family's influence on the *course* of mental illness. It does not pronounce upon the possible origins of schizophrenia in family life. A considerable amount of recent literature in this field has been concerned with the family's causative role in the disease process.

Prior to the mid-1950s research into the aetiology of mental illness was limited by a lack of concern with the total family as a unit. The case of schizophrenia illustrates this change of perspective. Most of the early research done was based on the view that the cause of the illness was to be found in the individual's own characteristics. Researchers then moved on to a concentration on the mother–child relationship, from there to the inclusion of a possibly pathogenic father, and eventually to a focus on the family as a 'pathological system of interaction' (Vincent, 1967).

The work of R.D. Laing has done much to popularize the view that schizophrenia is not so much an illness, as a label given to people who react to family life in a specific way (Laing, 1965; Laing and Esterson, 1964). The question 'what causes schizophrenia?' is to Laing a question about the social *meaning* of schizophrenia. As he puts it: 'Everyone who has made a close study of the families of schizophrenics appears to agree that much, or even all, of the apparent irrationality of the individual finds its rationality in its original family context' (Laing, 1969: 48). Through an analysis of the dynamics of 'schizophrenic families', Laing has been able to delineate the manner in which the family's whole system of emotional role-relationships is absorbed by each family member: 'to be in the same family means having the same family inside oneself' (Laing, 1967: 119). This internalization of the family's role-system by each of its members gives rise to an ever present possibility, one that is inherent in the structure of every family: the possibility that an individual's identity may become seriously confused through the conflicting images he receives of himself. The achievement of individual autonomy entails a breaking-out of this internalized system, a personal act that threatens the idealized autonomy of the family itself. Hence 'schizophrenic' behaviour, and the subsequent diagnosis of schizophrenia.

What goes on in schizophrenic families has been described as 'pseudo-mutuality': an appearance of harmony and flexibility which overlays an actuality of hostility, rigidity, and mutual destructiveness (Wynne, Ryckoff and Hirsch, 1967). Laing gives an example of such a family, which incidentally illustrates the research finding mentioned earlier — that the inclusion in the family of 'extra' adults may create problems of identity and loyalty for the children of that family.

A seventeen year old, Jane, experienced a change of personality from an active, friendly, involved adolescent, to an inactive, self-absorbed, and silent figure. In psychotherapy for a diagnosis of schizophrenia simplex, she revealed an image of herself as a tennis ball, being passed to and fro in a game of mixed doubles. This reverie was a metaphor for her experience of her family: father, mother, mother's father and father's mother, ranged against each other in a 'game of mixed doubles'. They would break off communication with each other for weeks at a time. During these phases, communication would be passed through Jane: 'Mother would turn to Jane and say "tell your father to pass the salt", Jane would say to her father "Mum wants you to pass the salt" and so on' (Laing, 1967: 122).

The task of the psychotherapist in Jane's case was to establish for her the connections between the world of the tennis game inside her head and the world of the family outside it: to convey to her the essential *rationality* of her response to this family situation.

Of course other interpretations of the family scenes Laing describes are possible. In the example of Jane and her family it could for instance be suggested that perhaps the child's behaviour was in some sense causing the tennis ball effect on other family members. Laing's work is interesting and thought-provoking, and an object lesson in how the source data can be given very different meanings by different individuals who bring to it their own prior assumptions and conceptual framework. But, sociologically speaking, his work is highly speculative.

However, other investigations of schizophrenic patients' families suggest patterns of communication that differ from those in other families. Just how they differ is not yet clear. Singer and Wynne's work on defects of communication among parents of schizophrenic, neurotic, and normal populations indicates that no 'schizophrenic' parents score in either the 'normal' or 'neurotic' range; in other words, that there may be particular patterns of communication among parents of schizophrenic people (Wynne, 1969). An attempt to replicate this finding by Hirsch and Leff concludes that a large proportion of schizophrenics have parents who show very little or no abnormality of speech, but that parents of schizophrenics produce significantly more words under test conditions than do parents of neurotics (Hirsch and Leff, 1971).

Laing's existential view, that the pathogenicity of the family inheres in the present and on-going experiences of its members within it, contrasts with the more established view that the pathologies of family members stem from their childhood experiences. Much of the research concerned with this hypothesis has focused on the role of the mother in the family. A wide range of illness syndromes and disturbed behaviour patterns have been attributed to inadequate maternal care: developmental retardation, affectionless psychopathy, delinquency, growth failure, and depression in adulthood among them (Rutter, 1972: 53). The paradox of these allegations is that, whether valid or not, they imply some criticism of the family as an institution.

If these various illnesses and disturbed behaviour patterns are not 'caused' by mothers, then perhaps the concentration of childrearing in the hands of women is a social arrangement based on a misconception of the needs of children and the duties of women. Mothers do not need to be any more tightly bound to their children than fathers could be. If, on the other hand, the mother's influence over the child's character formation and mental health is as great as these researchers propose, then the advisability of our present social arrangements is also called into question. Should the care of children be entrusted to people whose job it is to clean houses and service husbands in conditions of relative social isolation, with no financial recognition for the value of the work they do, and with only lip service paid to the status of motherhood as a profession? As the American feminist Charlotte Perkins Gilman asked seventy years ago:

'What is the real condition of the home as regards children ...? As a matter of fact, *are* our children happy and prosperous, healthy and good, at home? ... Follow the hours in the day of the housewife: count the minutes spent in the care and service of the child, as compared with those given to the planning of meals, the purchase of supplies, the labour either of personally cleaning things or of seeing that other persons do it ... "But" we protest "all this is for the child — the meals, the well-kept house, the clothes — the whole thing!"

Yes? And in what way do the meals we so elaborately order and prepare, the daintily furnished home, the much-trimmed clothing, contribute to the body-growth, mind-growth, and the soul-growth of the child?' (Gilman, 1972: 112–13)

Gilman observes that this polemic is geared to reality while the image conjured up in most people's minds by the term 'motherhood' is an idealized one: a warm picture of a mother and child united in mutual contentment and absorbed in the satisfaction of one another's needs.

What do we mean by 'motherhood'? Does a 'maternal instinct' exist? What does becoming a mother mean to women, and how do mothers experience the daily routines of caring for children? These questions which probe beneath the surface of the sentimental picture of motherhood are really only just beginning to be asked by social scientists, and clearly our knowledge of the reality of family life must remain deficient until they are answered.

It is possible to point to various contradictions surrounding motherhood in modern society. For example, it is generally thought that mothering skills come naturally to women, but there is evidence that this is not so: it has been estimated that about one in five of all mothers has difficulty in 'turning on' to the mother–child relationship (Kempe, 1970). This draws attention to the fact that biological drives do not necessarily bind mother and child together (Tomkins, 1965). Child-bearing and child-caring behaviours have separate and distinct origins (Steele and Pollock, 1968).

Another set of contradictions is involved in the transition to motherhood. While the ability to perform mothering tasks is considered a natural aspect of the feminine personality, pregnancy and parturition are increasingly treated as 'unnatural' processes. Hospitalized childbirth is the medical ideal: childbirth as a 'normal' process is thus given a primary association with illness. Rising induction rates, the increased use of monitoring in labour, of epidural analgesia, and other forms of medical intervention in the physiological process of giving birth, transform childbirth into an unnatural technological event. Other hospital rituals and procedures (for example, the pre-delivery shaving and enema routine, episiotomies, and forceps deliveries) through which the parturient woman passes may contribute to a loss of identity which makes adaptation to motherhood more difficult (Lomas, 1966).

Whilst many modern techniques in the management of childbirth undoubtedly make for greater safety, it is important not to lose sight of the psychological impact on the mother herself. Moreover, 'medical' or 'scientific' reasons for a particular mode of treatment may not be entirely rational. Many practices common in the management of childbirth today are so widely accepted that their use is rarely questioned, although examination of the way childbirth is managed in traditional small-scale societies raises questions as to their necessity, or even their advisability (Mead and Newton, 1967). For instance, the majority of these societies use upright positions for delivery, in which gravity is an aid to muscular efficiency. Although relatively little research has been done on the advantages and disadvantages of different positions, what has been done 'suggests that the flat supine position for delivery may make spontaneous delivery more difficult' (Mead and Newton, 1967: 214). The continuing popularity of this position (and the popularity of other procedures) has to be seen in the light of cultural attitudes to childbirth and to women generally.

A third example of the contradictions surrounding motherhood is found by considering medical attitudes towards breastfeeding. Usually the conventional medical approach is to allow the mother herself a free choice of feeding method, on the grounds that the infant will prosper equally well whether natural or artificial feeding is adopted. Yet this is, to say the least, controversial. Research has implicated artificial feeding in a number of disorders, including gastroenteritis, antibody response to milk, and hypocalcaemic convulsions (Davie, Butler, and Goldstein, 1972: 72). It seems that it is not simply the case that adequate hygiene precautions need to be taken with the artificially fed infant. Artificial milk formulae provide a dietary solute load which is at least twice that of breast milk and puts a considerable strain on the capacity of the immature kidney to maintain the normal tonicity of body fluids (Davies, 1973). Thus, even apparently healthy infants fed in this way may be on the verge of a crisis from only the mild degree of water loss accompanying any of the common infections of infancy.

One expert concludes that, on the basis of this kind of evidence 'perhaps the time has come for doctors to realise that there are firm, objective reasons for encouraging mothers to breast feed' (Davie, Butler, and Goldstein, 1972: 72). A Department of Health working party on infant feeding practices recently recommended that mothers should be advised to breastfeed for four to six months, and to delay the introduction of solid foods until this time. In particular the report deplored the promotion of substitute milks in a way that suggests that these are equal in value to human milk (Department of Health and Social Security, 1974). Nevertheless, the majority of doctors apparently continue to reassure non-breastfeeders that their choice of the bottle is a perfectly safe one. Looking at the evidence, however, the doctor's responsibility should really be to help women to breastfeed and to understand the importance of it — and a massive re-education programme is called for in the presence of what Jelliffe has termed the present 'trend towards world lactation failure' (Mead and Newton, 1967: 184). This does not, of course, mean that authoritarian pressures should be put on women to breastfeed. They should be given the facts. Certainly, in present conditions, the reluctance to breastfeed is in many cases a reasonable response to many factors, including a cultural context in which the breast is a sexual, rather than nutritional, object.

Contradictions and confusions such as these concerning motherhood are also to be found in the related and equally emotive area of 'maternal deprivation'. Pressure on women to adopt the stereotyped maternal role often stems from a belief that children who are not cared for full-time by their mothers will be 'deprived' in some clearcut and permanently damaging way. What do we mean by 'maternal deprivation'? What reliable research evidence do we have?

Certainly, in a family-oriented society, the loss of one or both parents may indeed be a condition of extreme vulnerability for the individual. In a fascinating study of Family Structure in Relation to Health and Disease, Chen and Cobb summarize the literature on parental deprivation (Chen and Cobb, 1960). They find that tuberculosis patients, accident victims, and people who make suicide attempts, report 'parental deprivation' (loss by death, divorce, or separation) two to three times as often as the general population of the United States. Since tuberculosis, accidents, and attempted suicide do not by any means form a single class of event, the connections between each of these and a background of parental deprivation must be different. Some evidence indicates that social isolation may be a common factor. Its importance in relation to suicide is well established; tuberculosis rates appear to be higher among those individuals who experience stress in conditions of isolation from their usual social contacts, and accident-prone workers in one study (Wolff, 1950) had a tendency to live in rooming-houses. But beyond this, we know very little about the precise factors responsible for the statistical relationships in these three instances.

Chen and Cobb advise caution in the interpretation of such relationships. Questions about how 'parental deprivation' is assessed, about the incidence of parental deprivation in the 'normal' population, and about a possibly spurious correlation with social class, need to be asked before definite conclusions can be drawn. The same cautions should be exercised in an assessment of the 'maternal deprivation' literature.

Historically speaking, the modern concern with mothering behaviour arose out of the study of institutionalized children — homeless children living permanently or semi-permanently in institutions. A variety of behavioural disturbances observable in such children were attributed to the lack of mother love, including withdrawal from social contact, stuporous sleep, persistent weepiness, hypertension, vomiting, wild screaming, and marasmus (wasting away) (Ribble, 1943). It was assumed that the basic cause was the absence of the child's mother, and there was little attempt to consider the wide range of different child-care arrangements possible in an institutional (non-family) setting. The concept of 'maternal love' or 'maternal care' and the corresponding concept of 'maternal deprivation' received quite inadequate attention in these studies. While it was clear that the pattern of child care current in institutions produced different results from the domestic pattern, the attribution of the difference to the presence of the mother in the home was a gross over-simplification of the variables involved.

Later on these observations of institutionalized children were extended to include children in hospital. Bowlby (1966) and others documented a syndrome of emotional withdrawal in hospitalized children which was similar to some of the behavioural disturbances seen in children living in institutions. The result was a general comparison between two alternative systems of child care (which were implicitly regarded as the only alternatives): child care in which the child is reared exclusively by its mother, and child care in an institutional context where multiple, changing mother-figures block the child's need to form one or more close and enduring relationships with adults.

It has become increasingly clear that this need can be met by arrangements other than the traditional mother–child relationship. Indeed, the consequence of the traditional assumption, that the upbringing of children is a woman's job, has been a failure to appreciate what it is exactly about 'mothering behaviour' that is necessary to a child's emotional and mental health, and to specify precisely under what conditions a child will be 'deprived'. The most important ingredients of 'mothering' are warmth and a degree of continuity, but these can be provided by persons other than the mother – most notably by the father (Rutter, 1972: 16). Another major component of mothering behaviour is stimulation: a simple difference in the amount of adult–child interaction is one of the largest differences between homes and institutions (Rutter, 1972: 24). A relationship in which the child can develop attachment is also crucial, but it too is a characteristic shared with other relationships besides that with the mother (Rutter, 1972: 17). The need for continuity should not be confused with the need to prevent separation. A national sample of five thousand children showed that by the age of four and a half, a third of the children had been separated from their mothers for at least one week; such separations are a normal part of childhood (Rutter, 1972: 22–3). As with many unquestioned assumptions in the 'maternal deprivation' field, the failure has been one of not comparing the incidence of the experience in question (maternal deprivation) in disturbed individuals with that in the normal population.

Thus the juxtaposition of maternal childcare (good) with institutional childcare (bad) poses a false dichotomy. A failure to provide for children's emotional needs is not endemic to institutional life, and not all mothers are able to provide ideal conditions for their children. For example, a depressed mother is often not in a position to consider her child's emotional or physical needs. Recent research shows a high incidence of accidents among children during periods of depression in the mother (Brown, personal communication). In considering mother-substitutes (when, for example, the mother herself wishes to take a full-time, paid job) success from the child's point of view depends on a range of variables: the quality of the surrogate, the child's age, the relationship between mother and surrogate, and so forth.

A similar need to take into account multiple variables exists when considering the effects of longer separations from the mother than those brought about by maternal employment. The term 'maternal deprivation' covers a wide range of different experiences, including short-term admission to a hospital or residential nursery, multiple separation experiences, and long-term institutional care (Rutter, 1972). In estimating the effects of any one of these experiences, crucial factors include the age of the child at the time of the separation, the nature of the mother—child relationship before separation (had a bond been formed, that was then disrupted, or had no bond yet developed?), the mother's reaction to the situation, the kind of environment (strange or familiar) in which it occurs, the presence or absence of other family members. Rutter says:

> 'It is most curious that studies of children in hospital or a residential nursery are nearly always considered as examples of separation from mother, when in fact they consist of separation from mother *and* father *and* sibs *and* the home environment. There are no studies of the short term effects of paternal absence and the influence of the father has been greatly neglected.' (Rutter, 1972: 48)

Research reported by Rutter elsewhere demonstrates that discord between the parents can be far more significant than separation from mother or father in the genesis of long-term disorder. Parental discord is associated with anti-social behaviour disorders in the children. Even in the emotive area of juvenile deliquency, a well-controlled study showed that broken homes resulted in significantly less juvenile delinquency than did unbroken but disharmonious homes (Rutter, 1971).

Rutter argues in his conclusion to *Maternal Deprivation Reassessed* against the supposedly special importance of the mother. This is a complex issue which requires urgent, unprejudiced research. Various studies now indicate that the human infant is not innately monotrophic (able to relate principally to only one person) but has a capacity for developing and maintaining several relationships simultaneously. Communal child-care systems, such as the Israeli *kibbutzim*, do, of course, utilize this capacity. A comparison of these systems with the nuclear family system, entailing

maternal child care, indicates that the former avoid the type of excessive
dependence on mother that is a clinically accepted pathology in our
culture (Bettelheim, 1971).

However, attached to the traditional notion of maternal child care is
our whole system of gender roles, both inside and outside the family.
What evidence is there that these roles are geared to the mental health
and happiness of men, women, and children, as individuals?

Gender Roles and Illness

It may be argued that the family's chief function in modern society is the
production of healthy people, and it is therefore worth asking how well its
internal system of relationships contributes to that end. Some evidence
suggests that what is usually considered both normal and desirable in
family roles may be pathogenic, not only for children but for adults also.

Sex-differentiated incidence rates for a variety of illnesses, all of which
could be broadly described as 'stress-related' have been noted for some
time. These include heart disease, ulcers of the stomach and duodenum,
depressive illness, and psychoneurotic disorders. The former two are
characteristically masculine illnesses (Dodge and Martin, 1970), while the
latter two are more typically feminine disorders (Gove and Tudor, 1973).
Obviously, a range of different variables are involved in each of these
categories of illness, and it is somewhat simplistic to group them together
in this way. The point of doing so is merely to suggest their possible links
with family role-behaviour.

A substantial literature on peptic ulcers and coronary heart disease links
the incidence of both these to properties of the masculine occupational
role (see for example Kasl and French, 1962). The hypothesized connection between these findings and the possible pathogenicity of the
family is that, in the ideal model, the husband—father's career role takes
precedence over his other roles, and occupies a key place in the family's
orientation to the social world. Whatever the actual direction of his
personal interests, social and economic pressures focus a man's attention
on the importance of occupational achievement. If housewifery as the
ideal form of feminine family behaviour assumes an equal involvement on
the part of all women in domestic skills, so a job or career as the ideal of
masculine family behaviour is based on the assumption that all men are
equally interested in, and fitted for, this role.

In practice, and even for the most committed, a life-long engagement in
a job or career structure is likely to hold particular stresses. There is the
primary necessity to keep one's job, so that the family standard of living
can be maintained. In the case of peptic ulcers, it is interesting that a
linear relationship between their incidence in males and the number of
children in the family has been found (Chen and Cobb, 1960). For the

middle-class male there is the desire to improve one's occupational position over time, which is likely to be a further source of stress.

Combined with the strains of the male's career role in the family are the social restraints that curb his emotional expressivity. It seems reasonable to speculate that this relative lack of emotional outlet (compared with the female) is not a factor that aids the male's ability to tolerate job related stress.

No firm evidence exists for rooting these sex-differentiated illness rates in different biological propensities.[5] Moreover, changes in rates of incidence over the half century from 1900 to 1953 indicate that, while for men, vulnerability to gastric ulcers and cardiovascular disease has increased, for women some feature of their social situation protects them to some extent from this response to the accumulating stresses of modern life (Dodge and Martin, 1970).

But while their family role may largely protect women from the experience of job stress, it carries other implications. In an analysis of American data on sex roles and mental illness, Gove and Tudor argue that the greater incidence of mental illness in the female population is linked with their social situation (Gove and Tudor, 1973). The authors' definition of mental illness is that it should involve 'personal discomfort ... and/or mental disorganization ... not caused by an organic or toxic condition' (Gove and Tudor, 1973: 812). Thus their classification includes the neurotic disorders and the functional psychoses, but excludes personality disorders and acute and chronic brain disorders.

Gove and Tudor begin by considering some of the findings of research on gender roles which demonstrate the problematic aspects of women's situation: the frustrations and restrictions of housewifery, their inferior occupational position, the strains of performing two roles of housekeeper and breadwinner, the contradictory social expectations with which women are confronted. The next step is an evaluation of mental illness rates with data derived from a variety of sources, including first admissions to mental hospitals, and the prevalence of mental illness in the practices of general physicians. Statistics from all these sources indicate that more women than men are mentally ill, that is, they are classified as suffering from the functional psychoses or neurotic disorders more often than are men.[6]

The British data generally accord with Gove and Tudor's conclusion. For example, in their study of *Mental Health and Environment*, Taylor, and Chave find that symptoms of what they term the 'subclinical neurosis syndrome' ('nerves', depression, sleeplessness, and undue irritability) were reported more often by women than by men (Taylor and Chave, 1964; see also Hare and Shaw, 1965). In a survey of three disparate communities two-thirds of those classified as manifesting the syndrome were female. At every age neurosis was more common among the women than among the men, and its maximum prevalence rate was in the group of women aged forty-five to fifty-four, a fact that Taylor and Chave attribute to the 'unemployment' among women in this age group consequent on the completion of their child-rearing role. A study by Porter of depressive illness in a general practice found that 85 per cent of patients treated for depression were women, and that the majority of these — sixty-seven out of seventy-nine — were married women (Porter, 1970). The rate of relapse was high, but many of the patients suffering from the 'milder forms' of depression were adequately treated with support and a placebo.

Again, evidence is lacking for the grounding of the female's apparently greater vulnerability to depressive and psychoneurotic illness in her bio-logical make-up. Murphy argues, on the basis of two small pilot studies among Eskimos and Mexican Indians, that the higher prevalence rate of psychiatric disorder among women may be a constitutional phenomenon (Murphy, 1962). However, a later study of the Yoruba of Nigeria demon-strated equal symptom prevalence in a different socio-cultural context (Leighton *et al.*, 1963). Regrettably, this relationship between mental health rates by sex and the differential cultural patterning of gender roles has not yet received systematic attention (with the exception of Murphy's and Leighton's studies).

So far as Western culture is concerned, the complementary hypotheses offer an explanation of the female's greater prevalence rate for depressive and psychoneurotic disorders. The first is that the feminine gender role is more congruent with the sick role than is the masculine role. A woman's complaint of depression, insomnia, or 'nerves' has a higher degree of social acceptability than does the same complaint on the part of a man — it is more in tune with expectations of femininity, with the aura of weakness and childish lack of control that imbues the feminine image generally.[7] Carne's observation, that depressed mothers sometimes present with the 'symptom' of a vomiting baby, draws attention to the possibility that a woman's depression may constitute a socially and medically acceptable form of response to the stresses of her family role (Carne, 1966).

The hypothesis that feminine role-behaviour and sick role-behaviour are closely allied is in agreement with the finding that women more often visit the doctor than men. Especially as consumers of psychotropic drugs, women assume a more important place than men in the doctor's surgery. An analysis by Balint and others of repeat prescriptions in general practice shows that in the ten years between 1957 and 1967, the consumption of these drugs increased by 80 per cent and that three quarters of these drug-users were women (Balint *et al.*, 1970: 176).

The particular situation of women in the family may account for some of their predisposition towards mental illness, particularly depressive illness. Gove has shown that the greater vulnerability of women to mental illness holds for the married population only (Gove, 1972). Though some disagreement between different studies exists, the majority report that male rates for mental illness are higher than females rates in the never-married, divorced, and widowed categories. Because mental health is better among women in the divorced/widowed as well as the never-married group (compared with the married group) it cannot simply be argued that it is the women with poorer mental health who marry in the first place. Contrary to the widespread expectation that unmarried women are frustrated and unhappy, it seems that avoidance of marriage for women may offer some protection against the risk of mental illness.[8] On the other hand, for men it may be that marriage is to be recommended (see also Bernard, 1973).

Marriage may also 'conceal' the mental ill-health of women in a rather subtle way — this is a separate issue from the question of what 'causes' the ill-health in the first place. Social norms sanction the married woman's restriction to the home, and 'deviant' behaviour may thus be less visible. From the husband's point of view, symptoms may be perceived as merely extreme instances of usual feminine behaviour. So long as the basic house-keeping services continue to be provided by his wife, he may feel there is no cause for the dissolution of marriage. In a study of schizophrenic patients, Brown *et al.* show that although twice as many female as male patients marry, only about half as many women as men subsequently obtain a separation or divorce (Brown *et al.*, 1966: 123). This is probably a situation in which the impact of mental illness on the marital relationship is mediated by gender-dependent conceptions of marital roles. In another context, Rogler and Hollingshead demonstrate how a Puerto Rican husband's schizophrenia may provoke more harmonious marital relations, simply because his sexual demands and marital infidelity are reduced (Rogler and Hollingshead, 1965: 338).

Although the modern marriage ideal is one of companionship, the social and economic differentiation of marital roles by gender is a reality opposed to this ideal. In their day-to-day lives the experiences of many husbands and wives are sharply contrasted, particularly during the early part of married life, when the children are young. The man daily leaves the home and its concerns for work involving social relationships; the woman's identification with a family role is reinforced by the greater amount of time she spends in the home. An American comparison of psychological stress symptom rates between housewives and unemployed men suggests that the similar high rates in the two groups may be related to restriction to the home (National Center for Health Statistics, 1970). Isolation from social contacts is the single most important consequence of full-time housewifery. But housework as a work role — a perspective hidden by the popular stereotype of housework as a 'feminine' role — also carries other dissatisfactions. A study by the present author suggests that it is intrinsic features of housework and the conditions under which it is done that act as dissatisfiers, and that the level of a woman's own domesticity, her educational background, and her social class grouping, may be much less important as variables influencing housework satisfaction/dissatisfaction than is usually thought (Oakley, 1974).

In the case of the housewife—mother, the effect of her social isolation as a houseworker, and the other dissatisfactions of housework as a work role, may be exacerbated by the demands of children who are not always all the sentimental ideal of motherhood makes them out to be.[9] Lack of any non-domestic occupation tends to intensify the housewife's involvement in the physical aspects of home-care, a pattern exemplified by the 'obsessional' or 'houseproud' housewife, who has a compulsive need to repeat the same cleaning routines over and over again. Although often socially branded as 'neurotic', these women can also be seen as responding in an extremely rational way to their situation. Since housework is unsupervized and largely unrewarded, the person who does it has to lay down rules for the standards to be reached and the routines to be followed. These are needed both as a way of making sure that housework gets done, and as a means of obtaining reward — self-reward — for the performance of it. Once formulated, these rules of housework behaviour tend to take on an air of objectivity: they compel obedience from the worker. Since the pursuit of reward or satisfaction with housework is a dynamic process, the rules tend to become more complex as time passes. The need to be satisfied with a role in which one's identity is bound up is constant, but the determination to *be* satisfied may grow as the frustrations of doing housework come to be felt more keenly.

A number of studies suggest that certain problems of the housewife role, including the danger of 'obsessionalism', are more likely to be experienced by working-class women whose marriages are characterized by a pronounced degree of role-segregation, than by those whose role-relationships with their husbands are more 'joint'.

A role-segregated marriage is one in which the duties and responsibilities of husband and wife are clearly demarcated and separate, and in which their leisure interests and social relationships are also divided. In her study of American family life, *Blue Collar Marriage*, Komarovsky presents a vivid and perceptive portrait of the institutionalized barriers to communication between man and woman that the structure of marriage can impose (Komarovsky, 1967). 'Are the husbands and wives friends?' she inquires of her fifty-eight couples: 'for almost a third of these men and women the answer to this question is clearly in the negative' (Komarovsky, 1967: 140). The marriage dialogue consists of abortive attempts at communication, frustrated by what one spouse experiences as the other spouse's unsatisfactory response. Komarovsky asked her respondents to enumerate the areas of reserve in marital communication, and the reasons why communication was not more complete. The wives reported worries about themselves, their health, dissatisfactions with self, hurts, and aspirations for self and family, as the major areas of reserve in their dialogue with their husbands, and said that the husband's lack of interest was the barrier that prevented their communicating more fully. The husbands listed satisfactions and dissatisfactions with their jobs, and worry about the economic situation generally, as the major areas of reserve, and they also said that the spouse's lack of interest was the reason for their lack of openness.

These areas of reserve reflect the roles of the sexes in marriage – the close involvement of the woman with the family, the identification of the man with his job. When these couples were asked to list the qualities of a good husband and a good wife, proper performance in the roles of provider, housewife, and parent, came first on the list. Second were 'human' qualities, such as kindness and consideration and third came psychological compatibility (Komarovsky, 1967: 122).

As Komarovsky observes, husband and wife do not need to occupy the same psychological world to understand each other, but there must be some overlapping of interests. In some of these marriages, virtually no overlapping occurred. A major reason was the institutionalized separation of home and work worlds. Eighty per cent of the wives had no social contact with their husband's work-mates. For the husband to talk about his job carried the connotation of 'griping', which was thought unmanly: the men perceived their jobs as too monotonous or too technical for them to constitute topics of marital conversation. Some husbands chose reciprocal reticence: 'It don't do no good to go home and belly-ache to your wife. If you don't want to know about what happens with the washing and with the neighbour's kids, you shouldn't ought to tell her about what goes on at the plant either' (Komarovsky, 1967: 154). A more fundamental explanation of poor communication in marriage proposed by Komarovsky is the differential socialization of the sexes, the contrast between the masculine and feminine roles that men and women bring to the institution of marriage. What Komarovsky terms 'the trained incapacity to share' is an aspect of masculine role-behaviour directly antithetical to the goal of psychological intimacy. As Komarovsky describes it: 'The ideal of masculinity into which they [the men] were socialized inhibits expressiveness both directly, with its emphasis on reserve, and indirectly, by identifying personal interchange with the feminine role ... In adulthood [these inhibitions are] ... experienced not only as "I shouldn't" but as "I cannot"' (Komarovsky, 1967: 156).

Marriages in which the husband cannot talk to his wife are statistically 'normal' marriages, as are those in which husband and wife have no interests in common. To the outsider – to society – only the failure of husband and wife to play their conventional breadwinning, housekeeping and parental roles, or some gross disturbance in the behaviour of family members, disturbs the gloss of normalcy such relationships possess. The segregated pattern of marital roles is a 'normal' one in our culture. Many studies of family life in Britain and the United States, aside from Komarovsky's, describe essentially the same pattern (see Klein, 1965: I, Sections 1 and 2). It is a possibility inherent in the structure of marriage itself, rather than a syndrome peculiar to particular communities. Recent descriptions of middle-class and dual carer marriages are not entirely without the same flavour of separation between husband and wife worlds that runs through Komarovsky's account of blue-collar marriage, and other portraits of working-class family life (see Pahl and Pahl, 1971; Rapoport and Rapoport, 1971). Moreover, this pattern of marital roles, though one in which both the man and woman suffer from a paucity of communication, is a situation that holds particular stresses for women. It continually reinforces their traditional identification with domesticity in a society that has reduced and devalued the rewards domesticity has to offer. The widening of opportunities for women outside the home which has occurred in recent decades has had very little impact on the lives of the majority of women, who are brought up to believe in marriage as a woman's life-goal, and who then find themselves restricted by marriage − by the segregation between husband and wife roles which marriage entails − to the sphere of domestic interests.

Conclusion

It seems to me very necessary that all who are interested in the family and its relationship with illness in modern society should speculate on what might be wrong with the family and marriage as institutions. This runs counter to the usual practice of eulogizing the family in an unthinking way and pontificating about its importance − a practice indulged in by those professionally concerned with the family, including sociologists and doctors.

The two questions 'why are people not critical of the family?' and 'why should they be?' have quite simple answers. Since most of us are brought up in families and all of us live in a society that is family-oriented, we tend to believe that the family is or could be the solution to every problem, that *in* the family, both personal and cultural salvation lie. As the various strains of modern living increase, there is a temptation to withdraw into the family, which seems increasingly the only escape from a competitive, hostile, and impersonal world. What has been called the 'sentimental model' of the family is a deeply rooted aspect of academic and popular discussion on the family in our society: the ideal of two parents and dependent children living in their own home in an atmosphere of mutual content. A social group that departs from this ideal in a positive sense − for instance, two women living happily together with their children, or a large household of mixed age and sex statuses − is either regarded as a 'failure' or a freak. There are actually many instances of statistical deviation from the sentimental ideal; not only single-parent families, but nuclear families without their own homes, one-person households or residential units comprising two or more persons whose bonds are not those of marriage or any form of kinship. These units are often referred to in derogatory terms, and are stigmatized for their failure to fit the normal pattern.

A search through the Census figures reveals a reality, for the family-sentimentalists, depressingly different from the popular image of a society made up of little families, each little family its own little intact, self-sufficient society. For instance, in Britain, about six in every ten households are non-nuclear family households, and one in twenty consists of a single-parent family (General Register Office, 1968: Table I, p. 1).

The Western industrial family type — that is the type portrayed in the sentimental model, is not 'natural' or 'universal' in any sense; it is merely one way of living among many that human beings have adopted (see Levi-Strauss, 1960). From a cross-cultural perspective, the modern nuclear family can be seen as a deviation from the more usual system which includes a large number of individuals in the social reckoning of family relationships and in the living arrangements of domestic groups.

In his interesting speculations on the American family, Birdwhistell proposes the metaphor of animals-in-their-cages to describe nuclear families isolated both spatially, in their separate homes, and by an ethic that limits meaningful emotional relationships to the small circle of family life (Birdwhistell, 1966). Cage-behaviour, he says, is 'interesting, but of little more than anatomical relevance to knowledge about the species'. It tells us how human beings act under certain circumstances, not how they should act, nor how they could act if their living conditions were different. Following this metaphor through, Birdwhistell suggests that the experts in our society who adhere to the sentimental model are behaving as 'zoo-keepers', or in more extreme cases as 'dog-catchers', 'returning malcontent escapees to the cage'. This suggestion, polemically phrased, surely merits serious attention from all those whose work brings them into contact with families.

Is the family the best source of help for the ill person? Is the role of families in the rehabilitation of the sick or disabled entirely beneficial? Are parents the ideal people to care for ill children? Is a married son or daughter the best person to care for an aged parent? Questions such as these — raised by some of the studies cited earlier in this chapter — need to be asked persistently and carefully, with the interests of each particular family in mind, rather than in the light of an idealized image of 'the family'. Unless they *are* asked, the concern of doctors and other experts is not with the well-being of people as individuals, but with the maintenance of the sentimental model of family life.

A critical approach to the family need not be either destructive or pessimistic. Its proper concern is simply the avoidance of false diagnosis and treatment based on erroneous premises. A plea for the reconsideration of conventional explanations and treatments is a plea for the discernment of the social causes of illness, where these exist. In the case of the family and marriage, sentiment probably gets in the way of science more than most of us realize.

Notes

1. Sears, Maccoby, and Levin (1957) is based on interviews with 379 mothers; Miller and Swanson (1958) on interviews with 582 mothers, Newson and Newson (1965) is a survey based on 709 interviews with mothers. None of these incorporate direct information from fathers about their role in child care.

2. 'It would appear ... that the opportunity to prepare oneself in anticipation of bereavement does affect the subsequent reaction to the event' (Parkes, 1972:130–31).

3. Komarovsky suggests that the severing of dependent ties with the family of origin is a task that the gender-role socialization of the female in our culture is structurally unable to accomplish successfully (Komarovsky, 1950).

4. As with other illness crises, the organization of gender roles in the family is critical. Townsend's classification of old couples without daughters as necessarily disadvantaged is based in part on the empirical observation that old people tend to live with, and be helped by, their daughters more than their sons. But it is also based on an assumption that the caring role is an inherently female one. It is interesting that in his study of institutions for old people, Townsend discusses future policy considerations, oriented to the community care system, solely in terms of a *female* network of caring people (Townsend, 1962: Chapter 16, 'Developing Future Policy').

5. Rutter (1971: 18) notes that the apparently greater vulnerability of the male to some forms of psychological stress, such as that involved in living in a discordant home, parallels the male's greater susceptibility to biological stresses. However, there is as yet no explanation as to why the parallel exists.

6. One of the few studies that finds similar symptom rates for men and women is Srole *et al.* (1962).

7. Parsons and Fox's analysis of illness in terms of a sick role uses the analogy of illness with 'childish behaviour'. These authors also suggest that illness is a 'compulsively feminine' mode of response to difficulty and frustration (Parsons and Fox, 1968: 377–90).

8. A particularly healthy group, according to Hinkle and Wolff, consists of middle-aged unmarried women with full-time jobs (Hinkle and Wolff, 1957).

9. The influence of the child's own characteristics on his upbringing and on parental attitudes towards him is a largely unresearched topic to date. Rutter (1971) cites some evidence that the child's temperament and personality influence the development of emotional and behaviour disorders.

References

Andrewski, I. (1966) The Baby as Dictator. *New Society,* 15 December.

Balint, M., Hunt, J., Joyce, D., Marinker, M., and Woodcock, J. (1970) *Treatment or Diagnosis: A Study of Repeat Prescriptions in General Practice.* London: Tavistock Publications.

Bell, W. and Vogel, E.F. (1968a) Toward a Framework for Functional Analysis of Family Behaviour. In Bell and Vogel (1968b): 1–34.
    A short statement of the functionalist approach.

— (1968b) *A Modern Introduction to the Family* (revised edition). New York: Free Press.

A massive collection of contributions to the sociology of the family, some very useful, some not so useful.

Bernard, J. (1973) *The Future of Marriage*. London: Souvenir Press.

Bernard argues that a wedding ceremony produces not one marriage but two: His and Hers. This is probably the best documented and best argued statement of the view that marriage is good for men and bad for women.

Bettelheim, B. (1971) *Children of the Dream*. London: Paladin books.

The *kibbutz* system seems to substitute dependence on peers for dependence on adults. Bettelheim's view is that the *kibbutz* system of childrearing is as viable as the family system: it simply produces different results in terms of personality structure.

Birdwhistell, R. (1966) The American Family: Some Perspectives. *Psychiatry* **29**: 203–12.

Bott, E. (1971) *Family and Social Network* (second edition). London: Tavistock Publications.

Bott's work on marital role-relationships and the social networks of families first introduced the concepts of 'joint' and 'segregated' conjugal role-relationships into the sociological literature. The basic theme in Bott's analysis of data on twenty London families is that the degree of segregation in the role-relationship varies directly with the connectedness of the family's social network. The 1971 edition includes a long section by Bott, 'Reconsiderations', in which she discusses the criticisms made of her work and subsequent contributions to the debate.

Bowlby, J. (1966) *Maternal Care and Mental Health*. This is a reprint of Bowlby's original work, together with Ainsworth, M.D., Andry, R.G., Harlow, R.G., Lebovici, S., Mead, M., Prugh, D.G., and Wootton, B. *Deprivation of Maternal Care: A Reassessment of Its Effects*. New York: Schocken Books.

Particularly useful are Mead's contribution A Cultural Anthropologist's Approach to Maternal Deprivation (236–54) and Wootton's paper A Social Scientist's Approach to Maternal Deprivation (255–65).

Brown, G.W. (1959) Experiences of Discharged Chronic Schizophrenic Mental Hospital Patients in Various Types of Living Group. *Milbank Memorial Fund Quarterly* **37**: 105–31.

Brown, G.W., Monck, E.M., Carstairs, G.M. and Wing, J.K. (1962) The Influence of Family Life on the Course of Schizophrenic Illness. *British Journal of Preventive Social Medicine* **16**: 55–68.

Brown, G.W., Bone, M., Dalison, B. and Wing, J.K. (1966) *Schizophrenia and Social Care* Maudsley Monograph no. 17. London: Oxford University Press.

Brown, G.W., Birley, J.L.T., and Wing, J.K. (1972) Influence of Family Life on the Course of Schizophrenic Disorders: A Replication. *British Journal of Psychiatry* **121**: 241–58.

Carne, S. (1966) The Influence of the Mother's Health on Her Child. *Proceedings of the Royal Society of Medicine* **59**: 1013–14.

Chen, E. and Cobb, S. (1960) Family Structure in Relation to Health and Disease. *Journal of Chronic Diseases* **12**: 544–67.

Chesler, P. (1971) Women as Psychiatric and Psychotherapeutic Patients. *Journal of Marriage and the Family* **33**, November: 746–59.

This paper presents a feminist interpretation of mental illness based on data from a number of sources. The 'diagnosis' of women as mentally ill and the treatment prescribed for them (or self-prescribed in the case of private psychotherapy) are analyzed in terms of the gender-role conditioning of women. Chesler's approach is a refreshingly novel one, and it is also very pertinent to a discussion of the connections between the 'sick role' and femininity.

Clark, A.W. and Sommers, P. Van (1961) Contradictory Demands in Family Relations and Adjustment to School and Home. *Human Relations* 14: 97–111.

Cooper, D. (1970) *Psychiatry and Anti-Psychiatry.* London: Paladin Books.

Davie, R., Butler, N. and Goldstein, H. (1972) *From Birth to Seven: A Report of the National Child Development Study.* London: Longman.

Davies, D.P. (1973) Plasma Osmolality and Feeding Practices of Healthy Infants in First Three Months of Life. *British Medical Journal,* 12 May.

Davis, F. (1963) *Passage Through Crisis: Polio Victims and Their Families.* New York: Bobbs-Merrill.

Department of Health and Social Security (1974) Present Day Practice in Infant Feeding. *Report on Health and Social Subjects* No. 9. London: HMSO.

Dodge, D.L. and Martin, W.T. (1970) *Social Stress and Chronic Illness.* Notre Dame, Indiana: University of Notre Dame Press.

Dyer, G.W. and Urban, D. (1969) The Institutionalization of Equalitarian Family Norms. In Edwards (1969): 201–11.

A useful critique of the assumption that modern marriage is characterized by task-sharing, based on data gathered from university students and their wives on the division of labour and allocation of power in marriage. Dyer and Urban show that the degree of equality varies a great deal between different areas of the marital relationship.

Edwards, J.N. (ed.) (1969) *The Family and Change.* New York: Alfred A. Knopf.

A useful compendium of articles on the family.

Elliot, K.C. (ed.) (1970) *The Family and Its Future.* London: J. and A. Churchill.

A valuable general symposium on the modern family.

Fink, S.L., Skipper, J.K.. and Hallenbeck, P.N. (1968) Physical Disability and Problems in Marriage. *Journal of Marriage and the Family* (30) February: 64–73.

The focus of this study is on need satisfaction and marital satisfaction as experienced by both spouses in marriages where the wife is severely disabled. An interesting suggestion made is that more problems in daily living may be experienced by disabled women who have a great deal of physical mobility than by those who have very little. The argument is that this former situation is more ambiguous, and thus more frustrating, for the partially disabled woman and her husband.

Ford, C.S. (1945) *A Comparative Study of Human Reproduction.* New Haven: Yale University Press.

A fascinating study of cross-cultural differences in attitudes to reproduction and the practices surrounding pregnancy and childbirth.

Friedman, S.B., Chodoff, P., Mason, J.W. and Hamburg, D.A. (1963) Behavioural Observations on Parents Anticipating the Death of a Child. *Pediatrics* 32: 610–25.

Gail, S. (1968) The Housewife. In Fraser, R. (ed.), *Work: Twenty Personal Accounts.* Harmondsworth: Penguin Books.

A statement of the disadvantages of domestication from the view-point of a middle-class housewife.

General Register Office (1968) *Sample Census 1966, England and Wales Household Composition Tables.* London: HMSO.

Gilman, C. Perkins (1972) The Home: Its Work and Influence. In Salper, R. (ed), *Female Liberation.* New York: Alfred A. Knopf.

Goldthorpe, J.H., Lockwood, D., Bechhofer, F., and Platt, J. (1968) *The Affluent Worker: Industrial Attitudes and Behaviour.* Cambridge: Cambridge University Press.

Gove, W.R. (1972) The Relationship between Sex Roles, Mental Illness and Marital Status. *Social Forces* 51 (1): 34–44.

Gove, W.R. and Tudor, J.F. (1973) Adult Sex Roles and Mental Illness. *American Journal of Sociology* (78) January: 812–35.

Hare, E.H. and Shaw, G.K. (1965) *Mental Health on a New Housing Estate.* London: Oxford University Press.

Hewett, S. (1970) *The Family and the Handicapped Child.* London: Allen and Unwin. A book that argues, on the basis of evidence from mothers with cerebral palsied children, that the adverse effects of a handicapped child on the family have been over-emphasized.

Hinkle, L.E. and Wolff, H.G. (1957) Health and the Social Environment. In Leighton, A.H., Clausen, J.A. and Wilson, R.N. (eds.), *Explorations in Social Psychiatry.* London: Tavistock.

Hirsch, S.R. and Leff, J.R. (1971) Parental Abnormalities of Verbal Communication in the Transmission of Schizophrenia. *Psychological Medicine* I (2): 118–27.

Hunt, A. (1968) *A Survey of Women's Employment.* Government Social Survey. London: HMSO.

Isaacs, B. (1971) Geriatric Patients: Do their Families Care? *British Medical Journal* 4: 282.

Janeway, E. (1971) *Man's World; Woman's Place: A Study in Social Mythology.* London: Michael Joseph.
A thorough and very readable look at contemporary ideals of gender roles and the myths to which they are linked.

Kasl, S. and French, J. (1962) The Effects of Occupational Status on Physical and Mental Health. *Journal of Social Issues* XVIII (3): 67–89.

Kempe, C. (1970) Cited in The Myth of the Madonna Mother. *The Times* 24 June, 1970.

Klein, J. (1965) *Samples from English Cultures.* London: Routledge & Kegan Paul.

Komarovsky, M. (1950) Functional Analysis of Sex Roles. *American Sociological Review* 15 (4): 508–16.

— (1967) *Blue Collar Marriage.* New York: Vintage Books.

Laing, R.D. (1965) *The Divided Self.* Harmondsworth: Penguin Books.

— (1967) Family and Individual Structure. In Lomas, P. (ed.), *The Predicament of the Family.* London: Hogarth Press.

— (1969) *The Politics of the Family and Other Essays.* London: Tavistock.

Laing, R.D. and Esterson, A. (1964) *Sanity, Madness and the Family.* Harmondsworth: Penguin Books.

Laws, J. Long (1971) A Feminist Review of Marital Adjustment Literature: The Rape of the Locke. *Journal of Marriage and the Family* 33 (3): 483–516.
An invaluable review of the sociological literature on marriage and family life, revealing the ways in which masculine bias informs the sociologist's approach to this topic.

Leighton, A.H., Lambo, T., Hughes, C.C., Leighton, D.C., Murphy, J.M. and Macklin, D.B. (1963) *Psychiatric Disorder among the Yoruba.* New York: Cornell University Press.
An attempt to apply Western methods for the study of the prevalence of psychiatric

disorder to the Nigerian scene; also a description of Nigerian concepts of mental health and disorder. A contrast with the Western situation, which the authors discuss, is the lack of ambiguity and discontinuity in the role of Yoruba women, and the uncertainty in the men's role evident in even the most 'integrated' villages.

Levi-Strauss, C. (1960) The Family. In Shapiro, Harry L. (ed.), *Man, Culture and Society*. New York: Galaxy Books.

Lomas, P. (1966) Ritualistic Elements in the Management of Childbirth. *British Journal of Medical Psychology* 39: 207.

Lomas compares primitive societies' rituals to do with the treatment of women in childbirth with those of modern society.

Marsden, D. (1968) *Mothers Alone: Poverty and the Fatherless Family*. London: Allen Lane The Penguin Press.

Mattinson, J. (1970) *Marriage and Mental Handicap*. London: Duckworth.

A study of the viability of marriage between disabled people.

Mead, M. (1952) The Contemporary American Family as an Anthropologist sees It. In Landis, J.T. and Landis, M.G. (eds.), *Readings in Marriage and the Family*. New York: Prentice Hall.

Mead, M. and Newton, N. (1967) Cultural Patterning of Perinatal Behaviour. In Richardson, S.A. and Guttmacher. F. (eds.), *Childbearing — its Social and Psychological Aspects*. Baltimore: Williams and Wilkins.

For anyone interested in cross-cultural variations in the treatment of childbirth, this paper is essential and fascinating reading. The book as a whole represents a close collaboration between the medical and social scientist, with the goal of understanding the relationship between the physiology of reproduction and social factors in the experience of the pregnant and parturient woman.

Meadow, K.P. (1968) Parental Response to the Medical Ambiguities of Congenital Deafness. *Journal of Health and Social Behaviour* 9 (4): 299–309.

Difficulties in diagnosing and treating congenital deafness are analyzed in terms of the strain they impose on the parents and on the doctor–patient relationship.

Miller, D.R. and Swanson, G. (1958) *The Changing American Parent*. New York: John Wiley.

Moore, B. (1969) Thoughts on the Future of the Family. In Edwards (1969).

Murphy, J.M. (1962) Cross-Cultural Studies of the Prevalence of Psychiatric Disorder. *World Mental Health* XIV (2): 53–65.

National Council for Health Statistics (1970). *Selected Symptoms of Psychological Stress*. United States Department of Health, Education and Welfare, August 1970.

Newson, J. and Newson, E. (1965) *Patterns of Infant Care in an Urban Community*. Harmondsworth: Penguin Books.

— (1970) *Four Years Old in an Urban Community*. Harmondsworth: Penguin Books.

Oakley, A. (1972a) *Sex, Gender and Society*. London: Maurice Temple Smith.

The aim of this book is the disentangling of biological facts about sex differences from social images of gender roles.

— (1972b) Are Husbands Good Housewives? In Barker, P. (ed.), *One for Sorrow, Two for Joy: Ten Years of New Society*. London: Allen and Unwin.

Information from housewives about their husbands' participation in domestic activities shows how the masculine role is perceived as a 'helping' role: the major responsibility for housework and childcare remains with the wife.

Oakley, A. (1974) *The Sociology of Housework*. London: Martin Robertson.

Pahl, J.M. and Pahl, R.E. (1971) *Managers and Their Wives: A Study of Career and*

Family Relationships in the Middle Class. London: Allen Lane The Penguin Press. The Pahls' study explores the rather unexplored relationship between home and work in modern society. They show the tension generated by the conflicting demands of the two spheres, many of which can only be resolved by the wife's family-oriented and husband-supportive behaviour.

Parker, S.R., Brown, R.K., Child, J. and Smith, M.A. (1967) *The Sociology of Industry.* London: Allen and Unwin.

Parkes, C.M., Benjamin, B., Fitzgerald, R.G. (1969) Broken Heart: A Statistical Study of Increased Mortality among Widowers. *British Medical Journal* 1: 740–43.

Parkes, C. Murray (1972) *Bereavement: Studies of Grief in Adult Life.* London: Tavistock Publications.

Parsons, T. (1956) The American Family: Its Relations to Personality and to the Social Structure. In Parsons, T. and Bales, R.F., *Family, Socialization and Interaction Process.* London: Routledge & Kegan Paul.

Parsons, T. and Fox, R.C. (1968) Illness, Therapy and the Modern American Family. In Bell and Vogel (1968).

Porter, A. (1970) Depressive Illness in a General Practice: A Demographic Study and a Controlled Trial of Imipramine. *British Medical Journal* 1: 773–8.

Rainwater, L., Coleman, R.P. and Handel, G. (1959) *Workingman's Wife.* New York: Oceana Publications.

Part 1 of this book 'The Psychosocial World of the Workingman's Wife' offers a valuable description of the wife's role in a traditional working-class role-segregated marriage.

Rainwater, L. and Weinstein, C.J. (1960) *And the Poor Get Children.* Chicago: Quadrangle Books.

This is a perceptive investigation of attitudes to the practice of contraception in working-class marriages. It shows how family planning behaviour is associated with patterns of relationships between husband and wife, and between parents and children.

Rapoport, R. and Rapoport, R. (1971) *Dual Career Families.* Harmondsworth: Penguin Books.

Five case-studies of dual career marriages make up the main body of this book, which also discusses the mechanisms that enable this family pattern to be created and sustained. A final section deals with issues raised by the dual-career family form, and the problems of social acceptance which it faces.

Ribble, M. (1943) *The Rights of Infants.* New York: Columbia University Press.

Rodgers, D.A. and Ziegler, F.J. (1968) Social Role Theory, the Marital Relationship and Use of Ovulation Suppressors. *Journal of Marriage and the Family* (30) November: 584–91.

An unusual approach to the family as an institution which limits excessive reproduction (rather than ensuring reproduction). The general view is that family role definitions are *boundary* conditions: within broad limits, husband and wife can negotiate their respective family roles.

Rogler, L.H. and Hollingshead, A.B. (1965) *Trapped Families and Schizophrenia.* New York: John Wiley.

A study of families living in the slums and public housing projects of San Juan, Puerto Rico. This is both a study of the culture of poverty in an emerging society and a study of the impact of schizophrenia on the family. It emphasizes the relationship between 'critical experiences' and the onset of schizophrenia, and shows that the impact of schizphrenia on family life differs according to the sex of the affected person.

Rowbotham, S. (1973) *Women, Resistance and Revolution*. London: Allen Lane The Penguin Press.

Rutter, M. (1970) Sex Differences in Children's Responses to Family Stress. In Anthony, E.J. and Koupern, C. (eds.), *The Child and His Family*. New York: John Wiley.

A useful report of work in progress on the impact of parental psychiatric disorder on children. Rutter finds that disturbance of family relationships is associated with antisocial disorders in boys, but not in girls.

— (1971) Parent Child Separation: Psychological Effects on Children. *Mental Health Research Fund*. Sir Geoffrey Vickers lecture 24 February, 1971.

— (1972) *Maternal Deprivation Reassessed*. Harmondsworth: Penguin Books.

Rutter, M. and Brown, G.W. (1966) The Reliability and Validity of Measures of Family Life and Relationships in Families Containing a Psychiatric Patient. *Social Psychiatry* 1 (1): 38–53.

Scully, D. and Bart, P. (1973) A Funny Thing Happened on the Way to the Orifice. *American Journal of Sociology* 78 (4): 1045–54.

A thought-provoking look at conventional medical attitudes to gynaecological patients.

Sears, R.R., Maccoby, E.E. and Levin, H. (1957) *Patterns of Childrearing*. New York: Harper and Row.

Shanas, E., Townsend, P., Wedderburn, D., Friis, M., Millhøj, P. and Stehouwer, J. (1968) *Old People in Three Industrial Societies*. London: Routledge & Kegan Paul.

Spock, B. (1957) *Baby and Child Care*. New York: Pocket Books.

Srole, L., Langner, T., Michael, S.T., Opler, M.K. and Rennie, T.A.C. (1962) *Mental Health in the Metropolis*. New York: McGraw-Hill.

Steele, B.F. and Pollock, C.B. (1968) A Psychiatric Study of Parents who Abuse Infants and Small Children. In Helfer, R.E. and Kempe, C.H. (eds.), *The Battered Child*. Chicago: Chicago University Press.

A detailed study of fifty-seven parents who had physically attacked their children, bringing out the parallels between abusing parents' styles of child-rearing and the styles in which they had themselves been reared. (This is an instance of the general tendency for family patterns to repeat themselves over generations.)

Stendler, C.B. (1960) Sixty Years of Child-Training Practices: Revolution in the Nursery. In Apple, D. (ed.), *Sociological Studies of Health and Sickness*. New York: McGraw-Hill.

Documents changing priorities in child-rearing.

Tavuchis, N. (1970) The Analysis of Family Roles. In Elliot (1970).

Taylor, Lord and Chave, S. (1964) *Mental Health and Environment*. London: Longman.

Tomkins, S.S. (1965) The Biopsychosociality of the Family. In Coale, A.J., Fallers, L.A., Levy, M.J., Schneider, D.M. and Tomkins, S.S., (eds.), *Aspects of the Analysis of Family Structure*. Princeton: Princeton University Press.

Tomkin's paper is by far the best answer to the argument that the family is, and must be, universal. He roots sociological theorizing in actual psychological and biological data on affectional systems in mammals, with particular reference to the mother–child relationship (always the lynch pin in the debate about the universality of the family).

Townsend, P. (1962) *The Last Refuge*. London: Routledge & Kegan Paul.

— (1963) *The Family Life of Old People*. Harmondsworth: Penguin Books.

— (1968a) Welfare Services and the Family. In Shanas *et al.* (1968).

— (1968b) The Structure of the Family. In Shanas *et al.* (1968).

Vincent, C.E. (1967) Mental Health and the Family. *Journal of Marriage and the Family* 29 February: 241—58.

Vincent, C.E. (1969) Familia Spongia: The Adaptive Function. In Edwards (1969).

A deliberately provocative statement of the thesis that in industrialized and industrializing societies the family's adaptive function is vital — not as the prime mover in social change, but as an institution that facilitates social change by incorporating the altered requirements of society into the on-going socialization of the child and adults in the family.

Wolff, E. (1950) Accident Proneness: A Serious Industrial Problem. *Industrial Medicine* 19: 419.

Wynne, L.C., Ryckoff, I.M., Day, J.L., and Hirsch, S.I. (1967) Pseudo-Mutuality in the Family Relations of Schizophrenics. In Bell and Vogel (1968).

Wynne, L.C. (1969) Family Research on the Pathogenesis of Schizophrenia. Presented at the International Symposium on Psychosis, Institut Albert-Probost, Montreal, 5 November, 1969.

Yarrow, M.R., Clausen, J.A., and Robbins, P.R. (1955) The Psychological Meaning of Mental Illness. *Journal of Social Issues* XI (4): 33—48.

Yudkin, S. and Holme, A. (1963) *Working Mothers and Their Children*. London: Michael Joseph.

Not a recent contribution to this debate, but still one of the best.

Chapter 4

David Tuckett

Work, Life-Chances, and Life-Styles

In this chapter I want to consider the life-experience of individuals and to introduce the notions of social class and social stratification in order to understand some of the differences in the experiences of individuals in different groups. Throughout this book discussion on the doctor–patient relationship, the causes of disease, the reasons why patients come to doctors, the patients' response to treatment, and many other areas of medical practice will emphasize the importance of the social background of the patient contributes for understanding the resulting processes.

In the first chapter I have already mentioned the studies of Imboden and his colleagues and Querido and his colleagues, all of which showed how the patient's social background could influence recovery from medical disorders (pp. 26–8). But, the social background can also cause individuals to acquire medical disorders in the first place.

One particularly striking way in which an individual's social background can *cause* disease and death is through the effects of working in a particular occupation. In the UK, every ten years, the Registrar General publishes statistics on occupational mortality. These statistics give standardized mortality ratios (SMRs) for different occupations and for different diseases. An SMR can be interpreted reasonably easily. The fact, for example, that coal miners have an SMR of 180 for all diseases means that they are 80 per cent more likely than the average person to die between the ages of fifteen and sixty-four. Had their SMR been 100, it would have meant they were as likely as the average person to die between fifteen and sixty-four. Had it been eighty, it would have meant they would have been 20 per cent less likely to die than the average person in this age group. *Table 1* sets out the most recent available occupational SMRs for death from various diseases. The relatively poor 'life-chances' of manual as opposed to non-manual workers are reasonably clear: an unskilled manual worker is 43 per cent more likely to die between the ages of fifteen and sixty-four than the average person; he is 85 per cent more likely to die of tuberculosis; 94 per cent more likely to die of bronchitis; and 93 per cent more likely to die from an accident (excluding motor and home accidents). A professional worker, on the other hand, is 24 per cent less likely than the average person to die between fifteen and sixty-four; 60 per cent less

Table 1 Standardized mortality ratios for different occupations in the UK, 1961 (men aged 15—64)

occupation	all causes	all TB	Lung Cancer	Coronary Heart Disease	Bronchitis	accidents other than motor vehicle and in the home)
A. (Manual)						
fisherman	144	171	188	115	148	480
coal face workers	180	294	140	144	293	522
engineering fitters	99	76	111	107	87	86
textile process workers	133	111	116	129	161	127
bus and train conductors	105	162	103	110	138	31
dock labourers	136	180	169	105	220	368
engineering labourers	139	169	151	115	217	112
kitchen hands	130	410	88	102	165	185
all semi-skilled manual workers	103	108	104	96	116	128
all unskilled manual workers	143	185	148	112	194	193
B. Non-manual						
mining managers	66	18	56	91	33	28
personnel managers	67	40	44	89	64	150
chemists, physical and biological scientists	88	21	56	111	33	65
government ministers	75	29	69	97	28	9
university teachers	56	50	12	65	—	43
judges, barristers, solicitors	76	33	40	93	24	53
medical practitioners	89	64	48	118	23	55
all intermediate non-manual occupations	81	54	72	95	50	56
all professional and administrative	76	40	53	98	28	43

Source: Registrar General, 1969: 91, 132—199

likely to die from TB; 72 per cent less likely to die from bronchitis; and 57 per cent less likely to die from an accident (excluding motor and home accidents). In short, when and how an individual dies is very much the product of the occupation he has. The point that your social class determines when you die was dramatically made many years ago at the time of the sinking of the *Titanic*:

'... recalling what happened when an 'unsinkable' trans-Atlantic luxury liner, the *Titanic*, rammed an iceberg on her maiden voyage in 1912 ... The official casualty list showed that only 4 first-class female passengers (3 voluntarily chose to stay on the ship) of a total of 143 were lost. Among the second-class passengers, 15 of 93 females drowned; and among the third-class, 81 of 179 female passengers went down with the ship.' (Lord, 1955: 107 quoted by Antonovsky, 1967: 31)

Figure 1   *Community diagnosis: inequality of mortality in first year of life in the different social classes. Scotland*

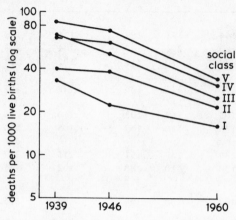

Source: Morris (1967: 57) – complied from data from various authors

Similar conclusions can be reached by an analysis of infant mortality. It is well known that the fall in infant mortality in the last 150 years has been dramatic – it is a major cause for the increase in the average expectation of life. Infant mortality for all occupational groups has fallen. However, the differential infant mortality between social classes, although narrowing slightly, still remains much as it always was. This is illustrated with figures for Scotland in *Figure 1*. The rate for social class 5 (unskilled manual) is still considerably higher than for the other social classes; indeed, although there is some narrowing of the gap between class 1 (professional and higher administrative) and class 2 (intermediate administrative) since 1946, there has been little narrowing otherwise. *Figure 2* shows a similar situation for the children of clerks and miners in England and Wales. In Chapter 9, where the evidence for a relationship between social factors and disease is reviewed, several other examples of a class differential for contracting disease are given.

As well as influencing the disease an individual gets, and the time at which he dies, an individual's occupation also influences his use of services. There is a considerable controversy over how far members of the lower[1] occupational groups under- or over-use medical services (see, for example, Titmuss, 1968; Rein, 1969; Tudor Hart, 1971; Alderson, 1970). The controversy arises from the fact that although the statistics of health care use show that, if anything, the lower occupational groups use the health service more frequently (Rein, 1969: 807), many commentators believe that the statistics, because they fail to take account of the *reason for an individual's visit,* are misleading. Tudor Hart (1971: 407), for example, argues that patients in the lower occupational groups make more 'administrative' visits (for example, for certificates) but do not use the services so

Figure 2   *Mortality at 4 weeks − 1 year of age in the children of miners and clerks, England and Wales*

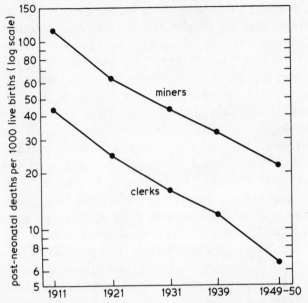

Source: Morris (1967: 57) − compiled from data from various authors

extensively for clinical purposes. People in higher occupational groups spend longer with the doctor and get more information out of him. Tudor Hart also argues that doctors' lists and medical facilities are much more inadequate in industrial and coal-mining areas where the majority of those in the lower occupational groups live (1971: 408).

In addition a number of studies indicate considerable variation in 'preventative' type services. Heasman (1961), for example, showed how those in the lowest occupational categories were less likely to obtain examination at a mass radiography session, despite the fact that they had a very much higher rate of tuberculosis. MacGregor, Fraser and Mann (1966) have shown how there was a gradient in the proportion of women remaining unscreened for cervical cancer (after several strong attempts to contact them) that ran from 5 per cent in the top two occupational categories to 16 per cent in the bottom two. Osborne and Leyshon (1966) also showed how the response rates were low in the bottom occupational groups, although once more the pick-up rate was higher. Marr *et al.* (1955) have argued that those in lower occupational groups make less use of facilities for immunization and prevention, of welfare clinics, and of supplementary foods and vitamins for children and pregnant mothers.

In a very recent paper Cartwright (1975) has reviewed the, by now, extensive literature on social class and use of the health service. She points out that Rein used evidence selectively to support his argument against class differences. In quoting Cartwright's own earlier study, for example, he failed to heed some of her reservations about the data and did not quote

other results — such as the fact that 14 per cent of middle-class patien.
were visited by their doctor compared with 4 per cent of working-cla:
patients. Cartwright's scholarly review of the evidence in fact leaves littl.
room for doubt that the middle class are the main beneficiaries of healt.
services. To select a few of the findings she reviews: they are more likel
to benefit from ante-natal examinations, more likely to attend a family
planning clinic, and more likely to discuss birth control with their GI.
Middle-class individuals are also more likely to have had post-nata
examinations. Middle-class old people are twice as likely to have had hel
from a chiropodist and a visit from their doctor. Middle-class individua.
are more likely to have their own teeth; they are usually found in th
better endowed geriatric and psychiatric hospitals; and stay for shorte
periods in general hospitals. Furthermore, doctors in 'well to do' area
write more expensive prescriptions and spend longer (on average 6.
minutes compared to 4.4 minutes) with middle-class patients. Finally
analysis of what happens in the general practitioner's consulting roo1
supports Tudor Hart's idea that middle-class patients are more successfu
there. Cartwright's evidence, therefore, overwhelmingly supports the view
that the health service operates to the greater benefit of middle-class (o
non-manual) families.

I have presented some data to show that occupational class can be a1
important determinant of the diseases individuals get and also of thei
use of services. In addition, it can influence the way individuals relate t
one another. Because the majority of medical students have fathers in th
higher occupational group — 34.5 per cent of those medical students qual
fying in 1961 and 39.6 per cent of those entering medical school in 196.
had fathers in professional or high administrative occupations, whereas onl·
2.8 per cent of individuals in the population have fathers in thos.
categories — and almost no medical students (less than 4 per cent) com.
from homes where their father was in social class 4 or 5 (Royal Commissio1
on Medical Education, 1968: 331), the experiences and modes of relation
ship that exist in 'lower' occupational groups may seem 'strange' to many
doctors.

To understand why differences of these kinds seem to operate, th.
remainder of this chapter will be concerned with a discussion of th.
different work situations, life-chances, life-styles, and modes of communi
cation found in different occupations. Since, from the data already
discussed, occupation is important I will start with a discussion of work

Work

Every day of the working week about 24 million people in Great Britair
go to work. They represent some 62 per cent of the population, aged
fifteen and over, with working men outnumbering working women by two
to one. About 3 million of these people work part-time (in part-time work

Table 2   Economic Activity in Great Britain (1966 sample Census Data[*])

population aged 15+	total	men	women
		thousands	
	total	*men*	*women*
economically active in employment			
full time	21,048	15,202	5,846
part time	3,121	373	2,748
not in employment			
out of employment	473	215	186
sick	214	134	
retired	2,411	1,911	500
students	1,266	675	591
others	11,508	450	11,058
total	40,041	19,030	21,011
% of population aged 15+			
economically active	62.1	84.1	42.2
retired	6.0	10.0	2.4
students	3.2	3.5	2.8
others	28.7	2.4	52.6
% of population aged 15+ as *% of total population*	76.6	75.2	77.9

[*] This was still the most relevant available information at time of going to press.
Source: Central Statistical Office (1972)

women outnumber men by 9 to 1). Some of this information is given in *Table 2*. From this table it is clear that those not involved in economically (recognized) active employment are largely women, students, or retired people. One important point to note is that an increasing number of married women are now working, so that by 1971 there were the same number of married women working as single, widowed, or divorced women. In the future there will be a greater proportion of married women working.

In order to discuss what is involved in different occupations, I am going to introduce the theoretical distinction between work situation and market situation (Lockwood, 1958). Work situation refers to the actual organization of work and the set of social relationships in which the individual is involved at work by virtue of it. It is thus concerned with the worker's role in the production process, the nature of the task he carries out, the satisfaction he derives from his task, the nature of his working conditions, the extent and style of his relationships with others in the factory, and so on. Market situation, on the other hand, refers to an individual's economic position, and is concerned with factors such as the source and size of income, the degree of job security, and the opportunity for upward mobility. It is suggested that readers attempt to analyse occupations they come into contact with along these lines; the characteristics of work and market situation are set out in juxtaposition to one

Table 3   Work and market situation

market situation	work situation
extrinsic rewards	intrinsic rewards
conditions of employment	work tasks
promotion prospects	work roles
	work conditions
more specifically:	*more specifically:*
wages and fringe benefits	size of plant (concentration of workers in one room)
hours of work	physical conditions (noise, danger, dirt, cold, etc.)

security of employment	control over the —
	   pace of work
	   method of production

chance of promotion	freedom of movement
lifetime earnings pattern	room for initiative
	length of task — is it routine, fragmented, monotonous, repetitive?
	contact with other workers
	amount and style of supervision

another in *Table 3*. Utilizing such a scheme, we are now in a position to categorize and compare types of occupations.

Manual occupations

Manual occupations comprise about 50 per cent of all occupations in Great Britain. Such occupations are distinctive in the sense that they consist primarily of tasks involving the use of physical effort. Car assembler, sheet-metal worker, dock labourer, carpenter, fitter, typesetter, bricklayer, tractor driver, porter, road sweeper, and agricultural worker are all manual occupations. A significant amount of manual work takes place in production activity in factories. Here, the shape of work tasks is predominantly influenced by the changing technological development of industry. Work tasks are designed to achieve the highest possible rate of output per man, and each task is organized in conjunction with an overall plan. Carefully developed work rules and discipline, supervision and regularity, are critical in assuring that each man fulfills his task within the total scheme of things. Consequently, industrialization has always involved a continuing process of rationalization. Work study, or the analysis of the time and movement involved in tasks, contributes to the discovery of the most efficient production methods. For example, component movements of a work task are studied (in the past this was done by observing workers with stereoscopic cine-cameras) and then the resulting conclusions become the basis for a mandatory system of work rules, enforced by supervisors and foremen. As a result of such rationalization, much factory work tends to be monotonous and to leave little room for initiative.

Within modern industry very different types of production systems are to be found, and it is known that the way in which people experience their work varies widely from one type of system to another (Blauner, 1964; Woodward, 1958). Three broad types of production may be distinguished: unit or small batch production, large batch or mass production, and process production. With unit or small batch production, it is possible to have forms of industrial work that are not far removed from the idea of craftsmanship. For example, workers making suits of clothes to order or constructing complicated apparatus to individual specifications, are likely to have a rather complex task and to have a certain degree of autonomy in their work. These workers tend to control the machines they use — rather than vice-versa — and as a result they are able to determine the rhythm of their work to some extent. Because products are produced in small batches or single units, the work task changes quite often, giving workers some variety in their day-to-day work experience.

Mass production and large batch production can involve assembly lines, which are quite common in industry as a whole. Such production methods simplify and rationalize the work task considerably. Through the logic of specialization, tasks are broken down to minimize operations and to maximize speed and efficiency. On a motor car assembly-line, for example, the longest tasks are measured in a few minutes, the shortest in seconds; and each task is repeated continuously throughout a shift. Through the logic of scale, products are produced in huge production runs of thousands. Through the logic of mechanization, materials are brought to the operatives. As Henry Ford said, 'walking is not a paying operation'. Thus, at Dagenham, the Ford production line that produces *Cortinas* and *Granadas* consists of over a mile of moving conveyor belts; in Detroit it is considerably longer. Tasks in mass production typically involve the repetition of single, usually minute, operations — the innumerable fragments into which the total work of production has been split up. Large concentrations of workers are characteristic, and evidence suggests that this can make it more difficult for workers to have a sense of identification with the firm. Big firms tend to have higher rates of absenteeism and accidents, a higher turnover of labour, and more strikes (Acton Society Trust, 1957).

With this form of production the worker is relieved of all necessity to make decisions and his autonomy is minimal. His work is all part of a complex plan requiring expensive machinery, which means that management is bound to be concerned with controlling his performances as precisely as possible.

On the assembly-line of a leading car manufacturer, for example, each worker generally has three tasks (at times when the line is operated at full speed he has two tasks, and an extra man is inserted in the line between every third man). One worker, observed when the plant was running at medium capacity, had the tasks of (1) putting on the nearside front wheel; (2) putting on the nearside back wheel; and (3) opening the boot of the

car. The man on the other side of the line did the offside front and back
wheels, and slipped the spare tyre into the already open boot. The fitting
of the wheels involved putting on eight wheel nuts as the car moved, with
the tyres dropping down at exactly the right moment to be put on. The
work had to be completed quickly. The three tasks took about one
minute, and the worker then had a minute and a half to rest before the
next car came along. These three tasks would be repeated throughout a
shift of about eight hours.

In industry as a whole, there is a great variation in the tasks within a
factory, and even mass-production plants differ substantially. However,
the work situation of such workers can be approximately generalized.
Most jobs have at least some of the following characteristics: the work
often takes place in large-scale plants, in noisy and dirty conditions; the
choice of techniques and work methods is determined in advance; the
pace of work is controlled externally, and the person's ability to move or
stop is often constrained by the need to keep the production-line flowing
(often a substitute has to be found before a worker can leave if he is sick
or needs to go to the lavatory); the work task tends to be intrinsically
unsatisfying, and there is little room for autonomy or for variation in the
quality and quantity of work. Because work tasks are often simple,
fragmented, and highly routinized, they lead to monotomy and make it
very difficult for the worker to absorb himself in what he is doing. Their
fragmentation leads to the worker's divorce from the final product of his
labour. In Alan Sillitoe's *Saturday Night and Sunday Morning*, for
example, Arthur Seaton endlessly produces small steel rods — components
of some end-product produced miles away, perhaps on the other side of
the world. Mass-production plants also tend to divorce the worker from
other people. There is little opportunity to contact others on the production line, the scale of the plant makes for impersonal relationships,
and the number of work rules makes for potential friction with management. Changes in technology in recent years have done little to improve
the situation of such workers, and the continuing rationalization and
increase in the scale of operations in industry suggest that more rather
than fewer workers will be employed in mass production in the immediately foreseeable future.

Process production involves an even more advanced level of industrial
technology, which, it has been argued, can be more conducive to satisfaction, at least for some workers. Automated production processes remove
even the need for physical effort, and the worker becomes largely an over-
looker, observing dials, taking simple measurements, and occasionally
making minor alterations to the process. The level of operative skill is
usually similar to that required in mass and large batch production —
although more background knowledge may be required — but tasks are
less likely to appear fragmentary and meaningless. The worker will usually
have more control over his own time and movement since he is not involved

directly in the production process. He is also likely to be employed in a situation that is capital intensive, where there is unlikely to be a mass concentration of workers. The chemical industry or the electricity supply industry are typical 'process' productions. However, such work does not yet account for a very high percentage of all occupations.

By no means all manual workers are employed directly in the production process; there are other groups of manual workers less directly involved. These include maintenance workers and other men whose jobs, though not requiring a great degree of skill and judgement, at least tend to be less repetitious and monotonous. There are also craftsmen (such as grinders, printers, and typesetters) both inside and outside factories, who are highly skilled in their work and whose jobs require several years of apprenticeship.[2] And then there are unskilled manual occupations, both inside and outside factories, such as sweepers and lavatory attendants, building workers, and farm labourers. Such unskilled jobs still account for quite a large number of occupations (perhaps 10 per cent).

There has been some change in the market situation of manual workers in the last fifty years. The growth of labour power, through the strengthening of trade unions and continued economic growth, has led to an improvement in income and other aspects of the workers' market situation. Trade-union power and government legislation have reduced the risk of victimization and have increased security for manual workers. Nonetheless, the market situation of all manual workers, when compared to all non-manual workers, still has certain salient disadvantages (within the manual category unskilled workers are usually more disadvantaged than semi-skilled and semi-skilled worse off than skilled). Most manual workers are paid hourly and liable to dismissal at very short notice. Although both social security legislation and progressive employment policies have eased their position, it remains the case that if, for example, there is a hold-up in supplies (such as during the 1973/4 fuel crisis) or a slow-down in the demand for products (as in 1975), the manual labour force in a capitalist society, such as our own, is liable to immediate cuts, depending on the approach of management. Firms do not necessarily pay manual workers if there is no work. They are sent home or put on 'short-time'. Even when they are given compensation, it is limited. Thus, in terms of security, the manual worker is in a relatively weak position. In addition, he has little chance of upward occupational mobility, certainly beyond the rank of foreman, and his income will not be subject to annual increments for experience. Generally, apart from wage increases to all workers and possible increases due to boom economic conditions (and hence opportunities for bonuses and overtime), his income will remain at the same level at which he started in the first month or so of the job. For those workers on assembly-lines there may actually be a decline in income in middle age if they can no longer stand the strain of the 'line' and have to move to less exhausting, less well paid, unskilled maintenance jobs.

Relative to previous times, manual wages (in real — or what you can buy — terms) have risen; and, for the better paid manual workers (particularly those doing work of a very monotonous and repetitive nature, which tends to be highly paid), there is a relative improvement in earnings as compared to the lower grades of non-manual workers (clerks, etc.). However, high wages (except for craftsmen) are usually associated with considerable overtime, shift work, and the taking of the most routine jobs. Goldthorpe *et al.* found that 'in order to gain parity in earnings with their fellow employees in clerical grades, the shop-floor men [we] studied might have to work up to as much as 25% longer (1969: 61)'. Less monotonous jobs off the 'line' are not as well paid, for the same level of skill, as the production-line jobs. Manual workers are thus often faced with a real dilemma: which should they choose — interesting work or good pay? Relatively few can command both.

In terms of hours worked, there are major differences between manual and non-manual workers. Almost all manual workers work more than forty-five hours a week, whereas almost all non-manual workers (even the longest working) work less than this (Central Statistical Office, 1972: 73). As I have argued above, overtime and shift work are normal for manual workers, and much work takes place at night and over weekends. Thus, those who have money may not have the time or energy to enjoy it. If manual workers must work long hours to gain a decent income, they will have less time and energy to spend with their families or on out-of-work activities. Those who have the time will not have the money.

Despite the fact that they work longer hours, manual workers are less likely than salaried non-manual workers to be included in occupational pension and sickness schemes. A recent survey showed that 46 per cent of manual workers were included in pension schemes and 63 per cent in sickness schemes; compared with 75 per cent and 93 per cent respectively of non-manual workers (Central Statistical Office, 1972: Table 44). Women manual workers fare even worse. Only 18 per cent and 47 per cent of them have occupational pension and sickness schemes respectively, compared to 47 per cent and 87 per cent of non-manual women workers (Central Statistical Office, 1972: Table 14). As government schemes become compulsory this difference will probably shift so that they will be in the least beneficial schemes.

Women in industry are badly paid compared to men. Their hourly earnings in the recent past have been about half those of men. Lower wages have been justified on the grounds that women are, at most, secondary bread winners in the family. This has never been true of a substantial minority of women, of course, and it is even less true today. In 1971 more than one in every five families was supported primarily by a women (Office of Population Census and Surveys, 1973). The *Equal Pay Act* (1970) has made it illegal for employers to pay women less than men if they are doing the same job — but there are snags. Employers have time to come into line, and they are still likely to segregate men and women in different jobs, reserving those with the lower wages for women. Progress towards 'equal pay' as defined by the *Equal Pay Act* is consistent with continuing and hefty disparities in actual earnings. Luise and Dipak Nandy (1975) examined one of the industrial agreements which, in the Department of Employment's terms, has shown encouraging progress towards equal pay — bacon curing.

'Roughly 45 per cent of the workforce was female. Nearly 4 per cent of the women were in managerial or supervisory positions, compared with just over 14 per cent of the men (which does not by any means place it at the bottom of the league). In January 1970, there was a collective agreement described as discriminatory — i.e., one which specified lower rates for women for similar jobs or lower minimum rates for women. The industry then embarked on an agreed phased plan towards equal pay. By the end of March 1972, the minimum women's rate was 80 per cent of the minimum men's rate; by the end of March 1974 it had increased to 93 per cent. The department expects it to have reached the target of 100 per cent by 29 December 1975.

In this industry, which is making encouraging progress towards equal pay, the average gross weekly earnings were £38.30 for full-time manual men and £20.80 for full-time manual women. When minimum rates for women were around the 90 per cent mark, average earnings were just above the 54 per cent mark.' (Nandy and Nandy, 1975: 247)

The reasons why women's earnings are likely ro remain substantially lower than men's for some time to come fall into three categories. First, until the Act becomes fully operative, there is direct discrimination. Second, there are the effects of past discrimination, such as the concentration of women in lower-skill grades and in sectors of industry (for example, woollen textiles) where low pay is prevalent. There is also a third reason: in 1970 the *New Earnings Survey* examined the reasons why employees lost pay in the survey period. They found that 7.8 per cent of the full-time manual women workers lost pay because of late arrival or early finishing, compared with 4.2 per cent of the men. This is an example of the way 'women's two roles' — the fact that even when working, women have ultimate responsibility for childcare and housework (see below p. 123) — influences women's life-chances. The same factor influences earnings in another way: women often cannot work the overtime and shifts that are necessary in order to take home the high earnings of men (see above p. 120). Until action is taken that puts women on an equal footing to men with regard to domestic responsibilities, for example by encouraging men to take real responsibility for childcare and housework by not penalising interrupted work records or in providing adequate childcare facilities, then discrimination will effectively continue (see Nandy and Nandy, 1975).

To summarize this discussion, which has necessarily been general, of the work and market situations of manual workers, the following passage from a recent study of the work experience of some of the best paid workers in British industry (some of whom are in automated industries or in craft jobs) describes very well the relatively disadvantageous situation of manual occupations:

'The industrial worker ... remains a man who gains his livelihood through placing his labour at the disposal of an employer in return for wages, usually paid by the piece, hour or day. Advances in industrial technology and management may in some cases result in work tasks and roles becoming more inherently rewarding, or at any rate less stressful; but it is by no means clear that any overall tendency in this direction is established. Certainly, new forms of industrial organization also give rise to new forms of strain or deprivation in work — as, for example, those associated with the imperative to scale, with multiple shift working, or with the blocking of promotion opportunities for men on the shop floor. Moreover, for many industrial workers, and especially for those who do not possess scarce skills, obtaining earnings sufficient to support a middle class standard of living may well mean taking on work of a particularly unrewarding or unpleasant kind — work, that is, which can be experienced only as labour. And indeed for men in most manual grades the achievement of affluence is likely to require some substantial amount of overtime working on top of a regular working week, which is already longer than that of white collar employees. Finally, it is evident that many types of industrial work, and often those that afford high earnings, exert a seriously restrictive effect upon out-of-work life; in this respect again, shifts and overtime are major factors and the impact of the former at least will become more, rather than less, widely felt.' (Goldthorpe *et al.*, 1969: 157—58).

For manual workers, the work that takes up a substantital proportion of their waking lives is typically experienced as 'labour', as something devoid of intrinsic satisfaction and pursued almost entirely for the reward that derives from it, namely pay. Thus it could be argued that Marx's characterization of the worker's experience of his work still stands as a not too exaggerated description of manual work in British industry:

'Work is external to the worker ... it is not part of his nature ... ; consequently, he does not fulfill himself in his work but denies himself, has a feeling of misery rather than well being, does not develop freely his mental and physical energies but is physically exhausted and mentally debased. The worker, therefore, feels himself at home only during his leisure time, whereas at work he feels homeless. His work is not voluntary but imposed, forced labour. It is not the satisfaction of a need but only a means for satisfying other needs.' (Marx, trans. 1963: 124—5)

Nonetheless, work, getting to work, preparing to work, and recovering from work take up about half of the manual worker's waking life (Young and Willmott, 1973: 139).

Housework

Before leaving this discussion of manual work, something should be said about the most common form of it, housework, even though those who do it, namely, four out of five women aged sixteen to sixty-five (Hunt, 1968: II, 3 and 5), are not *formally* employed in this work.

Evidence from a recent study suggests that women in the London area spend between forty-eight and 105 hours every week cleaning, washing, washing-up, making beds, shopping for household items, cooking, and mending. The average time that a woman spent on housework in this study was seventy-seven hours per week (Oakley, 1974: 148) which makes 'housewives' the longest-working occupational group in the UK. Furthermore, when Ann Oakley asked the women in her sample how they felt about their work in the home, she found that 75 per cent of them replied that it was monotonous (Oakley, 1974: 124). This finding is particularly interesting because she used the same form of question as that employed by Goldthorpe and his colleagues, who found that 41 per cent of the affluent manual workers they studied in Luton gave the same response. In fact 'housewives' experienced monotony even more often than assembly-line workers in Luton i.e. the group who experienced more monotony than any other, with 67 per cent of them reporting that they found work monotonous (Goldthorpe, 1958: 18). And to this finding should be added the fact that whereas the men could cope with this negative experience at work by going home and doing other things there, the women had no such alternative. It is important to note that the women studied felt that if they did not get through the amount of housework they did (which may seem excessive) they would not be adequately performing their roles as mothers and wives. It is also worth noting that very few husbands, particularly those with manual occupations, made much effort to help (Oakley, 1974: 137).

Non-manual occupations

Non-manual occupations comprise the remaining 50 per cent, approximately, of occupations[3] and can be usefully broken down into three categories: those described as routine occupations (such as wages clerks, shorthand typists, telephonists, account preparers, post office sorters, and shop assistants, etc.); intermediate occupations, which are considered to involve work requiring more individual initiative (for example, nurses, social workers, assistant school teachers, junior business executives and owners of small firms, as well as some freelance and self-employed people like journalists and actors); and finally, professional, scientific, and administrative occupations, which are elite occupations (doctors, lawyers, senior civil servants, university teachers, architects, accountants, and so on). The distinctions are crude, and, near the cut-off points, arbitrary, bu they are intended to give some indication of the degree of decision-making and responsibility involved. The three categories comprise about 25 pe cent, 15 per cent and 10 per cent, respectively, of occupations in Grea Britain. Most of the workers in the elite and intermediate occupations are men, and the majority of those in the routine occupations are women.

The occupations in the elite and, to a lesser extent, in the intermediate group will be fairly familiar to most readers. Their work situations are characterized by the considerable amount of responsibility they carry, by the authority they have over others, by the amount of variety in their work tasks, and by the relative absence of routinely repeated work (at any rate, compared with most manual workers, since each task tends to take much longer to perform and is not fragmented). Work usually takes place in an office and in a small group situation; there is often considerable opportunity for contact with other workers and only indirect supervision from above; the individual has considerable control over the pace of his work and the way he carries it out (the method of production); and there is room for discretion and initiative. Clearly those in elite occupations have the most responsibility and opportunity for initiative, while those in intermediate group occupations have somewhat less. With regard to the market situation, jobs tend to be secure for periods of time, on the basis of contracts, while incomes — in comparison to those in manual occu pations — tend to be high or very high and likely to increase by annua increments over time. There are usually considerable opportunities for promotion, some flexibility concerning hours and holidays, and a generally rising life-time earnings pattern. There are fringe benefits like pensions or superannuation schemes and, often, expense accounts to help meet current costs (Titmuss, 1962).

The work and market situations of routine non-manual workers may be less familiar. Traditionally, clerical workers, who account for a large pro portion of this group, were considered to be relatively skilled: reading writing, and arithmetic skills were at one time relatively scarce. But since the First World War, the development of mass education and the rapid expansion of bureaucratic organization associated with the increase in scale of firms and government agencies has brought about great changes Bureaucratization and rationalization have created a multitude of routin ized clerical type tasks, and increases in the scale of operations have led to workers being concentrated together in large groups such as in typing pools or in insurance and accounts offices.

Paper work has proliferated. Generally, when one buys something in a shop one is given a bill. The copy is processed. Before that, somebody somewhere wrote ordering the supplies from the wholesaler. He too supplied an invoice, as did the lorry driver who transported the goods Before that, somebody else ordered supplies from a manufacturer, and the manufacturer ordered supplies from another supplier, and so on. Other invoices and other lorry drivers were probably employed with the consignment details. At the manufacturer there is also a mass of paper work concerned with the operation of production lines. In addition to all these pieces of paper, records and accounts are kept for tax purposes and letters are typed and exchanged, answering queries and giving explanations. The development of various calculators and computers has reduced some of these operations, or rather the amount of manpower required to conduct them. However, computers, which extend human capacity by routinizing time-consuming operations, themselves generate more work by creating massive demands for people to process and programme the information fed in and taken out of them and to interpret the results. Many of these occupations are highly routine. Until someone develops a method of transferring the spoken word to paper directly, which is still some way off, clerical work will continue to expand.

Much clerical work is monotonous, like manual work, and incapable of absorbing the participant's full attention. Nevertheless, in other important ways, it is still different from manual work. The clerical worker, despite the typing pool and increases in the scale of the office unit, usually works in small concentrations of workers and is likely to be positioned near people carrying out different tasks. Executives, for example, have personal assistants and personal secretaries, each department has to have secretaries, and so on. They thus tend to mix with people doing different jobs, and also to have more contact with management, that is, with those who have the power in the organization. In principle, at least, it becomes possible for clerical workers to identify with their work and their employer's unit. These observations are confirmed by evidence that white-collar workers, unlike manual workers, give other reasons than the level of pay for staying in the job (Goldthorpe *et al.*, 1969: 57).

There has, however, been considerable rationalization and routinization of much office work over the past few years, and hence many tasks have become more monotonous. Nonetheless, the intensive mechanization of work tasks for office workers has not yet placed them in the same position as manual workers. This is because the types of machine used in office work are rather different from those used in the factory. Whereas most machinery in a modern factory involves subordinating human labour to the machine mechanism, this is not so in an office:

'The classification of modern office machinery clearly demonstrates that it is chiefly used to reinforce and support existing clerical functions ... First there are those machines which facilitate part of some complicated work, such as for instance the calculator used by a cashier. In his work the machine is not used full time, but is really an ancillary device which takes over the mental drudgery involved in routine addition, subtraction, multiplication and division. Secondly, there are those machines which are not used continuously, but where the operator really directs them after having thought out certain details of the performance. Typing is a good example of this kind of work; a typist is usually specialized in relation to the machine, but the work involves discretion, and the tempo of work is her own. Thirdly, there are those machines which are merely supplemented by the operator, the latter becoming really a cog in the machine. This is the role of the operator of an automatic duplicating machine, for example. It is really in this third type of operation that the clerk is reduced to the status of machine minder, which for Marx and Veblen was the distinguishing characteristic of modern factory labour. Thus the number of office machines which subordinate the work of the clerk to the tempo of the machine, which take over the larger part of the discretion involved in the operation, and which require full time, specialized attendance, is still extremely small.' (Lockwood, 1958: 88–9)

However, it is interesting to note that, although machines have been limited in their impact upon the actual nature of clerical functions, when compared with their influence in factory production, the rationalization of work procedures in relation to machinery has produced social consequences similar to those in the factory. This is especially true in large-scale and central office departments where there is a continuous demand for the recording and analysis of data. In such offices the standardization of methods of work, of the size of forms, and of the ways in which these are to be set out, etc., has been the main factor in speeding up and simplifying work for machine processing. It has also brought about considerable rationalization in the methods of grouping and supervising office workers. These developments have led to the growth of relatively large groups of semi-skilled employees who are concentrated together, separated from managerial and supervisory staffs. They typically perform continuous routinized and disciplined work, often rewarded in accordance with physical output, and they have little chance of promotion. In many ways similar to factory work, this work is, interestingly enough, likely to be carried out by the sisters and wives of the men in the factories.

With regard to the market situation, however, the clerical worker still enjoys advantages over the manual worker. Although manual workers' incomes have 'caught up' (and in some cases surpassed) those of many routine non-manual workers, it is still true that non-manual workers are on average better off in terms of the hours and conditions of work, security of tenure, pensions, and opportunities for promotion. The chances of promotion for men in non-manual work, for example, are quite good, though for women this is less true.

Table 4, which was the outcome of a recent piece of work at Imperial College (Wedderburn, 1970), aptly summarizes some of these differences in the market situation of different workers.

Table 4   Differences in market situation

	factory workers %	clerical workers %	senior managers %
holidays of 15+ days	38	74	88
normal working 40+ hours per week	97	9	22
pension — employers scheme	67	90	96
time off *with pay* for personal reasons	29	83	93
pay deductions for any lateness	90	8	0
no clocking-on or booking-in	2	48	94

Source: Wedderburn, 1970: 593 (adapted)

Power and Advantage

The discussion so far has analysed differences in the work and market situations of those in various occupations within the division of labour, and it has argued that an individual's position in the occupational structure has far-reaching consequences for his experience in many other areas of life as well.

In contemporary British society, which we may take to be reasonably typical of western industrial societies, advantages in almost every sphere of life consistently accrue to those occupying particular occupations, and also to their dependants. These people not only enjoy more advantageous work situations, but they also earn higher incomes, inhabit houses with the most convenient and decent amenities in the most salubrious areas of the country, possess more durable goods, have better transport facilities, send their children to better schools, have more responsibility and take more decisions, find it easier to influence governmental decisions (a motorway runs through Notting Hill and north Birmingham, but not Hampstead or Christ Church Meadow), and generally have greater opportunities for enjoying their lives. For example, because they have friends and acquaintances who control the production of many luxury goods and facilities which are scarce, they may find it easier to obtain tickets to the cup final, Wimbledon, or the opera.

It is in such a situation, where differentiation between occupations in the division of labour is associated with differences in advantages in other areas of life, that sociologists, following the early formulation of Karl Marx, begin to talk about social class. Social class is most generally conceived of as referring to a hierarchy of power and advantage (Dahrendorf, 1959); and to analyse further the distribution of power and advantage in a society, both at any one time and over time, it is useful to consider a conceptual scheme based on the work of the German sociologist Max Weber, who lived from 1863–1920 (Weber, trans. 1947). The schema can help us to think about social class, but I am uncertain about whether one could extract the dimensions empirically since they are always strongly inter related

Advantage here means the ability to control — or prevent others from controlling — scarce resources, be they material (goods and services symbolic (prestige and fashion), or physical (*force majeure*). Power, i this context, means the ability to mobilize, and prevent others from mobilizing, the same scarce resources. The two terms suggest two differen elements: the need to own and the need to be able to make use of what i owned.

The three main dimensions of power and advantage that can be di tinguished are the economic, the symbolic, and the physical. Althoug these will usually be strongly inter-related (the possession of symboli power or prestige may lead to economic power; economic power may lea to physical power through the possession of a private army or the abilit to influence the legitimate, coercive, power structure in any society, th state), it is also possible for divergence to occur. For example, clergyme tend to enjoy prestige quite disproportionate to their weak economi position. Workers can wield physical power through a trade union (fo example, they can withdraw collectively their labour and hence threate property or profits) even though they are well down the economic scale

Economic power involves the ability to control and mobilize scarc material resources, and a person's position in the economic hierarchy i often termed 'class' position, with class here having a narrow definition. I addition to the work and market situation of his occupation, economi power relates to his position as a consumer, his housing, and his possessio of land, capital, and consumer durables.

Symbolic power is concerned with deference, acceptance, and dero gation. Prestige or status permits an actor to wield power by 'creatin, favourable presumptions', by providing bases for exerting influence an for determining standards, tastes, and styles. Thus a virtually penniles aristocrat may be more credit worthy, may give more power to others b associating with them, and may influence standards of dress or musi more than a rich businessman. Such power, it should be noted, depend on social support or consensus: if the latter is not present, individual cannot wield symbolic power. It depends upon the existence of a share universe of meaning and value amongst the actors concerned. Symboli power therefore tends to be based on dominant cultural values. A person' position in terms of symbolic power is his 'status' position.

Physical power and advantage refer to the mobilization and control o resources through direct possession of *force majeure*. In societies such a our own, physical power is seldom exercised directly, but rather throug organizational and political hierarchies with legislative (and therefor legitimate) authority. For example, although from time to time a Prim Minister may fall back on direct force and call out the police or brin in the troops to enforce his authority, this is seldom necessary. Similarly top management seldom uses its power of 'giving the sack' or locking out the workers; and in the same way, trade unions threaten to strike far more often than they actually do. A person's position in terms of physical power is his 'authority' position.

As I have suggested, in societies like our own occupation is usually the key to an individual's power and advantage in each of these three hierarchies. The top civil servant has a high income, job security, and discretion at work; he enjoys considerable status and standing in the community; and he wields considerable authority in his work situation. An unskilled manual worker, on the other hand, has low income, low status, and little authority, at least in his work role.

There are, however, other factors that influence a person's position in the power and advantage hierarchy, of which some of the most important are associated with birth. For example, wealth may not be tied to occupation as much as to the material possessions of the family into which a person is born. Status too may be related to birth, or to such unalterable characteristics as race, colour of skin, or gender. Women, in most societies, have lower status and less authority than men. However, because they tend to live longer, they may, if they happen to be the associates of powerful men, own much property. Blacks, on the other hand, tend to be worse off than whites in all three hierarchies. Other determinants of social status and authority that can be important are religion and age. Discrimination against Catholics and Jews has at various times been a feature of British society and it is often suggested that entry into certain trades in places like Belfast is more difficult for Catholics. The effect of age is more complicated and is usually dependent upon prior social position. In other words, increasing age confers greater authority and exerts greater deference in some occupations, while in others the reverse is true.

In general, however, occupation is a good indicator of an individual's power and advantage. *Table 5* provides an indication of the way people tend to order a number of occupations according to their general desirability and probably reflects, in summary, the occupation's many different characteristics, that is, the intrinsic nature of the work; the conditions under which it is done; the income derived from it; its standing in the community; its security of tenure; the authority and status that accrue to its occupant, and so on. The last column of *Table 5* shows the proportion of the adult male population employed in the various occupational categories.

Life-Chances

Holding a particular occupation, as I have argued, confers power and advantage on an individual in a significant way. It is therefore interesting and important to ask what chance any particular individual has of obtaining a job in other occupations. This is known as the study of occupational mobility.

Table 5 The Hope—Goldthorpe occupational scale (recommended collapsed version)

rank order	descriptive title (and occupations of greatest numerical importance)	average scale value (i.e. median of scale values of constituent categories)	% in employed male population of England and Wales, 1% sample Census, 1971
1	independent professionals (doctors, lawyers, accountants, dentists, surveyors, architects, pharmacists, engineers, stock- and insurance brokers)	75	0.78
2	salaried professionals: higher grade (engineers, accountants and company secretaries, doctors, natural scientists, architects and town planners, university teachers, lawyers, airline pilots and crew)	71	4.78
3	administrators and officials: higher grade (managers in large commercial enterprises and public utilities, sales managers, senior civil servants, local authority senior officers, also includes company directors, n.e.c.)	69	2.88
4	industrial managers: large enterprises (managers in engineering, extractive industries, general manufacturing and construction, personnel managers in all large establishments)	66	1.40
5	administrators and officials: lower grade (police officers, radio and telegraph officers)	65	0.88
6	technicians: higher grade (work study engineers, computer programmers, draughtsmen, laboratory technicians)	64	2.84
7	large proprietors (working owners of large shops and service agencies)	63	0.02
8	industrial and business managers: small enterprises (managers in commerce, public utilities, engineering, extractive industries, general manufacturing and construction, personnel managers in all small establishments)	62	2.41
9	independent professionals: lower grade (parochial clergy, entertainers, artists, journalists)	62	0.33
10	salaried professionals: lower grade (primary and secondary school teachers, civil service executive officers, social welfare workers, male nurses, public health inspectors, journalists, commercial artists)	61	3.01
11	farmers and farm managers	58	0.79

Table 5 (continued)

rank order	descriptive title (and occupation of greatest numerical importance)	average scale value (i.e. median of scale values of constituent categories)	% in employed male population of England and Wales, 1% sample Census, 1971
12	supervisors of non-manual employees: higher grade (supervisors of clerical employees)	57	0.41
13	small proprietors (working owners of small shops and service agencies, small builders, painters and decorators, hoteliers, boarding-house keepers and restauranteurs)	57	2.75
14	managers in services and small administrative units (managers of shops and service agencies, office managers, hotel and restaurant managers)	53	3.02
15	technicians: lower grade (electrical and electronic engineers, post office technicians, auto engineers, radio engineers, fire brigade men)	51	3.69
16	supervisors of non-manual employees: lower grade (supervisors of sales personnel)	48	0.26
17	supervisors of manual employees: higher grade (foremen in engineering, construction, communications and mining)	47	3.03
18	skilled manual workers in manufacturing: higher grade (maintenance and other fitters, millwrights, tool makers, pattern makers)	46	5.89
19	self-employed workers: higher grade (shopkeepers, painters and decorators, carpenters and joiners, jobbing builders, publicans)	43	3.69
20	supervisors of manual employees: lower grade (foremen in warehousing, distribution, transport, chemicals and food products)	42	1.74
21	non-manual employees in administration and commerce (clerical workers, cashiers, commercial travellers)	40	7.68
22	skilled manual workers in manufacturing: intermediate grade (machine setters, sheetmetal workers, precision instrument makers, printers and compositors, glass and ceramic formers, also includes 'other ranks' in the armed services	38	3.55

Table 5 (continued)

rank order	descriptive title (and occupation of greatest numerical importance)	average scale value (i.e. median of scale values of constituent categories)	% in employed male population of England and Wales, 1% sample Census, 1971
23	skilled manual workers in construction (carpenters and joiners, painters and decorators, bricklayers)	38	4.04
24	smallholders without employees	37	0.72
25	service workers: higher grade (cooks, stewards, hairdressers)	37	0.50
26	semi-skilled manual workers in manufacturing (machine-tool operators, press operators, assemblers and routine inspectors, chemical process workers, food and other process workers)	36	6.33
27	skilled manual workers in transport, communications and services, and extractive industries	36	2.84
28	service workers: intermediate grade (shop salesmen and assistants)	35	1.39
29	self-employed workers: intermediate grade (taxi drivers, carriers, cafe owners, entertainers)	35	0.90
30	skilled manual workers in manufacturing: lower grade (plant and engine operators, locksmiths, engravers and other metal working craftsmen, moulders, furnacemen and forgemen, sawyers and woodworkers, butchers, bakers)	33	4.97
31	agricultural workers	31	1.22
32	semi-skilled manual workers in construction and extractive industries (roofers, asphalters and cable layers, demolition workers, surface workers in mining and quarrying)	30	1.38
33	semi-skilled manual workers in transport, communications, and services (lorry drivers, warehousemen, packers, and labellers, storekeepers, postal workers, bus drivers and conductors, roundsmen, ambulance men, deck hands, railway lengthmen, gardeners and groundsmen, dry cleaners and pressers)	28	10.40
34	service workers: lower grade (caretakers, doormen, guards and attendants, telephone operators, waiters, barmen and counter hands)	27	1.71

Table 5 (continued)

Rank order	descriptive title (and occupation of greatest numerical importance)	average scale value (i.e. median of scale values of constituent categories)	% in employed male population of England and Wales, 1% sample Census, 1971
35	unskilled manual workers (general labourers, factory labourers, building site labourers, railway porters, kitchen porters, office and industrial cleaners, messengers)	18	6.11
36	self-employed workers: lower grade (street vendors, jobbing gardeners)	18	0.23

Source: Goldthorpe and Hope, 1972: 134—43
This table should in no circumstances be used as a coding frame.

One way of analysing occupational mobility is to look at the lifetime experience of individuals and the types of occupations they hold. Such work, known as the study of *intra-generational* mobility, suggests that the opportunities for occupational advance (or conversely, demotion) are significantly small within a person's lifetime. Between 1953 and 1963 the Social Survey Department of the government carried out a study (Harris and Clausen, 1966) analysing job changes in the UK over a ten-year period.

From this study it can be seen that the majority of job changes made by individuals do not involve a change to another occupational group (the seven occupational groups used in this study are outlined in *Table 6*). Nonetheless the total number of changes in occupational group was quite considerable. Nearly 20 per cent of respondents in the national sample had a job in an occupational group that was different from that of ten years before. However, such *frequency* data exaggerated the degree of openness within the occupational structure; if the extent of movement in terms of the distance individuals travelled (the *range*) is concerned, there are only a very small number of long-range movements and the majority of moves are seen to be of short distance. Thus, of those moving out of the top category about 85 per cent went to category 2 or 3.1 (both non-manual categories), leaving only 15 per cent who all became partly-skilled manual workers. Conversely, of those moving out of category 4 (partly skilled manual workers), 60 per cent went to the other manual categories (3.2 or 5), and only one third entered any sort of non-manual occupation (2, 3.1, 4.1).

In fact, from this study, there are three over-riding impressions that are important if it is life-chances that are being considered. First, there were considerable limitations on the distances individuals could rise or fall in the occupational structure; second, there was a particularly strong barrier to entering from below either of the top two categories (1 and 2 — particularly 1) or the top manual category (3.2); and third, there was very limited movement from manual to non-manual categories, and vice versa. Indeed,

Table 6   Occupational groups used in the social survey (1953–63) and the L.S.E. (1948) enquiries into occupational mobility

Social Survey (Harris and Clausen)	L.S.E. (Glass)
1. professional and administrative	1. professional and high administrative
2. managerial, executive, and minor professional	2. managerial and executive
	3. inspectional, supervisory and other non-manual, high grade
3.1 intermediate non-manual	
3.2 skilled manual	4. inspectional, supervisory and other non-manual, low grade
4.1 routine non-manual	
4.2 partly-skilled manual	5. skilled manual and routine grades of non-manual
5. unskilled	
	6. semi-skilled manual
	7. unskilled

Source: Glass, 1954: 182
Harris and Clausen, 1966: 49

manual and non-manual categories are in effect like two non-competing occupational systems, each with its own elite. Thus the first job that someone gets is likely to determine the occupational level of all his or her subsequent jobs.

A second way of looking at occupational mobility is to consider the chances of differences between the occupational groups of parents and their children. As yet, however, such studies of what is termed *inter-generational* mobility have all been restricted to comparisons between fathers and their sons.

In considering the question of inter-generational mobility, the most recent data that is available is from the study that David Glass and his associates made at the London School of Economics in 1948. In this study a seven category occupational ranking-scale (see *Table 6*) was constructed; the occupation of each respondent in a national sample was placed in one of the categories and then compared with the category into which the occupation of the respondent's father had been placed. The extent to which the fathers' and sons' occupations were associated was then calculated.

Interpretation of the results, which are expressed in *Table, 7,* once again depends on the extent to which it is the frequency or the range of mobility that is considered. In the first place, it can be calculated that the manual/non-manual division was much less significant in inter-generational terms than it was during the individual's lifetime. About 30 per cent of the sons whose fathers were manual workers had held non-manual occupations, and vice versa. However, such mobility was likely to be of short-range. When there were changes in the occupational level of father and son, the son's occupational level was usually in one of the groups adjacent to his father's. Thus of those who were in category I in 1948, nearly two-fifths had fathers who held jobs in the same category, and a further

Table 7 The distribution of fathers' occupations compared to those of their sons, in 1948.

Each cell shows two percentages: the row percentage (son's distribution for a given father) and the column percentage.

fathers' status category	sons' status category*							Total
	1	2	3	4	5	6	7	
1	38.8 / 48.5	14.6 / 11.9	20.2 / 7.9	6.2 / 1.7	14.0 / 1.3	4.7 / 1.0	1.5 / 0.5	100.0 (129)
2	10.7 / 15.5	26.7 / 25.2	22.7 / 10.3	12.0 / 3.9	20.6 / 2.2	5.3 / 1.4	2.0 / 0.7	100.0 (150)
3	3.5 / 11.7	10.1 / 22.0	18.8 / 19.7	19.1 / 14.4	35.7 / 8.6	6.7 / 3.9	6.1 / 5.0	100.0 (345)
4	2.1 / 10.7	3.9 / 12.6	11.2 / 17.6	21.2 / 24.0	43.0 / 15.6	12.4 / 10.8	6.2 / 7.5	100.0 (518)
5	0.9 / 13.6	2.4 / 22.6	7.5 / 34.5	12.3 / 40.3	47.3 / 50.0	17.1 / 43.5	12.5 / 44.6	100.0 (1510)
6	0.0 / 0.0	1.3 / 3.8	4.1 / 5.8	8.8 / 8.7	39.1 / 12.5	31.2 / 24.1	15.5 / 16.7	100.0 (458)
7	0.0 / 0.0	0.8 / 1.9	3.6 / 4.2	8.3 / 7.0	36.4 / 9.8	23.5 / 15.3	27.4 / 25.0	100.0 (387)
Total	100.0 (103)	100.0 (159)	100.0 (330)	100.0 (459)	100.0 (1429)	100.0 (593)	100.0 (424)	100.0 (3497)

* For definition of category, see Table 6

Source: Glass, 1954: 183

two-fifths had fathers who held jobs in categories II, III, or IV; only one-fifth came from families where the father was a manual worker (categories V, VI and VII). This was true despite the fact that in 1948 occupations in the manual groups accounted for well over two-thirds of all occupations. Finally, it can be seen that certain occupational groups tended to be recruited, to a very large extent, from among the children of those already in the group. This is particularly noticeable in categories I and V where about 40 and 50 per cent, respectively, of the children came from families where their father was in the same group.

This remarkably high degree of internal recruitment into certain categories could, of course, be accounted for in two ways. It could be the case that fathers were able to pass on advantage to their children — for example, by sending them to a 'good' school or giving them money; or, alternatively, it could be spurious — the result of the statistical fact that if one occupational group accounts for a disproportionate number of all jobs at *both* the points in time when comparisons are being made, then there must automatically be a high probability that people born into that category will remain there. To choose between these hypotheses and estimate the extent to which internal recruitment occurs because of unequal opportunities, it is necessary to develop a method for taking into account the way in which the distribution of fathers' and sons' occupations at two points in time can mask the results. Glass and his colleagues developed such a technique, which they termed an index of association (Glass, 1954: 188). It takes into account not only the way in which the distribution of jobs in the occupational structure can affect results, but also the way in which changes in the distribution can produce a misleading estimate of the openness or closedness of different occupational groups. Using this method, it is possible to argue that the degree of internal recruitment was thirteen times greater for category I, six times greater for category II, twice as great for category III, and two and a quarter times greater for category VII, than would have been expected if it was only chance that determined occupational selection. Category VI turned out to be rather open, which can be explained by the fact that the previous finding (which suggested that half the people in category V themselves had fathers in category V) was the result not of internal recruitment, but of the fact that category V accounted for somewhere near half the jobs in the sample at both points of comparison (see *Table* 7).

Therefore, from the L.S.E. study of inter-generational mobility, it is possible to conclude — as was suggested in reference to intra-generational mobility — that there were considerable barriers to occupational choice and particularly to entry into the top categories on the occupational scale.

The Glass study, which was undertaken in 1948, is of course now quite dated, and does not take into account any occupational mobility that may have resulted from the war and the educational reforms of the post-war years. The preliminary results from a new study undertaken in Oxford during 1973 seem to indicate that inter-generational mobility has increased somewhat (Goldthorpe, 1973). Nonetheless, although the study suggests, that in 1973, more mobility takes place, and that the degree of internal recruitment in the upper categories has been reduced quite markedly, society is still by no means an open one, and occupational choice is still significantly affected by the occupation of a person's father. Considerable inequality of opportunity for those in the lower part of the occupational hierarchy remains, notwithstanding the fact that it is possible for some of their fellows to reach the top categories. This apparent contradiction is possible because, whilst the lower groups in the occupational hierarchy account for a very high proportion of those in the population, the higher groups are very much smaller (see *Table* 7). If some form of equal opportunity were to prevail, the top category could be expected to be *very largely* made up of those with fathers from the lower occupational groups. This was certainly not the case in 1973.

Life-Styles and Social Class

The differences in the material life-styles of individuals from different occupations are so commonplace that they are rarely described. But a drive through Walton-on-Thames, Haslemere, Hampstead Garden Suburb, or Brentwood (to name places in the South-East that I am familiar with) has a very different quality than a drive through Willesden, Camberwell, Holloway, Dalston, or Southfields — not to mention Tower Hamlets or Hackney. One defining characteristic that differs between such areas, and which Young and Willmott have illustrated, is physical space:

'So important is it that one could, if one made the measurements on a large scale, tease out an index of prestige based on space alone which would tally pretty well with other scales, and perhaps even serve as a general indicator of social class as useful as occupation. We did just that by way of example with three tolerant informants at different levels in the hierarchy of a particular furniture company. The manager had a London house of about 4,600 square feet, a cottage in Sussex of 2,500 and an office of 600 (or 900 if his secretary's suite was added in), making some 8,000 square feet whose entrances and exits he controlled. An accounts clerk had a suburban house of 950 square feet, and an office 'space' of 150, making 1,100 in all, while a machinist had a flat of 550 feet and a work space of 150, or 700 in all. Judged by this ready reckoner, the manager had seven times more prestige than the clerk or eleven times more than the machinist.

The Civil Service had (and has) a particularly famous grading system. At the time of the survey a Permanent Secretary was entitled to an office of 500 to 550 square feet; a Deputy Secretary to 400 to 450; an Under Secretary to 250 to 350; a Principal to 150 to 200; right down to the depths of the Clerical Officer or Scientific Assistant with an allowance of 55 to 65. The ratio was something like eight or ten to one ... in general people's homes corresponded in size with the scales at work. Some worked, lived and travelled first class; others others. With the homes one difference, in London, was that if they were high up in the air, in blocks of flats, they did not have the same cachet at all. A home territory in the air was far less of a satisfaction than if it was planted on the "solid" ground, as the phrase sometimes went. An electrician in Ealing lamented about his children — "Living up here they've never played with the earth, they've never played with a worm." To play with a worm was self-evidently a natural right of which those perched on a pile of steel and concrete were deprived.

From a tower block the view did not compensate for the psychic vertigo. But a view did add to the value of a house which also had the advantage of being on the ground. Many of the sites with open space in front of them had been appropriated by the rich. Almost every one of the great common lands of London — Hampstead Heath, Wimbledon Common, Blackheath, Hyde Park, Green Park, Regent's Park, Epping Forest, Hadley Wood, Richmond Park, Ham Common — was public for walking on within the prescribed hours but private all the year round and all the clock round for the views over it. Public property gave a spatial bonus from the community to those who already had private privilege.' (Young and Willmott, 1973: 43–5)

The contrast between the 'executive homes' of the commuter belt or even the well-ordered, suburban 'semi-detacheds' in Barnet and the average working-class terrace or council estate suggests great differences in life-experience. For many individuals in semi-skilled and unskilled occupations life is still a fight for survival typified by low income and inadequate and overcrowded living conditions. Again, Willmott and Young provide examples:

'Miss Fernando from Trinidad was an informant in Deptford. She lived with her three children in a "lodging house", a once-majestic Victorian building which besides her contained fourteen single men and three other small families. She had arthritis and was unable to work. She could not even go outside, since, if she did, her stiff joints would have stopped her climbing back up the rickety stairs. Her income was £12 per week in sickness benefits, family allowances and supplementary benefits. After paying £4 per week for her two rooms she had £8 left for everything else. Her only heating came from a single paraffin heater. It had been knocked over not long before the interview; the fire which broke out was extinguished just in time to prevent the house burning down.' (Young and Willmott, 1973: 60)

'Aged thirty-eight Mr. Crawley was a Senior Development Engineer at a plant in Slough. He lived about twenty miles away in a sixteenth-century house, converted out of three former farm cottages, in rural Berkshire. There was a wood at the back of the house and two large farms within about a quarter of a mile. "The man that way, " said Mr. Crawley, "is a weekend farmer. I met him at a cocktail party last weekend and we were talking about dining out. He said, Are you ever down during the week? I ask you! This is our home." Mr. Crawley travelled to Slough by car most days, but about once to twice a week had to go to meetings in Central London — to the firm's head office — or to "a meeting at the Ministry". One evening during the week before the interview he had, as he put it, "stayed in Town to have dinner with an old University friend. He lives in Sussex, and it's about the only chance I get to meet him." He had, on another evening, gone home after work to collect his wife and then driven her into Central London "to go to the Festival Hall". He explained, "We've got our hi-fi here, but there's nothing quite like hearing it live." The next Saturday, they planned to go out to dinner at a restaurant in Henley, about ten miles away; "We're going to meet some friends who used to live near us when we lived in Kensington. They now live at Maidenhead." There was no trouble about baby-sitting. "We've got the au pair, you see." (1973: 61–2)

'The Wests had few of the Crawley's advantages. They were in their early thirties and had four children under eleven. Mr. West earned £18 a week as a labourer in a builder's yard. When they got married twelve years earlier, they had first lived for a while with Mrs. West's parents in Hackney. "We found it didn't work," said Mrs. West. "There wasn't much room anyway, and after a while troubles started blowing up, mainly between my husband and my mother. We put down to move to Harlow New Town. My husband got a job there working for the council and that meant we could get a house. We lived there for four years. It was lovely. I had a big garden and a modern house. But we had to come back because of the work. There's plenty of jobs in these new towns for the more intellectual sort of people — draughtsmen and engineers — but not for people without a trade. My husband was out of work for fourteen months and we had to come back. We tried to get a council flat but in the end we were desperate and all we could get was this."
"This" was four rooms above an ironmonger's shop in Acton. The West's front door was beside the shop door. Behind it there was a long corridor, with bare cream walls and a single exposed light bulb. The stairs, with a rectangle of grey linoleum on each tread, led up to four rooms. On one floor was a kitchen/dining room and what Mrs. West called "the front room" facing on to the street. The kitchen had an Ascot water heater over the sink which also served as wash basin (there was no bathroom), a modern white gas stove with eye-level grill and transparent door, a tall kitchen cabinet, a red plastic-topped kitchen table and four matching chairs. The other room contained two beds, neither of them as large as standard double size and one much smaller, a two-year-old asleep on it

with a dummy in her mouth and a bottle beside her. It was a chilly
April day and Mrs. West wore thick cream-coloured socks and a long
green cardigan over a yellow-and-white flowered dress with an uneven
hem. She explained how they used the rooms. "We watch TV in this
room and sleep here. The baby sleeps where she is now and my husband
and I in the other bed. The other three children are in one of the rooms
upstairs. We don't use the other one because there's damp coming
through the walls. You can smell the damp as soon as you go into the
room." The Wests had no car. They had stayed in on every evening but
one during the previous week.' (Young and Willmott, 1973: 62–3)

Young and Willmott, supporting earlier findings on the significance of the
'home' in individual's lives, found that both married men and women
(working or not) spent more than half their weekday time (men spent 55
per cent of their time, working women 71 per cent, and other women 87
per cent of their time) and well over two thirds of their weekend time
(men, 60 per cent on Saturday and 76 per cent on Sunday; working
women 75 per cent and 85 per cent; and other women 82 per cent and 87
per cent respectively) at home (Young and Willmott, 1973: 99). Yet, as
the quotations above indicate, the quality of these homes varied greatly.
Serious housing problems, according to one recent study are four times as
frequent among the lower half of the occupational structure as among the
top. An example of a 'housing difficulty' from this study was one woman
who had been living for several years with her husband and two adult
children in a flat with only one bedroom. The noise made by the neighbours upstairs had for a long time made life intolerable. The family had
complained to the police and to the Citizens Advice Bureau, but this produced no change in the disturbance they experienced while trying to sleep.
After four years they had finally succeeded in obtaining a council flat.
(Brown, Ní Bhrolcháin, and Harris, 1975: pp. 225–55).

The notion of 'social class' is intended, among other things, to convey
some of the differences in life-experience that I have described in the
preceding paragraphs. In addition, however, a great deal of sociological
work suggests that individuals not only differ by being 'advantaged' or
'disadvantaged' by the material implications of holding different occupations but that they also differ in their life-styles and attitudes — in other
words, norms of behaviour and attitudes are different according to occupational group. Studies imply that these differences in attitude and
behaviour are the product of the different material situations of individuals,
but this is rarely demonstrated or discussed.

The most clear-cut differences in norms and values among occupational
groups are those between manual and non-manual workers. There are, of
course, other differences within these categories but, nonetheless, the
manual/non-manual distinction remains the most significant.

One reason why individuals from manual and non-manual occupations
differ in their behaviour and attitudes more than do other occupational

groups may be the fact that there is an effective segregation of contact. They rarely mix except in formal role-defined (for example, manager— worker) situations. At work, the work situations and the canteen arrange- ments are usually segregated for manual and non-manual workers. In leisure time there are many informal modes of segregation; for example 'public' bar as opposed to 'lounge' bar; watching football from the terrace rather than a seat. Furthermore, residential districts and school populations are often quite highly segregated — there are not many non-manual workers on housing estates and, indeed, Goldthorpe and his colleagues (1969: 160, footnote 3) found that none of their forty-two manual respondents with children of secondary school age, had a child at Grammar school. Informal social contacts between manual and non-manual workers are extremely limited. In fact Goldthorpe and his colleagues found that 66 per cent of the manual workers they studied (who lived in an unusually unsegregated residential area — Luton) had no sparetime companions in non-manual occupations, and the proportion was as high as 76 per cent when contacts with kin were disregarded. Eighty-two per cent of the manual respondents reported that they had never entertained any couple who were non-manual and not kin in their homes. Furthermore, when the same authors examined the character of formal associations in which manual respondents participated (evening classes, clubs, societies), they found that they were largely of two kinds: 'Ones that were likely to be almost entirely working-class in membership, such as working-men's club, angling or allotment societies' or, if somewhat more mixed in their social composition, 'ones which had some fairly specific function — religious, charitable, sporting — and also some formalised internalised hierarchy in which respondents rarely held superior positions' (Goldthorpe *et al.*, 1969: 109–111).

Findings such as those reported in the previous paragraph suggest that what Disraeli called *The Two Nations* still exists today. The small amount of overlap between individuals in manual and non-manual occupations and the fact that intra-generational or inter-generational mobility is limited, together with the different norms common in the two groups, may be responsible for some of the difficulties that arise when individuals from these 'two nations' interact, as in the doctor's surgery (assuming as is most likely that the doctor is from a non-manual background). In a recent study of social work, for example, the authors concluded that the failure of the (also predominantly middle-class) social workers to help their clients was primarily due to the fact that neither the working-class clients nor the middle-class workers had much idea of what the other was on about. This is what two of the clients who were interviewed reported:

'Once I got talking to the social worker, I felt at ease, but then I realized that she wasn't entering into what I was saying at all. And I thought, "You are not really listening to me. You are not really interested." She just wasn't giving me an answer or any advice at all ... She just kept saying, "Yes, yes" in a quiet sort of way and nodding her head and would I like to come back and that sort of thing.'

'I was disappointed when the social worker remarked, "We don't give advice, as you notice. Also I don't really know you." Which of course she did not, to be fair — as it was the first time I had come in. But with the training that I understand these welfare officers have, they must be a pretty good judge of character ... The point is, I personally can judge whether I would trust a person or not ... If you came in to me with problems, I would listen to your problems. And if I felt it was genuine and quite honest, I would give advice there and then as to what should be done.' (Mayer and Timms, 1969: 36).

The research workers argued that the reasons clients gave for the social workers' failure to act in a so-called appropriate manner were of particular interest. They suggested that the clients were almost totally unaware that the social workers' approach to problem-solving was fundamentally different from their own, and they argued that the clients attributed their own cultural perspective to their caseworkers (Mayer and Timms, 1969: 36).

The authors of the research suggested that:

'... the social workers were unaware that the clients entered the treatment situation with a different mode of problem solving and that the clients' behavior during treatment was in part traceable to this fact ... Viewed from a distance, the worker—client interactions have the aura of a Kafka scene: two persons ostensibly playing the same game but actually adhering to rules that are private.' (Mayer and Timms, 1969: 37)

Following Goldthorpe and Lockwood (1968), it is useful to distinguish three areas where manual and non-manual workers have different norms: in attitudes, in communication styles, and in patterns of life-style and sociability. The differences are supported by a great deal of social research in the UK, the USA, and elsewhere (for example, Rainwater, 1960; Komorovsky, 1962; Bott, 1971 (revised edition); Willmott and Young, 1962; Willmott, 1963; Goldthorpe *et al.*, 1969; Hoggart, 1957; and Young and Willmott, 1973). Two books that summarize many of the findings are Frankenberg's (1966) *Communities in Britain* and Klein's (1965) *Samples from English Cultures* — the latter's chapter on the new working class, however, has been superseded by the findings of Goldthorpe and his colleagues. The great majority of these authors argue that, despite changes in affluence and industrial work, it still makes sense to draw a quite sharp distinction between the life-experience and norms common among manual and non-manual workers respectively. Nonetheless, it is often the case that differences reported, although statistically significant, are small (for example, Goldthorpe and his colleagues found that 14 per cent of manual couples reported that they regularly entertained couples who were neither kin, neighbours, nor workmates as compared to 26 per cent of non-manual couples (1969: 88)). It is possible that these small differences reflect a considerable overlap between occupational groups. Alternatively, they may reflect weak measurement: most studies use schedule interviews which are much less likely to allow sensitive measurement of the subtle differences in entertaining (or other aspects of life-style) that may exist (see above pp. 61—3). In my view the emphasis on frequency measures of life-style, common in most studies, exaggerate the similarities between occupational groups. I suspect that it is the quality, for example, rather than the frequency, of interaction in certain social relationships, that is important (some small evidence for this can be found by analysing 'confiding relationships' see below p. 131 and pp. 322—3). However, it is not possible to choose between these explanations on the basis of current work. Measures of the quality of a relationship, although possible, as I argued in Chapter 2, are much more time-consuming and complex. We can have little confidence in measures based simply on (unvalidated) schedule interviewing. Results are too gross. [4]

Attitudes and Aspirations

Goldthorpe and his colleagues (1969: 118—121) have abstracted characteristics of 'typical' working-class (manual) and middle-class (non-manual) conceptions of the world and these are laid out alongside each other in *Table 8*. There are, I think, three main points to be emphasized in this conceptualization: notions about the *purpose* of life; the extent to which *the future can be controlled;* and the emphasis placed on *individual effort.* Whereas the typical non-manual worker sees life in terms of an individual project in which to create what he wants, the typical manual worker sees life in terms of making the most of what comes along. Although Goldthorpe and his colleagues (1969: 121—2, 145—156) found some changes in this traditional attitude in Luton (particularly a much more active orientation towards the future and a willingness to 'follow the money' by moving to new areas and new jobs) their study, designed to find change, failed to show any real switch from working-class to middle-class attitudes. A number of their findings illustrate this quite well.

With regard to their future orientation, it is clear that manual workers are still 'making the best of it' rather than 'planning for some future good'. Fifty-five per cent of the Luton manual workers and their wives, as compared to 29 per cent of the non-manual ones did no planning ahead at all, other than to provide for payment of regular bills or holiday expenses. On the other hand, 42 per cent in the non-manual group as compared to 13 per cent in the manual (three times as many) planned ahead for purchases in three or four months' time. It should be remembered that in Goldthorpe's study manual and non-manual workers were sampled so that

Table 8   Typical class attitudes

working-class (manual) perspective	*middle-class (non-manual) perspective*
(i) The basic conception of social order is a dichotomous one: society is divided into 'us' and 'them'. 'They' are people in positions in which they can exercise power and authority over 'us'. The division between 'us' and 'them' is seen as a virtually unbridgeable one; people are born on one side of the line or the other and very largely remain there. Life is seen as something to be 'put up with'.	(i) The basic conception of the social order is a hierarchical one: society is divided into a series of levels or strata differentiated in terms of the life-styles and associated prestige of their members. The structure is, however, seen as a relatively 'open' one: given ability and the appropriate moral qualities — determination, perseverance, etc. — individuals can, and do, move up the hierarchy. What a man achieves in the end depends primarily on what he 'makes of himself'. Moreover, it is felt that the individual has an obligation to assume responsibility for his own life and welfare and to *try* to 'get on in the world' as far as he can.
(ii) Complementary to the idea of 'putting up' with life is that of 'making the best of it'; that is, of living in and for the present. As Hoggart (1957) observes, 'working class life puts a premium on the taking of pleasures now, discourages planning for some future good'. This emphasis on the present and the lack of concern for 'planning ahead' are, moreover, encouraged by the view that there is in fact little to be done about the future, that it is not to any major extent under the individual's control. A certain amount of fatalism and acceptance, as well as an orientation to the present thus hold together as a mutually reinforcing set of attitudes.	(ii) The emphasis placed on 'getting on' implies on the part of the individual or family, a marked orientation towards the future. Major importance is attached to looking and planning ahead and, where necessary, to making present sacrifices in order to ensure greater advantages or benefits at a later stage. Such deferring of gratification, say, in the furtherance of a career or business undertaking — is approved of as a matter of morality as well as expediency.
(iii) In so far as it is felt that purposive action can be effective, the emphasis is placed on action of a *collective* kind aimed at the protection of collective interests — trade unionism being, of course, the most developed form. A prime value is that set on mutual aid and group solidarity in the face of the vicissitudes of life and the domination which 'they' seek to imposed. This value in turn confirms the shared, communal nature of social life and constitutes a further restraint on attempts by individuals to make themselves 'a cut above the rest'. Such attempts, in the form, say of conspicuous consumption or occupational advance, are likely to be interpreted by the community as threats to its solidarity, as expressions of group or class disloyalty. Even in the case of children, parental concern that they should 'do well' is confined to achievement within the context of working-class values and life-styles — as, for example, in becoming established in a 'trade' or a 'steady' job. Aspirations do not extend to levels of education nor types of job that would result in children being taken away from their family and community in either a geographical or a social sense.	(iii) The middle-class social ethic is thus an essentially *individualistic* one: the prime value is that set on individual achievement. Achievement is taken as the crucial indicator of the individual's moral worth. However, achievement is also regarded as a family concern: parents feel an obligation to try to give their children a 'better start in life' than they themselves enjoyed, and then anticipate that their offspring will in turn attain to a still higher level in the social scale. In other words, the expectation is that advancement will be continuous — between generations as well as in the course of individual lifetimes. Indeed, through parental aspirations for children, it is possible for desires and hopes for the future to become virtually limitless.

(Adapted from Goldthorpe *et al.*, 1969: 118–121)

each group was as 'well off' financially as the other. Attitudes to family planning and to the children's education also showed differences. The children of manual workers and their wives were likely to be born nearer to each other, and, although the manual workers and their wives had high hopes for their children's educational attainment, they had rarely taken any active steps (like going to talk to a teacher) to achieve them (Goldthorpe *et al.*, 1969: 121—155). Such findings are common in much other work. For example, we know that the completed size of working-class families tends to be larger than that of middle-class ones (for example, Douglas, 1964: 168) and Brown, Ní Bhrolcháin, and Harris 1975) found that 43 per cent of the women they studied in the lower occupational group had three children under eleven, compared to 14 per cent in the higher group. Ann Cartwright (1970: 194—5) found that working-class women were much more likely to report unintentional pregnancies (13 per cent for non-manual; 22 per cent skilled manual; 31 per cent semi-skilled manual; 37 per cent unskilled manual). Three fifths of all such contraceptive failures resulted from irregular or improper use (1970: 17) and the use of methods varied with social class. Withdrawal, for example, was practised by about three times as many manual couples as non-manual. In general, manual couples used the least effective measures (1970: 17). These findings support those of Rainwater in the USA, who argued that the lack of contraceptive use was not so much a product of ignorance or poor education, but of, among other things, a fatalistic present-orientated perspective (Rainwater, 1960: 167—8).

A lack of planning for the future on the part of manual workers is associated with a *collective* rather than an *individualistic* outlook on action. Manual workers in the Luton sample showed little desire to be promoted, and even where they did, the reasons given related to immediate financial objectives rather than the long-term advancement mentioned by white-collar respondents (Goldthorpe *et al.*, 1968: 125—7). The men in the Luton sample who anticipated a rising standard of living in the years immediately ahead (two-thirds of the total) did not see this as coming about from their own actions. Rather, they attached importance to the economic fortunes of the country as a whole or of their particular firm or industry (Goldthorpe *et al.*, 1969: 123). In this respect, as with many aspects of the working-class and middle-class perspectives, their beliefs and aspirations are strictly realistic. As we saw above, while middle-class individuals do have chances to be socially mobile, this is rarely possible for working-class individuals.

Communication Styles

Further differences between manual and non-manual workers may be found in the communication styles and the methods of bringing up children that are typical in the two sub-cultures:

> 'If a social group by virtue of its class relation, that is, as a result of its common occupational function and social status, has developed strong communal bonds; if the work relations of this group offers little variety or little exercise in decision-making; if assertion, if it is to be successful, must be a collective rather than an individual act; if the work task requires physical manipulation and control rather than symbolic organisation and control; if the diminished authority of the man at work is transformed into an authority of power at home; if the home is over-crowded and limits the variety of situations it can offer; if the children socialize each other in an environment offering little intellectual stimuli; if all these attribures are found in one setting, then it is plausible to assume that such a social setting will generate a particular form of communication which will shape the intellectual, social and affective orientation of the children.' (Bernstein, 1971: 143)

Bernstein has argued that particular features of the social context in which the middle- or working-class child grows up differ in an important way. For example, mothers in middle-class families tend to use toys in a certain way, and the way in which the child is disciplined or taught how to carry out basic social routines, such as using knives and forks, seems to vary. Middle-class parents tend to see the use of toys and play as part of a developmental sequence; working class parents tend to use toys only to keep a child busy. Similarly, whereas discipline and the exercise of authority in the working-class home tends to be concerned with sets of isolated incidents or transgressions and the need to correct them, the middle-class parent is at pains to build up a set of rules of behaviour for the child to operate within. Such differences, it is argued, lead to quite different styles and expectations with regard to communication and specifically with regard to the uses of language. Whereas most middle-class children become oriented towards receiving and offering universalistic (context-free) meanings in certain contexts, working-class children are oriented largely towards specific or particularistic meanings.

These differences in communciation and the use of language can lead to serious problems when a working-class individual, accustomed to the style of the working-class culture, comes into contact with the middle-class style that dominates social institutions such as schools and hospitals.

It is argued that a working-class communication code will tend to:

> 'emphasize verbally the communal rather than the individual, the concrete rather than the abstract, substance rather than the elaboration of processes, the here and now rather than exploration of motives and intentions, and positional rather than personalized forms of social control. ... [however] to say this about a communication system is not to devalue it, for such a communication system has a vast potential, a considerable metaphoric range and a unique aesthetic capacity. A whole

range of diverse meanings can be generated by such a system of communication. It happens, however, that this communication code directs the child to orders of learning and relevance that are not in harmony with those required by the school. Where the child is sensitive to the communication system of the school and thus to its orders of learning and relation, then the experience of school for this child is one of symbolic and social development; where the child is not sensitive to the communication system at school then this child's experience at school becomes one of symbolic and social change. In the first case we have an elaboration of social identity; in the second case, a change of social identity. Thus between the school and community of the working class child, there may exist a cultural discontinuity based upon two radically different systems of communication.' (Bernstein, 1971: 143)

The considerable variation in day-to-day experience, the fact that informal contact between manual and non-manual occupational groups is rare, and the variations in outlook and communication styles, mean that cross-class interaction in a number of settings is associated with difficulties. Strauss and Schatzman (1960) drew attention to this with regard to research interviewing with working-class respondents; Mayer and Timms (1969), in the study quoted earlier, have shown difficulties that arise in social work with working-class clients; and Overall and Aronson (1963) have indicated problems that arise in psychotherapy.

A recent study, which has been made into a film by the Open University, illustrates the difficulties very well. A television camera was placed high up in the roof of Paddington station and two actors impersonating middle- and working-class people were told to select individuals in the station at random and ask them the way to Hyde Park. A tiny microphone recorded the conversation. From the film it was quite clear that there were significant differences in the encounters depending on the class identity of the people involved and who was asking or answering the question. For example, shorter time for the interaction, a smaller amount of eye contact, and a considerable extent of anxiety and fidgeting were observed when actors dressed as individuals in middle-class occupations (suit, tie, and hat) confronted working-class rather than middle-class travellers. Middle-class travellers conducted the interaction much more formally — ending it with a clear signal after establishing that the information had been received and understood. Working-class travellers, on the other hand, conducted the interaction in a much more 'muddled' and informal way and rarely gave a clear end-signal or established that the 'lost' traveller had correctly understood directions. (Open University, 1971). Such differences in communication style can easily be mistakenly understood as 'rude' or 'offhand'.

Patterns of Leisure and Sociability

Reference has already been made (above p. 140) to the fact that the main characteristic of individuals' leisure time is that it takes place in the home. This 'privatization' of social life and relationships (we have already noted that visitors to the home are quite rare) was emphasized by Goldthorpe and his colleagues in their study in Luton. 'Privatization' not only involves a form of sociability where a high proportion of time is spent in the home but also an emphasis on social activities in the home at the expense of those outside — social contacts of all types being limited (Young and Willmott, incidentally, found women to have even fewer social contacts than men (1973: 229)).

Among individuals with manual occupations the emphasis on the home is particularly noticeable. Asked about social activities in the two days and the weekend prior to interview, manual workers and their wives replied that 62 per cent of activities took place in the home: doing chores and odd jobs, watching television, doing the shopping, making improvements to the house, and so on (Goldthorpe *et al.*, 1969: 102). Among the wives of manual workers, a home-based activity such as knitting while watching television was the typical spare-time activity.

Activities outside the home were rare in both manual and non-manual occupational groups. For example, during the two weekends before interview as many as 23 per cent of all couples had engaged in no activity in the company of people living outside the household (usually husband, wife, and any children), and 60 per cent mentioned no more than two people from outside the household with whom they share their spare time. Most couples found it hard to name even three friends with whom they 'most often spent spare time' (Goldthorpe *et al.*, 1969).

Young and Willmott (1973: 212–219) examined the way in which individuals used their leisure time. Watching television was by far the most frequent activity in all occupational groups and happened every day. Even in the spring and summer months (when the study took place) individuals watched for at least twelve hours a week, although the rate for professional and managerial occupations was somewhat lower. An interesting class difference that emerged was the finding that watching television was cited by one out of five unskilled manual workers as the leisure activity they 'most enjoyed'. The proportion saying this in other groups was negligible.

Young and Willmott (perhaps because their research approach focused only on the frequencies of activity) found few significant differences in the way individuals from different occupations use their leisure time in the home — watching television; playing with children; listening to taped, recorded, or broadcast music; home-decorating and repairs; car cleaning and car maintenance (all practised at least twelve times a year by more than 30 per cent of those interviewed). The two main differences that did emerge were in gardening (practised by 70 per cent of professional and managerial workers; 62 per cent of clerical workers; 66 per cent of skilled manual workers; and only 50 per cent of unskilled and semi-skilled workers) and in reading books (done by twice as many (65 per cent) of those in the non-manual categories compared with those in the manual categories). Where activity outside the home (also engaged in on twelve or more occasions in a year) was concerned the members of higher occupational groups (particularly professional and managerial workers) were much more likely to go out for dinner, go to the theatre, take evening classes, and visit museums and art galleries. Manual workers, on the other hand, were much more likely to play darts (25 per cent compared to 12 per cent) than non-manual workers. In general, manual workers were less likely to engage in activities outside the home. This probably reflects lack of desire, lack of resources, and the effects of hard physical work and long hours of overtime and shift work.

The pattern of sociability of the manual and non-manual workers studied by Goldthorpe and his colleagues had other features. In the first place, male manual respondents were more likely than male non-manual respondents to report 'neighbours' (individuals living within a ten minute walk) as people with whom 'they most often spent spare time' (this was in fact reported by one fifth of the male manula respondents but by almost no non-manual respondent). For the wives of the workers studied the same difference existed but was not so great. It appears that whereas manual workers spend more time with neighbours, non-manual workers spend more of their time with 'friends' or couples who are neither kin, neighbours, or workmates (42 per cent of the non-manual workers most often spent spare time with such individuals compared to 21 per cent of manual workers). Similar large differences were reported in the choice of spare-time companions by wives, and by husband and wife together). In both groups kin played an important role, accounting for between a quarter and a third of spare-time companions with a slightly higher tendency among the wives (Goldthorpe *et al.*, 1969: 88).

A second difference emerged by analysing the frequency and character of patterns of entertainment in the home — although, again still greater differences might have emerged if more attention had been given to the quality of such interaction. In the first place, entertaining at home was more common among the non-manual couples, who could name on average 3.4 couples they regularly entertained compared to the 2.36 named by manual couples. It was also more frequent for manual couples to entertain kin, although kin were most frequently entertained by both groups. In fact, 42 per cent of the manual couples (compared to 24 per cent of the non-manual couples) reported entertaining at home *only* couples who were kin and another 33 per cent mentioned no more than one couple apart from kin whom they would entertain in this way. Entertaining at home was not at all frequent among manual respondents: only 17 per cent of the manual respondents compared with 31 per cent of the non-manual reported that they entertained at home at least once a month on average *and* mentioned two or more couples who were so entertained and who were not kin (1969: 92).

These findings on entertainment and on the most frequent spare-time companions, combined with the fact that manual workers and their wives are much less likely to join formal associations, suggests that the manual workers studied by Goldthorpe and his colleagues are similar to those described by other workers in more traditionally working-class settings, such as the East End of London (for example, Young and Willmott, 1957). As Goldthorpe and his colleagues put it:

'... the couples who figured in our critical case, despite their affluence and the characteristics of their community setting, remain in fact largely restricted to working-class styles of sociability, and in the form-ation of their friendship relations are for the most part neither guided by middle-class norms nor aided by middle-class social skills. To the extent that kinship could not provide the foundation of their social life, these couples turned most readily for support and companionship to those persons who, as it were, formed the next circle of immediate acquaintance — that is, to persons living in the same neighbourhood. Thus, in much the same way as working-class people in more traditional contexts, they would appear to build up their friendship relations largely on the basis of social contacts that are in the first instance 'given'. Actually *making* friends — through personal choice and initiative — from among persons with whom no structured relationships already exist could not be regarded as at all a typical feature of their way of life.' (Goldthorpe *et al.*, 1969: 91)

Until quite recently, because most families lived in overcrowded circum-stances, working-class social life was stongly influenced by the need to create physical and psychological space. Consequently, inviting anyone other than kin to the home was rare, and this kind of entertaining was reserved only for very special circumstances. Sociability, or the act of being friendly, took place outside the home in such places as the shops, pubs and working-men's clubs. As one respondent in an earlier study (Young and Willmott, 1957: 85) put it:

'I've got plenty of friends around here. I've always got on well with people, but I don't invite anyone here. I've got friends at work and friends at sport and friends I have a drink with. I know all the people around here, and I'm not invited into anyone else's home either. It doesn't seem right somehow. Your home's your own.'

There is an interesting difference between the nature of working-class and middle-class friendship patterns which is illustrated by the quotation above. In the first place, working-class friendships tend to be specific rather than to be generalized across situations. Thus there are friends at work, in the street, or in the pub, but these do not tend to be the same people (Weiss, 1969). 'Friendship' as such seems to be a different kind of concept from that experienced by middle-class individuals.

Conclusion

I have suggested that social class exerts an important influence on people's everyday lives and have tried to describe some of the differences in outlook and experience that exist, particularly between manual and non-manual workers. Social class is important, in an 'objective' way in differentiating individuals in terms of their material well-being, i.e. the sort of job they get, the income they derive from it, the sort of housing conditions in which they live, the opportunities they have for promotion, and the opportunities that their children have for getting a job at a different occupational level. It is also important as a means of differentiating life-styles and ideas about the work, and I have described some studies that indicate substantial differences here, between manual and non-manual groups of workers. Finally social class is important in relational terms and an understanding of it in this way can help to isolate the potential difficulties that can occur when individuals from different class backgrounds meet.

In relation to health and medicine, social class is important in each of these three ways. In the first place, such objective features of everyday experience as the quality of job, condition of housing, and opportunities for promotion can have an important influence on the causes of illness and the chances of recovering from it. Further research supporting such associations is reviewed in Chapter Nine. As we have seen, access to higher-ranked occupations is not equal, and it may therefore be concluded that the system of social stratification in our society not only provides unequal chances for obtaining the material benefits of existence but also significantly affects who shall survive how long and who shall get a number of diseases.

Second, features of the life-style of individuals within different social classes can be important in many ways. Once again they can influence an individual's susceptibility to disease. For example, the fact that manual workers and their wives are less likely to plan their families by spacing births (see above p. 145) and the fact that the early years of their marital relationship are unlikely to be of the kind where the partners feel they can confide in each other about *any* kind of problem means that they are more vulnerable to depression following a life-crisis (below pp. 322–3). Similarly, the fact that the perspectives of working-class people do not emphasize *individual* action to secure future ends, offers one reason for working-class parents being less likely to visit welfare clinics with their children (Douglas and Blomfield, 1958) or to take preventive action in relation to pre-natal (Donnebedian, 1961; McKinlay, 1973) or dental care (Kegeles, 1963).

Finally, features of the social class from which individuals are drawn influence their communication style and hence their ability to relate to those from a different class. Basil Bernstein's (1971) work in relation to the school, Mayer and Timms (1969) work in relation to social work, and Overall and Aronson's (1963) work in relation to psychotherapy have been reviewed to suggest some of the difficulties that can occur. These kinds of difficulties may account for such findings as the fact that mentally subnormal children from higher social classes are more likely than children from lower social classes to receive the 'appropriate' education in a special school (Stein and Susser, 1960). The same types of dangers certainly exist in medicine, since (while doctors continue to come from predominantly non-manual backgrounds) the majority of consultations are between doctors from a middle-class background and patients from the working class. Knowledge of the set of values and meanings inherent in different occupational groups and the ability to recognize that these are *different* and a response to a different kind of situation, rather than odd or inferior, is likely to be important for those trying to provide any service.

Notes

1. 'Lower' refers to semi- and unskilled manual workers. The justification for regarding these as 'lower' is given below (p. 129).
2. The precise meaning of 'skilled' is sociologically complex. In this context it is intended to imply degrees of training, experience, and responsibility. Thus highly-skilled jobs might require an apprenticeship of at least a year, skilled jobs might require a month or so of training, and semi-skilled jobs a few days. Many other definitions are also used.
3. A list of occupations and their distribution in the population appears in *Table 5*.
4. Young and Willmott (1973: 331–92), for example tried to measure changes in the quality of marital relationships by asking 'Does your husband help at least once a week with any household jobs like washing up, making beds, helping with the children, ironing, cooking or cleaning?'. On this basis, any husband who had *ever* helped with housework or childcare may be rated as 'sharing'. This misleading inference has been demonstrated by Oakley who, with a flexible and much more precise interviewing technique (that established who did what in a detailed way) showed that husbands' participation in housework was still very low. Only 20% of middle class husbands and 10% of working-class husbands participated in housework in any equal manner. Although the proportions for childcare were somewhat higher, the idea that marriages are 'joint', 'equal', or 'symmetrical' is obviously false (Oakley, 1974: 137). By failing to cross-question their respondents and really establish what went on, Young and Willmott drew quite incorrect inferences.

References

Antonovsky, A. (1967) Social Class, Life Expectancy and Overall Mortality. *Millbank Memorial Fund Quarterly* **XLV**: 31–73.

Acton Society Trust. (1957) *Size and Morale Part II. A Preliminary Further Study of Attendance in Large and Small Establishments.* London: Acton Society Trust.

Alderson, M.R. (1970) Social Class and the Health Service. *The Medical Officer* 124: 50–52.

Bernstein, B. (1971) A Socio-Linguistic Approach to Socialisation with Some Reference to Educability. In B. Bernstein (ed.), *Class, Codes and Control* Vol. 1. London: Routledge & Kegan Paul.

— (ed.) (1973) *Class, Codes and Control. Vol. II.* London: Routledge & Kegan Paul.
These are two volumes of papers describing the work of Bernstein and his group at the Institute of Education.

Blauner, R. (1964) *Alienation and Freedom: The Factory Workers and His Industry.* Chicago: Chicago University Press.
Demonstrates the effect on work experience of different kinds of technology.

Bott, E. (1971) *Family and Social Network* (second edition). London: Tavistock.
A classic description of family differences among manual and non-manual workers.

Brown, G.W., Ní Bhrolcháin, M., and Harris, T. (1975) Social Class and Psychiatric Disorder among Women in an Urban Population. *Sociology* 9 (2): 225–55
See Chapter 10.

Cartwright, A. (1970) *Parents and Family Planning Services.* London: Routledge & Kegan Paul.

— (1975) Social Class Variations in Health Care and in the Nature of General Practitioner Consultations. London: Institute for Social Studies in Health Care (mimeo).

Central Advisory Council (for Education) (1959) *The Crowther Report.* London: HMSO.

Central Statistical Office (1972) *Social Trends.* London: HMSO.
An excellent source for social statistics which is published annually at the end of each year.

Dahrendorf, R. (1959) *Class and Class Conflict in Industrial Society.* London: Routledge & Kegan Paul.
An elegant analysis of the utility of Marx's and Weber's approach to stratification.

Donnabedian, A. (1961) Some Factors Influencing Pre-Natal Care. *New England Journal of Medicine* 265: 1–6.

Douglas, J. (1964) *The Home and The School.* London: McGibbon & Kee.
A study of a large sample of children born in March 1946 and their subsequent development. This report (one of a series) describes the experience of the children at the time when they were allocated to the various types of secondary schools. The study looks at the effect of family background, social situation and IQ on their achievement and selection.

Douglas, J. and Blomfeld, J. (1958) *Children Under Five.* London: McGibbon & Kee.
An earlier report in the same series as the 'The Home and the School.'

Frankenberg, R. (1966) *Communities in Britain.* Harmondsworth: Pelican Books.

Glass, D. (ed.) (1954) *Social Mobility in Britain.* London: Routledge & Kegan Paul.
See text pages 134–6.

Goldthorpe, J. (1973) Paper presented to the British Sociological Association at Guildford.

Goldthorpe, J., Lockwood, D., Bechoffer, F., and Platt, J. (1968) *The Affluent Worker: Industrial Attitudes and Behaviour.* Cambridge: Cambridge University Press.

— (1969) *The Affluent Worker in the Class Structure.* Cambridge: Cambridge University Press.
Two parts of the report of a study of well-paid manual workers in Luton, completed in the early sixties. The study demonstrated major differences between

manual and non-manual workers — in work experience, in economic position, in attitudes and behaviour, and in the relationships they had with each other. The study therefore refuted any simplistic claim that 'rising affluence' was leading to the erosion of the working class and their assimilation into the middle class.

Goldthorpe, J. and Hope, K. (1972) Occupational Grading and Occupational Prestige In K. Hope (ed.), *The Study of Social Mobility: Methods and Approaches.* London: Oxford University Press.

Explains the Oxford study of occupational ranking and therefore the underlying basis for table four.

— (1974) *The Social Grading of Occupations.* London: Oxford University Press.

Harris, A. and Clausen, R. (1966) *Labour Mobility in Britain: 1953—63* (An enquiry undertaken for the Ministry of Labour and National Service in 1963). London: HMSO.

See text pages 133—4.

Heasman, M.A. (1961) Mass Minature Radiography. *General Register Office Studies on Medical and Population Subjects,* No. 17. London: HMSO.

H.M. Government (1973) *New Earnings Survey.* London: HMSO.

Hoggart, R. (1957) *The Uses of Literacy.* Harmondsworth: Penguin.

An insightful description of working-class life by someone who was brought up in working-class conditions to become Professor of English Literature at Birmingham and then a Director of UNESCO.

Hunt, A. (1968) *A Survey of Women's Employment.* Social Survey Report (2 vols.). London: HMSO.

Kegeles, S. (1963) Why People Seek Dental Care: A Test of a Conceptual Formulation. *Journal of Health and Social Behaviour* 41: 166—173.

Klein, J. (1965) *Samples from English Cultures* (2 vols.). London: Routledge & Kegan Paul.

A well documented account of the day-to-day experience of people in British society using information gathered in a range of other studies. The chapter on the new working class is, however, superceded by the Luton studies which suggest that the drift of Klein's argument is fallacious (cf. Goldthorpe *et al.,* 1968, 1969).

Komarovsky, M. (1962) *Blue Collar Marriage.* New York: Random House.

A superb account of working-class life in America which is interesting to read and methodologically convincing.

Lockwood, D. (1958) *The Blackcoated Worker.* London: Routledge & Kegan Paul.

An example of what can be done using secondary data. This is one of the best accounts of the situation of routine non-manual workers.

Lord, W. (1955) *A Night to Remember.* New York: Henry Holt.

McKinlay, J. (1973) Social Networks, Lay Consultation and Help-Seeking Behaviour. *Social Forces* 51: 275—92.

MacGregor, J.E., Fraser, M.E., and Mann, E.M.F. (1966) The Cytopipette in the Diagnosis of Early Cervical Carcianoma. *The Lancet* i: 252.

Marr, J.W., Hope, E.B., Stevenson, J.D., and Thomson, A.H. (1955) Consumption of Milk and Vitamin Concentrates by Pregnant Women in Aberdeen. *Proceedings of the Nutritional Society* 14: 7.

Marx, K. (trans. 1963) *Early Writings.* Translated by T.B. Bottomore. London: Watts & Co.

Mayer, J. and Timms, N. (1969) Clash in Perspective between Worker and Client. *Social Casework,* January: 32—40.

Morris, J. (1967) *The Uses of Epidemiology* (revised edition). London and Edinburgh: E. & S. Livingstone Ltd.

Oakley, A. (1974) *The Sociology of Housework.* London: Martin Robertson.

Nandy, L. and Nandy, D. (1975) Towards True Equality for Women. *New Society* **31**: 246–49.

Open University (1971) Psychological Views of Social Class (film).

Office of Population Censuses and Surveys (and General Register Office, Edinburgh) (1973) *Census for 1971. Great Britain.* Summary Tables based on 1 per cent Sample. London: HMSO.

Osborn, G.R. and Leyshon, V.N. (1966) Domicillory Testing of Cervical Smears by Home Nurses. *The Lancet* **i**: 256.

Overall, B. and Aronson, M. (1963) Expectations of Psychotherapy in Patients of Lower Socio-economic Class. *American Journal of Ortho-Psychiatry* **43**: 41.

Rainwater, L. (1960) *And the Poor get Children.* Chicago: Quadrangle Paperbacks.
An extremely readable account of the attitudes of American working-class families to sex and contraception.

Registrar General (1969) *Decennial Supplement, 1961: Occupational Mortality Tables, England and Wales.* London: HMSO.

Rein, M. (1969) Social Class and the Health Service. *New Society,* November 20.

Royal Commission on Medical Education (1968) *Report.* London: HMSO.

Stein, Z. and Susser, M. (1960) Families of Dull Children. Parts II, III and IV. *Journal of Mental Science* **106**: 1296–1319.

Strauss, A. and Schatzman, L. (1960) Cross-Class Interviewing. In R. Adams and J. Presiss (eds.), *Human Organisation Research.* Homewood, Illinois: Dorsey Press.

Titmuss, R. (1962) *Income Distribution and Social Change: A Study in Criticism.* London: George Allen and Unwin.

 (1968) *Commitment to Welfare.* London: George Allen and Unwin.

Tudor Hart, J. (1971) The Inverse Care Law. *The Lancet* **i**: 405–12.

Weber, M. (trans. 1947) *The Theory of Social and Economic Organisation.* Translated by A. Henderson and T. Parsons and then revised by Parsons. New York: Free Press.

Wedderburn, D. (1970) Workplace Inequality. *New Society* **15**: 593–5.

Weiss, R. (1969) The Fund of Sociability. *Transactions* **9**: 36–43.

Willmott, P. (1963) *The Evolution of a Community.* London: Routledge & Kegan Paul.
An account of life in Dagenham – thirty years after its completion.

Willmott, P. and Young, M. (1962) *Family and Class in a London Suburb.* London: Routledge & Kegan Paul.
An account of life in Woodford Essex.

Woodward, J. (1958) *Management and Technology.* Department of Scientific and Industrial Research, Problems of Progress in Industry No. 3. London: HMSO.

Young, M. and Willmott, P. (1957) *Family and Kinship in East London.* London: Routledge & Kegan Paul.
An account of life in Bethnal Green and Greenleigh – a housing estate to which East End working-class families were being moved.

 (1973) *The Symmetrical Family.* London: Routledge & Kegan Paul.
A study of work and leisure in the Greater London Area – ten years after the first Institute of Community Studies survey (Young and Willmott, 1957).

Part III

Areas of Medical Sociology

Chapter 5

David Tuckett

Becoming a Patient

In the first chapter I drew attention to the fact that general practitioners regard a great deal of their work as 'trivial', 'unnecessary', and 'inappropriate' – the usual estimates varying from half of their work upwards (Cartwright, 1967: 44). The same phenomenon, although less well-documented, exists in the hospital outpatient clinic where many consultants feel they are wasting their time having to deal with cases the general practitioner should never have referred. At the same time evidence is accumulating from a number of sources that many patients with severe medical difficulties do not consult the doctor at all (below pp. 163–4). In this chapter, therefore, I will review the available evidence concerning these issues and consider the factors involved in 'becoming a patient'. A review of this evidence, although not answering the question as to when and under what conditions individuals consult a doctor, does, I think, have important implications for the practice of medicine.

The Problem of 'Illness'

Morris (1967:82) has argued that 'Needs have to be felt as such, perceived, then expressed in demand'. But what are the medical needs of the population? How many people suffer from disease? Do they take their complaints to the doctor?

The assessment of morbidity in a population poses complex theoretical and methodological problems, which sociologists and doctors are quite a long way from answering. Is someone 'diseased' if they have the clinical signs and symptoms of disease but do not themselves (at least as yet) feel they are 'ill'? [1] Is someone who feels 'ill' diseased? Is a disease 'serious' because, as medically understood, the prognosis involves severe disability or death, or is it serious because the individual suffering (or his friends and relatives) feels it to be serious? Is 'trivia' a set of conditions defined as such by patients or by doctors? Consider those diseases that doctors are unable to treat. Should people seek help from them? Should the individual with cancer symptoms, which do not yet inconvenience him, be placed 'in treatment' even if there is little or no likelihood of its 'success'? Just what *should* patients come to doctors for, and when?

The answers to these questions are complicated by the fact that individuals can experience enormous suffering from a condition which medically does not exist (in the sense that no pathological abnormality can be found). Similarly, individuals who have never experienced any 'illness' have been found, post mortem, to have had serious problems, such as advanced malignant neoplasms or circulatory abnormalities, although these were not the cause of death. The picture is also complicated by the particular characteristics of the diseases that now constitute the bulk of the doctor's work. In the typical infectious diseases, which formerly accounted for so much medical work, the sufferer passes in a very short space of time from a state of being healthy to feeling unwell, and he recognizes that he is 'ill' soon after the disease process begins. Rapidly it becomes clear to him that he really is 'ill'. The typical course of those diseases that are now most frequently brought for medical attention is altogether different. The time scale is increased. 'Deviations from a normal state of health are small, and may appear quite trivial. For example, an outcrop of boils, an unexpected bout of indigestion, or transient giddiness may be tolerated for years' (Wadsworth *et al.*, 1971: 86). For some people such incidents may be considered sufficiently disruptive for them to get worried, for others they may not. The symptoms may be tolerated for a long time because the individual accommodates gradually to each deterioration – this accommodation is aided by self-medication, 'taking it easy', and by the individual otherwise altering his pattern of life. Often symptoms (like an upset stomach) may gradually disappear. At other times they may be a sign of something rather serious. From a lay point of view, many of the symptoms of 'chronic' and 'degenerative' disease – headaches, stomach aches, chest pains – are difficult to distinguish from self-limiting 'minor' illness. Wadsworth and his colleagues suggest that the same problem can exist for doctors 'who sometimes find that only when looking back after a diagnosis has been made does the meaning of a pattern of different symptoms presented over a period of time become explicable' (Wadsworth *et al.*, 1971: 87). The fact that the early diagnosis of many conditions which have a gradual onset is advantageous further complicates the situation.

Many surveys have now estimated the extent of illness and disease in the population. The methods employed have varied from clinical examination and laboratory testing to questionnaires, interviews, and the collection of information on medical care utilization (visits to various medical services or sickness absence certificates) to name but a few. The results of all the surveys are confused by the difficulty of defining 'illness' and 'disease' mentioned above. All have weaknesses. Sickness absence rates and visits to medical services, for example, reflect the factors that determine whether people seek help as well as their experience of 'illness' and 'disease'. Not all who feel unwell stay away from work or bother to get a certificate from their doctor. Similarly, questionnaires may measure 'illness' and 'disease' by asking about interference with routine activities but in this case there is again confusion over whether we are measuring 'illness' or 'disease' — many individuals seem to carry on just the same despite 'feeling' really quite 'ill'. One American woman put this particular problem very succinctly:

> 'I wish I knew what you mean by being sick. Sometimes I felt so bad I could curl up and die, but I had to go on because of the kids who have to be taken care of, and besides, we didn't have the money to spend for the doctor. How could I be sick? Some people can be sick anytime with anything, but most of us can't be sick, even when we need to be.' (Koos, 1954: 30)

This articulate woman makes the point that 'illness' and 'disease' are defined according to a set of values and norms — the point at which an individual ceases to fulfil obligations, feels his life is not satisfactory, feels he cannot do what he wants, depends in part on the situation he is in and the norms and values that are attached to different behaviours. The quotation also suggests another point, there seem to be two stages involved in seeking medical care: recognizing that one is 'ill', and then deciding to do something about it. These issues will be returned to.

The Extent of 'Illness' and 'Disease'

As the results of several epidemiological enquiries, using many different methods and many different definitions, we have become aware (surprising as this may seem to the already overworked general practitioner or consultant) that the medical services deal with a rather small proportion of the symptoms of disease experienced by members of the community. Stocks (1949) reporting the Survey of Sickness undertaken by the Government found that only 25 per cent of all people recording an illness or injury during a month had consulted a doctor during that time. Horder and Horder (1954) studying their own general practice discovered that 'under one third of the units of illness ever reach any medical agency'. Brotherston's (1958) analysis of sickness on a new housing estate revealed a long list of complaints for which a doctor was consulted in less than half the instances. Furthermore, these findings have been confirmed by more recent enquiries (Dunnell and Cartwright, 1972: 10–12; Epson, 1969; Wadsworth *et al.*, 1971; Brown, Ní Bhrolcháin, and Harris, 1975).

Figure 1 illustrates the results of a recent epidemiological survey carried out on the health of a London borough population (Wadsworth *et al.*, 1971: 32–42). The results of the study, which are in broad agreement with the other studies mentioned above, suggest that in a community of a thousand members over the age of sixteen, the vast majority (750–900) of them would have, in any given two weeks, at least one painful and distressing symptom. However, of these 750–900 people, only about 200, or less than

Figure 1   *The 14 day incidence of symptoms and subsequent illness behaviour for 1000 randomly*
selected persons in two London boroughs

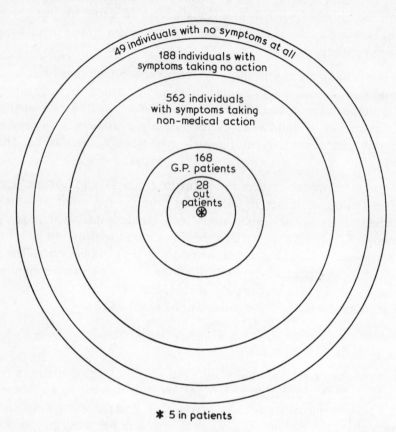

✻ 5 in patients

Source: Wadsworth, Butterfield, and Blaney (1971: 32–42)

one third, would have visited any type of doctor during the same period, about twenty-eight of them would have attended as an out-patient in a hospital, and only five would have been an in-patient.

The knowledge that the medical services deal with such a small amount of symptoms of disease in the community prompts a very interesting question. Why do some of those with distressing symptoms seek care from doctors while others with similar symptoms do not?

It might be supposed that there is one reasonably obvious answer to the question: it is those in the community with mild symptoms who have not visited their doctor, while those with the more severe symptoms are likely to be in hospitals as in- or out-patients.

The surveys conducted suggest a much more complicated picture than that compatible with this answer. Many people who do not seek medical care are nonetheless seriously ill. At the same time many of those who do consult a doctor do not have symptoms which medicine can alleviate or cure – let alone severe ones.

The medical officer of the London Borough of Southwark carried out a screening survey of 1000 randomly selected individuals who lived in the borough. A battery of tests were administered in a specially converted caravan which was taken to various parts of the borough during the four months of the study. The survey consisted of collecting the following information and carrying out various tests: a social history, a medical history, a haemoglobin estimation, blood pressure test, urine test, measurement of height and weight, vision test, cervical smear offered to women over twenty-five years, a general physical examination by a doctor, and a chest X-ray. All individuals selected in the sample were visited, although not all finally attended – the study population was underrepresented, (compared to the census data for the borough) for males and for individuals in the lower social classes. This shortcoming could be expected to have provided an underestimate of the disease found. In any case the study revealed many diseases that had previously been untreated. Altogether 52 percent of persons screened were regarded, by the doctors concerned, as needing further investigation and possibly treatment (which they were not already having (Epson, 1969)).

The Southwark findings, far from being remarkable, confirm earlier studies in Peckham, Kent (Pearse and Crocker, 1944) and in the USA (Commission on Chronic Illness, 1957) where it was found that, roughly, for every person in care with any given condition, there was at least one, and in many cases several, other persons outside care, with a symptom that was regarded as equally serious by the doctors who completed the study.

Studies of specially selected populations confirm this picture. Two hundred individuals aged sixty-five and over were studied by Williamson and his colleagues (1964) in Edinburgh. Investigators found, on clinical examination and after tests, that a high proportion of medical difficulties of a serious kind were not known to general practitioners working in the area. For example, of the four individuals who were bedridden one was unknown to the doctor (1964: 1119); three out of seventeen severe visual defects were unknown (1120); ten out of forty with chronic bronchitis were unknown (1120); thirteen out of thrity seven individuals with heart disease were unknown – including a man of seventy-three with atrial fibulation, hypertension, and congestive failure who was actualling attending a hospital for physiotherapy for quite another condition (1120); sixteen out of forty cases with alimentary system disability were unknown – including a seventy year old man living along and in very poor health due to hepatic cirrhosis. This man had severe generalized œdema but had not consulted his doctor although he was feeling quite miserable (1120). There were many more findings reported in this and other similar studies. In short, whether we consider minor medical problems (for example, feet problems: Clarke, 1969); potentially serious ones (for example, streptococcal pharyngitis: Goslings *et al.*, 1963; Valkenberg *et al.*, 1963); or major ones (for example, diabetes: Butterfield, 1968) and whether studies are done in a 'free' service, such as that in Britain, or in a 'fee-for-service' system, as in the USA, there are always a very large number of individuals with serious medical problems who have not sought help with them. Many of the individuals are quite aware of their disability and their lives are not infrequently totally disrupted by it.

Of course one reason why the extent of disease and illness in the community is similar to that in medical care, is that, as several studies have demonstrated, many patients remain in hospital when they no longer need nursing and medical attention (Jenkinson and Pearson, 1967), and some are there because there is no other satisfactory place for them to go (Lowe and McKeowen, 1960); others because consultants pursue policies of discharge that are unnecessarily conservative (Pearson *et al.*, 1968). Furthermore, as I have already stated, in general practice many patients have what their doctors consider to be relatively trivial complaints, and these are hard to distinguish from those possessed by the rest of the population who do not consult doctors.

Having symptoms and the extent of their seriousness, therefore, although a common reason, is by no means a sufficient one to explain why and how somebody becomes a patient and where he will receive treatment.

Tolerance, Definition, and Alternative Action

One reason why some people in the community can have quite severe symptoms and still not consult a doctor is that those people can tolerate considerable pain and the disruption that pain can cause in their lives. Similarly, some families are able to tolerate considerable disruption caused by a seriously ill member. As I have suggested earlier, this tolerance is made easier by the fact that many conditions have a gradual onset and are therefore easier to adapt to than those with a dramatic onset.

For symptoms, which are recognized by the medical profession as signs of disease, to be taken to the doctor they must first be perceived as a problem, then defined as something to be taken to the doctor, and then actually taken there. This process of *recognition*, *definition*, and *action* can, of course, be influenced in a powerful way by members of the individual's family or others in a position close to him. Symptoms can be other, as well as, self defined. Looking at the large number of symptoms experienced by people who are not in care, it seems that the majority of individuals do not necessarily define as problems symptoms that most doctors would identify as pathological. At least, this was the finding of Suchman and Phillips (1958) in New York when they compared the symptoms listed by a random sample of the population, in response to a health questionnaire, with the judgements made by doctors of the seriousness of the symptoms listed. One out of five respondents reported themselves in 'unfavourable' health despite the doctor's 'favourable' report, while as many as two out of three who were rated as 'unfavourable' by the doctors gave themselves 'favourable' health.

There can also be a wide discrepancy between the views of families and doctors concerning the presence or absence of mental disorder within a particular family member. This was suggested in a study of discharged schizophrenic patients in three areas of England where it was shown how relatives were less likely than psychiatrists to define a person's behaviour as problematical (Brown *et al.*, 1966: 208–10).

Another factor is that pain is itself a complex phenomenon and that there is no simple relationship between the objective severity of a symptom or injury and the individual's subjective experience of pain and discomfort. Observers, such as the American anaesthetist Beecher (1959, 1965), for example, have noted that quite discrepant amounts of morphine were required to relieve pain in people with apparently similar injuries. Beecher's early recognition of this arose during the Second World War when he was a doctor with the American forces landing on the Anzio beach-head. At that time he noticed the great difference in the complaints made by the battle casualties he was looking after and those he was accustomed to hearing from patients with similar injuries but resulting from abdominal surgery, in the USA.

Beecher argued cogently that the common belief that wounds are inevitably associated with pain, that the more extensive the wound, the worse the pain, was not supported by observations made 'as carefully as possible' in the battle zone.

'The data state in numerical terms what is known to all thoughtful, clinical, observers: there is no simple direct relationship between the wound 'per se' and the pain experience.
The pain is in a very large part determined by other factors, and of great importance here is the significance of the wound. .. In the wounded soldier [the response to injury] was relief, thankfulness at his escape alive from the battlefield; to the civilian, his major surgery was a depressing, calamitous event.' (Beecher, 1959: 165)

But individuals may also be found outside care either because they do not see their difficulties as suitable for medical attention, or because even when they do, they do not actually visit the doctor. For example, they might take patent medicines or, like the Africans in Lusaka, Zambia studied by Frankenberg (1969) who decided that certain symptoms were not suitable for treatment by Western medicine and were better dealt with by the traditional *Nganga* (witchdoctor), consult an alternative source of help. In Western societies *Nganga's* can be found in the shape of herbalists, christian scientists, scientologists, chiropodists, radionics practitioners, clergymen, masseurs, osteopaths, or other such sources of specialist advice. Many individuals also consult friends, relatives, and others in a lay-referral system where a doctor is only one of many potential specialists (Freidson, 1961). Other individuals, even when they do feel their problem ought to be taken to a doctor do not necesarily do so. They may, for example, be frightened what the doctor will say (Blackwell, 1963), feel that there is little that can be done (Cartwright, Hockey, Anderson, 1973: 87), or simply be too busy (Koos, 1954: 30; Zola 1973: 677).

A Conceptual Scheme

In an elegant and extensive review of the available literature Kasl and Cobb (1966) have developed a conceptual scheme to try to understand under what conditions individuals will, and will not, take their symptoms to the doctor. The scheme attempts to combine a good number of the earlier research findings in the area and contains over two hundred references.

Figure 2   *The postulated relationship between symptoms and illness behaviour*

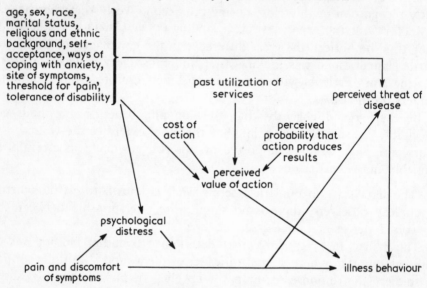

Source: Kasl and Cobb (1966: 252, 258)

The scheme, which is presented schematically in *Figure 2*, focuses on the circumstances that will lead an individual to perceive a symptom as a threat and those that will lead him to value a visit to the doctor as a way of reducing that threat. The idea is that if the individual sees the symptom as a threat and perceives a visit to the doctor as likely to reduce it he will seek medical aid. In other words the individual must first become aware of a symptom as a problem and must then also choose a visit to the doctor as the appropriate action. A whole range of factors influence the way in which he defines the value of visiting the doctor.

Social and cultural factors influence both the definition of a symptom as a threat and the value attached to a particular action. Age groups, sex groups, marital status, racial groups, religious groups, and ethnic groups can all influence the perception of symptoms as a problem.

The early studies of illness behaviour (activities undertaken by a person who has symptoms in order to define the state of his health and discover a suitable remedy) which have been extensively reviewed by Mechanic (1968: 117–128) as well as by Kasl and Cobb (1966), were able to identify particular groups of individuals who were under-utilizers of medical services and who were found to be more likely to tolerate the symptoms of disease, have definitions of symptoms that were different from those of the medical profession, be likely to consult their friends and relations or practitioners of fringe medicine, be frightened about going to the doctor, feel that little could be done about their condition, or be too busy to make a consultation. Investigators found that these 'intervening' variables, which mediated between the presence of symptoms and consulting a doctor about them, were often patterned according to social and cultural groups (for example, Koos, 1954). For example, the ability to tolerate pain, which Beecher suggested could vary according to the 'significance' of the wound, has been found to vary across cultures and ethnic groups. Melzack (1973: 22–24) quotes the example of differences in childbirth experience between Western culture and South American culture:

'In Western culture, for example, childbirth is considered by many to be one of the worst pains a human being can undergo. Yet anthropologists (Kroeber, 1948) have observed cultures throughout the world which practise *couvade*, in which the women show virtually no distress during childbirth. In some of these cultures a women who is going to give birth continues to work in the fields until the child is just about to be born. Her husband then gets into bed and groans as though he were in great pain while she bears the child. In more extreme cases, the husband stays in bed with the baby to recover from the terrible ordeal, and the mother almost immediately returns to attend to the crops.
Can this mean that all women in our culture are making up their pain? Not at all. It happens to be part of our culture to recognise childbirth as possibly endangering the life of the mother, and young girls learn to fear it in the course of growing up.'

The same author provides another example:

'One of the most striking examples of the impact of cultural values on pain is the hook-hanging ritual still in practice in parts of India (Kosambi, 1967). The ceremony derives from an ancient practice in which a member of a social group is chosen to represent the power of the gods. The role of the chosen man (or "celebrant") is to bless the children and crops in a series of neighboring villages during a particular period of the year. What is remarkable about the ritual is that steel hooks, which are attached by strong ropes to the top of a special cart, are shoved under the skin and muscles on both sides of the back. The cart is then moved from village to village. Usually the man hangs onto the ropes as the cart is moved about. But at the climax of the ceremony in each village, he swings free, hanging only from the hooks embedded in his back, to bless the children and crops. Astonishingly, there is no evidence that the man is in pain during the ritual; rather, he appears to be in a "state of exaltation". When the hooks are later removed, the wounds heal rapidly without any medical treatment other than the application of wood ash. Two weeks later the marks on his back are scarcely visible.'

In another study Zborwski (1952) suggests that the ethnic origin of an individual influences his perception and interpretation of symptoms. Americans of Italian origin were found to be concerned mainly with the immediate pain experience, while Jewish Americans focused upon the symptomatic meaning of pain and its significance for their health and welfare. 'Old-stock' Americans also showed future-orientated anxiety about pain, but were much more optimistic about its outcome than Jews.

The distinction between ethnic groups in America in the significance they attached to painful or distressing symptoms was confirmed by Zola (1966) who found that Italian, Irish, and Anglo-Saxon Americans differed in the type of symptoms they needed to have in order to seek medical aid. The Italian Americans would be most concerned about symptoms that interfered with social and personal relations (such as their relationship to boy friends or girl friends). Irish Americans needed someone else to approve their action and Americans of Anglo-Saxon origin saw a doctor when the symptom was considered to be interfering with their work or physical activity.

These differences have been confirmed in other studies. Saunders (1954) described in some detail the difference in attitudes and responses to symptoms that he found among 'Anglos' and Spanish-speaking persons in the American south-west. Whereas the 'Anglos' preferred modern medical science and hospitalization for many symptoms the Spanish speaking people were more likely to rely on folk medicine and family care and support. As a result, Spanish speaking people, Saunders argued, had lower rates of medical care utilization than did the 'Anglos'.

Again, in their study of schizophrenia in the families of Puerto Ricans, Rogler and Hollingshead (1965: 314–331) found that a comparatively large proportion of married male schizophrenics could be tolerated in families without causing disruption. They interpreted this finding by asserting that the various symptoms of withdrawal associated with schizophrenia and exhibited by the husbands were actually valued by the wives because it improved a wife's otherwise subordinate position in the household. It was when wives had schizophrenia that a serious problem existed because a sick wife could not carry out the role in the household that a husband in Puerto Rico insisted on.

The perceived value of action to deal with symptoms is also something individuals learn from membership of a social group. Freidson (1961), for example, has described the 'lay-referral' system which varies between social groups, but through which individuals seek advice about their symptoms from friends and relatives, and McKinlay (1973) has described the way this is done by expectant mothers in Aberdeen. McKinlay suggests that the more extensive the social network a person is involved in, that is the extent to which day-to-day activities are typically carried on with reference to a wide and interlocking circle of friends and relatives, the less likelihood that she will be a high utilizer of antenatal care. This, he suggests, is because that person can share the experience of pregnancy (for our purposes here equivalent to symptoms) and have anxiety articulated, or reduced, in conversations with others who have shared the experience and who can advise about action. By contrast McKinlay found that people who are relatively isolated may need to visit a doctor frequently so that they can come to terms with the day-to-day changes in their body and other experiences. The advice given, and the action recommended, amongst those with extensive social networks, will be an influence on the response to symptoms and other bodily changes. Nevertheless, none of the differences reported by McKinlay is particularly large. Another example concerns American Roman Catholic students who were consistently found in several US studies to be less likely than Protestant students, with the same type of symptoms, to use student mental health services. The reason for this, it was argued, was that Roman Catholics confess to a priest rather than to a psychotherapist (see, for example, Schlingensiepen and Kasl, 1970).

In short the recognition of a symptom as a problem and the patterns of appropriate action to deal with symptoms are socially construed and maintained in much the same ways as are (to choose varied examples) patterns of courtship, the order of dishes at a meal, appropriate behaviour at weddings, and methods of settling disputes over ownership. Different social groups have different norms and values concerning the recognition of symptoms and what it is appropriate to do about them.

In Kasl and Cobb's scheme the 'perceived value of action' does not only depend on these socio-cultural variables. It will also depend, they suggest, on an individual's prior experience of medical services and his estimate of the costs and benefits that will come to him from a visit. They do not develop this idea but it is possible again, that past experience of medical care also varies according to social group. Strauss (1970), for example, has argued that the actual experience of having medical care, among lower income groups in America, acts as a deterrent to future visits to services. Medical care simply is not organized for their needs and expectations.

The importance of past medical care for explaining the 'perceived value of action' is demonstrated in a study of the last year of life of 785 people who died in the UK in 1969 (Cartwright, Hockey, and Anderson 1973). The investigators found that many of the individuals had not sought medical aid for many of the symptoms they had prior to their death. One reason for not consulting the doctor might have been that symptoms were felt to be relatively trivial or of short duration. But this was by no means the complete explanation. Twenty-nine per cent of all the symptoms about which no advice had been sought were described as 'very distressing' and 37 per cent had been present for a year or more. Comparable proportions for symptoms about which general practitioners' advice had been sought were, 53 per cent regarded as 'very distressing' and 50 per cent present for a year or more.

In fact the explanation for people's failure to consult lay in their, often realistic, assessment of the degree to which doctors could help. Cartwright, Hockey, and Anderson showed a clear relationship between the proportion of individuals with particular symptoms who had consulted and the proportion of those consulting with particular symptoms who had been helped (1973: 87). This result was reflected in some of the comments that the dying person's relatives made when asked why they had not sought advice:

> 'Knew he couldn't do anything.' (Loss of appetite – had sarcoma of femur (1973: 87.))
> 'It was part of his illness and nothing could be done for his condition.' (Depression – had cancer of the prostate (1973: 89.))

Another important variable Kasl and Cobb consider is the role of psychological distress. But this could operate in different directions. High anxiety, for example, could lead to frequent help-seeking for comparatively minor symptoms or to a denial of some symptoms and a long delay. Blackwell (1963) in a review of studies on delay in seeking treatment for cancer provides examples of the latter.

Finally, Kasl and Cobb, emphasize the importance of the symptoms themselves. As Zola's work suggested (above p. 168) particular types of symptoms are more threatening to some people than to others.

Rosenstock (1967) in a further review of the literature has suggested a very similar scheme to that proposed by Kasl and Cobb and to his own earlier formulation (1960) for interpreting illness behaviour. Although primarily intended to explain health behaviour (actions by healthy people designed to take preventive action against future disease) Rosenstock argues that the scheme he puts forward can also be applied to illness behaviour. For our purposes the significant addition to Kasl and Cobb's approach is the notion of a 'cue' to action. But Rosenstock does not develop this idea beyond stating it is important.

For Rosenstock an individual must first be 'psychologically ready' to take action and must perceive a need for it; second, he must believe that the action is going to reduce the threat; and third, a cue or stimulus must occur to 'trigger' this response from the individual. In support of this third variable Rosenstock quotes Zola's work but focuses on the need for a 'critical incident' rather than Zola's culturally patterned 'triggers'. Zola suggested that individuals made appointments to consult their doctors after disagreements with their mother, difficulties at work, unfortunate incidents at social gatherings and so on (Zola 1966, 1973).

Both Kasl and Cobb's, and Rosenstock's, schemes, although an important contribution to the clarification of research findings in the field of illness behaviour do have certain difficulties. The two schemes do provide us with a framework for thinking about the problem of how people take decisions to go to doctors, but they are limited in usefulness because there is no estimate of the weight to be attached to any of the variables. They only really comprise lists of possible variables rather than a model of how they interact. Most of the empirical evidence reviewed is introduced to support the possibility of a particular causal link rather than to assess its importance relative to another variable. It must be admitted, however, that there is little research evidence that would allow such comparison between variables.

The bulk of the evidence that does exist, and which is presented by Kasl and Cobb, concerns the influence of socio-cultural factors on the perceived threat of symptoms and the perceived value of visiting a doctor. But, while the studies reviewed above show that illness behaviour is usefully understood as a piece of social action and therefore as something influenced by features of an individual's social location, the results of such studies do not permit us to answer the question posed at the beginning of this chapter: why do some of those with distressing symptoms seek care from doctors while others with similar symptoms do not? Although there are important differences in the way particular ethnic or religious groups tolerate pain, perceive symptoms, or take action to get help with them, the differences, as I suggested when discussing McKinlay's work, are not sufficiently large to explain the medical care utilization of the majority of people. Large numbers of high and low utilizers of medical care can be found in all the relevant ethnic, social class, or religious groups (Mechanic, 1968: 120).

Thus, the limited importance that can be attached to demographic background factors, considered as variables in their own right, is supported by a small-scale study completed in one general practice in the UK by Kessell and Shepherd (1965). They attempted to compare the differences between attenders and non-attenders (defined as all those who had not sought medical care from the practice doctor or any other doctor for two years or more) but with largely negative results. There was no significant difference between attenders and non-attenders, for example, in relation to social class, employment status, marital status, and size of household. Differences where they existed seemed to be small, such as the fact that non-attenders included proportionately more old people, less young people, and fewer women. Although the external validity (pp. 48–9) of this one study in a possibly un-representative practice may be limited, all the evidence considered up to this point suggests that it is unlikely that socio-cultural factors of the broad demographic type will be found to play a major role in determining who does, and does not, seek medical aid.

The Actor's Point of View

The schemes that Kasl and Cobb and Rosenstock outline are, essentially, a conceptual framework with which to think about the problem posed at the beginning: why do some of those with distressing symptoms seek care from doctors while others with similar symptoms do not? So how helpful are they? As I have suggested, sociocultural factors are unlikely to explain much of the variation in help-seeking and, since the authors place their major emphasis on these factors, this in itself must restrict the usefulness of their approach. More fundamentally, I think the schemes have serious weaknesses in their emphasis: there is inadequate concern with the problematic nature of the reasons why individuals chose to visit doctors and too little attention is paid to the complex and ongoing relationships that individuals have both with their symptoms and their doctors. In terms both of explaining why people do, and do not, go to the doctor, and of drawing conclusions of medical practice, these weaknesses are critical. I will first expand these criticisms and then argue that an understanding of the reasons individuals have for visiting doctors, and the complex ongoing interaction of symptoms, doctor, and community — precisely the points that the two schemes underemphasise — provides the best way forward.

The first criticism I have made of Kasl and Cobb, and Rosenstock, is that the scheme they outline is biased in its emphasis, if not in its intentions, by an assumption, which might at one time have seemed 'rational', that the reason people go to doctors is because they are threatened by the symptoms of disease and want the doctor to reduce that threat. This assumption that what is rational for the observer will also be so for the actor, which may be regarded as normatively biased because it is derived from only one of many possible views on why a patient visits a doctor, is reflected in much of the work they review. Yet individuals may have other reasons for going to a doctor. For example, they may want company, want advice from the doctor on how to obtain a council house, or get on better with their husband, or wish to reduce pressure that is being put on them by friends or relatives. As argued in the first chapter illness behaviour is social action (pp. 21, 22–4) and as such is likely to benefit from being comprehended in terms of the meaning that the action may have for the actor. The difficulty with Kasl and Cobb or Rosenstock is not that they deny the central significance of the actor in the decision to consult but that, by not considering the full range of conceivable reasons for seeking aid, they make an implicit assumption about the actor's subjective intent.

The second criticism I would make of the two schemes is that they tend to create a misleading abstraction. Symptoms are largely conceptualized in terms of isolated (and probably rare) incidents which appear from time to time in a normally healthy individual. In fact, however, as the discussion of Rosenstock's paper at the Chicago conference indicated:

'Whereas health itself is in reality an elusive concept in much of the research the stages involved in seeking medical care are conceived as completely distinct. ...In this broad perspective everybody, in Leighton's terms, would appear to be a case, and exhaustive studies of the total process of seeking care would appear most timely.' (Mainland (ed.), 1967: 127)

As was suggested earlier, symptoms seem to be a recurrent feature of day-to-day life and a conceptual scheme for understanding illness behaviour is likely to be misleading unless it recognizes this.

Finally, the emphasis of Rosenstock (but in a lesser way Kasl and Cobb) can also be criticized for tending to abstract the decision to consult from the individual's ongoing relationship with his doctor and other medical services. Yet certainly in the UK, where individuals have family practitioners whom they tend to see over a period of time, the ongoing relationship between doctor and patient, and a person's past experience of being a patient, may be critical. In fact, decisions to consult take place in the context of an ongoing negotiation between doctor and patient that has been succintly described by the general practitioners attending the Balint seminars (Balint 1957) and in a recent paper by Ann Cartwright (1974). Let us look, briefly, at the evidence which is relevant to these three issues.

The management of disease

The picture that we have of the extent of disease in the population suggests that the management of symptoms without recourse to medical treatment must be part of the quite routine daily life of many people. Thus in a recent study Dunnell and Cartwright (1972: 11—15) found that a random sample of adults throughout Britain reported on average 3.9 symptoms each during the two weeks prior to interview. Altogether 91 per cent of the adults reported symptoms in this two-week period but only 16 per cent were then found to have consulted a doctor during that time. In fact as many as 28 per cent said they had not been to a doctor at all during the previous twelve months.

A much more common reaction was to take medicine. More than half the adults (55 per cent) said they had taken or used some medicine during the *twenty-four hours* before interview. In fact during the two-week period these adults had on average taken 2.2 different items each (Dunnell and Cartwright, 1972: 13). A similar finding was reported by Jefferys, Brotherston, and Cartwright (1960) when they surveyed a working-class housing estate in 1954—5 and by Wadsworth and his colleagues (1971) when they studied two London boroughs. Furthermore, Dunnell and Cartwright found that it was self-medication using patent medicines that was much more frequent than the use of prescribed medicines. In their study (1972: 14) they report that for every prescribed item taken in the two-week period there were two non-prescribed ones. In fact two-fifths of the adults had taken something prescribed whereas two-thirds had taken a non-prescribed medicine.

There is no conclusive evidence as to how far self-medication and pre-scribed medication are alternatives or on how far self-medication is an alternative to visiting the doctor. Jefferys, Brotherston, and Cartwright (1960) found that individuals tended to use self-medication and prescribed medication together and this finding was supported by Kessel and Shepherd's 1965 study of non-attenders in one general practice, although it was reversed, to some extent, when Dunnell and Cartwright (1972: 31—3) looked at prescribed and non-prescribed medicines according to the number of symptoms an individual had. One explanation may be that there is a large group of individuals — the majority — who for any level of symptoms they experience use self-medication regardless of whether or not they visit the doctor, that there is also a smaller group who use self-medication as an alternative either to taking prescribed medicines or visiting the doctor, and that finally there is also another group, quite large, which although often having symptoms rarely self-medicates or visits the doctor.

Certainly, when we remember that Dunnell and Cartwright found so many people with symptoms in a two-week period (91 per cent) and so many who had taken medicines the day before interview (55 per cent), but so few (16 per cent) who had consulted a doctor in the two weeks before, the most important conclusion we must draw is that for the majority of individuals visiting a doctor is a rather rare method of managing the symptoms of disease.

Seeking medical attention
The evidence of the last section suggests a pattern of ongoing accommo-dation to symptoms within the community that is only rarely interrupted by seeking medical aid. However, this does not mean that individuals never go to see their doctors or experience being a patient. On average, men in the UK made about three visits, and women about four, during the year studied by Dunnell and Cartwright (1972: 34). In fact only about a fifth to a quarter of those interviewed had not made a visit in the year. What does happen, however, is that individuals only present their doctors with some of their symptoms. At a recent conference the director of the General Practice Unit at St Thomas's Hospital suggested that individuals probably took about one in every ten symptoms to a doctor (Morrell, 1973). Fur-thermore, to see a doctor about one condition does not necessarily mean that the individual will ask about other problems (Lance, 1971). It is also worth remembering that the epidemological evidence suggests that the symptoms that are taken for help are not necessarily those that a doctor would consider the most serious.

In any case, individuals seem to be most reluctant to define themselves as ill and in need of medical attention. This is illustrated not only by the rarity of visits to the doctor, given the number of symptoms an individual will have, but also by the reluctance they display, as described in studies of how people go about defining themselves, or others, as in need of medical help.

Yarrow and her colleagues (1955) have described the way in which the wives of mental patients resisted the definition of their husbands as 'ill' and, instead, attempted to normalize their husbands' symptoms for as long as possible. That the wives of mental patients (even accounting for the stigma of mental illness) are not exceptional, was demonstrated by Davis's (1963) study of the way in which families dealt with the symptoms of polio in one of their members. Davis presents one family as typical of his sample.

'Well, [Norma Jean] had a little, slight cold that week ... But that week, all that week, why, she went to school. We even asked her one morning, I believe, if she wanted to stay home. She said no ... She didn't want to lose any time, she said. She didn't seem sick. And Saturday is when we noticed that — you know, she felt worse. But of course she's — Lord, I mean — years previous she's been sicker than that and went to school. We never noticed anything, never given anything like polio a thought. And then Saturday I was working daylight shift and when I came home from work she was out in the lady's yard next door. ... She said, "Hi, Dad." She acted all right to me, and I didn't even give it a thought about her being sick. Then when she come in, why she started laying around and she acted to me maybe more like she had an upset stomach than she had a cold ... And that night ... I give her a dose of milk of magnesia, just a small dose. And the next morning, why her bowels hadn't moved, and I give her another small dose, and still thinking that it was more of a upset stomach than it was a cold — see, because you could have took it either way. Well, she just laid here on the sofa all day. She watched television. That day some time she started complaining about her leg feeling heavy. And she went upstairs to the bathroom two or three times, without any assistance. I didn't give it a thought, and that Saturday night (the previous evening), though, I told my wife, not giving a thought in the world that anything could happen to us, I said, "You know, I'm always scared about polio." I didn't give it a thought in the world she had it — I'm just thinking, you know ... But I didn't think it'd happen to us. And so she laid around all Sunday, and we put a pad on her leg, and I rubbed her leg some. ... Couple of times I started to rub it, you know, and she told me to stop. And she went to bed, I guess about 9.30 or 10 o'clock, something like that ... She ate a good supper and, well, you know, we figured she was eating and all, she was just feeling punk ... I told my wife that night, I said, "Well, if she don't feel too good in the morning, call Dr. S." So the next morning she seemed to have a temperature ... A little later on her temperature dropped and my wife told her that if her temperature come back again she was going to call Dr. S. And it come back. She called Dr. S and I don't — I just forget what the temperature was. It was a little high — wasn't even too high, I mean, but it was a little along. And Dr. S come. She (Norma Jean) didn't want him to come, you know. Now that's one reason my wife was holding off, because she was afraid he was going to give her a needle, see! Any my wife was just trying to please her ... So after she saw that the temperature did come back ... she got a little worried, and then she called Dr. S and he came ...' (Davis 1963: 15—16)

It seems that a considerable accommodation can develop between individuals, their symptoms, and the patterns of relationships and activities they are involved in. Recognizing this Zola (1973) argued that to understand a visit to the doctor it is necessary to consider what can lead to a breakdown in this accommodation.

'Virtually every day of our lives we are subjected to a vast array of discomforts. Only an infinitesimal amount of these get to a physician. Neither the mere presence nor the obviousness of symptoms, neither their medical seriousness nor objective discomfort seem to differentiate the episodes which do and do not get professional treatment. In short, what then does convert a person to a patient?...' (Zola 1973: 678—9)

There are considerable methodological difficulties involved in studying any breakdown in accommodation after it has occurred because of the problems involved in *ex post* reconstruction. Techniques that were developed for *ex post* measurement of life events are discussed elsewhere in this book (above, pp. 58—9 and below pp. 314—16), but that approach, which could afford to limit itself to major life events, because it was considered that they were likely to produce an onset of depression, would be difficult to apply to the study of consultation. The 'triggers' that Zola describes as important are much less obvious and dramatic and much more idiosyncratic. In this situation it would be difficult to establish a proper comparison group because the list of possible 'triggers' to be covered for comparison and the number of patient groups involved would be just about infinite.

However, the alternative longitudinal approach to this kind of 'C' type error (above, pp. 46—8) — in which investigators might observe people periodically as they experienced and coped with symptoms — in addition to being expensive, also has its difficulties. The main problem is the fact that data-collection at one point in time tends to be obtrusive and can therefore influence data collected at subsequent times. Filling in a health diary or being regularly questioned about health could *create* a new pattern of illness behaviour — in short, improved internal validity could threaten external validity (above, pp. 48—9). For this and other reasons, therefore, it is hard to evaluate studies such as that of Robinson (1971), who investigated randomly selected families in South Wales over a period of several months and compared the families' illness experience with the action taken to manage it. In fact, Robinson made little effort to establish whether his presence might have influenced the results. He could have studied a group of individuals in different ways (some without actual contact) and then compared results. It would then have been possible to assess whether particular kinds of bias were introduced by particular methods of study. Considerable advances might then have been made.

Because of these methodological difficulties, and the fact that investigators have made insufficient progress towards overcoming them, our knowledge of how the accommodation to symptoms breaks down has not advanced a great deal beyond the pioneering work of Stoeckle, Zola, and Davidson (1963, 1964; Zola 1963, 1966, 1973) which was carried out in several out-patient clinics at the Massachusetts General Hospital in the early 1960s. The methodology of the Massachusetts studies (which were of the retrospective type) does not give great confidence since little formal attention was paid to considering possible alternative, but conflicting, explanations of the findings. The studies need replication, but nonetheless provide a stimulating account of how patients behaved, and one which compares favourably with observations made by some clinicians (Balint, 1957). Furthermore, because patients were seen very soon after making the decision to consult possible biases arising from the patient's later reconstruction of what happened would be reduced.

The authors' basic claim was that the decision to seek medical aid was based on a break in the accomodation to symptoms and did not necessarily occur at the point where the individual felt most ill. As Zola put it:

> 'I do not mean by this that the symptoms were unimportant. What I mean is that they function as a sort of constant and that when the decision to seek medical aid was made the symptoms alone were not sufficient to prompt this seeking.' (Zola, 1973: 681)

Zola illustrates this argument by quoting the case of a woman who was diagnosed as having Choriorenitinitis O.S. (permanent partial blindness) — 'lesion present much longer than present symptoms'.

> 'Mary O'Rourke is forty-nine, married and is a licensed practical nurse. Her symptom was a simple one, "The sight is no good in this eye ... can't see print at all, no matter how big." This she claimed was due to being hit on the side of the head by a baseball four months ago, but she just "couldn't get around to a doctor before this". Why did she decide now, did her vision become worse? "Well ... about a month ago I was taking care of his (a client's) mother ... he mentioned that my eyelid was drooping ... It was the first time he ever did ... If he hadn't pointed out I wouldn't have gone then." "Why did you pay attention to his advice?" "Well it takes away from my appearance ... bad enough to feel this way without having to look that way ... The same day I told my husband to call." (Zola 1973: 683)

Zola pointed out that no 'drooping' was actually noticeable to either the interviewer or the examining doctor. He then went on to isolate several different 'triggers' which, he argued, were important in the decision of these patients to seek help. Triggers could be (1) an interpersonal crisis; (2) a discovery that symptoms could interfere with social or personal relationships; (3) sanctioning, by which he meant an occasion when some other person advised or insisted that an individual make a visit to the doctor; (4) the discovery that symptoms could interfer with vocational or physical activity; and (5) what he called a kind of temporalizing of symptomatology.

Jennie Bella was an example of someone who sought help as the result of an interpersonal crisis:

'Jennie Bella was forty, single and had a hearing difficulty for many years. She said that the symptoms have not gotten worse nor do they bother here a great deal (Diagnosis: Non-supporative Otitis Media) and, furthermore, she admitted being petrified of doctors. "I don't like to come ... I don't like doctors. I never did ... I have to be unconscious to go ..." She can nevertheless not pinpoint any reason for coming at this time other than a general feeling that it should be taken care of. But when she was questioned about her family's concern, she blurted out, "I'm very nervous with my mother, up to this year I've been quiet, a stay-at-home ... Now I've decided to go out and have some fun. My mother is very strict and very religious. She doesn't like the idea of my going out with a lot of men. She doesn't think I should go out with one for a while and then stop. She says I'm not a nice girl, that I shouldn't go with a man unless I plan to marry ... She doesn't like me keeping late hours or coming home late. She always suspects the worst of me ... This year it's just been miserable ... I can't talk to her ... She makes me very upset and it's been getting worse ... The other day ... last week we (in lowered tones) had *the* argument." Miss Bella called for an appointment the next morning.' (Zola 1973: 683)

Harry Gallo was an example of someone who sought help as a result of a perceived interference with his social or interpersonal relations:

'Harry Gallo is forty-one, married, and a "trainee" at a car-dealers. "For a very long time my trouble is I can't drink ... tea, coffee, booze ... eat ice cream, fried foods. What happens is I get pains if I do have it." (Diagnosis – peptic ulcer). He becomes very dramatic when talking about how the symptoms affected him. "It shot my social life all to pieces ... we all want to socialize ... and it's a tough thing, I want to go with people, but I can't. Wherever we go they want to eat or there's food and I get hungry ... and if I eat there, I get sick." Of course, he has gone off his "diet" and has gotten sick. Most of the time he watches himself and drinks Malox. He saw a doctor once two years ago and has been considering going again, but, "I kept putting it off ... because I got lazy ... there were so many things ... I've just been starting a new job and I didn't want to start taking off and not working but this last attack was *too much* !" He then told me how day after day the "boys at work" have been urging him to stop off with them for a few quick ones. He knew he shouldn't but he so wanted to fit in and so "I was with the boys and the other salesmen ... I drank beer ... I knew I was going to have more than one ... and *it* happened on the way home..." Storming into his home, he asked his wife to make an appointment at the hospital, stating almost exasperatingly, "if you can't drink beer with friends, what the hell..." (Zola 1973: 684)

There are other examples, including the important trigger of 'sanctioning' – for example, a visit being precipitated by the influence of someome else, perhaps a relative – which serve to remind us that the patient role can be self or other defined, but Zola presents enough evidence to suggest that looking at help-seeking as the result of a breakdown in the accommodation to symptoms seems to be useful. Further studies will need to replicate and extend the work before it will have significant implications. What does become clear is that individuals ceased to cope with symptoms themselves and started to define themselves as patients, or be defined by others, because of the inability of the social and interpersonal network in which they were involved to contain them. The definition of a problem as one requiring medical attention was inextricably bound up with changes in the patient's social and emotional environment. The implication is striking: action directed at allowing the network to accommodate the symptoms, or some change in the network's ability to do so, can remove the need for a visit. In fact, many visits to the doctor may be as much about the social and interpersonal network in which a patient is located as about the symptoms which, as Michael Balint (1957) has pointed out, need be no more than a presenting complaint, a ticket to obtain help with difficulties of a social, interpersonal, or emotional kind.

Expectations of the patient role

The research of Zola, or Balint, suggests that patients do not simply view the doctor as someone to remove the threat of illness. The research suggests that patients' conceptions of their role in relationship to the doctor may be much more important than might be concluded from the Kasl and Cobb or Rosenstock schemes.

It seems possible that patients can be concerned not only with the *perceived value of action to reduce the threat of symptoms* but also with the *perceived value of action to solve other problems* that they have. Thus the way people think about their potential role as patient and the way they conceive of the doctor's role is likely to be an important influence on whether they seek help. The way people think is also likely to influence their behaviour as a patient and produce potential conflict with medical routines, definitions, and requirements.

Research on the way patients see their own or the doctor's role is no[']
very well advanced. A great deal of work has used research instruments o[']
dubious demonstrated validity — such as the semantic differential tes[']
(Robinson, 1971) or highly structured hypothetical questionnaire[s]
(Mechanic and Volkart, 1961; Gordon, 1966; Robinson, 1971) —which d[o]
not permit great confidence that the conclusions reached regarding patients
views were not merely artefacts of the method used to investigate them
Both Robinson and Gordon, for example, use hypothetical question[s]
describing illness situations to find out how individuals see their own rol[e]
and might behave towards others. Yet how the respondents interprete[d]
the questions and how far they are referring to the situations the investigators intended is a matter for conjecture. Hypothetical questions use[d]
in other studies have often proved to have difficulties. Dunnell an[d]
Cartwright (1972: 55), for example, reported that 72 per cent of respondents would consult a doctor if they had a constant feeling of depression.
Yet we have good grounds for believing that these respondents would not
behave in that way. In a recent study in Camberwell, Brown and his colleagues (1975) found that only about half of those with serious symptoms
of depression (that had been present for some time) were actually receiving
any form of aid for these symptoms. It seems quite likely therefore that
answers to hypothetical questions cannot be taken literally. This is not to
suggest that such questions are useless. In fact Cartwright used the data
she collected in her study to show very effectively (by comparing answers
to a similar question several years earlier) that people's attitudes to depression were changing (Cartwright, 1974: 3). Dunnell and Cartwright also
used hypothetical questions (see *Table 1*) to assess differences in the
seriousness that doctors and patients attached to different symptoms.
They were then able to show that 'adults often may not consult doctors
about depression, persistent headaches, acute sore throats and boils when
doctors feel this appropriate. On the other hand they may consult about
sleeplessness and heavy colds more often than doctors feel reasonable'
(1972: 66).

Hypothetical questions, therefore, can be useful, but, like any other
research instrument, if they are to be helpful in interpreting what people
do and think in specific circumsrances, it would be necessary, before the
main study gets under way, to compare answers to such standard questions
with those obtained from a more lengthy and flexible style of interviewing
where the respondent's meaning can be more fully drawn out (pp. 61—3).
For the time being, because of such methodological difficulties involved in
existing research, how patients see their own or the doctor's role remains
largely speculative.

Much work suggests that patients use doctors for help with problems
other than those simply caused by the 'threat' of symptoms. Silver (1963),
for example, in a study of a health team approach to 'family' medicine in
the USA, has shown that a large proportion of patients are unwilling to

Table 1 Comparison of doctors' and adults' views on self-treatment in various circumstances

	a constant feeling of depression for about three weeks	difficulty in sleeping for about a week	a heavy cold with a temperature and running nose	a headache more than once a week for a month	a very sore throat for three days and no other symptoms	a boil that doesn't clear up in a week
proportion of doctors who thought each condition suitable for people to treat themselves without consulting a doctor	9%	58%	86%	17%	27%	12%
number of doctors (= 100%)			307			
proportion of adults who thought they would do something themselves (including nothing) without consulting a doctor	26%	45%	70%	40%	55%	22%
number of adults (= 100%)			1,412			

Source: Dunnell and Cartwright, 1972: 65)

present emotional problems in a non-medical context. They were more willing to talk to doctors than social workers. The observations of Balint (1957), Zola (1973), Satin (1971, 1972), and much of the experience of established clinicians suggest that patients often wish to talk about their families, housing, jobs, or friendships. Indeed, there seems little doubt that many of the complaints presented to many general practitioners are of this type and this may explain why so many doctors in general practice complain about being called upon to treat trivia.

Another influential factor may be the individual's own expectations of his role as patient. One salient feature of this role (for example, Parsons, 1951: 422) may be that it usually involves submitting to the authority of the doctor. This entrance into a dependent role may not be welcomed.

Second, in entering the patient role an individual may be placing himself in a position not only of dependence but also of uncertainty. This will be exaggerated in importance by the potentially highly charged emotional atmosphere that surrounds disease. An individual will usually lack the technical skill to ascertain whether what is being done for him is appropriate and adequate. In this connection his past experience of medical care and his past treatment by doctors may be important. The lack of information given by doctors is so widespread that it has become part of folklore and the main complaint of patients in UK hospitals (Cartwright, 1967: 75). The experience of 'being kept in the dark' probably increases the feeling of helplessness and reduces the willingness to put oneself in the same position again.

Another feature of the patient role described by Parsons (1951: 437), and which may influence a person's unwillingness to assume it, is the fact that the patient role is 'stigmatized'. That is, the role is defined as undesirable (Parsons argues this is necessary to society in order to prevent a too frequent or too immediate assumption of the patient role). 'Being a patient' is not socially valued and can reduce an individual's status either temporarily or permanently. This is more serious for patients with some diseases – particularly mental illness – than for others. But this 'symbolic' cost of being a patient may be important in explaining some of the reluctance to visit doctors that exists.

There are other 'costs' involved in taking the patient role. In many countries it costs money. But, in any case, a person may have to take time off work or risk loss of earnings or potential discredit (in the sense that he may imagine that others will think 'less of him' for 'being ill'). Robinson (1971: 14–15) describes one patient who counted the 'cost' of taking time off as greater than the gain from obtaining treatment.

'Mr. and Mrs. M obviously shared quite a clear notion of when it was appropriate for Mr. M to be sick and when to consult a doctor. When Mr. M (the previous month) had been with his old employer as a laundry delivery-van driver it would have been quite proper for him to have taken time off from work, consult a doctor and get the necessary medical certificate to legitimise his absence. [Also he could have been sick.] During that time between jobs when Mrs. M could have looked after her husband and, because rest was all that Mr. M was considered to require, he "wouldn't have needed the doctor." However, Mr. and Mrs. M felt that the demands and obligations of being in his new job as a machine operator were such that it was impossible, even though the condition was worsening, for Mr. M to take time off from the aluminium factory even if he had been able to obtain the official approval of the doctor [which would readily have been given], Mr. M had quite severely torn ligaments in his knee.' Robinson, 1971: 14–15)

Financial loss is important for other people, particularly if they have to support a family. In this connection it is worth recording Cartwright's (1967) finding that patients in hospital received quite inadequate sickness benefit.

'For 44% of these patients (who were the main breadwinners) absence from work meant cutting off their normal income completely, 36% continued to receive full pay, and 20% received something from their employers, but less than their normal wage. Full pay usually meant the basic rate less the amount payable to the man from the National Insurance Scheme, this amount either being deducted from the wages paid or returned to the firm later by the employee. Even these people may, in fact, receive less than usual while they are sick, as payments for overtime and piece-work are not normally included.' (Cartwright, 1967: 152–3)

A South-Wales general practitioner, Tudor Hart (1971: 408), has argued that a large number of visits to the doctor by working-class patients are 'administrative' — that is they are concerned with the legitimation of illness by a doctor's certificate, and these patients are therefore primarily concerned not with their health but with their income. Using the consultation rates provided by Ann Cartwright (1967), Tudor Hart points out that middle-class patients at ages under forty-five had a rate that was 53 per cent less than that of working-class patients; but at ages over seventy-five they had a consultation rate 62 per cent higher than the working-class patients of that age. Between forty-five and seventy-five there is a regular progression so that the middle-class rapidly catch up. He argues that it is reasonable to interpret Cartwright's findings as evidence 'that middle-class consulations had a higher clinical content at all ages, that working-class consultations had a higher clinical content at all ages, that working-class and that the middle-class was indeed able to make more effective use of primary care'. Tudor Hart's evidence cannot be regarded as final but it does raise an important point. If many working-class individuals do visit for 'administrative' reasons then it might provide another explanation for the frequent complaints about 'trivia' in general practice.

People anticipate other gains from obtaining patient status. Some will expect a reduction of the threat from their symptoms. This can occur through treatment, but, equally important, a visit to the doctor and obtaining a diagnosis can serve a function of 'labelling' the patient's problem. The label or diagnosis received has the effect of ruling out other (perhaps worse) labels or diagnoses that the patient may have feared (see Chapter 10). Alternatively, like one man who was referred to a consultant psychiatrist at a West London hospital because (he said) he wanted to keep his wife happy (Tuckett, forthcoming), becoming a patient temporarily may be a device adopted to satisfy the demands of others. The same man, once pronounced 'well' — as he thought he was — was able to use this in negotiation with his wife.

Adopting the patient role can also help to 'legitimate' a person's behaviour (for example, a wife who feels her husband is too sexually demanding may need a doctor to justify her refusal) or it may help to qualify someone for a council house in a situation where priority is given to those who are 'sick'. Both these situations were found among patients attending the West London hospital I studied.

Much more research into the wide range of possibilities that exist is needed. For the patient the meaning of his symptoms and of a visit to the doctor, and the implications of 'being ill' may be very different from those that the doctor imagines. Entry to the sick role may present all kinds of advantages and problems. The difficulty that doctors have had in appreciating the patients' point of view, together with their own conception of

their role, is in my view the general explanation for the complaints about
'trivia' and the frustrations that many doctor's now experience. The
implicit 'rational' perspective that I have discussed, and which seems to
inform so much medical research and thinking, has been a serious obstacle
to the recognition of the appropriate causes of this problem. Assertions
about 'trivia' are statements about the conflict between patients' and
doctors' conceptions of the doctor's role.

The influence of the doctor

Finally, it should be noted that, particularly in the UK where most people
see their doctor at least once a year (p. 174), the decision to consult takes
place within the framework of an ongoing relationship with a doctor. A
study surveying 171 doctors in the UK showed variations from 2.7 to 9.2
consultations per patient per year (Logan and Cushion 1958). These variations could not be adequately explained by differences in age or sex of
patients, or location of the practice, and must be due in part to different
types of interaction between patients and doctors. Certainly doctors feel
they can influence consultation rates among their patients. At least, this
seems an implication of the work of Dunnell and Cartwright (1972: 66–7)
who found that doctors who considered visits trivial could correspondingly
reduce consultation rates. Furthermore Cartwright, Hockey, and Anderson
(1973: 89) reported that when doctors gave the impression that they were
busy or uninterested there did seem a tendency for patients to be less
likely to seek their advice. These results are based on a small amount of
research work and much more needs to be done.

   When an individual does visit a doctor he will often be in a position to
choose which symptoms or problems to present. Korsch and her colleagues
(1968), who studied 800 patients visiting the walk-in clinic of the Children's Hospital in Los Angeles by tape-recording the consultations and
interviewing the patients afterwards, found that only a quarter of patients'
main worries were specifically mentioned to the doctor during the visit.

   Although the way in which the doctor reacts to the patient's concerns
and the way that the doctor-patient relationship is handled over time, may,
therefore, be significant in determining which symptoms a patient presents
to the doctor much more careful study is needed. An indication of the
possibilities that exist in this direction is indicated by Zola (1963) who
suggested that where the doctors at the Massachussetts out-patient clinic
failed to be concerned with the 'trigger' that brought a patient to come
and see them, patients either left treatment prematurely, or kept returning
with different symptoms. The doctor-patient relationship, however, is the
subject for the next chapter.

Conclusion

In conclusion, why some people choose to take their symptoms to doctors, and others do not, is a complicated issue which we do not, as yet, fully understand. Some of the difficulties have been outlined and some lines of further research indicated. However, what we can be reasonably sure of is that trying to understand why people come to doctors, and paying attention to the reasons involved, is likely to be important both in determining individuals' future responses to symptoms, and in analysing the relationships between doctors and patients. It is hoped that such an understanding will allow doctors to be less frustrated by what is now termed 'trivia'.

If the findings of investigators like Zola and Balint are confirmed the study of 'illness behaviour' may lead to a re-evaluation of some aspects of the doctor's role and of ideas about appropriate forms of medical care and of treatment. This is one reason for my arguing rather strongly for a re-emphasis in the Kasl and Cobb and Rosenstock approaches to the problem. On the face of it, their schemes, in particular Rosenstock's, have rather different implications from the emphasis that I have suggested. Rosenstock's scheme, for example, would suggest that more attention to the health education of patients might be appropriate and he even helps to identify where this effort might be directed. Special education programmes could be mounted (perhaps among specific ethnic or other groups) to increase the 'perceived threat' of disease or the 'perceived' value of visiting a doctor. The emphasis that I have suggested, on the other hand, would indicate changes in medical practice and in the way that the complaints that do reach doctors are handled. The doctor might become as concerned with the trigger as with the patient's symptoms. Future research will no doubt help to suggest what can be done both in health education, medical education, and in the organization of medical care.

There is one other important point that needs to be made as a result of considering individuals' differential responses to symptoms. It is clear that if those in treatment are there because they have reacted to the signs and symptoms of disease in a different way to those who have not sought treatment, then in studies attempting to understand the causes of particular illnesses by examining treated populations (for example, interviewing patients, using medical records, and so on), there will always be a strong possibility that results suggest not causes of illness, but causes of illness behaviour. To exclude this alternative explanation, investigations into the aetiology of different diseases will need at some point to take a random sample of those with the symptoms in the general population. The same applies, of course, to research or teaching in a teaching hospital. The special process that an individual undergoes in order to reach a teaching hospital may well suggest that patients there may differ from those in general hospitals.

Note

1. The terms 'disease' and 'illness' are used in the sense defined on pp. 32–3, that is,

'illness' is a subjective category felt by patients to be appropriate, and 'disease' is an observer-defined category used by doctors to indicate the presence of a pathological process.

References

Balint, M. (1957) *The Doctor, His Patient, and the Illness.* London: Tavistock.
A fascinating account by Balint, a psychoanalyst, who describes his work with a group of general practitioners. The account is, however, anecdotal. See also Chapter 6.

Beecher, H.K. (1959) *The Measurement of Subjective Responses.* New York: Oxford University Press.
An account of research on pain by one of America's leading anaesthetists.

— (1965) Quantification of the Subjective Pain Experience. In. P. Hoch and J. Zubin, (eds.), *The Psychopathology of Perception.* New York: Grune and Strutton.

Blackwell, B. (1963) The Literature of Delay in Seeking Medical Care for Chronic Illnesses. *Health Education Monographs* 16: 3—32.

Brotherston, J. (1958) Some factors affecting the Use of General Practitioner Services on a Housing Estate near London. In J. Pemberton, and H. Willard, (eds.), *Recent Studies in Epidemiology.* London: Oxford University Press.

Brown, G.W., Ní Bhrolcháin, M., and Harris, T. (1975) Social Class and Psychiatric Disturbance among Women in an Urban Population. *Sociology* 9 (2): 225—254

Brown, G., Bone, M., Dallison, B., and Wing, J. (1966) *Schizophrenia and Social Care.* London: Oxford University Press.

Butterfield, W.J.H. (1968) *Priorities in Medicine.* London: Nuffield Provincial Hospitals Trust.

Cartwright, A. (1967) *Patients and their Doctors.* London: Routledge & Kegan Paul.
A study of patients' attitudes to their general practitioners.

— (1974) Prescribing and the Relationship between Doctors and Patients. Paper presented at the Toronto Conference on Alchoholism and Drug addiction. Proceedings to be published by the Alcoholism and Drug addiction Research Foundation.
An intriguing account of the kinds of relationship that can transpire between patients and their doctors.

Cartwright, A., Hockey, L., and Anderson, J. (1973) *Life Before Death.* London: Routledge & Kegan Paul.
A study of the last year of life of nearly a thousand people, selected at random, who died in Britain during 1972.

Clarke, M. (1969) *Trouble with Feet.* Occasional Paper on Social Administration No. 29. London: G. Bell and SMS.
A survey of the problems of mobility reported by old people.

Commission on Chronic Illness (1957) *Chronic Illness in a Large City. Chronic Illness in the United States.* Vol. 4. Cambridge (Mass): Harvard University Press.

Davis, F.M. (1963) *Passage Through Crisis.* Indiannapolis: Bobbs Merrill.
A detailed description of twelve families and the way they reacted to one of the children contracting polio.

Dunnell, K. and Cartwright, A. (1972) *Medicine-Takers, Prescribers, and Hoarders.* London: Routledge & Kegan Paul.
A description of the way people use medicines and deal with symptoms, with and without the doctor's help.

Epson, J.E. (1969) The Mobile Health Clinic: An interim Report on a preliminary analysis of the first 1000 patients to attend. Mimeo. London: London Borough of Southwark Health Department.
1000 people selected at random in the Southwark area were subjected to a battery of screening tests and examinations.

Fock, S. (1960) South American Birth Customs in Theory and Practice. *Folk* 2: 51—69.

Frankenberg, R. (1969) Man Society and Health: Towards the definition of the role of Sociology in the development of Zambian medicine. *African Social Research*, 8th December.

Freidson, E. (1961) *Patients Views of Medical Practice.* New York: Russell Sage Foundation.

Gordon, G. (1966) *Role Theory and Illness: A Sociological Perspective.* New Haven: College University Press.

Goslings, W.R.O., Valkenburg, H.A., Botts, A.W., and Lorrier, J.C. (1963). Attack Rates of Streptococcal Pharyngitis, Rheumatic Fever and Glomerulonephritis in the General Population. I. A Controlled Pilot Study of Streptococcal Pharyngitis in one village. *New England Journal of Medicine* 268: 687—94.

Horder, J. and Horder, J. (1954) Illness in General Practice. *Practitioner* 173: 177—87.

Jefferys, M., Brotherston, J., and Cartwright, A. (1960) Consumption of Medicine on a Working-Class Housing Estate. *British Journal of Preventive and Social Medicine* 14: 64—76.

Jenkinson, V. and Pearson, R. (1967) Report to the Steering Committee of the Liverpool Project. Medical Care Research Unit, University of Manchester.

Kasl, S. and Cobb, S. (1966) Health Behaviour, Illness Behaviour and Sick-Role Behaviour (in two parts). *Archives of Environmental Health* 12: 246—66 and 531—41. See text.

Kessel, N. and Shepherd, M. (1965) The Health and Attitudes of People who Seldom Consult a Doctor. *Medical Care* 3: 6—10.

Koos, E. (1954) *The Health of Regionsville: what the People felt and did about it.* New York: Columbia University Press.
An early study of people's attitudes to health, illness, and help-seeking.

Korsch, B., Freeman, B., Negrete, V.F., and Daws, M. (1968) Gaps in Doctor-Patient Communication: 1 Doctor-Patient Interaction and Patient Satisfaction. *Pediatrics* 42: 855.

Kosambi, D.D. (1967) Living Pre-history in India. *Scientific American* 216: 105.

Kroeber, A.L. (1948) *Anthropology.* New York: Harcourt, Brace and Ward.

Lance, H. (1971) Transport Services in General Practice. Supplement to the *Journal of the Royal College of General Practitioners* 21(3).

Logan, W. and Cushion, A. (1958) *Morbidity Statistics in General Practice.* Studies in Medical and Population Subjects. No. 14. London: HMSO.

Lowe, C. and McKeown, T. (1960) The Care of the Chronic Sick: II Social and Demographic Data. *British Journal of Social and Preventive Medicine* 4: 61—74.

Mainland, D. (ed.) (1967) *Health Services Research.* New York: Millbank Memorial Fund.

McKinlay, J.B. (1973) Social Networks, Lay Consultation, and Help-Seeking Behaviour. *Social Forces* 51: 255—92.

Mechanic, D. (1968) *Medical Sociology: A Selective View.* New York: Free Press.
Includes a comprehensive review of factors of influencing illness behaviour.

Mechanic, D. and Volkart, E.H. (1961) Stress, Illness Behaviour, and the Sick Role.

American Sociological Review 5: 51—58.

Melzack, R. (1973) *The Puzzle of Pain.* Harmondsworth: Penguin Education.
An excellent statement of the evidence on the causes of pain.

Morrell, D. (1973) Paper presented at the Annual Conference organized by the Department of Social Medicine, St. Thomas's Hospital Medical School.

Morris, J.N. (1967) *Uses of Epidemiology.* Edinburgh: Livingstone.
A standard test which is informative and incisively written.

Parsons, T. (1951) *The Social System.* London: Routledge & Kegan Paul.
Chapter ten presents Parsons' view on medical issues.

Pearse, I. and Crocker, L. (1944) *The Peckham Experiment.* London: G. Allen and Unwin.
A pioneering epidemiological study aimed at assessing the effect of new medical care facilities.

Pearson, R., Smedley, B., Berfenstan, R., Logan, R., Burguins, A.M., and Peterson, O (1968) Hosptial Caseloads in Liverpool, New England, and Uppsala: An International Comparison. *The Lancet*, September 7: 559—66.

Robinson, D. (1971) *The Process of Becoming Ill.* London: Routledge & Kegan Paul

Rogler, L. and Hollingshead, A. (1965) *Trapped: Families and Schizophrenia.* New York: John Wiley.

Rosenstock, I.M. (1960) What Research on Motivation suggests for Public Health *American Journal of Public Hygiene* 50: 295—302.

— (1967) Why People Use Health Services. In D. Mainland (ed.), *Health Services Research.* New York: Millbank Memorial Fund. Reprinted from *Millbank Memorial Fund Quarterly* (1966) 44: Part 2.

Satin, D. (1971) 'Help': Prevalence and Disposition of Psycho-social Problems in a Hospital Emergency unit. *Social Psychiatry* 6(3): 105—13.

— (1972) 'Help': Life Stress and Psycho-Social Problems in the Hospital Emergency Unit. *Social Psychiatry* 7: 119—26.
Two interesting but unconvincing studies which suggest similar conclusions to those of Zola but do not overcome any of the methodological hurdles.

Saunders, L. (1954) *Culture Differences and Medical Care.* New York: Russell-Sage Foundation.
Another early American classic which illuminated the relationship between culture and the way symptoms are handled.

Schlingesepien, W. and Kasl, S. (1970) Help Seeking Behaviour of Male College Students with Emotional Problems. *Social Psychiatry* 5: 25.

Silver, G. (1963) *Family Medical Care.* Cambridge (Mass): Harvard University Press.
A study of an experimental project in the Bronx district in New York.

Stoeckle, J., Zola, I., and Davidson, G. (1963) On Going to See the Doctor: the Contribution of the Patient to the Decision to Seek Medical Aid: A selective review. *Journal of Chronic Disease* 16: 957.

— (1964) The Quality and Significance of Psychological Distress in Medical Patients — Some Preliminary Observations about the Decision to Seek Medical Aid. *Journal of Chronic Disease* 17: 959.

Strauss, A. (1970) Medical Ghettos. In A. Strauss (ed.), *Where Medicine Fails.* Chicago: Aldine.

Stocks, P. (1949) *Sickness in the Population of England and Wales.* Studies on Medical and Population Subjects No. 2. London: HMSO.

Suchman, E. and Phillips, B. (1958) An Analysis of the Validity of Health Questionnaires. *Social Forces* 26: 223–32.

Tuckett, D. (forthcoming). An account of a study of psychiatric out-patients in London.

Tudor Hart, J. (1971) The Inverse Care Law. *The Lancet* i: 405–12.

Valkenburg, H.A., Goslings, W.R.O., Botts, A.W., de Moor, C.E. and Lorrier, J.C. (1963) Attack Rate of Streptococcal Pharyngitis, Rheumatic Fever and Glomerulonephritis in the General Population II. The Epidemiology of Streptococcal Pharyngitis in one Village during a two-year Period. *New England Journal of Medicine* 268: 694.

Wadsworth, M. Butterfield, W.J.H., and Blaney, R. (1971) *Health and Sickness: The Choice of Treatment.* London: Tavistock.

A report of a recent study looking at the experience of symptoms and methods of dealing with them in a population around Guy's Hospital in London.

Williamson, J., Stokoe, I.H., Gray, S., Fisher, M., Smith, A., McGhee, A., Stephenson, E. (1964) Old People at Home: Their Unreported Needs. *The Lancet* i: 1117–20.

Yarrow, M.R., Schwartz, C.G., Murphy, H.S., and Deasy, L.C. (1955) The Psychological Meaning of Mental Illness in the Family. *Journal of Social Issues* 11: 212–24.

An early description of the way American wives interpreted the developing psychiatric symptoms experienced by their husbands.

Zborowski, M. (1952) Cultural Components in Response to Pain. *Journal of Social Issues* 8: 16–30.

Zola, I.K. (1963) Problems of Communication, Diagnosis and Patient Care. *Journal of Medical Education* 38: 829–38.

– (1966) Culture and Symptoms: An Analysis of Patient's Presenting Complaints. *American Sociological Review* 31: 615–30.

– (1973) Pathways to the Doctor: From Person to Patient. *Social Science and Medicine* 7: 677–89.

Originally given at the 1st International Conference on Social Science and Medicine, Aberdeen (September 1968).

Chapter 6

David Tuckett

Doctors and Patients

'Well they don't tell you anything hardly. They don't seem to want to. I mean, you start asking questions and they say, "Well, I only have about three minutes to talk to you". And then the things that you ask, they don't seem to want to answer you. So I don't ask them anything any more.' (Davis, 1963: 57–8)

'He'll say well, we'll talk about it next time. And next time he'll talk fast, he out-talks you — and rushes out of the room and then when he's out of the room you think, well, I was supposed to ask him what he's going to do about my medicine ... you run in the hall and he has disappeared that fast.' (Tagliacozzo and Mauksh, 1972: 177)

This chapter is concerned with the role of the doctor and the nature of the relationships between doctors and patients. Now there are various ways of looking at the relationships that develop between doctors and patients. However, the perspective I want to introduce is that focusing on the structural or situational elements in the relationship: that is, to consider the underlying processes and the constraints on action that operate if the relationship is to be 'successful'. The word 'successful' is chosen quite deliberately. It serves to beg what may well be the most important question in considering any relationship: success from whose point of view? This is certainly an important question to ask when considering the relationships between doctors and patients.

Roles

When sociologists examine the interaction of individuals they have found it useful to conceive of those individuals as actors performing roles. A role — that of doctor, nurse, patient, social worker, cleaner, Prime Minister, manager, father, or daughter — has duties, or at least expectations of carrying out particular tasks and activities, attached to it. The analogy is to a play. The actors and director start with a script, performing their roles, but they do depend on the script. Now just as different playwrights give more or less room for interpretation, so the discretion available to a person playing a particular social role will vary. There is more room for personal interpretation (the influence of an individual's *personal role* conception) in some roles than in others. We can study the different interpretations and ask to what they are due. But it is also important to look at the regularities in the way that most actors who occupy particular occupational or other roles perform (the influence of the *social role* itself). What are its requirements? How does it relate to other roles?

Consider, from the point of view of some of the actors involved, the situation where someone is about to die. A number of individuals might be involved in a variety of different roles: the dying person, other patients, nurses, doctors, relatives, friends, employers, work-mates, hospital administrators, cleaners, undertakers, etc. The situation will look different to the occupants of each of those roles. For the patient his impending death is a unique and overwhelming experience. For his relatives, depending on how close they are to him, it will also be a specific and significant experience, although of a different kind than that experienced by the patient. It may well have profound implications for their way of life and many other aspects of their lives. Friends, neighbours, other ward patients, will each have a different view of the event which is to come.

The situation of doctors and other health workers will be different again. Death is part of the routine experience of their role. Its management is part of their job and can happen several times a week or even a day. Nurses and doctors cannot afford to become too deeply involved and they cannot go into mourning or be relieved from their normal activities. There will be another patient in the same bed very soon and a whole set of operations will have to be performed once the person actually dies. Delay and inefficiency caused by emotional upset at this person's death may cause another death if there is somebody in urgent need of a bed. Similarly, the reactions of other people, for example, that of the undertaker, will be influenced by the requirements of their roles in relation to the dying person. Hence, the notion of role can be useful. It sensitizes us to the common features of certain individuals' tasks and activities. Being a doctor, a nurse, father, or a patient means that the individual is placed in a certain situation, and this implies certain prescribed actions.

This chapter is going to focus primarily on the doctor's role and on the conflicts that are innate to it — conflicts that are built into the fulfilling of the work tasks. However, one other general notion which sociologists use to try to understand human interaction is helpful.

Role performance is negotiated. That is, not only are there regularities that derive from the social role itself, and personal interpretations deriving from that role, but also the final performance depends on the audience

that the person in the role has. In order to perform as a doctor one has
to have people who are prepared to be patients. Doctors, like anyone else
in a role, are partially dependent on their audience. Their own 'role
identity' — being a doctor — is, as it were, up for negotiation. They have
got to find patients who accept that what they are doing is being a doctor.

At the first encounter between two actors, the doctor and the patient
each will tend to give the other clues about how he wants to behave and
expects the other person to behave. They will both try to find out how
the other person defines the situation. Some of the clues come from the
setting itself. For example, the doctor often wears a white coat and sits
behind a desk. He may get up from behind his desk when the patient
enters the room or he may not. Whatever he does he will be offering
a clue as to the equality of the relationship that is being created. In the
negotiation which follows, there are several possible outcomes. The doctor
and patient may have defined the situation identically from the start
and continue to do so; after starting with different definitions they may
move towards a common one, either as a result of the doctor moving
towards the patient's conception or the patient moving towards the
doctor's conception, or by a process of some adjustment on the part of
both. Alternatively, they may totally fail to reach agreement, in which
case the transaction is likely to be broken off altogether. Again they may
disagree at the outset and then never reach anything more than a very
minimal agreement which allows them to carry on a relationship but with
an enormous amount of irritability and dysfunctional frustration for a
considerable period of time. Many such possibilities can be observed in
doctor-patient interaction.

What happens in the bargaining process will often be influenced by
power: by the relative ability of each participant to apply rewards and
sanctions to the other. In this exchange the patient is generally at a
disadvantage. Whereas the doctor has all the procedures of medicine as
well as his own considerable social status and authority, the patient has
only negative sanctions: he can refuse to co-operate, refuse to be cured,
or drop out of treatment. But most of these actions only affect the doctor
indirectly, and in any case, he is only one patient and the doctor can gain
rewards from others. The type of bargaining, which takes place in doctor-
patient interactions, therefore, tends to be influenced by this inequality.

However, there is nothing particularly remarkable about these conceptual notions of role and role negotiation. Every social role has
underlying constraints and conflicts within it. Every role performance
also involves features of the personal roles of the participants (interaction
does not take place in a vacuum) and every area of social interaction
involves bargaining and negotiation, in an attempt, or otherwise, to reach
a working agreement. In this chapter, however, I concentrate on the
doctor's role, and particularly the conflicts within it, rather than the
role of mother, nurse, or boy friend.

Conflict in the Doctor's Role

Built into the social role of being a doctor there are a whole series of conflicts that are innate to it and that are part of the script which the actors have to work with.

First, there is the conflict that the doctor has to resolve between the interests of any individual patient and the interests of patients as a group. This is the problem that came into focus in the discussion of the dying patient. The needs of the individual dying patient have to be balanced with the need to keep a ward situation functioning efficiently for others. A doctor will often have to choose between taking considerable care and attention with one patient and neglecting the others. Telling a parent that a child has a fatal disease like leukemia, for example, may lead to a whole series of difficulties and upsets which the doctor could help the parent with but could mean that somewhere else another patient was not getting attention. The doctor may decide to let the parents find out by themselves. In such circumstances to say that the doctor *must* put the patient first is not a great deal of help. The fact is that there is an inevitable conflict and that while the doctor

'will be struggling to adjust or fit any single case to the convenience of practice (and other patients), the patient will be struggling to gain a mode of management more specifically suited to him as an individual irrespective of the demands of the system as a whole.' (Freidson, 1970: 322)

In hospitals and, indeed, in medical practice generally, the essence of managing patients is the routinization of care. Hospitals are organized to help patients with particular diseases and problems, and standard rules and procedures have been developed to ensure that each patient obtains the appropriate treatment by doctors and nurses trained to carry these out. Patients are diagnosed and they are placed in a category of people for whom a particular course of management is prescribed. However, no individual is ever likely to fall perfectly into any one category and this will tend to create tensions. Rosengren and DeVault (1963), for example, observed that in one maternity hospital the staff attempted to maintain a definite spatial and temporal organization of its work irrespective of individual variations in condition. In the traditional movement from admitting office to preparation room, then labour room, no step was skipped even when the patient was well past the need of it; instead she was moved through the stages more rapidly than she would otherwise have been. By the same token, the staff tolerated the expression of pain by the patient only in the labour room, where it was considered appropriate to the 'illness' and where it could be managed by anaesthetics; elsewhere it was deprecated and ridiculed. In order to maintain the 'routine' tempo of work flow established by the staff (there would be other patients to follow), the laggard women were helped along (with forceps, etc.) to get them to deliver on schedule.

In another study Roth (1963) showed how the staff had conceptions of how long it 'should' take to get cured in a tuberculosis hospital and the steps in management were organized, not on the basis of laboratory tests, but on an institutional timetable. It is suggested that whether or not actual instances of this sort always obtain there will inevitably be continual tension between the routines created to provide good care for all patients and the fact that few patients perfectly fit the category to which they are assigned.

The same kind of conflict between individual and group needs will also arise over the practice of research and teaching. Research will usually benefit patients as a group but the submission to trials and test procedures will often not be 'in the interest' of the individual patient. Again, the same point can be made about using patients for teaching students. Undoubtedly, students need to have opportunities to observe, experiment, and ultimately practise, but this may be against the interest of the individual patient.

These examples suggest a second conflict. Not only is there the need to resolve the interests of any individual patient with patients as a whole (with a consequent potential loss of the individual needs of each patient), but also to allocate what are almost always scarce resources of time, skill, and materials between individual patients. If they have too few resources to treat all patients the same doctors have to choose exactly who is going to benefit from the most complicated life-saving procedures. There are usually insufficient resources for everyone: thus doctor time, scarce technical resources (like kidney machines), psychotherapy, and new drugs have to be rationed.

In the Casualty Departments of two American hospitals described by Sudnow (1967) doctors were actually involved in determining the distribution of death in the population, when they had to decide who to save and who to leave when patients arrived Brought in Dead (BID or in the American usage DOA – Dead on Arrival):

'...there seems to be a rather strong relationship between the age, social background, and the perceived moral character of patients and the amount of effort that is made to attempt revival when 'clinical death signs' are detected (and for that matter, the amount of effort given to forestalling their appearance in the first place)...

Generally speaking, the older the patient the more likely is his *tentative* death taken to constitute *pronounceable* death. Before a 20-year old ... [arriving] ... in the E.R. [emergency room] with a presumption of death attached in the form of the ambulance driver's assessment will be pronounced dead by a physician, very long listening to his heartbeat will occur, occasionally efforts at stimulation will be made, oxygen administered, and often times stimulative medication given. Less time will elapse between initial detection of an inaudible heartbeat and non-palpitating pulse and the pronouncement of death if the person is 40 years old, and still less if he is 70...

The driver's announcement of a "possible" places a frame of interpretation around the event, so that the physician expects to find a
dead person and attends the person under the general auspices of that
expectation. When a young person is brought in as a "possible", the
driver tries to convey some more alarming sense to his arrival by
turning the siren up very loud and keeping it going after he has already
stopped, so that by the time he has actually entered the wing,
personnel, expecting "something special" act quickly and accordingly...
...the older the person, the less thorough is the examination he is given;
frequently, elderly people are pronounced dead on the basis of only a
stethoscopic examination of the heart. The younger the person, the
more likely will an examination preceding an announcement of death
entail an inspection of the eyes, attempt to find a pulse, touching of
the body for coldness, etc. When a younger person is brought to the
hospital and announced by the driver as a "possible" but is nonetheless
observed to be breathing slightly, or have an audible heart beat, there
is a fast mobilization of effort to stimulate increased breathing and a
more rapid heart beat. If an older person is brought in in a similar
condition there will be a rapid mobilization of similar efforts; however,
the time which will elapse between that point at which breathing
noticeably ceases and the heart audibly stops beating and when the
pronouncement of death is made will differ according to his age.

One's location in the age structure of the society is not the only factor
that will influence the degree of care he gets when his death is
considered possibly to have occurred. At County Hospital a notable
additional set of considerations relating to the patient's presumed
"moral character" is made to apply ...

Among other categories of persons whose deaths will be more quickly
adjudged, and whose "dying" more readily noticed and used as a
rationale for apathetic care, are the suicide victim, the dope addict,
the known prostitute, the assailant in a crime of violence, the vagrant,
the known wife-beater, and, generally, those persons whose moral
characters are considered reproachable.' (Sudnow, 1967: 103–5)

A third area of conflict concerns the doctor's need to balance the
interests of any one patient at any point in time with the same patient's
interest in the future. The difficulties that arise in this respect were
illustrated in Duff and Hollingshead's study in New Haven, Connecticut
when they argued that patients with a poor prognosis were often treated
at the expense of their future interests.

'Patients and physicians commonly had a tacit agreement that the real
situation would not be confronted. This course may have seemed,
superficially, to be the most comfortable one for a time, but several
questionable consequences followed. The patient or his family often
asked for or encouraged treatment which brought about false hope,

prolonged suffering, lingering death, and high expenses. A realization of the true diagnosis and the limitation of treatment possibly may have resulted in an "appropriate" giving up of life to shield the patient from utter exhaustion and the gross indignities of extreme physical and emotional pain. The choices were not clearly reasoned but shaped, in part, by evasion of the truth. The patient wished to avoid the pain of illness and death. The physician wished to avoid conceding failure; he considered it a physician's duty to fight disease, and he expected the patient to do likewise regardless of his exhausted condition and imminent death.' (Duff and Hollingshead, 1968: 369–70)

Duff and Hollingshead argued that 'the evasion of truth' could be very dysfunctional in the long run both for patients, relatives, the staff, and good care. Because of such an 'evasion' patients and relatives may be denied the opportunity for gradually coming to terms with and accepting the fact of death. They are not given the opportunity to adjust gradually to their loss but have to experience it suddenly at the end.

One study on parents anticipating the death of a child from leukemia (Friedman *et al.*, 1963) showed that if the doctors and staff provide an opportunity for patient and relatives to work through their grief while the child is dying it is possible to reduce the stress at the time of death. This is important because periods of loss which are experienced as stress can lead to a raised susceptibility to a number of diseases (Rahe, 1969; Brown *et al.*, 1973; Parkes, 1969).

If there is a poor prognosis then there may be a conflict between what the patients and relatives want in the present (good news) and what their needs may be if there is to be successful management of the illness or crisis in the long run (the truth). Doctors have, perhaps not surprisingly, found this a very difficult dilemma to be faced with and have often simply ignored the problem (for example, Davis, 1963: 6).

Similar situations arise frequently in medicine. A psychiatrist sometimes thinks he knows, and probably does know, better than the patient, what is good for him. Surgeons have to weigh up pain, discomfort, and handicap in the present with the long-term survival interests of the patients, and so on. In such situations the patient's 'best interests', which the doctor should be working for, are uncertain. There is an ever-present danger of taking an easy way out, or for that matter, of rigid authoritarianism.

A fourth set of related problems involves the doctor's concern for the patient's welfare as against his concern for the patient's household or relatives. At what point does a doctor take the relatives' side and admit a mental patient compulsorily? When does a doctor interfere in a family on the patient's side? Once again there are no clearcut answers.

A fifth set of problems surrounds situations where the doctor is unable to help the patient and thus live up to his own view of his role as a curing one. This can occur either because the doctor is at a loss in terms of his technical abilities or because the patient is demanding help that the doctor cannot give. An untreatable disease is an example of the former and a patient complaining about a boring job, bad housing, or an appalling marriage, is an example of the latter. Often, of course, as was discussed in the previous chapter, such problems as the latter will be presented in disguised form. In such situations there is a conflict between how the doctor defines his role — and in time doctors may come to define themselves as able and willing to act in such areas — and the way the patient does. Such situations are almost certainly very common, but because doctors see themselves, and are seen, as active interveners, they often feel particularly threatened when they cannot help their patients and intervene positively. What can happen is that, although they do not necessarily accept that the patient's problem is a 'medical' one that they are competent to deal with, they continue to search for biological causes which could be dealt with medically, and, by recommending a specialist or prescribing a drug, prop up their own self-image but encourage the patient to continue to think in terms of an 'illness' (Balint, 1957: 22–23).

Often, doctors know perfectly well that the action they take is of a placebo kind — a ritual or practice that can have an effect on patients independent of the direct pharmacological or surgical effect — which will not really alter the underlying situation (for example, the marital or housing problem) or get to grips with the patient's problems. Where a doctor takes 'medical' action by referring or prescribing, one effect of his behaviour is to encourage the patient's belief that his problems are 'medical ones' and thus discourage other beliefs and, consequently, other action. Paradoxically, the growth of medical technology has probably increased this conflict between what the doctor can do and what his patients would like him to do. The rapid growth of surgical and pharmacological techniques has provided doctors with a large armoury of weapons for intervention and, together with the immense publicity that has accompanied the discovery of great life-saving techniques and procedures, has given a much greater illusion of medicine's efficacy than is actually the case. The contribution of scientific medicine to the reduction of death and suffering from disease, insofar as it can be measured, has not been that great (McKeown, 1965; Powles, 1973; see Chapter 11). Yet doctors themselves have made remarkably little attempt to document and publicize the limits of their knowledge. They have tended instead to make dogmatic pronouncements and to accept what Balint (1957) terms the 'apostolic' function and collude with their patients' suggestions that they are omnipotent. In this connection many technical procedures can be used to convince doctor and patients that he is doing something and thus conceal the lack of knowledge and the lack of effective treatments.

The tendency of doctors towards active intervention has been frequently discussed (Parsons, 1951: 466–9; Freidson, 1970: 244–77;

Dowling, 1963; Scheff, 1963: 97–107) and is well illustrated by studies of prescribing in general practice. Brotherston and Chave (1956), for example, found that on one housing estate ninety-nine prescriptions were issued for every 100 consultations and that only 5 per cent of the registered population consulted a doctor without obtaining a prescription. It is likely that a great many of those prescriptions had only symbolic value. Of course much of the pressure towards chemical intervention comes from patients' expectations built up over the years. For example, in a recent study, Ann Cartwright found that four-fifths of the elderly patients studied said they expected or hoped to be given a prescription, and only one in seven were not given one. Interestingly, half of those expecting a prescription were not given one compared with one in twenty of those who did get one (Cartwright 1974: 15).

Another set of conflicts, intrinsic to the role of many doctors, is that between his obligation to help an individual patient and his duties as an agent of the state or some other agency. Doctors have certain duties which derive from past actions on the part of the profession. The profession, for example, has become the legitimator of illness. A psychiatrist has the power to certify someone as mad rather than sane and gives evidence in court about people's mental state. This may confer disadvantage on a patient as well as any advantage that is derived from correct diagnosis, leading to effective treatment (see Chapter 10, pp. 357–59). Conflicts arise. When does a psychiatrist break 'clinical confidence' and go to the police? When does the general practitioner decide not to give a 'malingerer' a sickness certificate? Whose interest should be uppermost in his mind, and when?

A different group of conflicts are those between the doctor's responsibility in any particular appointment that he takes up and his own career needs. This is a problem well recognized in other occupations. It may well be one of the most significant in the relationship of doctors to patients in hospitals. A doctor's presence on any one particular ward or his task with any one patient has to be seen within the perspective of his whole career. In both Britain and the USA, for example, the majority of work in hospitals is done by relatively junior doctors — house officers, interns, registrars, residents — who are only employed in one hospital job for a short time and where they are supposed to gain experience and further training before specializing as a consultant or entering private practice. In fact, taking into account the short time such hospital posts are held, and considering that patients will often see a different doctor each time they visit the hospital or follow-up clinic, it may be stretching the point to talk about a single doctor-patient relationship in hospital at all.

Doctors who are just passing through a ward or a clinic, on the way to becoming a consultant, or achieving other career ambitions, may have difficulties carrying out their work and will sometimes find themselves in a conflict between their own career interests (which from their point of view is one reason they are there) and those of their patient. In New Haven, Duff and Hollingshead found that:

'...the physicians were not able to identify with [some] patients. To be well, young, and vigorous was to be in a very different position from that of an older, sick, or dying patient. The future of [those] ward patients was usually dismal; that of their ...[physicians]... offered an extreme contrast. The young physicians looked with anticipation toward a career in medicine. They hoped for the time when they would not have to do so much work and associate with "crocks" and "crud". Meanwhile they learned in the ward accommodations but indicated their awareness of the patients' situation in various ways such as naming these wards "the zoo".' (Duff and Hollingshead, 1968: 133).

The difficulty of resolving the conflict between patient and career in favour of the patient, is exacerbated by the fact that, on the whole, the reward structure of medicine will not operate to encourage career orientated young doctors to engage in good quality, all-round, medical care. They are unlikely to gain position, wealth, or status by being successful in improving the experience of patients on a back ward in a geriatric hospital, although the situation is improving. Similarly a young doctor or medical student will notice that it is not general practitioners who command the most respect in the profession. To obtain high prestige they will need to do research or specialize. If they do specialize they will be likely to stand a better chance of success in the profession if they work in some area of techno-scientific skill (as in surgery), where their achievements are more tangible, rather than in an area emphasizing the whole personality (as in psychiatry), where the outcome of treatment is much harder to measure. The emphasis in medicine is still very much on the rather narrow study of disease with only lip service paid to the broader context of the person:

'To be sure these young physicians realised that the problems of patients were great; they realised the chief task of a physician is to treat disease, but they were students who had to learn how to become physicians before they could treat people. When we asked them about the patients, they usually knew the nature of the patient's disease and something about his ongoing treatment but they knew little about the patients as human beings. Thus, our questions embarrassed them. Some told us we were choosing the less ill patients who required less time to care for or that they had been assigned to the patient in question for only a few days and had had little contact with him. One intern was more precise in his views. He ended a rather non-productive interview with this comment: "I cannot answer your questions. You're interested in patients: I'm interested in the disease in the body in the bed." ' (Duff and Hollingshead, 1968: 128).

What is suggested is that, quite apart from how good or bad a doctor this man was, the situation which he was in and the rewards he could expect in a medical career set up this conflict between his interests and those of the patient.

A final set of conflicts in the doctor role are ones that again arise in any occupational role, and probably any role at all: the conflict between that specific role and the remainder of roles which a person may have, for example, as father, husband, and tennis club player. Such conflict is particularly important in medicine because illness and death do not take weekends and holidays. Doctors may have to deal with emergencies at any hour.

Interaction between Doctors and Patients

Turning away from a direct focus on the doctor's role I now want specifically to examine the relationships that develop between doctors and patients. One commonly quoted discussion of doctor-patient relationships is the analysis done by two doctors, Szasz and Hollender (1956: 585–592), who distinguished between three types of doctor-patient interaction: activity-passivity; guidance-co-operation; mutual participation. They argued that these are the three types of relationship that will transpire depending on the disease condition the patient has and the therapy the doctor considers appropriate.

In the activity-passivity type the doctor is active and the patient passive. This type of situation originates in, and is appropriate for, emergencies (severe injuries, marked blood loss, delirium, or coma). The patient is more or less completely helpless as the doctor completes procedures and treatments on him. The medical work requires minimal interaction between doctor and patient: attendants, straps, anaesthesia, and other forms of restraint make certain the patient is thoroughly immobilized and passive – quite submissive to the doctor. Treatment takes place regardless of the patient's contribution. One can think of surgery or electro-convulsive therapy as examples. It should be noted, however, that even with surgery, this model rarely applies in its entirety. As I reported in an earlier chapter, Egbert *et al.* (1964) showed how the patient is an active agent in his recovery from major abdominal surgery. Where patients were warned what to expect, and how to obtain relief from pain prior to surgery (in other words, not treated as passive recipients), they recovered more quickly and needed less morphine than a comparison group of patients. In other words, in that instance, if the surgical patient was treated as passive, treatment was less effective. It is a finding that may well have implications for other forms of surgery.

The guidance-co-operation model usually underlines the doctor-patient relationship when the circumstances are less desperate than those discussed above. It applies to most acute disorders and especially to those of an infectious type. Although the patient is sick, he is keenly aware of what is going on, is capable of taking instructions and of exercising judgment, and has to be taken into account as a person. In essence, in this situation the patient is expected to recognize that the doctor knows best, that is why he is there, and he wants to be told what to do so that he can follow instructions and get better. This is the type of relationship most writers assume when discussing doctor-patient interaction. It is compatible with the 'rational' conception of the sick role discussed in Chapter 5.

Finally, in the Szasz-Hollender scheme, there is the relationship of mutual participation. This approach is regarded as essential for the management of chronic illness in which the treatment programme is carried out by the patient with only occasional instruction from the doctor (as, for example, in most cases of diabetes mellitus or psoriasis). Psychotherapy falls into this category of relationship. According to the model, the doctor helps the patient to help himself. For the purpose of completing the treatment the doctor needs the patient and the patient needs the doctor. Thus, in diabetes mellitus, for example, the patient needs the doctor's expertise, but the doctor needs the patient to monitor his blood sugar levels, to diet, and to alter his dose of tablets, or insulin, when necessary.

Logically, as Freidson (1970: 317–8) pointed out, Szasz and Hollender's scheme should not end with these three types of relationship. There are other possibilities they have not thought of (or do not consider important): guidance-co-operation where the patient guides and the doctor co-operates; activity-passivity where the patient is active and the doctor passive. There could also be mutual non-co-operation; mutual passivity; and so on. Szasz and Hollender's selection of possible relationships unwittingly perpetuates what in the previous chapter I termed the 'rational' or 'normatively-biased' model of doctor-patient interaction, the practice of tacitly assuming that the patient shares the observer-doctor's assumptions about what he wants from the doctor (above p. 172). Presumably it did not occur to Szasz and Hollender that a situation where the doctor was not at least jointly in charge could obtain. Yet there are situations where the doctor simply does what he is told: he writes a prescription or makes a referral in response to a patient's request. In one study I conducted, for example, several patients described how they had dictated a referral letter to their GP (Tuckett, forthcoming). Also, in situations where the doctor is dependent on the patient (for example, for his fees), or the patient is particularly prestigious, or the doctor is in some other way dependent, the doctor's ability to control the interaction is limited. Indeed this view of the doctor as passive, as someone to carry out a request, may be quite commonly held. Many patients, like the clients of social workers described by Mayer and Timms (1969), probably want doctors 'to put sense' into their husbands or to help with their housing situation. Such patients have made up their mind about their problem and do not therefore feel they need the doctor to tell them. From their point of view the doctor's job is to co-operate with them.

I would, therefore, agree with Freidson who suggests that the three types of doctor-patient relationship analyzed by Szasz and Hollender should be considered not as types of relationship that actually obtain (although they sometimes will) but as types of relationship that doctors wish to create with patients suffering from different conditions. Analysis may then focus on the conflict, bargaining, and negotiation that takes place as doctors try to create these types of relationship. If we add in the patient's point of view we can consider the mutual bargaining over roles and goals that occurs. What patterns of interaction do doctors or patients wish to create? What social circumstances are the prerequisite for such patterns and how is it that doctors or patients set about establishing them? What happens if the patient or the doctor does not play the expected part — as they often do not? How does a psychiatrist deal with patients who should be active, in psychotherapy for example, but want just to lie down and have their problems 'whisked' away? What happens with patients who should be passive but do not want to be? Adding further questions that Szasz and Hollender ignore, how does the patient set up the type of inter-action he wants? How will he attempt to manipulate the doctor into activity or passivity? An analysis and consideration of these questions will, I think, contribute to understanding and therefore improve doctor-patient relationships.

In the previous chapter I discussed some of the research that gives us an idea of what patients may be trying to get from doctors. But what, in addition to the factors already discussed, will the doctor attempt with the patient? Looked at from the point of view of his role a doctor typically has two tasks to perform: he must first diagnose the problem which a patient presents, in order to determine the appropriate treatment, and he must then get the patient to agree with his diagnosis and act on his advice, including sometimes the advice that there is nothing really wrong. In diagnosis, the doctor has to obtain information of the sort relevant to medicine. However, this information may not be the sort that the layman is typically used to providing. The doctor has, therefore, to specify exactly what information is required and to help the patient to give it in a form that can be translated into medical data despite problems in recollection, vagueness, and so on. In treatment there are more complicated problems. The patient may disagree with the doctor's recommendations, not be accustomed to regulating his life in the appropriate manner, or share other different conceptions of the sick-role and of the doctor's role.

The doctor is in a complex and ambiguous situation. On the one hand, since his role is to help the patient, it is his task to listen to what the patient has to say and to help the patient to communicate with him. On the other hand, since the patient's view of what he should present, how he should behave, and how his problem should be treated may not always (indeed, not often) agree with the doctor's judgement, the doctor has to try and persuade the patient to change his view or his behaviour.

There are various ways in which doctors appear to try and control this dilemma and reduce conflict. One strategy is to restrict themselves to patients who are unlikely to differ in views, for example, those from a similar social and educational background who will share, to a large extent, their norms and values and may more readily agree with their recommendations. Many do seem to take this option. Tudor Hart, for example, has argued that practices with a more middle-class clientele are much more popular among doctors and get the best qualified new recruits (Tudor Hart, 1971: 406–7). But not all doctors could solve the problem this way. It is therefore interesting that Cartwright (1975: 15) after tape-recording consultations found that doctors spent longer talking with middle-class patients, taking up 6.2 minutes on average, compared to 4.7 minutes for working-class patients. Since working-class patients have more complaints this is an important difference. In fact, Ann Cartwright (1975: 19) concluded a discussion of doctor-patient relationships by saying:

'Altogether the data suggest that doctors have a rather less sympathetic and understanding relationship with their working-class patients, and we would speculate that a middle-class patient is more likely to regard the doctor as a peer, to be more confident about his own opinions on the importance of his problems and so insist on their being discussed. This would suggest that working-class patients are likely to find it more difficult to raise additional problems at a consultation; and our observations that working-class patients discuss fewer problems, and are no more likely to talk about social problems although more of them regard these as appropriate issues to discuss with their doctor, support this.'

(1975: 19)

Whether they are dealing with middle-class or working-class patients doctors seem to be most happy when they are in control of the situation. This is my interpretation of another finding by Cartwright, who also reports that doctors are more satisfied where consultations are kept short (1975: 19–20). A doctor has various ways in which he can control the relationship he has with patients and minimize the need to interact with them if he so desires. Doctors can and do 'educate' their patients to bring appropriate complaints to them in various ways. Seventy-six per cent of general practitioners in an earlier Cartwright study (1967: 31) agreed that a 'good general practitioner can train his patients not to make unnecessary or unreasonable demands on him'. One way doctors can control how often patients see them is by repeat prescriptions. If a patient is given a prescription which lasts for four weeks he may be discouraged from returning in two. The doctor can see the patient regularly but not too frequently. A repeat prescription for a medicine can ensure a regular dose of doctor. A patient may be more hesitant to return if not given a reason he can readily accept. As one doctor said about a patient in Cartwright's more recent study: 'It offers her a regular and legitimate occasion to come and see me — gives some structure to her life and she feels someone is bothering' (Cartwright, 1974: 18).

Cartwright provides in a more recent paper further examples of the way doctors control their interaction with patients. Here are two tape-recorded consultations where the doctor cuts short the interaction:

'Doctor: Apart from these palpitations you're really very healthy, aren't you?
Patient: Yes, yes. Well, I mean, I have varicose veins you know?
Doctor: Oh yes.
Patient: And I've got a small ulcer, but it's dry now.
Doctor: Mm.
Patient: On my right leg I have a small ulcer.
Doctor: Yes, that's very good.
Patient: But it's drying up gradually. One day I think it's gone completely but it hasn't. It comes back. But...
Doctor: Now here's the letter to see about your eyes.'

'Doctor: Righto, well that's it. Very good.
Patient: One or two other aches and pains but I suppose that's — old age, I suppose? A bit of rheumatism in my shoulder.
Doctor: O.K.
Patient: As I say, the thing is that, well this here, though I've had these pains I've felt so good in myself, you know ...
Doctor: That's right.
Patient: I've had — well ...
Doctor: That's right, if you develop further trouble, come back. Otherwise you don't need to, just keep going.' (1975: 16)

These are negative examples but doctors can also encourage patients to bring up additional problems or symptoms. Cartwright quotes an example from the beginning of a consultation:

'Doctor: You've been spitting blood?
Patient: Yes.
Doctor: It comes when you cough?
Patient: Yes, but not always.
Doctor: Any other trouble?
Patient: Well, when I've taken that medicine I've been prescribed that all comes up with it.
Doctor: Have you noticed any other trouble at all?
Patient: In what way?
Doctor: Any other complaints?
Patient: No.
Doctor: Any pains anywhere?
Patient: No.
Doctor: Any trouble with your joints or your hands?
Patient: Only my feet.' (1975: 16–17)

and another from the end of a consultation:

'Doctor: Now was there anything else that you might like to talk about?

Patient: No, I dont't think so thank you.

Doctor: Jolly good, fine. How's your wife by the way? Is she alright?

Patient: I think that the fact that I've not been well has done her the world of good.

Doctor: Oh good. Busy looking after you.' (1975: 17)

If a doctor is not confident that a patient will carry out the agreed treatment he can attempt to extend the scope of his intervention in a patient's life in order to exert direct control and thus ensure recommendations are carried out. For example, patients can be brought into the hospital as in-patients or the doctor and other health workers can visit them in the home. A similar strategy would involve enlisting the support of relatives or others in the treatment and 'control' process. A further alternative is to try and by-pass the patient to a large extent. The need to obtain reliable information from him, for example, can be circumvented by using tests and laboratory techniques that are largely independent of anything but his minimal co-operation. The need to involve the patient in treatment can be similarly reduced by using long-acting or slow-releasing drugs.

This examination of the ways doctors try to control the doctor-patient relationship should not hide the fact that patients are by no means passive. The point is made in Cartwright's 1974 paper where one doctor felt that patients often actively try to create their own diagnoses. Describing one consultation this doctor felt it was:

'a "success" because the reason for the consultation was openly recognized as being for marital problems and depression. Two others he felt did not have this insight. One had been told he had asthma by the hospital – but the doctor did not think this was an appropriate diagnosis. In his view she had shortness of breath brought on by anxiety or hysteria. A third woman also suffered from depression and a dry mouth. She reckoned the dry mouth was caused by the drugs she was taking for depression. In the doctor's view the dry mouth preceded the treatment for depression and was "a classical Jewish symptom of depression." But he did not explain this to her as he felt it would be tantamount to calling her a liar. In the doctor's view these three consultations illustrated the way in which patients create their own diagnoses. They also show how doctor and patient may agree or disagree with an interpretation or collude.' (Cartwright, 1974: 8).

A second patient, but from a different doctor, provides an example of the mutual negotiation that can go on:

' "The doctor classified three of this patient's six prescriptions has 'his' and three as 'mine'. He's one of the few who has barbiturates. He says it's the only thing that gives him sound sleep. Ephedrine tablets are very important to him. I think they are useless. When he first came I wasn't going to give him barbiturates. I tried others which were useless — then Mogadon. Then I accepted barbiturates. It's an amicable arrangement." ' (Cartwright, 1974: 17)

As I pointed out at the beginning of this chapter the basic consideration in situations of bargaining and negotiation is where the power lies. This is a complex issue which has been much under-researched.

In one sense the patient is often in a weak power position. After all, his illness may literally make him powerless. More frequently, however, he has some latitude when deciding whether to visit the doctor. But according to Parson's (1951) view of the sick-role (above p. 181), if the patient does seek help he places himself in an inferior position and accepts the doctor's superior wisdom. Like Szasz and Hollender's analysis I think this view of Parson's accords more with what the doctor hopes will happen (the rational model again) than with the facts. We have already seen that patients have their own ideas and this is confirmed by my own experience that patients often visit a doctor without having finally made up their mind that they will accept help. The doctor's right to determine what is wrong and what to do about it, in short his right to carry out what he sees as his task, is one issue that the patient will be out to negotiate in the consultation. Correct, or not, this view is a possibility. In any case what is certain is that if patients do not give up their right to determine their future then the doctor, if he wishes to persuade a patient, will need to establish he is in authority. Ritual activity in the consulting room and the hospital helps the doctor to do this. Through various devices, such as making patients wait, the white coat, the filling in of forms, and other administrative procedures, the patient and doctor are marked as of different status. Factors such as social class and the doctor's high prestige in society will be of help to a doctor wishing to establish his authority, although conversely, they may hinder a relationship of mutual participation, such as attempts at psychotherapy, with working-class patients.

There are a number of studies that analyze the negotiation and bargaining that can occur between doctors and patients and the strategies that each use to advance their points of view. Goffman's (1968) participant observation study in a mental hospital and Roth's (1963) participant observation (he developed tuberculosis whilst a Ph.D student) in a tuberculosis sanitorium provide sensitive descriptions of the way patients and hospital staff manipulate one another. The work of Davis (1963) on children with polio, Duff and Hollingshead (1968) in an American teaching hospital, and Sudnow (1967) and Glaser and Strauss (1963) on dying are also especially interesting.

The relative power of doctor and patient, and hence the ability of each to get their way in the consultation, depends on a number of variables. In my view the most basic determinants are the relative needs of the actors involved. In the language of economics it depends on each actor's preference or utility function – on their wants in the interaction. If the patient does not particularly need the doctor's help, for example, if he is simply going to the doctor in order to placate a relative or friend, he will not be in a situation where he has much to win or lose. Conversely if his wants are great, if he has to get a sickness certificate or is in terrible pain, he needs the doctor's help very much and is thus dependent on him.

A doctor's utility function can be examined in the same way. He may need to succeed with some patients very badly. One need may be financial and, in their relationship with rich or powerful patients, doctors have often been in a difficult situation. If they insist on an unwelcome treatment the patients may leave. As Freidson (1970: 305–16) points out, the institutional arrangements through which doctors and patients meet will influence the doctor's power to carry out his wishes regardless of a patient's status. It is not surprising, therefore, that doctors in countries like the USA, where they are dependent for their income on the patient returning to them, have sought to limit the number of doctors and therefore improve their competitive position. A reduction of reliance on the patient is one of the gains that a doctor derives from the National Health Service, where he is paid in effect adequately regardless of the patient's views.

However, the rewards in a situation are not only financial. Doctors may wish to succeed for other reasons, for example, they may want to help patients in order to improve their own self-esteem or because they care for others. The point, for the purpose of this discussion, is that the doctor's power will be reduced the more his utility function depends on the patient, for example, a doctor who 'cares' not only that the patient does not come back but that he actually stays well and successfully carries out his various roles, will be much more dependent on his patients than one who does not. It is conceivable that a reward system for doctors could be designed (based on financial or other incentives) so that doctors gained from 'caring' in this way. Such a system would very much increase the power position of patients.

From the discussion so far it must be clear that patients often tend to be in a much weaker position than doctors. Their power is largely negative (they can refuse drugs or give up treatment or can simply sit it out in the doctor's surgery by bothering him until something happens) and depends very much on the doctor's utility function. Furthermore, patients are often likely to need the doctor's help badly. Also, for the patient, the patient role is more all-embracing (his 'illness' may affect all his other roles) whereas for the doctor his role is only one of several others he plays. Finally, whereas the patient is often dependent on one doctor, as in most systems there is a shortage of doctors or an agreement between doctors that shopping around is bad, the doctor has the opportunity of seeking rewards from other patients. For all these reasons the distribution of power in doctor-patient relationships, unless controlled by compensatory institutional arrangements, is potentially highly skewed.

Goffman (1969: 107–182) provided a model of social relationships which he termed strategic interaction* and which may help us to think further about the relations that develop between doctors and patients. I shall briefly present it because I think it may help to provide a more useful way of looking at relationships than does the present alternative – the 'rational' or 'normatively biased' model. Relationships between doctors and patients, I suggest, are likely to be very frustrating for both parties if they assume the other is going to act in a 'sensible' manner.

Goffman's model is appropriate to a situation of 'mutual impingement', that is, where the actors involved have something to win or lose by interacting with one another (as we have seen this assumption may be unwarranted in the case of some doctors and some patients). Goffman conceives of a set of interactions (that is, consultations) *as* a game (he does not mean they *are* a game) in which individuals try to maximize rewards (he is therefore following the assumptions of exchange theorists who assess the costs and benefits to be derived from interaction). Individuals maximize rewards by making moves – that is acting in some purposive way. Before, and as they move, however, each player (an actor in the game) assesses the situation in various ways. The emphasis is on mutual assessment.

Each player attempts to assess the other player's *moves*, trying to find out what decisions he has taken and what plans he has for the game (why the patient has come, why the doctor does not get up when the patient enters the room, etc.). They each attempt to assess the *operational code* that the other is using, that is, the orientation towards the game that a player has and his preference pattern or utility function. This has been discussed earlier. What aims and goals does each player have and how does he order them in terms of possibilities? What is he willing to give up? What constraints are imposed on him by his values and norms (for example, religious or ideological or professional beliefs)? Another assessment can be made of each player's *style of play*, this is the particular way he presents himself in the situation. As I noted in an earlier chapter social class is likely to influence such styles of communication (above pp. 145–7). Then there is the need to assess each other's *resolve* – how far is the individual willing to go in the game? What is he willing to put up with or lose? For how long will he persevere? Is he sincere?

Players will also wish to know each other's *information state* – what does each think the other knows about his own situation? Then there are the *resources* each has to help them play; records of past games (for example, patient records), techniques for discovery (for example, laboratory

* This way of clarifying my thoughts was suggested to me by my colleague, Uta Gerhadt.

tests), and so on. And most important, in Goffman's view (1969: 121), there is the assessment of *gameworthiness* — the ability of an individual to assess all possible consequences of action and also his ability to act in the manner required by his judgement of the situation. Finally, there is the assessment of *integrity*, 'that is the strength of their propensity to remain loyal to [each other's] agreed interests once they have agreed to play ... and not to instigate courses of action on behalf of [some other] interests, usually their own' (1969: 123).

These assessments are the elements of the situation that each player tries to *'dope-out'* in order to embark on courses of action. Actual moves will be made according to those assessments and according to the *position* in the game the players have arrived at (the history of the relationship). Moves and positions may be *viable* or *nonviable* depending on how far they sacrifice the game should they prove unsuccessful. At a certain point there is no turning back.

Goffman concentrates on the way in which assessments are made. Assessments are made by interpreting *expressions given off* by the other actor as well as by *communication transmitted*. In other words there are verbal and non-verbal elements of communication. Both may be intentional and a major concern of the actors involved will be to try and discriminate their *'correctness'*, whether or not they accord with the facts or are being created to make an impression. A great deal of the assessment that takes place will concern the *credibility* of information received. Is what the doctor says true? Is he really trying to help?

No study that I know has yet analyzed doctor-patient relationships in terms of strategic interaction but I would regard it as a highly relevant perspective for doctors.[1] What is the patient's *operational code*? Does the doctor understand the patient's *style of play*? How much *resolve* does a patient have? What *moves* has he made? What are his *resources* and his *information state*?

Certainly, whether or not doctors make these kinds of assessments, implicitly or explicitly, or find them useful, patients do. For example, in my own interviewing of psychiatric patients and in observation of general practice, I have been struck with the way patients are very sensitive to the *expressions given off* by doctors. Whether or not the phone rings in the consultation, the amount of time the doctor spends with a patient, the kinds of questions that are asked, all these are assessed by patients and not necessarily in ways one might expect. Different patients, for example, interpreted long consultations as indicating they really were 'mad' whereas actually the psychiatrist was simply concerned to carry out a thorough interview. Other aspects of the consultation and of treatment, as well as the doctor's behaviour, were given all sorts of interpretation by patients (Tuckett, forthcoming). Given the fact that doctors and patients often come from very different backgrounds and often have opposing ideas about what consultations are about there can be many false assessments of operational codes, moves, resolve, and the like. This often leads to frustration for doctors and patients. Thinking of what is happening in terms of strategic interaction, or some other similar model, may help to create a less frustrating situation.

The Drug 'Doctor'

The factors underlying the doctor-patient interaction have become all the more significant in recent years with the increased recognition that the actual relationship is itself a highly effective therapy. The importance of doctor-patient relationships is illustrated by a number of studies. For example, Egbert *et al's*. (1964) study showing how pre-operative encouragement and instruction of patients can dramatically improve treatment efficacy has been quoted (pp. 25–6), so was Friedman *et al's*. (1963) attempt to intervene to help the parents of dying children cope with their loss (p. 196). Other studies can be considered. Skipper and Leonard (1968) showed how a particular sort of social interaction with hospital personnel, providing information and emotional support, can reduce a mother's experience of stress and that this in turn will have profound indirect effects on the child's social, psychological, and even physiological responses to hospitalization and recovery. Zola's (1963) suggestion, that failure to recognize the 'non-medical' element in help-seeking leads to drop out of treatment, may be put alongside Michael Balint's (1957) work arguing that harm is done to the patient through treating physical symptoms alone without recognizing they are part of a wider presenting picture.

Furthermore, work with the placebo response underlies the significance of the doctor-patient interaction as a powerful therapeutic agent. Beecher (1955; 1961) in reviews of this literature suggests, for example, that up to one third of the success of any drug or procedure may be attributable to placebo, that is to the patient's belief that something is being done for him. One of the more interesting studies he cites is one where a 'pretence' operation, involving no more than an incision and sewing up again, produced both subjective and objective improvement in a substantial proportion of patients. To what extent and for how long such placebo improvements can take place is still very much a matter for debate (Wolf, 1959), but research indicates that:

'The doctor's relationship to the patient is basic to an understanding of the placebo effect. The interested doctor who imparts confidence, who is friendly and reassuring to patients, who performs a thorough examination and who is not anxious, conflicted or guilty about the patient or his treatment is more likely to elicit positive placebo reactions.'
(Shapiro, 1964: 80)

However, several studies suggest that patients feel doctors are often unaware of their point of view (for example, Tagliacozzo and Mauksch,

1972). One reason suggested, for example, by the two patients quoted at the beginning of this chapter, is that doctors do not have sufficient time. This may be so but another reason is that many doctors have been too quick to start on the complicated (and for that matter time-consuming) medical procedures that they have at their disposal:

'From the viewpoint of the doctors, Mrs. O'Pell was a model patient, co-operative and forbearing. She made no demands and seemed to accept without any major challenge their explanation of her illness. She responded dramatically to treatment which was most gratifying to all, and finally she was discharged as "cured" from the medical clinic. The doctors felt they had learnt much whilst practising splendid medicine ... they knew nothing of Mrs. O'Pell's doubts and fears about her illness. Although the pulmonary disease was treated successfully, regardless of its nature, the management of this patient did involve some risks of treatment (anticoagulant therapy) which she almost certainly did not require and which was costly to her and her family... The management of the physicians had the effect of increasing the severity of her hypo-chondriasis; she went to more doctors, incurring higher costs, and her fears (*the main reason for her coming*) were never successfully relieved.'

(Duff and Hollingshead, 1968: 131)

Similar incidents are cited by Balint (1957) in his study of general practice. For example, one general practitioner reported the case of,

'Mrs. C., aged 32 years; married, childless. This patient has been on my partner's list since early 1946. She complained then of epigastric and chest pains. My partner sent her for investigation to an eminent physician in April 1946, who reported, "You will be glad to hear that this patient's chest X-ray is quite normal. She seems very pleased at this and I think most of her symptoms are functional, and hope that the reassurance I have given her may be of some help."

A short while after, the patient was unhappy about the condition of the chest as the pain returned, and she was sent for chest X-ray to a chest clinic. The physician to the chest clinic reported in May 1946, "You will be pleased to learn that there is no evidence of pulmonary or pleural tuberculosis. I think the epigastric pain originates in the abdominal wall, that is, it is probably muscular or fibrous in origin. Massage might now be tried." Massage was accordingly tried, but with little success. She was a frequent visitor to the surgery and was seen by me first in October 1946. I thought then that her symptoms might be due to "chronic appendicitis". I referred her to a gynaecologist first, who wrote in 1947, "This lady is rather puzzling. She has been under Dr. L, who had her completely investigated and found nothing, and I must admit I can find nothing abnormal, and from the gynaecological point of view I have drawn a blank. Whether in view of her constant pain in the right side and her chronic constipation there is the possibility of an appendix, it is difficult to say, but if you wish I will ask one of our surgeons ..." A surgeon was accordingly asked, and he said in October 1947, "...I have advised her to come into hospital for the removal of her appendix." Appendicectomy was carried out in December 1947. She came to see me then practically every week with a variety of pains, sometimes in the right iliac fossa, sometimes in the back, and drove me frantic with seemingly irrelevant chatter and unwillingness to leave me during a busy surgery. I sent her to see a well-known orthopaedic surgeon on account of her persistent backache. He said in January 1948, "She has a supple back, although there is some slight tenderness in her lumbar muscles. I am arranging for her to have some treatment in the physiotherapy department."

Mrs. C. attended my surgery regularly every week, had still the same complaints as before, and began, to my puzzlement, to be rather aggressively flirtatious with me. I then told her one day, rather abruptly, that there was little more I could do for her and that it would be best if she went back to her job as a sales assistant and would not come back to see me for some time, and I did not see her again until 1950. She came then with her old complaints of pains again, and in the attitude of a penitent child ("Didn't you miss me?" and "I hope you won't be cross with me any more."). She still came every week, again became flirtatious and tried to put her foot on mine, and one day put her hand on mine. I rebuked her then, and she cried out; went, only to come back the following week, and in subsequent weeks. She received five to ten minutes' chat and a bottle of medicine on each occasion.

Since then, due to a greater awareness of personality disorders on my part, she has been given a one-hour interview in which, *inter alia*, she told of her childhood, of a father who was in the Navy and away from home most of the time, of a much loved younger brother who died at the time of the onset of her symptoms, of her dyspareunia since the beginning of her marriage, and of her complete inability to have sexual intercourse since her brother's death. Further investigations are in progress. Her attitude to me since that interview has much changed, there are no more efforts to flirt and there is an improvement in her symptoms. But it took four years to get to that hour, and an appendicectomy. *Mea culpa!*' (Balint, 1957: 11–12)

In his book Balint argues that patients like Mrs. C are interested in talking about their worries rather than being subjected to medical treatments. They require what he terms a dose of doctor. Balint and his group have argued, therefore, that by paying quite deliberate attention to the communication between doctor and patient, the patient's way of thinking and the problems as the patient perceived them, much more 'effective' medical care could take place. In this respect Balint argues (p. 109 *et seq.*) that doctors can be profoundly hindered by some aspects of their training:

'Our experience has invariably been that, *if the doctor asks questions in the manner of medical history-taking he will always get answers — but hardly anything more.* Before he can arrive at what we called "deeper" diagnosis, he has to learn to *listen.* This listening is a much more difficult and subtle technique than that which must necessarily precede it — the technique of putting the patient at ease, enabling him to speak freely. *The ability to listen is a new skill, necessitating a considerable though limited change in the doctor's personality.* While discovering in himself an ability to listen to things in his patient that are barely spoken because the patient himself is only dimly aware of them, the doctor will start listening to the same kind of language in himself. During this process he will soon find out that there are no straightforward direct questions which could bring to light the kind of information for which he is looking. Structuring the doctor-patient relationship on the pattern of a physical examination inactivates the processes he wants to observe as they can happen only in a two-person collaboration.'

(Balint, 1975: 121)

What is needed, Balint continues, is a:

' "mutual investment company"; it was this that enabled Mrs. O to talk to her doctor on the first occasion offered her, and likewise enabled Mr. Y, though only at the very end of the interview, to mention what really had brought him to the surgery.' (Balint, 1957: 121)

Balint contrasts the doctor's traditional rather paternal reassurances with a genuine attempt to 'listen' to the difficulties of patients.

'...."listening" during a "long interview" represents a very large part of psychotherapy and is, moreover, an indispensable requisite, almost in the same way as diagnosis is indispensable for a rational therapy.'

(Balint, 1957: 135)

The type of approach suggested by Balint, leads to a re-emphasis on the human skills a doctor possesses rather than on technical and clinical intervention. Although it may appear to be time-consuming, Balint argued, his approach could actually save the doctor time.

'If we take it that Mrs. O came to the surgery about three times a month, needing from five to ten minutes attention on each occasion, her disappearance from the surgery saved the doctor between one and two hours' work in four months. Even if the "long interview" is set against this, the saving was considerable; moreover, the follow-up report showed that it continued. Another aspect is the *cessation* of the drudgery and irritation caused to Dr. G, and the relief to him when Mrs. O changed from a complaining, depressed and dissatisfied patient into a friendly and cheerful acquaintance. Still more important, the "long interview" caused his understanding of his patient's problems to be better and safer.' (Balint 1957: 126)

Nonetheless, although concerned about the implications of giving some patients 'long interviews' in an otherwise hurried general practice, the Balint group (Balint and Norrell, 1973) have developed further techniques for the consultation such as concentrating on the 'flash' which can be used in a short interview of only a few minutes. I have little doubt that work of this kind, which is still at a very preliminary stage and needs careful assessment, will eventually contribute greatly to the skills a doctor can use in general practice.

Of course, the Balint group's work, which is not yet based on controlled studies, has important implications for practice. The implication, as elsewhere in this work, is that the doctor should be more concerned with the social and emotional background of his patients than has usually been the case. However, recognition of this social and emotional background may accentuate the fifth conflict I described above (pp. 196—8). The doctor may come to recognize that because the true cause of the patient's problems lie in social and economic forces apparently beyond his control, in many cases what he can do is extremely limited. This conflicts with his wish to be active and effective and may be one reason why many doctors have been unwilling to see the complex relationship of disease and the social environment, prefering rather to label most of their work as 'trivia'.

The Professional Image

If a doctor is to carry out his task effectively he will often be placed in a position of quite unusual power and intimacy with his patients. For example, he will often need to probe quite deeply into their most intimate thoughts and behaviour, he may need to examine parts of their body such as their genitals, and he will on occasion require the power to command them to carry out his orders even though this does not necessarily seem right to patients at the time. These requirements and the fact that the power of healing is of immense significance to individuals make the role of the doctor a particularly special one which has attracted great interest among sociologists.

In one particularly elegant analysis the American sociologist Talcott Parsons (1951: 428—79) has suggested that in order to carry on his task effectively a doctor has to present himself in a particular way. He is expected to perform his role in a way that is 'collectivity' rather than 'self-oriented' and base his actions on 'universalism, functional specificity and affective neutrality'. In other words, doctors rely on generally accepted scientific standards rather than on particularistic ones, restrict their work to the limits of their technical competence, work objectively without emotional involvement, and finally, put the patient's interests before their own. 'By defining his role in this way it was possible to overcome or minimise resistances which might well otherwise prove fatal to the possibility of doing the job at all' (Parsons, 1951: 459). Although Parsons may be right and it is helpful to doctors trying to carry out their task that they may be seen in this way, as Freidson (1970) argues, it is certainly not the case that a doctor's performance of his role is unambiguously characterized by functional specificity, universalism, affective-neutrality, or a collectivity orientation.

First, let us consider the universalistic aspect of the clinical doctor's role. How far is the practice of medicine itself scientific? It is apparent that in contrast to the research doctor the clinician's work is practical and applied, rather than theoretical. Whereas 'scientists' attempt to arrive at general solutions the practitioner is concerned to apply them. His work is with individual problems and their solution. Since his attention is focused in this way on concrete problems he is often obliged to carry on even when he lacks an adequate scientific foundation for his activities: the doctor is there to he helpful and has an orientation towards intervention, towards trying to do something. In fact he must try to act irrespective of the state of knowledge (the patient's illness will not wait for the research scientist to produce the answer). Furthermore, even where scientific knowledge is available the fact that science is based on probabilistic relationships involving aggregates means that it can only give general guidance not infallible proof that what he prescribes for an individual is right. The doctor will always be looking for the exception and will base this search on 'personal first hand examination' of every individual case. This is then evaluated in terms of the doctor's experience. But clinical experience, of course, far from being objective and universalistic, is of its very essence subjective and particularistic. In this connection it is interesting to note the great importance attached, in medical schools and in the medical hierarchy, to clinical experience and the doctor's individual responsibility and personal experience. In the American study of medical education in Kansas (the conclusion of which, in this respect at least, is not I think a long way off describing any London medical school), clinical experience was generally emphasized as far more significant than general scientific knowledge. In Kansas students learnt to treat 'science' with circumspection. Those who argued 'from the book' were frequently the subject of ridicule and faculty members would delight in telling of their own contrary experience.

> ' "Clinical experience" refers to "actual experience" in dealing with patients and disease ...[which] even though it substitutes for scientifically verified knowledge, can be used to legitimate a choice of procedures for a patient's treatment and can even be used to rule out some procedures that have been scientifically established.' (Becker *et al.*, 1961)

In terms of this argument only greater experience was acceptable and this also formed the main basis of hierarchy in the hospital. In the same way individual responsibility was frequently stressed by faculty members who would make great play of catching out students who had omitted some precaution or procedure.

Just as the doctor's role tends towards particularism rather than universalism, towards personal judgement rather than scientific deduction, so is it also more functionally diffuse than specific. That is, it involves intervention in more areas than might be suggested by applying strictly medical skills. The present so-called shortage of doctors in Britain or the USA would end overnight if doctors were to concentrate only on areas where they are technically competent by virtue of their training. Many of the problems faced in clinical work, and particularly in general practice, are outside the doctor's formal competence. General practitioners complain that many complaints brought to them are 'trivial' or in areas such as housing, marriage, sex, and friendships which are not strictly relevant to the application of medical skills.

Even in strictly 'medical' cases the doctor has often to act well outside any clearly established scientific procedure because patients have a strong expectation of his success. These expectations are complicated by the high degree of emotional involvement surrounding illness and death. Such situations are those typically associated with the development of magic and ritual with which, of course, medicine and its ancestry has always been associated. Until very recently almost all medical procedures were probaby placebos and a great number of present activities no doubt still are (Siegerist, 1951). The use of the placebo is in fact a great potential strength of the doctor (see above).

Situational factors in the doctor's role, insofar as he is a clinician, therefore, lead him to use particularistic standards, and at the same time, notably if he is a specialist or doctor of 'first contact', he is typically led to play a 'pontifical, functionally diffuse role', not really limited by his training or qualification. In having to rely heavily on his own individual clinical experience with specific individuals the doctor comes more and more to rely in essence on the authority of his own senses, independently of the general authority of tradition or science. At the same time the doctor exists in a situation of more than usual uncertainty and vulnerability which is intensified by the strong emotions that are generated in the area of illness and death. The need to be secure, leads in many cases to rigidity and a claim to omnipotence, and hence to fear of outside criticism.

When discussing the conflict that a doctor faces when he has to arbitrate between the interests of two or more patients it was suggested that doctors have to be concerned with the distribution of scarce resources. In such decisions, as in all others, doctors are expected to act with 'affective neutrality': that is not to become emotionally involved or ideologically biased. In practice, however, there is considerable evidence to suggest that doctors, inevitably and understandably, tend to apply the value judgements of their social class and culture in their decisions. Thus the doctors in Sudnow's study (see p. 194—5) were less likely to make great efforts to save the old, the socially deviant, or those from the less reputable areas of the city.

Another instance of value judgements entering into the way doctors worked was from the same study at County Hospital where the degree of medical interest intrinsic to a case affected what happened:

'On the medical wards, on the basis of general observation, it seems that one could obtain a high order correlation between the amount of time doctors spent discussing and examining patients and the degree of unusualness of their medical problems.' (Sudnow, 1967: 106—7)

Many other examples could be given of the way in which value judgements other than 'affectively neutral' ones enter the doctor-patient relationship through (often implicit) decisions about the allocation of resources. Individuals with a low socio-legal status, drug addicts, tuberculosis patients, certified mental patients, and others confined against their will, will often tend to be less well treated. Similarly someone seen as less than a responsible human being like the senile, psychotic, retarded or otherwise 'deficient', are at risk for less than adequate treatment. Socio-economic resources are important as well. Money and status gain special care, the best doctors, private rooms, and the most prestigious hospitals. In an American study, Duff and Hollingshead (1968) found, for example, that top nurses and doctors, despite their formal attachment to the whole hospital, were rarely seen on the general wards where the lower-class patients could be found. In socialistic countries political status may be the significant variable.

Finally, just as the analysis of the first three 'pattern' variables enumerated by Parsons has led us to suspect that far from being functionally specific, affectively neutral, and universalistic, the doctor's role tends to be one based on particularism, individualism, and the need for quite definite value orientations, so it appears that the collectivity orientation – placing the interests of patient before self – is questionable. The situational structure of the doctor's role will frequently, as has been suggested earlier, put him in conflict with his patients and it is by no means clear that this conflict will be resolved in the patient's interest. Fred Davis (1963), in a study of the illness and treatment experience of twelve children, and their families, as the children went through the various medical services during an attack of polio, makes the point very clearly. In order to make their job easier, and arguably to be more efficient, doctors withheld prognostic information from the parents and children:

'At the end of [a] six-week-to-three-month period, [after hospitalization] all the important [medical] findings were in, and meaningful and fairly accurate estimates could be made of the type and degree of the child's residual incapacity. By then uncertainty had been greatly reduced for the treatment personnel. Was it also reduced to any significant extent for the parents?

... were the parents of those children whose affected muscles showed "moderate or little return of strength at the end of this period" told that the child "would probably never make a complete recovery"? ... Few of these parents were told by treatment personnel that the child would be handicapped to some extent. Nor were they told the contrary. Their questions on outcome were, for the most part, hedged, evaded, rechanneled, or left unanswered, such as they had been in the diagnostic period. By and large the parents were left to "find out for themselves, in a natural sort of way". Only gradually – in some instances, as much as a year and a half following the child's discharge from the hospital – did most of them come to learn the true extent of their child's impairment.' (Davis, 1963: 63)

In terms of their personal roles the doctors no doubt felt as distressed about the child's plight as anyone else. They may have wanted to put off coming to terms with the bad prognosis and the fact that medicine had been unable to help. But just as fundamentally, from the point of view of their (social) role (as doctor), they appeared to weigh up the fact that the cost to them of breaking the bad news would, as likely as not, lead to them having a 'weeping and emotional' parent on their hands, a situation which many doctors find extremely difficult because it is time-consuming, difficult to handle, and disruptive of their tight routine. Davis argued:

'Uncertainty is to some extent feigned by the doctor for the purpose of gradually – to use Goffman's very descriptive analogy – "cooling the mark out", i.e. getting the patient ultimately to accept and put up with a state of being that is initially intolerable to him.' (Davis, 1963: 67)

Indeed the most frequent complaint amongst patients concerns the lack of information they receive from doctors and other medical staff.

In a study of patients who had been in hospital, three-fifths of those interviewed reported some difficulty in getting information while they were in hospital (Cartwright, 1964: 74); and in another study of mental patients' attitudes towards hospital the lack of information was one of the few complaints they had (Raphael and Peers, 1972: 21). Complaints like the following were the main criticisms patients voiced about the general hospital service.

' "I wanted to know why I kept having the abortions, but the doctors were too distant to talk to." (Cartwright, 1964: 75)
"I'd like to have known just what was coming in me, which kidney it was and if I'd be completely cured. Also I wanted to know if I could have any children. They just jump down your throat if you ask them."
                                                                                          (75)
"I think I should have been told straight out why they had to do a total (hysterectomy). There must have been some reason."   (75)
"I had a heart specialist – he took an electrocardiograph of my heart. I

asked him what was the matter. He said, 'You'll be all right,' I might
just as well not have asked." (75)

"I would have liked to have been told *when* I was going down for the
op, but they didn't. Nobody knew when we were going down. For six
days this went on." (75)

"I would like to have her told after the operation what they had done
like. All the staff were the type you couldn't speak to a lot really. When
I did ask once they just said 'scrape'. I don't know what that was except
from hearing old wives' tales from other patients." (76)

The secrecy surrounding information is particularly acute with dying
patients and those who have cancer. It is rare in British, as in many other
hospitals, for doctors to tell patients straight out. This is particularly true
if they have cancer (Cartwright, Hockey, and Anderson, 1973: 164). Yet
most patients do find out at some point. One interviewer in Ann
Cartwright's 1964 study described an example:

'When I asked Mrs. A. "What were you in hospital for?" there was a
slight pause before she said she had had a radical mastectomy. She then
sat watching me, as though looking for my reaction. It was evident that
she hated telling me this, and the thought of it still worried her deeply.
It was impossible to ask the next question, "What was the name of your
condition?" When there was no reaction from me and I did not ask for
further details she became less reserved, and later glad to discuss her
sense of shock when she discovered she had had a radical. "The G.P.
thought it was mastitis — A common complaint in a woman of my age.
I was quite convinced I was going in for a minor job. It was a great shock
to me. The houseman didn't come for two days. The sister didn't tell
me either. I did feel somebody could have spared just two minutes to
explain! I can see now that it had to be but I wasn't very happy about
it at the time."
It was obvious that part of the shock was lying fearing that radical
mastectomy indicated a malignant growth, and facing that fact alone.
"Personally I would much rather be told about things than lie and
worry. To me the known is much better than the unknown. I would
have liked things explained more — although they knew that I and my
husband were in touch with my own doctor, who really explained
things very fully. I did ask the sister once or twice — little things —
and she'd say: 'Ask Mr. B when he comes in.' Well, these surgeons
haven't the time and you can't discuss things as fully as you'd like.
They're at the foot of the bed and on to the next patient before you
know.
Mr. B said, 'Don't worry. We'll find out when we get the results from
the path lab.' But it was my own doctor who explained that six weeks
later.'
There was a pause each time she mentioned the path report. Talking
about it at all was painful for her. It was not until nearly the end of the

interview that she told me she had had post-operative deep X-ray as an out-patient at — hospital (a cancer hospital). She again watched my reaction when she mentioned this hospital. It was quite impossible for her to say "They found it was malignant — I had cancer." She knew that I realised the nature of her condition.' (Cartwright, 1964: 9—10)

There are many arguments for and against providing medical information to patients but so little is provided, and practices are so haphazard, as to leave little doubt that one reason why poor prognoses are not communicated is the one suggested by the Davis study (above pp. 217—18). That is, doctors, partly no doubt because they have not been given the appropriate skills in their training, simply find it easier not to tell. One way in which staff in British hospitals avoid giving information to patients is by evasion of responsibility.

' "I said to my own doctor, 'Why in hospital when you ask a perfectly straightforward question do they just sidetrack you?' What I wanted to know was, shall I be able to carry on as I did before or shall I have to get a lighter job, and will I have a recurrence of this. The doctors wouldn't tell me anything. I asked the first in command, the second in command and they all sidetracked you. In the end they say, 'Your local doctor will be informed; he'll tell you'." (Cartwright, 1964: 110) "They didn't seem to want to tell you anything. They'd put you on to someone else and to someone else. I asked the sister and one of the nurses. The nurse said, 'Ask Sister.' Sister said, 'Ask Doctor', and when the specialist came he just laughed in a nice way and that was that." '
(110)

The general practitioners, also, are sometimes left in the dark.

'Other general practitioners described the disadvantages of this system, or lack of system. "If patients don't ask, the staff think someone else has told them." "There's always the complication that you don't know what the patient has been told. With fatal illness you've got to have some understanding between hospital doctors, nurses and the G.P. This doesn't exist at the moment." "Very much explaining is left to the most junior probationer nurse, who imperfectly understands the process herself." ' (*Op cit.*: 110)

Summary and Conclusion

In this analysis of the role and situation of practising clinicians it has been shown that the doctor's role is one of immense conflict and difficulty. He is continuously having to arbitrate between a single patient's interests and those of all his patients, between one patient and another, between a patient's interests now and in the future, between patient and family, between patient and society or community, between the patient's interests and his own interests, between his own interests as a doctor and his interests in other roles. In making these choices the doctor does not rely on affective neutrality, universalism, functional specificity, and his collectivity orientation. His scientific knowledge offers no way of telling him (after a certain point at least) which patient should have a kidney machine; it is usually inadequate as a framework for treating individuals, and it is not developed enough to solve many of the problems he comes up against. Even if he would wish to limit his tasks to those that are functionally specific to his training his patients would not let him. As a result of his situation he often develops a stance which will tend towards individualism and particularism, encouraged in this connection by his own middle-class values. He will often tend to develop a thick skin and a belief in his own wisdom — how else can he act effectively in tight corners — and there will be a tendency, because of the varied demands made on him, to pontificate and give advice in areas in which he has no more expertise than anybody else.

In all this the doctor, himself, will be aware, somewhere, of the thinness of the crust upon which this edifice stands. The lip service that is played to the 'scientific basis of medicine, to universalism, affective neutrality, functional specificity, and collectivity orientation, serves, at least in part, as a smoke-screen. It is bad enough to be in this situation, not least with matters of life, death, and the highest emotions involved, without having to justify one's every action.

The patient also likes to believe in the 'fair' doctor acting on universalistic, affectively neutral, functionally specific, and collectivity oriented principles. If the doctor could not be observed in this way, trusting him with the sort of things he is trusted with, would be difficult. The belief that the doctor's role is free of conflict is a coping device developed on the one hand by doctors who have to cope with the problems and the uncertainty of medical procedures, but actively colluded with by patients.

1. The attempt of Stimpson and Webb to do this became available after this book went to press.

References

Balint, M. (1957) *The Doctor, His Patient, and the Illness.* London: Tavistock.
  A fascinating account by Balint, a psychoanalyst, who describes his work with a group of general practitioners. See pp. 211–14. The account is, however, anecdotal.
Balint, E., and Norell, J.S. (eds.) (1973) *Six Minutes for the Patient.* London: Tavistock.
  A stimulating discussion of a group of GPs' experiments with different styles of doctor-patient interaction.
Becker, H.S., Greer, B., Hughes, E.C., and Strauss, A.L. (1961) *Boys in White: Student Culture in a Medical School.* Chicago: Chicago University Press.
  A distinguished team of American sociologists observed medical students in training in a medical school in Kansas, USA.

Beecher, H. (1955) The Powerful Placebo. *Journal of the American Medical Association* **159**(1): 602—6.

— (1961) Surgery as Placebo. *Journal of the American Medical Association* **176**: 1102—7.

Brotherston, J. and Chave, S. (1956) General Practice on a New Housing Estate. *British Journal of Preventive and Social Medicine* **10**: 200.

Brown, G., Sklair, F., Harris, T., and Birley, J. (1973) Life Events and Psychiatric Disorders. Part 1: Some Methodological Considerations. *Psychological Medicine* **3**(1): 74—87.

See Chapter 10.

Cartwright, A. (1964) *Human Relations and Hospital Care.* London: Routledge & Kegan Paul.

A survey of the attitudes to hospital treatment of a national sample of patients.

— Cartwright (1967) *Patients and Their Doctors.* London: Routledge & Kegan Paul.

A second national survey, this time of the attitude of patients to their general practitioners.

— 1974 Prescribing and the Relationships between Patients and Doctors. Mimet published by the Alcoholism and Drug Addiction Research Foundation.

A description of some ongoing work investigating the way in which patients and their general practitioners use drugs and each other in an ongoing relationship. Data included taped patient-GP consultations.

— (1975) Social Class Variations in Health Care and in the Nature of General Practitioner Consultations. London Institute for Social Studies in Medical Care (mimeo).

An excellent summary of the way in which class factors can influence medical care — including the doctor-patient relationship.

Dowling, H.F. (1963) How do Practising Physicians use New Drugs? *Journal of American Medical Association* **cixxxv**: 233—36.

Duff, R. and Hollingshead, A. (1968) *Sickness and Society.* New York: Harper & Row.

A fascinating account of the experience of a sample of patients referred to the Yale University Hospital.

Egbert, J., Battit, G.E., Welch, C.E., and Bartlett, M.K. (1964) Reduction of Postoperative Pain by Encouragement and Instruction of Patients. *New England Journal of Medicine* **270**: 825—27.

See Chapter 1.

Freidson, E. (1970) *Professions of Medicine.* New York: Dodds Mead and Co.

An elegant and well worked out analytical treatment of the situation of patients and doctors. It provides fascinating insights and has been heavily drawn on in this chapter.

Friedman, S.B., Chodoff, P., Mason, J.W., and Hamburg, D.A. (1963) Behavioural Observations on Parents Anticipating the Death of a Child. *Pediatrics* **32**: 610—25.

Glaser, B., and Strauss, A. (1963) *Awareness of Dying.* Chicago: Aldine.

An account of observations of deaths in hospitals all over the world.

Goffman, E. (1968) *Asylums.* Harmondsworth: Penguin Books.

A group of insightful essays into the situation of patients in large mental hospitals in the USA. Goffman's observations are based on a period working as an attendant in a number of hospitals.

— (1960) *Strategic Interaction.* New York: Ballantine Books.

The second essay is the one discussed in this chapter.

Mayer, J. and Timms, N., (1969) Clash in Perspective between Worker and Client. *Social Casework*, January: 32—40.
A report of follow-up interviews designed to discover why working-class clients had dropped out of social casework.

McKeown, T. (1965) *Medicine in Modern Society*. London: George Allen and Unwin.
A book by the Professor of Social Medicine at Birmingham about health care planning within the context of assessing the effectiveness of medical care. The early chapters on the nineteenth century improvement in health conclude that the medical contribution to this improvement was limited.

Parkes, C.M. (1969) Broken Heart: A Statistical Survey of Increased Mortality among Widowers. *British Medical Journal* 1: 740—43.

Parsons, T. (1951) *The Social System*. London: Routledge & Kegan Paul.
Chapter 10 of this theoretical treatise contains one of the earliest systematic analyses of the situation of doctors and patients.

Powles, J. (1973) On the Limitations of Modern Medicine. *Man, Medicine, and Society* 1: 1.
See Chapter 11. Powles summarizes some of the evidence on the impact of modern medicine on disease.

Rahe, R. (1969) Life Crisis and Health Change. In P. May and J. Witterborn (eds.), *Psychotropic Drug Response: Advances in Prediction*. Springfield: Charles Thomas Publications.
See Chapter 10. Rahe produces some evidence that major life crises may cause the onset of a whole range of medical disorders for up to two years afterwards.

Raphael, W. and Peers, V. (1972) *Psychiatric Hospitals Viewed by Their Patients*. London: King Edward's Hospital Fund.

Rosengren, W. and DeVault, S. (1963) The Sociology of Time and Space in an Obstetrical Hospital. In E. Freidson (ed.), *The Hospital in Modern Society*. New York: Free Press.

Roth, J.A. (1963) *Timetables*. Indiannapolis: Bobbs-Merrill.
A fascinating account of a hospital for the treatment of tuberculosis patients in the USA. Roth's observations are based on his own forced admission to the hospital when he was a Ph.D student.

Scheff, T. (1963) Decision Rules, Types of Error, and Their Consequences. *Behavioural Science* 8: 97—107.

Shapiro, A. (1964) Factors Contributing to the Placebo Effect. *American Journal of Psychotherapy* 43: 73—88.

Siegerist, H. (1951) *A History of Medicine*. New York: Oxford University Press.

Skipper, J. and Leonard, R. (1968) Children, Stress, and Hospitalisation: A field experiment. *Journal of Health and Human Behaviour* 9: 275—86.

Stimpson, G.V., and Webb, B. (1975) *Going to See the Doctor: The Consultation Process in General Practice*. London: Routledge & Kegan Paul.

Sudnow, D. (1967) *Passing on: The Social Organisation of Dying*. New York: Prentice Hall.
A fascinating account of death and dying in two different types of hospital, one fee-paying and one state-owned.

Szasz, T. and Hollender, M. (1956) A Contribution to the Philosophy of Medicine: The Basic Models of the Doctor-Patient Relationship. *Archives of Internal Medicine* 97: 585.
See this chapter.

Tagliacozzo, D. and Mauksch, H. (1972) The Patients View of the Patients Role. In G. Jaco (ed.), *Patients, Physicians and Illness* (2nd edition). New York: Free Press.

Tuckett, D. (forthcoming) Observations based on a study of referrals to the psychiatric department of a general hospital which is being analysed.

Tudor Hart, J. (1971) The Inverse Care Law. *The Lancet* i: 405—12.

Wolf, S. (1959) The Pharmacology of Placebos. *Pharmacological Review* 11: 689—704.

Zola, I. (1963) Problems of Communication, Diagnosis and Patient Care. *Journal of Medical Education* 38: 829—838.

See Chapter 5. Zola suggests that unless the doctors' approach takes account of the patient's reasons for coming to treatment the patient may leave prematurely or return with more symptoms.

Chapter 7

David Tuckett

The Organization of Hospitals

Large-scale organization of activities is wide-spread in many societies, not only in industry and commerce, but also in government, education, politics, religion, and sport. The modern large-scale, or, as it is often called, bureaucratic type of organization can be found in most spheres of life and it has not left medicine untouched, influencing the relationships between doctors and patients, between doctors and members of auxiliary professions like social workers or nurses, and finally between the medical services and the community as a whole (Titmuss, 1958).

Elaborate equipment, complex procedures, and specialized skills have necessarily accompanied the introduction of scientific developments in medicine over the last century. Radiology and radiotherapy have required expensive machines and a specially trained staff; metabolic investigation has involved the combined efforts of persons skilled in several disciplines: physics, biochemistry, physiology, and engineering. However, the new technologies and the treatment that they offer, cannot be utilized economically in an individual context. They become available to all individuals only when organized on a large scale. The modern hospital is an institution organized for this purpose, and during this century it has become the dominant institution in medical care, training, and research. Nonetheless, this is a considerable enlargement of its previous functions, for until recently, the hospital was a place of charity, a refuge for the sick and homeless, or for the dying poor (Rosen, 1963, 1964; Abel Smith, 1964).

Consider a patient in his bed on a ward in a modern general hospital. Every member of the staff in the hospital must successfully perform his or her function. The patient's food has to arrive at the right time (cooks, porters), it must be of the right sort (dietician), clean linen must be available (launderers, porters), supplies of drugs must come up to the ward (pharmacists, porters), materials must be sterilized (porters, sterilisers), laboratory tests must be completed (technicians, pathologists), X-rays must be taken (radiographers), records of the patient's past treatment must be available (clerical staff), orders for food and equipment must be prepared (administrators), nurses must be available night and day to monitor his condition and tend to him in emergencies. In order to carry out his role in the way he expects, a doctor in a modern hospital needs all these different workers to be functioning effectively.

225

Table 1 Personnel in hospitals, Great Britain

	no.	% *hospital workers*
doctors (whole time equivalents)	30,685	4
of whom:		
consultants	11,046 (36%)	
of whom (approximately):		
in general medicine	9%	
general surgery	9%	
traumatic surgery accidents and emergency	6%	
radiology	6%	
anaesthetics	13%	
pathology	4%	
obst. and gynae.	6%	
all psychiatry	12%	
nurses and midwives	378,941	47
of whom:		
in psychiatric wards (approx.)	76,000 (20%)	
professional and technical workers social workers, opticians lab. technicians psychologists, occupational therapists, pharmacists, physiotherapists, etc.	46,506	6
ancillary staff porters, domestics, catering, works and maintenance, orderlies, laundary, etc.	270,107	34
administrative and clerical (inc. secretaries, etc.)	71,676	9
Total		(100)

Source: DHSS, 1974: 28, 35, 37, 46.

In fact, in September 1970 about two-thirds of a million people were employed in hospitals in England and Wales. They carried out a multitude of tasks and it is interesting to see from *Table 1* that only about one in twenty-five of them were doctors. Obviously, the co-ordination of all the different groups of people who work in a hospital, and in the health service as a whole, is a major task. In Chapter 8, Draper, Best, and Grenholm, discuss the organization of the service, while in this chapter I shall be concerned with the organization of hospitals. However, many of the problems that are discussed also apply to health centres, out-patient clinics, local authority clinics, social service departments, and other organizations.

Technology and Structure

One theme of the chapter will be to illustrate the interdependence of technology and structure and the way in which they exert an influence on each other. Following Perrow (1965), it will be argued that the most effective utilization of a given technology depends to some extent on an appropriate organizational structure. From the doctor's point of view, the most effective application of his therapeutic skills will depend, amongst other things, on whether the structure of the organization in which he works is appropriate to it. But, since I shall be using the terms *organization, structure,* and *technology* in a rather special way, I will first explain how they are used.

Organizations can be seen as 'systems which utilize energy (given up by human and non-human devices) in a patterned, directed effort to alter the condition of basic materials in a predetermined manner' (Perrow, 1965: 913–4). Often, in the case of a hospital, a primary task will be to alter the state of human material and in order to do so, people are co-ordinated to make use of a body of techniques drawn from medical and related sciences.

It will be useful to distinguish between actions taken by organizations in an attempt to alter the condition of basic material, which I shall term the *technology,* and the way in which people and things are organized to bring the technology to bear, which I shall call *structure.*

If action is to be part of a *technology,* rather than some other form of behaviour, five elements are necessary. There must be some knowledge that the actions will cause changes in specified circumstances. There must be some way of assessing the consequences of action. It must be possible to demonstrate that the actions 'work' in the manner intended, *and* that this will happen sufficiently often to make it worth doing. Lastly, the actions must be such that anyone could carry them out with the desired effect, provided they were adequately trained. Therefore, *technology,* in the circumstances of a hospital, amounts to a therapeutic strategy that has been shown to work in some definite way and can be utilized and monitored by properly trained hospital staff.

By *structure,* on the other hand, I have in mind how an institution is organized. That is, the way in which tasks are broken down and allocated to different office-holders, the beliefs and skills that members of an organization have, the rewards that are offered to those who work in it, and the manner in which the institution monitors and controls its performance.

Rosengren and Lefton (1969: 119–44) looked at the therapeutic actions (*technology*) of different medical teams in terms of their differing intentions and related them to hospital organization (*structure*). They argued that the nature of medical intervention varies along at least two dimensions. A team's interest in its patients can range on one dimension from a very short space of time — for example, the casualty clinic in a general hospital which is generally concerned with only immediate first-aid work — to an indefinite span of time — as in some of the work for mental patients on long-stay wards, chronically ill patients, and so on. Rosengren and Lefton refer to this distinction in the temporal reference of medical intervention as the longitudinal dimension. A second dimension, which they term lateral, is that of the patient's life-space. Some types of medical intervention — for example, the practice that takes place in some psychiatric hospital units, or in those concerned with the rehabilitation of severely handicapped patients, such as the old, or those incapacitated by a factory or car accident — tend to have a broad interest in many aspects of a patient's life. Rosengren and Lefton argue that others, like the short-term general hospital 'acute' ward, usually have a more narrow concern with the patient's life and concentrate on limited areas of his person — for example, just his symptoms — rather than focus on the patient's whole pattern of life and social relationships. On the other hand, in hospitals such as those dealing with psychiatric patients, Rosengren and Lefton argue, it is the wider perspective that is important. In any case, using their approach it is possible to derive a typology for hospital intervention.

The creation of such a 'property space' (Barton, 1965) is a useful exercise because it suggests to us the full range of logical possibilities in a situation and helps us not to be restricted by our own preconceived notions.

Given the logical alternatives, it is then possible to consider possible empirical examples and the way we would expect the dimensions to combine for different therapeutic strategies. Hospitals, or parts of hospitals, which have a similar orientation as far as the time dimension

Figure 1   *Types of intervention*

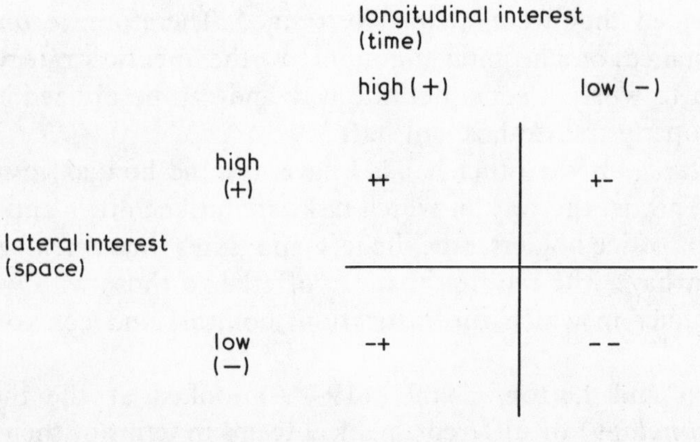

Source: adapted from Rosengren and Lefton (1969: 125)

is concerned, should have certain features in common, even if they differ markedly along the lateral dimension. For instance, a long-term psychiatric ward could be expected to resemble a tuberculosis ward in some aspects, even though the former may have more of an interest in the patient as a person (lateral dimension).

Using Rosengren and Lefton's approach, we can consider the possible conflicts that may exist between the hospital's (or a part of a hospital's) conceptions of space and time, and those of the patients or staff members, and also consider what organizational needs the hospital has because of its particular longitudinal or lateral orientation.

In addition to considering how intervention can vary along longitudinal and lateral dimensions within a hospital, it may be useful to take account of intervention extending outside the hospital. There are several reasons why the therapeutic task in many medical conditions may extend outside the hospital in space and time. First, a decline in the relative significance of many infectious diseases, together with an increase in the frequency of diseases like arteriosclerotic heart disease, has meant that there has been a change in the type of conditions that doctors are called upon to treat in hospital. Many hospital admissions are caused by complaints of the type that tend to be chronic in course and often are treated by long-term chemical or other intervention, which in itself can create iatrogenic difficulties. Diabetes mellitus, for example, is not cured, but managed, by dieting, and/or by the prescription of insulin by mouth or by injection. Associated with diabetes and its treatment, in the long term, are diabetic retinopathy and raised blood pressure, both of which may require further treatment and certainly demand constant monitoring. Therefore, the time perspective for intervention in diabetes mellitus is prolonged, and intervention is extended outside the hospital.

Second, the growth of knowledge relating aspects of an individual's life-style to a number of diseases like heart disease, rheumatoid arthritis, lung cancer, and depression (reviewed in Chapter 10) suggests that medical workers, even if they themselves do not take action, may be concerned with preventive work which will attempt to influence the patient's life-style outside the hospital. Giving up smoking, for example, is likely to reduce substantially an individual's risk to coronary heart disease, lung cancer, bronchitis, emphysema, and other problems (Royal College of Physicians, 1971). Similarly, the fact that the way families handle hostility and authority within their midst produces greater or lesser vulnerability to rheumatoid arthritis when the children are grown up (Kasl and Cobb, 1969), or that a lack of intimacy in an individual's marriage increases the risk of a depressive onset at times of bereavement (see Chapter 10) suggests that work within the hospital should be linked to intervention extending outside.

Also, we know that some individuals are hospitalized primarily because they have social difficulties (Lowe and McKeown, 1960; Abel Smith and

Titmuss, 1956: 139—52) and that in such circumstances a concern with the home situation can be an important part of the treatment. In the same way, the evidence that was reviewed in Chapter 1 suggested a range of variables, inside and outside the hospital, that can affect treatment and rehabilitation (for example, Querido, 1959; Imboden *et al.*, 1961).

Now if the structure of hospital organization is conceptualized as a system involving the allocation and specification of tasks to those working in it, the training of these workers, and the process of co-ordination and control necessary for monitoring what is happening, then it is reasonably clear that the type of lateral or longitudinal intervention which is the basis of medical technology for any condition will tend to influence organizational patterns.

A therapeutic perspective which emphasizes a long time period, for example, should[1] place great weight on an accurate system of records, on follow-up appointments, on the development and maintenance of a continuing relationship to general practitioner and domicilliary support services, on motivating patients to keep coming back to the hospital, on devising ways of looking after patients over long periods of time, on motivating staff to take a long view rather than a short perspective which cuts corners, and so on. Furthermore, as Rosengren and Lefton suggest, if patients keep returning to hospital, or have to stay there for a long time, activities will have to be devised to give them possibilities for carrying on their lives so that they do not become depersonalized and institutionalized (Wing and Brown, 1970). Of course, many of these concerns are voiced in several hospital specialities whether or not they have a therapeutic orientation that emphasizes considerable longitudinal intervention. But the point is that there are always priorities in medical care and those medical teams who do emphasize considerable intervention over time will place some things higher on the list of priorities than they would if they had a different emphasis. It is in this way that the therapeutic orientation, the available *technology*, influences organizational *structure*.

In much the same way, a therapeutic perspective that emphasizes a substantial lateral orientation will also have organizational implications. Where doctors are concerned not only with the patient's body but also with him as a social and psychological being they will need an appropriate range of skills and techniques amongst themselves and other staff, and they may need to bring in and co-ordinate, for example, social workers, psychologists, home-helps, dieticians, and other professionals. Furthermore, they will need organizational patterns that permit and encourage co-operation between staff in the collection, exchange, and use of necessary information. But let us look more closely at the way hospitals are organized.

Organization for Work

With every technical innovation in medicine, new specialists have appeared, often with a separate department, so that responsibility and authority can be properly defined, and hence instant response and life-saving precision predicted within the hospital organization. In this way, departments of radiology, radiotherapy, clinical pathology, chemical pathology, cardiology, neurology, thoracid surgery, endocrinology, paediatrics and paediatric surgery, geriatrics, and many others have developed in only a generation. This tendency has been very apparent in the UK but even more so in the USA.

As a result, the same patient may be dealt with by a number of doctors, both inside and outside the hospital, as well as by other persons in auxiliary medical professions, as with welfare and similar serivces. Problems at once arise of how to allocate responsibility for the patient, and who is to exercise final authority for his care.

As Susser and Watson (1971: 237) point out, it may not be clear whether responsibility for a patient rests with the orthopaedic surgeon who advises physiotherapy for an effusion in the knee joint which a general practitioner has diagnosed and referred to him), or with the specialist in physical medicine who is in charge of the physiotherapists who give the treatment. The goal of treating the whole patient, and ministering to all the needs, physical, psychological, and social, that bear on his medical problem, is often lost within the restricted aims and authority of the specialist departments which share responsibility for the patient, and do not always take up sole responsibility. The fragmentation of authority has been much criticized (*Lancet*, 1959, for example) and has caused many doctors, particularly those working in departments of social and community medicine, to put forward ideas that emphasize 'human medicine' and the 'whole' patient. In a study of patients' attitudes to hospital care, Cartwright (1967: 78—86) reported that the most common complaint of patients was that they were not given enough information about their condition and treatment, and that was the result, in part, of the fact that no one, of the many hospital workers involved in their care, admitted responsibility.

Therefore, in the modern hospital there is a great need for co-ordination between different medical specialities, and between medical specialists and the many other workers in a hospital who were listed in *Table 1*. As a result, a complex administrative system is required to allow a hospital to function, especially since facilities have to be available twenty-four hours a day seven days a week.

Now, a basic question in any administrative system is one of authority, that is, how the power to manage people and tasks is distributed and legitimized. Max Weber (1946) suggested that there were three main ways of disposing authority. First, there is traditional authority, as with chiefs and monarchs, that is hereditary, and acquired by individuals through birth and succession. Here the chief's authority is bounded by tradition, his rule is personal, and he appoints whom he wishes to help him in administrative affairs. Second, there is charismatic authority, which depends on an individual's capacity to convince others that he is entitled to their obedience, and which is often acquired by religious and political leaders, through extraordinary personal qualities. Charisma is typically achieved, and the leader has to demonstrate over and over that he has it in order to exact continued obedience from his followers. Third, there is bureaucratic authority consisting of a system of officers, arranged in a hierarchy of authority of each office, those at the top having more authority than those at the bottom. Weber described this as a 'rational-legal' system, and considered it the most 'efficient' form of administration, in that it rationally organized the means to achieve ends. The hierarchy of offices is based on a continuing system of rules and regulations, which precisely define the authority of each office, so that centralization and continuity of control are assured. Therefore, a bureaucracy does not depend on the vagaries of individual behaviour, and although individual functionaries may come or go, their specialized tasks can be performed by their successors, since their functions are subject to rules and repeatedly recorded in writing, and human behaviour is thus made predictable.

The typical person in authority in bureaucracy is therefore an officer, and each lower officer is controlled and supervised by a higher one. Orders pass from above downwards, and statements of grievances or rights of appeal from lower to higher. Officers can be specialists, and are personally free and subject to authority only in respect to their impersonal official obligation. An officer obeys authority because he holds an office defined by rules, and what he obeys is the law; he obeys not a person but an impersonal order. The most obvious example of this is the way the soldier 'salutes the uniform' of a commissioned officer and not the man who wears it; personal feelings are theoretically irrelevant. Each office is filled by appointment, in principle on the basis of free competition, so that the person best fitted to exercise the role is selected. In many bureaucracies capability is tested by examination, or guaranteed by certificates of competence. Accordingly, specialized training is necessary for appointment to official positions.

Several analysts have developed Weber's model of the 'ideal' bureaucracy and in doing so they have concentrated on the need to make sure that each office is well defined, that is, specifying what has to be done (which involves sub-dividing the goals that members of the organization have devised and allocating particular tasks or sub-goals) and by whom (for example, Rowbottom *et al.*, 1973). Many difficulties in hospitals and other organizations have been attributed to a failure of responsibility, that is a situation where nobody was quite sure whose job the overlooked task was. Thus, Stanton and Schwartz, in one of the earliest systematic attempts to analyse a large mental hospital, suggested that deficiencies or ambiguities in the decision-making machinery and in the co-ordination of work of different groups, accounted for many of its problems. A paragraph from their book sums up some of their main findings:

> 'The hospital suffered conspicuous inadequacies in its decision-making; the whole subject was rarely discussed and then was usually treated in a most unrealistic way. A corollary of this was the inadequate arrangements for locating difficulties, diagnosing them and changing the conditions that had brought them about. Appraisal was informal and unplanned; it had to occur almost continuously, but it was a most bungling process — inaccurate, poorly directed, hit or miss and unnecessarily painful. The emotional cost of this and similar inadequacies in the hospital was heavy; it would have been at least partly avoided if a clearer understanding of its origins had existed ...' (Stanton and Schwartz, 1954: 405).

One reason why the allocation of responsibility in hospitals is a particularly complicated matter is that hospitals have dual lines of authority. On the one hand, administrative and policy decisions come down to the individual on the ward from the Department of Health through Regional and District Area Health Authorities, Management Committees, and the professional hierarchy he is part of (medical, nursing, administrative, etc.), and on the other, individuals from different professional hierarchies work together usually under the direction of a doctor on specific clinic tasks. Now, dual authority of this type is not in itself particularly unusual in organizations. For example, the relation of line and staff officials in industry has been studied by Dalton (1959). But what is unusual is the fact that the doctor's own authority is not only bureaucratic in Weber's sense, as head of a team, but also charismatic. The doctor, by virtue of his special relationship to death, dying, and life-saving, and his need to have power over patients so that they carry out his advice, has charismatic authority based on his proved experience. He is therefore difficult to fit into a bureaucratic system of authority and will often be able to subvert or undermine it. Rowbottom and his colleagues describe the situation at one hospital they studied in this country:

> 'For administrative staff, difficulty lay in the fact that each consultant could independently approach whichever member of staff he thought most appropriate on any matter he wished to raise, there being no organization among medical staff to collate and select from their individual requests the most representative in any given sphere. Consultants therefore approached the House Governor, the Deputy House Governor, and Hospital Secretaries, as they thought best, a procedure that was time-consuming and made necessary much cross-informing to avoid confusion. Formulation of policy was made more difficult under these circumstances.
> Similar problems were found by senior nursing staff at CNO, PNO, and SNO[2] levels, who would be asked by consultants to provide services for which no policy existed, but initially on so small a scale that refusal

would be unnecessary, although subsequently it might be found that demands were building up to quite considerable proportions, necessitating decisions on policy which might have been more useful if taken at an earlier stage.

The problem of dealing with requests and suggestions from consultants and other medical staff was complicated by the feeling that such requests, sometimes, though not always, carried the force of instructions. Ward sisters felt that consultants had authority over them, for example. So also did paramedical staff, such as the dietician. Administrative staff felt that requests from medical staff carried special weight. The relationship of the medical staff to the rest of the hospital was however not specified. Their authority over ward sisters was felt to differ from that of the PNO. Similarly, a consultant's request to a Hospital Secretary was felt to differ from the instructions he received from the House Governor. What these differences between medical authority and other authority were based on, and how they affected the relationships between medical and non-medical staff, was not known. The feeling that authority was one of the elements in the relationship added to the difficulty of keeping a clear view of the lines of executive authority.' (Rowbottom *et al.*, 1973: 84–5).

The 'creeping developments', described in this quotation, can lead to great inefficiency in the allocation of resources and also considerable friction and dissatisfaction among staff. For instance, nurses sometimes feel orders are coming from too many places at once, and doctors feel that nurses, who may be acting according to instructions from Senior Nursing Officers, do not care sufficiently about their patients' welfare.

As well as illustrating the rather special authority of the doctor, the quotation from Rowbottom's book also raises a further issue: the fact that doctors themselves do not have the same type of hierarchy as the other professionals. Although each 'firm', which is headed by a consultant, will have a clear line of authority from the consultant down through senior registrar, registrar, and houseman, each consultant is an individual in his own right and his professional colleagues at consultant level are equals, not superiors (Freidson and Rhea, 1963).

Current policy in the management of hospitals in the National Health Service has been to encourage the development of hierarchies within the various professions (Ministry of Health 1966, 1967; Home Office, 1968; Department of Health and Social Security, 1972) and to institutionalize contacts between the occupational groups at top management levels. However, this type of approach can cause difficulties when, for example, requests for action between lower-level personnel in two hierarchies can only be resolved by going up one hierarchy for decision-making, and then be passed across at top level, before coming down the second hierarchy to the person who will carry out the task. However, the approach does have the advantage that people know who is responsible for what, and allows conflict to be resolved at high levels where nursing or administrative staff may be more able to resist 'creeping developments' resulting from 'charismatic' medical authority.

Such a system of authority, considerably simplified in our discussion, is based on the formal structure of organization, on the organization of people for work. A second, complimentary perspective on organizations is based on the notion of analysing organizations in terms of what actually happens and how work is carried out in practice. This perspective tends to emphasize a distinction between formal and informal authority, between official and unofficial patterns of work.

The Performance of Work

In this second approach the organization is conceived of as a social system (Etzioni, 1961; March and Simon, 1958). It is viewed as an institution in action. Analysis centres on the actions of the various workers in the institution, its clients, and on the aims, goals, and behaviour of individuals in the institution as these emerge in the complex interplay of day-to-day work.

Of course, in terms of getting things done, a hospital, or for that matter any organization, has no entity in itself. It is a collection of people working within it in different tasks and in different roles. The many different occupational groups in a hospital have been mentioned in *Table 1*. Now, each group is in a different situation, and their interests may in some senses be different. For example, whereas ward staff may be concerned with all the patients on their ward and want resources for them, hospital administrators have to be concerned with the allocation of resources throughout the hospital and balancing various sources of pressures. Within occupational groups there can be other divisions based on situational factors such as divisions between day and night staff, between chronic and acute ward staff, between operating theatre staff and surgical ward staff, and so on. At other times, groups that differ in one way have certain attributes in common. For example, patients may be in competition with one another for the attention of nursing and medical staff but have a common interest when it comes to improving the food. Nurses and doctors may be at one when dealing with a difficult patient or hospital administrator. The doctors in one hospital may be quite united when dealing with an attempt to take away members of their staff or merge their hospital with another, and so on.

Hospitals, like large business firms, medical schools, or universities, are an amalgamation of interests and pressures. For example, medical work is usually organized on a ward or departmental basis known as the 'firm' system — an interesting metaphor since firms in the outside world are generally in competition with one another. Usually, each consultant has his own medical team, which treats patients in his beds, and is effectively independent of his peers. Furthermore, because he has ultimate clinical authority a consultant can, as I suggested above, bring pressure on medical and nursing staff to carry out his orders and suggestions by implying that death or other harm might come to a patient if they do not. But at the same time his firm is often part of a department and that is part of the hospital in which there will be many other firms or departments competing for resources. In this situation, a consultant has to barter and negotiate in order to obtain the resources he wants and also participate in settling the general strategy of the hospital and its priorities. Each consultant can have his own conception of what the hospital goals should be, for example, a greater emphasis on community care, or a belief that the creation of a reasonably acceptable 'institutional life' may be preferable to trying to discharge all mental patients, and he will then try to obtain them through argument, persuasion, and the forming of alliances with other consultants and members of management committees. Other consultants and workers in the hospital, such as those in the nursing, social work, and administrative positions, as well as representatives of trade unions, will have their interpretations of the way they and those they represent should work, and their ideas will in turn influence hospital policy.

Decision-making Behaviour

The actual disposition of power and authority, and hence the policies and goals of the institution, will differ from hospital to hospital and depend on a host of organizational and personal factors. Decision-making within the hospital can take place in a process of making and breaking coalitions. The representatives of the various hierarchies: the consultants in the various specialties, nurses, administrators, trade-unionists, lay representatives, and others on management committees, may form different allegiances on different issues, and although the non-specific goals of the hospital will be reasonably clear — perhaps 'good' patient care, a 'good' atmosphere, 'effective' co-ordination between departments and with other branches of the health service — once the time comes to carry out or plan particular strategies, there will often be difficulties and disagreements. For example, 'good care' can be interpreted in many different ways. Furthermore, some of the interpretations, and even some of the non-specific goals themselves, may be in conflict with one another when it comes to determining policy. Decisions will tend to have different implications for the work and prestige of different members of staff. For example, there may be a dispute as to whether or not to have an intensive-care unit. There might be arguments in favour. Top quality nursing staff may be in short supply and there could be a suggestion to concentrate them in one place where their skills could be vitally needed. However, money may be short as well, and the only way to have an intensive-care unit might be to put it in place of one of the four surgical units that could already exist in the hospital. This would not actually reduce the total number of surgical beds very much because many surgical cases would go into intensive care. It would, however, reduce the number of beds solely available to the surgical department and lessen its status. In such circumstances the innovative proposals can often be defeated. The reduction of beds in the surgical department would reduce the relative power and status of the surgeons within the hospital.

Although hospitals in the UK have fairly strict financial constraints imposed on them from outside, by ministry and Regional and Area Health Authority decisions, nonetheless, there will often be ways round. For example, ministry circulars, although not uncommon, often merely make suggestions, and even when they do go further, guidance may well be sufficiently vague as to leave the way open to conflicting interpretation. For example, the Regional Health Authority may decide to improve facilities in a mental hospital (perhaps one outside a big city) by introducing an EEG unit and a consultant to run it. Early on, however, it can be pointed out that it might be difficult to obtain a top-class consultant at such a hospital and therefore the appointment ought to be made jointly with a prestigious teaching hospital in the city. But, at the teaching hospital concerned, there might then be some concern in the department in which the new consultant would be located, that the introduction of a further EEG specialist would upset the balance of departmental interest. The consultants who felt this, therefore, might suggest in sub-committee that although they themselves did not see the appointment as a top priority they would not object provided it was understood that this appointment would never have to be paid out of hospital funds. Then, at the District Management Committee, at which the appointment might be discussed, it could be pointed out that under the NHS re-organization the appointment would be bound to be paid for, in the end, out of the hospital's allocation. The suggestion could therefore be referred back to the sub-committee — much to their delight — with a suggestion that they should only push for the appointment if they saw it as top priority. This might have the effect of killing the proposal. Thus, even when money is available, a group of consultants are able to get round a higher-level decision at Regional Authority level.

In any case, in the manoeuvering and negotiating that takes place in decision-making, the members of committees can have different aims, and will be more and less energetic, personable, and persuasive in putting over their point of view. It is in this sort of rather complex setting that organizational goals are interpreted, defined and set, and as we have seen, financial constraints sometimes only increase the intensity of manoeuvering.

In such situations, individuals with the most rewards to offer and withhold, with reputations, or with external support, will most likely influence policy decisively. Certainly, anyone not represented, with little to give or withhold, and without outside sanctions, will be unlikely to exert much influence. In this connection it should be remembered that information and knowledge can be power. For example, the need for new resources will often rest solely on figures provided by the advocate. If these are tied to his professional person (say a surgeon claiming that new equipment is needed) it may be difficult for his colleagues, let alone lay-committee members, to question his judgement. Added to this the medical man may be able to rely on vague but nonetheless real moral imperatives. As we have discussed, people *may* die without some life-saving equipment.

The decisions that are taken in hospitals will be strongly influenced by those with the most power. Now, in the present organizational structure of hospitals in this country, and to a greater degree in many others, this is unlikely to be the people whom the hospital exists to serve, at least in a formal sense, the patients. Doctors are in the majority on both ministry and local committees. Patients themselves are only by chance on hospital-management committees and the 'community health councils' which are the National Health's administrative units intended to represent patients, do not (at least as yet) have administrative power. Thus, although patients may be mentioned in any argument, this will often be only because one or other professional interest uses them to attempt to build up ammunition for its case. As is pointed out in Chapter 8, in the recent re-organization of the National Health Service £220,000 was spent on commissioning a management survey of the service, but nothing was done to make a serious attempt to find out the views of consumers.

Therefore, the way in which decisions are taken in hospitals is likely to lead to some form of the well-recognized process of 'goal-displacement'; the decisions which are taken and the tasks which are carried out, involve a move away from one set of goals — the formal aims of serving patients — towards another — representing the providers of care. These providers, quite naturally, interpret their goals and their tasks in terms of their interests. This need not occur in a dramatic manner. Small changes are constantly occurring in an organization along the lines of the 'creeping developments' discussed above (p. 234). Often these changes are apparently trivial solutions to minor difficulties. For example, a porter retires and is not replaced because of some temporary financial crisis, or an out-patient clinic at a neighbouring town is suspended because there is no available registrar. However, such temporary changes based on expediency have a remarkable tendency to become permanent because at the same time they tend to add up to the advantage of some particular group-interest in the hospital. There need be no Machiavellian-type plot, but only a failure to resist change or struggle to restore the *status quo ante*. Some practices in a hospital which in the fullness of time may seem grotesquely inappropriate when looked at dispassionately may well have been built up in such ways. For example, for a number of historical reasons children were often admitted for tonsillectomy as a group and parents and children were taken through a whole series of stages for many hours, with no sense of useful purpose or explanation. In one case this culminated in a long wait while each child was bathed in the single bath on the ward. Nobody need have worked out that such inhuman batch treatment produces a great saving of staff-time and trouble, but once it had occurred the extra staff and money needed to change the practice would have had to compete with other plans, often of a more exciting life-saving nature.

In most hospitals, as in other institutions, the basis of power and decision-making is never stable and this means decisions will tend to be taken on an *ad hoc* basis and often a decision, at one point, will not be related to other decisions before or after. This is particularly likely when it is remembered that members of committees have to live and work with each other on a day-to-day basis and will probably want therefore to minimize open conflict in order to make day-to-day life more pleasant. Thus Cyert and March (1963) have concentrated on such 'latent' conflict. They describe the way in which institutions cope with latent conflict through its 'quasi-resolution'. Differences in view between members of decision-making committees, or in the non-specific goals of the organization, can be avoided by paying attention to one issue at a time and having policy carried out by separate departments of the institution.

Thus one 'firm' may be trying to speed up the discharge of patients and try to get them to do things off the ward in preparation for returning home, and another may retain certain patients in order to justify its continued control over beds. Again, while some doctors are making strenuous efforts to improve the experience of patients who come to them, by instructing appointments staff to keep some space for a few non-medical emergencies who need to be seen quickly before they lose the will to come, their receptionists or appointments staff may be breaking the spirit of the agreement and in effect reducing 'input' by keeping a long waiting list except for 'emergencies'. It is very easy in such circumstances to 'have one's cake and eat it'. Higher-echelon workers may drift out of contact with what is going on and yet have the comfort of believing all is well (that the procedure is liberal and reformist) while, because of the unrecognized (or more likely half-recognized) shortcuts made by lower-echelon personnel, also have the benefits to their own work arrangements of 'reactionary' procedures. This kind of arrangement can get quite out of hand with 'gate-keepers' (for example, the university professor's secretary or the general practitioner's receptionist) exerting very great influence.

Another problem for those who have to implement policies, and one that is often due to the need to minimize conflict in negotiating the policy, is that decisions, when they come down from policy makers, can be left deliberately vague. For example, a decision to increase social-worker support or to teach behavioural science to medical students may (as a result of a 'quasi-resolution') be made without a discussion of the consequences. Vague guide lines may be offered mentioning only, for example, the need for community care or the changing nature of the doctor's role. The problems of implementation, which may well be critical if the policy is to be successful, are left and the differences in view among the decision-makers not articulated. This is sometimes not a deliberate policy but occurs as the result of the closing of ranks to an innovation which it is hard to oppose but which would be unwelcome if it were implemented.

Achieving Compliance

The potential conflict, between the organization's needs and those of its staff, is one source of 'inefficiency' and cause of lack of co-ordination in hospitals and many other institutions. The staff, whether at upper or lower levels of the hierarchy, have to interpret, achieve, and create the hospital's goals and procedures and some staff have to get others to co-operate with them. Now, since it cannot be assumed that all the staff will share the same aims and ideas about what is to be done and how, the theme of compliance is one that is extremely interesting. How do members of an organization create a situation where they co-operate with one another? In the remainder of this chapter it is suggested that such 'compliance' can be facilitated by the creation of an organizational *structure* that is appropriate to the *technology* available. This relationship between *structure* and *technology* is important and in the discussion that follows I will concentrate on examples of situations where incongruities in the relationship of *structure* to *technology* caused major difficulties in hospitals. I will look at organizational structure in terms of the appropriate training of staff, the specification of tasks and rewards, and the operation of an effective system of monitoring.

The Training of Staff

A critical problem, faced by an institution, is the need to inculcate the appropriate attitudes and ideologies (the term socialization can be used to describe this process) in the staff it selects to carry out tasks. Appropriate socialization, which includes paying careful attention to selecting people who will most easily be trained to carry out tasks 'appropriately', is particularly important in institutions for the chronically ill (for example, long-stay patients with major mental or physical handicaps) which, because they emphasize much more longitudinal and lateral intervention than has been typically prepared for in medical and nursing training, have rather different aims and procedures than those that many of the staff will have brought in from outside. Yet the number of hospital beds taken up by such patients is extremely large, and it is suggested that the experience of such institutions is increasingly relevant to many more medical institutions where there is a growing tendency towards more longitudinal and lateral intervention (above, pp. 4–11). The need for careful attention to socialization is emphasized by the further fact that institutions such as those caring for the old or the mentally ill, are also faced with the need to impose their own values on staff because lay as well as professional ideas may be at variance.

Dominant in the traditional attitude of either nurses or patients, for example, is the idea of 'cure', and, if this is not modified considerably in long-stay units from which patients may never leave 'cured', staff will tend to become dispirited. Coser (1963) ascribes the apathy and alientation of a group of nurses caring for long-stay patients, who could not be cured by existing *technology*, to their inability to implement the goal of 'curability', so dominant in the motivation of medical men. She examines two types of adaptation to this situation: the first being ritualism in which active striving has been given up though 'one continues to abide almost compulsively by institutional norms'; and the second being retreatism, in which there is an abandonment of culturally approved means as well, that is, an escape from active involvement in either goals or means. The nurses are faced with one or other of these adaptations because the goal orientations they bring with them are inappropriate. Patients do not on the whole go bouncing back home after a medically engineered intervention; neither does the structure of the hospital unit provide an alternative goal to motivate nurses. The nursing staff on the ward studied by Coser lacked any clear idea of what could be done for a patient or how to judge how well they were doing. In this situation any definition that was used to describe a patient was seized upon as a clue to action. Since the organizational *structure* failed to provide an adequate definition that could be acted upon, medical definitions, that were intended to describe the patient for quite other purposes, were used. For example, if the patient was defined as a 'terminal' case, then this gave the clue to actions so that activities relevant to obtaining his discharge were abandoned for more simple custodial actions necessary until he died. 'What is considered disruptive in one situation is considered rewarding in the other. If patients are defined as "terminal and custodial", plans to discharge them are seen as disrupting activities' (Coser, 1963: 235). In this sense 'stated beliefs' about a patient can provide a definition of the situation relevant to its *technology*. This ward organization gave away the chance of providing a 'belief' that would allow the nurses to undertake meaningful action.

When the aim of discharge is not seen as feasible, or as only likely to lead to readmission, and when no alternative worthwhile goals are supplied, work is said to be defined 'instrumentally' and it is seen 'not as a means of satisfaction' but as a 'job to be done'. Coser describes what she calls means-orientated as opposed to goal-orientated attitudes and behaviour, which are similar to the institutionally-orientated as opposed to child-orientated patterns of behaviour noted by King (1971) and his colleagues in their study of the care of subnormal children. In Coser's study nurses who were means-orientated tended to avoid the human implications of their work; their work was mechanical. As one of the nurses explained, 'Well, my dear, I don't know. There isn't anything that I find unpleasant. I have done it for so long. I just automatically do it' (1963: 237). Pessimism may take many forms and need not be clearly articulated; most commonly it simply leads to lack of interest. It is easily conveyed not only to patients by nurses but also to nurses by doctors. Indeed most of the attitudes ascribed to nurses in certain situations can be applied to doctors on the occasions in which they are in similar circumstances. This is well illustrated in a study by Roth.

'A question we might raise is — how can an active therapy or rehabilitation programme operate in a setting where the bulk of the population are "poor candidates for rehab" who must be taken on the programme because there are no better ones around. By the staff's own working definition of success and failure, they fail in the majority of cases ... That is one reason why mental hospitals, institutions for the retarded, homes for the aged, and training schools for the delinquent are often considered the backwaters of the health and welfare field, and the recruitment of competent personnel is difficult. They commonly have a goal of restraining inmates to a "society" which really doesn't want them.

Farewell Hospital has an enormous turnover among its professional staff, many of whom come there right after their formal training programme to get a short period of "experience" before moving on to more agreeable and rewarding positions elsewhere. Those staff members who stay around for a number of years come to more or less accept the limited selection of patients, the delays, the institutional assaults upon the patient's initiative, and the fact that their rehabilitation programme has little relationship to the larger institution where most people end up feeling rejected and abandoned. It is not surprising therefore that most of the more experienced staff members turn their backs on the therapy programme and spend as much of their time as possible building professional enclaves of research, administration, and teaching — activities which, in part, serve as an escape from a treatment programme which offers little satisfaction and reward.' (Roth, 1970: 62–3).

In a recent paper Brown (1973) has argued forcible that the traditional beliefs of psychiatrists in this country, which, at least until recently, have been more concerned with aetology than treatment, have limited their ability to help patients.

'The need for doctors to collaborate with other groups in the search for worthwhile goals and to become intimately involved in the work at ward level has been indicated. There are various ways in which such collaboration can be achieved. But there is a conflict that should perhaps be more honestly faced. A good deal can be said for the view that many handicapped patients need little more than that given by "moral treatment", which rests on a set of basically optimistic ideas about what could be done and conveying a sense of hope to the patient. In practice it meant "kind, individualistic care in a small hospital with occupational therapy, religious exercises, amusements and games, and in a large measure a repudiation of all threat of physical violence and infrequent resort to mechanical restraint" (Grob 1966). This is a reasonable aim for most, if not all, chronically handicapped patients. Perhaps it is enough. *The trouble is that it is not necessarily seen as professionally challenging and demanding.*' (Brown, 1973: 417 — italics added)

Brown goes on to argue that as a result of training, the care of long-term handicap may not greatly interest someone who is medically qualified and who will often want to set in motion processes which make his work interesting but which deal with only part of the patient (1973: 421). It seems unlikely, on the other hand, that an appropriate basis for the care of the handicapped can be found without the belief that something can be done, that the patient can be influenced in some way. Among doctors, as well as nurses, therefore, there is a need for medical aspirations to move away from the traditional ideas of care based on immediate intervention usually of a chemical or physical kind.

Indeed, Brown has suggested that there are good grounds for believing that care outside the medical system, based on non-medical common sense humanitarian principles might be the most effective solution for patients with long-term handicaps. Similarly, King, Raynes, and Tizard (1971) discuss the shortcomings of a nursing training, for example, for the care of sub-normal children. In their study, what they perceived as the most effective hostels were managed by staff trained for local authority childcare work. However, untrained voluntary workers did even worse than nurses, so the suggestion is that a particular training, not necessarily to provide systematic knowledge, but to give some sense of purpose to those involved in the work, is necessary.

It appears that one of the persistent failures of many of those that work in institutions for the care of the chronically handicapped has been to ignore the need for setting, in conjunction with other professional groups, a sufficiently graded series of goals which staff could use to make their work appear meaningful and rewarding.

'For this it is unnecessary to cure a patient. Once it is recognized how little can be done a worker can be greatly rewarded by quite slow progress. The level of aspiration and the kind of feedback and reward provided by the organization is critical. The extreme case is where no change in the patient can be expected but where care can prevent deterioration. Here, since change cannot be perceived, recognition of what is going on must flow from institutional definitions of reality. Heartening progress has been made along these lines (Wing 1967), but the aim must be to make it general throughout *all* psychiatric institutions.' (Brown 1973: 416).

Of course where institutional beliefs about goals diverge in certain respects from those of the wider society, the beliefs that an institution wishes to inculcate in its staff will need to be strongly socially supported. But, provided this happens, and staff can agree about aims great progress can be made. An instance, concerning one nurse at Severalls Hospital, showed how even the most (apparently) inhuman beliefs about patients are malleable. At the interview this nurse cried openly about life on the ward she had been running for many years before a new superintendent took over.

> 'She said she had known in a way that what had been going on was wrong; that her patients had not really needed to sit around the walls of the ward day in and day out like cabbages doing nothing. But no one had told her. This nurse had worked at the hospital for many years and I suspect had not been unduly worried by such thoughts. Deeply felt humanitarian views which are present in most hospital workers will need strong social support to become generally effective.' (Brown, 1973: 414).

Tasks and Rewards

The ways in which an individual can be rewarded for carrying out a task varies. Following Etzioni (1961) and others (Homans 1961; Blau 1961) it is possible to conceive of dimensions along which rewards can be classified, including negative rewards or sanctions. There is a relationship between the type of rewards or sanctions that an organization applies to its staff and the way in which the staff orientate themselves towards their tasks and carry them out.

Table 2 illustrates the three dimensions along which rewards and sanctions can be received (readers of Chapter 4 will see that they are similar to the dimensions discussed in relation to the distribution of power and advantage in a society) and further subdivides them into those that are *intrinsic* — obtained from the nature of the task itself — and those that are *extrinsic* — part of the context of the task.

Any particular task is likely to involve a combination of such rewards — for example almost all jobs in a hospital are paid by a wage or salary — but often the mix of rewards and sanctions that is offered will vary from task to task. The type of mix can affect the involvement staff have with the organization and this in turn can affect the way tasks are carried out.

The 'instrumental' orientation to work described by Coser and discussed above is one that suggests an individual has become primarily concerned with extrinsic rewards. Work is carried out largely for the sake of what can be done when it is finished. Such workers, as was the view of

Table 2 Some rewards and sanctions offered by organizations

	'economic'	*'symbolic'*	*'force-majeure'*
intrinsic	e.g. conditions of work	e.g. satisfaction gained through emotional and personal involvement in the carrying out of the work task itself.	e.g. power and authority within the organization, powers of dismissal and promotion, etc.
extrinsic	e.g. level of pay, bonuses, incentive payments.	e.g. status in the community derived from work.	e.g. authority in the community derived from position at work.

Karl Marx (trans. Bottomore 1963), are alienated from their work, which is seen not as the 'satisfaction of a need but only a means for satisfying other needs'. Obtaining rewards in the work situation ceases to be a concern of such workers who wait to obtain satisfaction outside it. They opt out of becoming emotionally involved in work.

As was suggested in Chapter 4, situations where workers are 'alienated' are quite common in British industry. Work is seen not as a central life interest but as something to be undergone and suffered in return for extrinsic rewards. In industry opting out can be serious and lead to inadequate care in production but this is not always so. In any case where the care of human beings is concerned, as in hospitals, such an outcome can be disastrous.

'Apathy and general lack of interest as such cannot be conveyed to a component of a car, but they can to a patient; and yet often patients are treated essentially as objects. The common decencies and rituals of every-day life are either ignored or performed in so perfunctory a manner as largely to negate them. There is insufficient involvement for any kind of genuine appreciation of the person's needs — even to the degree of becoming beware of them in the pragmatic sense of a good clinician or interviewer so that the job of influencing the person may be more efficiently achieved. Minor aspects of the task tends to dominate as with the labour exchange clerk concerned only to send people out to a job (so he can chalk up a "contact") quite ignoring the match of person and job (Blau 1955).' (Brown, 1973: 410).

Alienation at work can occur because the orientations that staff bring to their work from outside either prevent them from finding rewards in their work (as was, to some extent, the case with the nurses described by Coser in the previous section, who, because of their professional training, did not possess a way of being satisfied with the intrinsic nature of their work task) or because they are not looking for intrinsic rewards, or at least have relegated this to a low priority (like the car-workers in Luton described by Goldthorpe and his colleagues (1968: 33)). But it can also occur because the organization does not make it possible for them to find the intrinsic rewards they would need in order to become involved in their work.

In the case of institutions such as hospitals, which are orientated towards the care of human beings, if there is emphasis on the importance of the relationship between staff and patients in the therapeutic task, and staff cannot afford to treat patients like objects, it will be necessary for at least those members of staff who deal with patients to be orientated, to a large extent, towards the pursuit of intrinsic rewards.

Herzberg (1968) has noted that something must actually be achieved if workers are to receive intrinsic rewards deriving from feelings of achievement and successful accomplishment that stem directly from the work task. Because of this both *technology* and ideology can be a great limitation. For example, a good deal of thought and effort has gone into the creation of intrinsic involvement in industry. But very strong constraints are set by socially based value judgements concerning the division of labour derived from outside the organization. Top management do not see themselves as cleaning lavatories or doing routine work. *Technology* sometimes means work is lacking in intrinsic reward. Certainly in medical institutions there are constraints of this type. The tasks of a nurse are to some extent dependent on what a doctor will and will not do. The job of a nursing auxiliary is strongly influenced by what a nurse will not do, and so on. Furthermore, the nature of the disease or handicap and the availability of effective therapy and management sets limits on the task. Dramatic life-saving cannot be built into most tasks in institutions for the long-term care of patients in mental hospitals, geriatric units, or indeed in many other medical situations. A large proportion of the people in such institutions will not get better, but will remain chronic cases, or will not rejoin the community again.

However, provided the institution takes care to indicate to its staff the goals that *can* be achieved, hospitals or certainly the medical and nursing staff within them, have far fewer constraints when it comes to devising intrinsically satisfying tasks, than do organizations in industry. Much more dramatic investments would be required to alter substantially the opportunity for intrinsic rewards that exist in, for example, the motor car industry, than are needed in hospitals.

The most difficult nursing jobs are demanding but can also be made rewarding. People are being dealt with and this introduces continuous variation in the work since each is an individual who can usually respond in some way to what is done — at least if the worker is trained to notice these responses which may often, as with the mentally subnormal, appear rather small and insignificant if not taken in context. Indeed, as suggested in the last section, an important characteristic of medical and nursing work is that there is considerable scope for the beliefs 'surrounding the output', or achievements in a task, which can be inculcated in training, to influence the nature of the work and therefore the intrinsic rewards obtained.

In other words, intrinsic rewards, the receipt of which can be important in preventing staff from treating patients like objects, are not solely a function of the nature of a specific task but also depend on the meaning given to it. When creating tasks and devising rewards, therefore, an organization needs to pay attention to the varied implications of different approaches. Over-definition from others can make a task appear monotonous and unrewarding; so too can a lack of well-specified routines, conventions, and well-understood procedures. Both imply a loss of meaning, making it very difficult for a worker to involve himself in his work. One nurse from a mental hospital (Robb, 1967) recounted some of the day-to-day problems she faced because of a lack of specification and routine on her arrival at a hospital: a lack of clear guidelines meant that various doctors failed to accept that patients were their responsibility; that food failed to arrive from the kitchen on a regular basis; that scheduled drugs were not routinely available; that staff frequently failed to turn up on duty; that syringes which had just been laid out to be used would be taken by the out-patient department, without notice; that bread could be delivered for several days to the wrong ward without anyone making an attempt to do anything about it; that towels failed to appear; that because an assistant nurse handed out all the drug doses on the ward from memory it was difficult to get antibiotics; that there was no standard procedure for putting a banging door to rights; and that twenty odd requests to the engineers failed to produce the necessary action; and so on. In the situation described by this nurse a lack of clear routine and established procedures in the work situation made her task extremely unrewarding.

Another important factor is the degree of autonomy and responsibility a person has and the extent to which he can use his initiative. But in order to provide responsibility problems of authority must be overcome. For example, if nurses have more discretion, doctors have less control. In another context, if bosses take all the decisions and refuse to do any typing then their action, backed by their authority, defines the role of the secretary. These sorts of inter-relationships can be overlooked when discussing the problem of job satisfaction. What is known as the problem of 'lower-order involvement', whereby workers low down in the hierarchy of an organization are less motivated, may be a direct reflection of a higher status group's refusal to carry out the more simple and monotonous tasks. Such 'political' issues within an organization prevent 'interesting tasks' from being shared out more equitably so as to improve the intrinsic satisfaction possible in the 'lower' echelons of work organizations.

The problems that arise where 'power-sharing' is introduced into institutions have been well illustrated in attempts to create new therapeutic milieu – just as they have been in discussions of industrial democracy. Such movements are not successful, and are even counter productive, if they are not accompanied by genuine changes (Rubinstein and Lasswell, 1966; Etzioni, 1960; Brown, 1974: 410). Where there are changes in the distribution of authority it can cause difficulties with higher status groups. For example, once it is recognized that everyone on a ward has an important part to play or everyone is equally valuable why should some people be paid so much more than others? Because such conflicts of interest are often involved in task specification it is not surprising that institutions do not always adopt the most rational solutions and are therefore not as effective as they might be.

Monitoring and Feedback

Socialization procedures and the reward system in operation are two very important parts of organizational structure, but there is also a third: a system for providing feedback so that the extent of the actions undertaken in the organization can be monitored, assessed and, if need be, modified.

The provision of feedback and monitoring is irretrievably linked to the division of responsibility and the flow of information within an organization and is often dependent on a set of work rules defining roles and responsibilities. However, although these rules may appear to ensure 'formal' compliance with the organization, this is not necessarily the case.

Rules themselves can dominate institutions so that it becomes almost impossible to get any action from anyone and yet still leave tremendous room for the staff and workers to act in quite other ways than those intended in the spirit of the rules. Crozier in a study of a particular state-owned French industry has described an instance where workers, maintenance engineers, low level supervisors, and other groups fought to preserve and enlarge the area over which they could have discretion by actually sticking to the rules that those above them had designed for their control, thus preventing interference and surveillance from above:

'Conformity is not a one-sided process. Subordinates will bargain with their conformity and use it as a tool with which to bind argument. This is just another aspect of the fight for control. Subordinates tacitly agree to play the mangement game, but they try to turn it to their own advantage and to prevent management from interfering with their independence. When this double pressure is stabilised and leaves very little freedom for adjusting difficulties, then an organization has become deeply rigid. This was the case with an earlier ritualistic clerk who made a point of following his instructions to the letter and ignored the reality with which he had to deal, not only because of his "trained incapacity, but because he needed protection against too harsh treatment in the case of error".' (Crozier 1964: 185).

The way in which railwaymen work to rule in order to bring pressure on management is another example of how rules can be used for a purpose opposite to that for which they were originally intended.

The study that first emphasized the distinction between 'formal' and 'informal' structure and the use of work-rules to realize other ends than those intended was undertaken in the Bank Wiring Room of an electrical plant at Hawthorne by a team of American social psychologists. They said that the group of workers being studied made use of 'ostracism, ridicule, and physical punishment ('binging')' in order to control the conduct of its individual members. But

> 'the chief mechanism by which they attempted to control ... outsiders, supervisors, and inspectors, who stood in a position of being able to interfere in their affairs ... was that of daywork allowance claims' [part of the system of work rules determining payment].

One inspector, for example,

> 'refused to be assimilated and they helped to bring about his removal by charging him with excessive amounts of daywork. This was the most effective device at their command. Interestingly enough it was a device provided them by their wage incentive plan. The mechanism by which they sought to protect themselves from management was the maintenance of uniform output records, which could be accomplished by reporting more or less output than they produced and by claiming daywork.' (Roethlisberger and Dickson, 1939: 523)

Certainly one explanation for the fact that information rarely flows smoothly between parts of an organization, and actions do not necessarily have the intended effects, is that there are differences of interest between workers and between different departments. The type of struggle that can result was well illustrated in a study of promoting change in a psychiatric hospital, undertaken by the Cummings (1956). In this case older staff were greatly threatened by the ideas of the new, and younger, staff. They sought therefore to maintain the status quo and to subvert the innovations that the new staff tried to bring in. They tended to see the new young doctors as their enemy and did their best to conceal what was going on from them. They emphasized the disadvantage of the innovations and the way in which they threatened routine and the cleanliness, tidiness, and orderliness (actually meaning activity) of the wards.

But another reason why organizations often suffer from a lack of feedback and take an inordinately long time to correct malpractices or discover they are ineffective, is that there is often a collusion amongst members of the staff not to enquire too far into what is going on and how successfully the aims of the institution are being achieved. As well as preventing the correction of mistakes, of course, this deliberate reduction of feedback also has the disadvantageous effect of preventing staff from being rewarded by the sight of what they are achieving.

> 'In the mental hospital if there is general pessimism about what can be
> done for the patient there may be actual co-operation between status
> groups to reduce relevant rules to a few general principles, such as
> safety of the patient and cleanliness of the ward, so that all groups can
> live with the situation with a minimum of fuss. All parties will have an
> interest in reducing the flow of information about what is "really going
> on" ... The widespread pessimism will rob doctors and other non-ward
> personnel of significant work and there will be general agreement to let
> nurses get on with the job ... Lack of communication will also enable
> those outside the ward to avoid having to recognise what is really going
> on; and they will then not be tempted to increase surveillance. This is
> not simply a matter of ignorance. Almost certainly most know reason-
> ably well what is "going on". If, however, they never have to deal with
> a formal "complaint", they can directly avoid having to face what is
> going on and the resulting pressure to act upon the knowledge.
> Malinowski gave a classic description how in one Melanesian village all
> were aware that for years a fundamental rule was being broken by their
> chief (giving important favours to his sons and not to his sister's sons)
> but nothing was done until the sister's sons in exasperation over a
> particular crisis shouted out at night what was happening for the whole
> village to hear (Malinowski, 1962). Then those directly involved acted
> − Malinowski, I think, would argue had to act.' (Brown, 1973: 412−3).

Summary and Conclusion

Enough has been said to show that behaviour in organizations is extremely
complex. I have tried to show how understanding organizational functioning depends on both an analysis of the formal structure of the organization
− the way tasks are specified, the way authority is distributed, the types
of rewards that are organized, and so on − as well as of the way that the
people within it perform their work as part, not only of the organization,
but also as individuals who are part of sub-groups and the wider society.
Some of the difficulties that arise in organizations, and particularly those
in institutions for the care of the long-stay patient which have been considered in detail, come from organizational factors and others from values,
norms, ideologies and conflicts that exist outside the hospital. The aim
of this chapter has been to give some indication of the factors that operate,
and to help to begin to understand some of the implications of working in
large diverse groups. This should help to reduce frustration among those
working in hospitals and allow them to provide better care for patients.

Notes

1. Of course, this does not mean they will. In fact, efficient records systems, close

contact with referral agencies and other elements required for longitudinal intervention may actually be discouraged in some institutions so that staff can limit their activities in order, for example, not to recognize the great difficulties involved in long-term intervention, and to reduce their work-loads. This is very common in institutions that logically 'ought' to have longitudinal perspectives.
2. CNO, Chief Nursing Officer; PNO, Principal Nursing Officer; SNO, Senior Nursing Officer. The Chief Nursing Officer is the most senior grade followed by the Principal Nursing Officer and then the Senior Nursing Officer.

References

Abel Smith, B. and Titmuss, R.M. (1956) *The Cost of the National Health Service.* National Institute of Economic and Social Research Occasional Paper. Cambridge: Cambridge University Press.
Abel Smith, B. (1964) *The Hospitals 1800–1948: A Study in Social Administration in England and Wales.* London: Heineman.
An excellent account of the way English and Welsh hospitals developed and of the factors leading to their nationalization in 1948.
Barton, A.H. (1965) The Concept of Property Space in Social Research. In P. Lazarsfeld and M. Rosenberg (eds.), *The Language of Social Research,* New York: Free Press.
Blau, P.M. (1955) *The Dynamics of Bureaucracy: A Study of Interpersonal Relations in two Government Agencies.* Chicago: Chicago University Press. A classic account of observations made in a labour exchange in the USA.
— (1964) *Exchange and Power in Social Life.* New York: John Wiley. An important statement of exchange theory: the view of social interaction as being based on the exchange of goods and services.
Brown, G.W. (1973) The Mental Hospital as an Institution. *Social Science and Medicine* 7: 407–24.
Presents a review of the way organizational factors can be important determinants of the treatment that mental patients receive. See text.
Cartwright, A. (1967) *Human Relations and Hospital Care.* London: Routledge & Kegan Paul.
A survey of the views of patients in UK hospitals.
Coser, R. (1963) Alienation and the Social Structure: A Case Analysis of a Hospital. In E. Freidson (ed.), *The Hospital in Modern Society.* New York: Free Press.
Crozier, M. (1964) *The Bureaucratic Phenomenon.* London: Tavistock.
A fascinating report on two pieces of observation in French bureaucracies. One of the sociological classics on organizations.
Cumming, E. and Cumming, J. (1956) *Closed Ranks.* Cambridge, Mass.: Harvard University Press.
An account of attempts to change a mental hospital in the USA.
Cyert, R. and March, J. (1963) *A Behavioural Theory of the Firm.* Englewood, N.Y.: Prentice Hall.
A stimulating attempt to develop an economic theory of large firms based on behavioural theories of organizational functioning.

Dalton, M. (1959) *Men Who Manage: Fusions of Feeling and Theory in Administration* London: Chapman and Hall.
A classic of participant observation in American industry.

Department of Health and Social Security. (1972) *Report of the Working Party on Medical Administrators* (Hunters Report). London: HMSO.

Etzioni, A. (1960) Interpersonal and Structural Factors in the Study of Mental Hospitals. *Psychiatry* 23: 13–22.

Etzioni, A. (1961) *A Comparative Analysis of Complex Organisations: On Power Involvement and their Correlates.* New York: Free Press.
Presents a detailed sociological statement of organizational functioning.

Freidson, E. and Rhea, B. (1963) Processes of Control in a Company of Equals. *Social Problems* 11: 119–31.

Goldthorpe, J., Lockwood, D., Bechoffer, F., and Platt, J. (1968) *The Affluent Worker Industrial Attitudes and Behaviour.* Cambridge: Cambridge University Press.
The first volume of the Luton studies on the attitudes and experience of highly paid manual workers in car assembly, ball bearing and chemical plants. See Chapter 4

Grob, G. (1966) *The State and the Mentally Ill: A History of the Worcester State Mental Hospital, Massachussetts 1830–1920.* Chapel Hill: University of North Carolina Press.

Herzberg, F. (1968) One More Time: How do you Motivate Employees? *Harvard Business Review* 46 (i): 53–62.

Homans, G. (1961) *Social Behaviour: its Elementary Forms.* London: Routledge & Kegan Paul.
A classic of exchange theory – the analysis of social relationships in terms of the exchange of goods and services.

Home Office. (1968) *Report of the Committee on Local Authority and Allied Personal Services* (The Seebohm Report). Cmnd 3703. London: HMSO.

Imboden, J.B., Cauter, A.B., Cluff, L.E., Trevor, R.W. (1961) Symptomatic Recovery from Medical Disorders. *Journal of the American Medical Association* 178: 1182–4

Kasl, S. and Cobb, S. (1969) The Intra-familial Transmission of Rheumatoid Arthriti – 6. Association of Rheumatoid Arthritis with Several Forms of Status Inconsistency. *Journal of Chronic Diseases* 22 (4): 259–78.

King, R., Raynes, N., and Tizard, J. (1971) *Patterns of Residential Care.* London Routledge & Kegan Paul.
A first class account of the treatment of the mentally subnormal.

The *Lancet* (1959) Editorial: Specialisms i, 625.

Lowe, C.R. and Mckeown, T. (1960) The Care of the Chronic Sick: II. Social and Demographic Data. *British Journal of Preventive and Social Medicine* 4: 61–74

Malinowski, B. (1962) *Crime and Custom in Savage Society.* London: Routledge & Kegan Paul.

March, J. and Simon, H. (1958) *Organizations.* London: Chapman and Hall.
A classic statement of organizational theory.

Marx, K. (Trans. 1963) *Early Writings.* Translated by T.B. Bottomore. London: C Watts and Co.

Ministry of Health. (1966) *Report of the Committee on Senior Nursing Staff Structure* (Salmon Report). London: HMSO.

– (1967) *First Report of the Joint Working Party on the Organization of Medical Work in Hospitals* (Cogwheel Report). London: HMSO.

Perrow, C. (1965) Hospitals, Technology, Structure, and Goals. In J. G. March (ed.)

Handbook of Organization. Chicago: Rand McNally.

Querido, A. (1959) An Investigation into the Clinical, Social and Mental Factors Determining the Results of Hospital Treatment. *British Journal of Preventive and Social Medicine* **13**: 33–49.

Robb, B. (1967) *Sans Everything.* London: Nelson.
  A polemical but incisive account of life in institutions for the elderly.

Roethlisberger, F. and Dickson, W. (1939) *Management and the Worker: An Account of a Research Program Conducted by the Western Electric Company, Hawthorne Works, Chicago.* Cambridge, Mass.: Harvard University Press.
  A classic piece of industrial observation and experimentation.

Rosen, G. (1963) The Hospital: A Historical Sociology of a Community Institution. In E. Freidson (ed.), *The Hospital in Modern Society.* New York: Free Press.

— (1964) The Impact of the Hospital on the Physician, the Patient and the Community. *Hospital Administration* (Chicago) **9**: 15–33.

Rosengren, W. and Lefton, E. (1969) *Hospitals and Patients.* New York: Atherton Press.
  An excellent introduction to sociological ideas about hospitals.

Roth, J. (1970) The Public Hospital: Refuge for Damaged Humans. In A. Strauss, (ed.), *Where Medicine Fails.* Chicago: Aldine.

Rowbottom, R., Balle, J., Cang, S., Dixon, M., Jacques, E., Packwood, T., and Tolliday, H. (1973) *Hospital Organisation.* London: Heineman.

Royal College of Physicians of London. (1971) *Smoking and Health Now.* London: Pitman Medical.

Stanton, A. and Schwartz, M. (1954) *The Mental Hospital.* London: Tavistock.
  An important and very readable account of a large mental hospital in the USA.

Susser, M. and Watson, W. (1971) *Sociology in Medicine* (revised ed.) London: Oxford University Press.
  Chapter 7 has a good account of organizational issues in the NHS.

Titmuss, R.M. (1958) *Essays on the Welfare State.* London: George Allen and Unwin.
  An excellent analysis of issues in social policy — including the development of the health service.

Weber, M. (1946) *From Max Weber: Essays in Sociology.* Translated by H. Gerth and C. Wright Mills. London: Routledge & Kegan Paul.
  Includes Weber's original statement about bureaucracy and the types of legitimate authority.

Wing, J. (1967) Social Treatment, Rehabilitation and Management. In A. Coppen and A. Walk (eds.), *Present Developments in Schizophrenia.* London: Royal Medico-Psychological Society.

Wing, J. and Brown, G. (1970) *Institutionalism and Schizophrenia.* Cambridge: Cambridge University Press.
  Demonstrates that many of the symptoms exhibited by patients in large mental hospitals are the result not of a primary biological condition but of their lives in the hospital.

Chapter 8

Peter Draper, Gary Grenholm, and Gordon Best

The Organization of Health Care:
A Critical View of the 1974 Reorganization
of the National Health Service

Introduction

It is easy to forget how massively health care has changed over the past
few generations. The most dramatic and obvious aspects of this change
have been in the development of a 'health industry' and the increased
effectiveness of certain kinds of medical care at the physical or biological
levels. We have the capability today of preventing and treating some
categories of pathology that ravished mankind less than a century ago.
The other side of the coin is that vast numbers of people are now subject
to the degenerative diseases, and to those still ill-defined 'diseases of
civilization', presumably the sequelae of stress, noise, and of living within
enormous aggregates of people who have few human bonds among them.

As health care has developed in certain technical, biological respects,
it has also become more complex. Around the turn of the century, most
of the known arts, sciences, and skills of medicine could be mastered by
one person in a relatively short time. Virtually all the benefits of medical
care, such as they were, could be provided by any practitioner. Practitioners were essentially equal in the fund of knowledge they had available to help people.

Today the fund of medical knowledge is so vast, and increasing at such
a rate, that no one practitioner can master all aspects of medical care.
Some kind of different social arrangement has been made necessary by
the changed nature of available care. An arrangement that can replace
the age-old pattern of medicine that mainly named diseases and predicted their course, and in which the practitioner himself or the relative
'treated' the individual patient.

Such 'social arrangements for getting care to people' are sometimes
referred to as health-care delivery systems. The systems vary widely
from one nation to another, and indeed can, and do, differ within a
single country. These differences, however, are largely *social* differences;

the technological and scientific components of the medical care provided within the different systems of industrialized countries is remarkably similar.

The specific form of a health-care delivery system will therefore throw light on a society's political and economic conditions as well as its history and traditions: it will, to varying degrees, reflect the values and commitments of a total society and of the groups within it. It will also reveal something of the influence that particular segments of society are able to exert on the whole. It often reflects the stratifications present in a society and indicates the bases of the stratification system (e.g. monetary, occupational, ascribed class, race, religion). It also reflects such societal characteristics as the extent of authoritarianism or non-authoritarianism present; the extent to which social influence is centralized or shared; and whether decision-making occurs on an inclusive or exclusive basis. In short, a health-care delivery system can be seen as something of a social 'mirror', a mirror that reflects what a society stands for.

The relationship between a health-care delivery system and the society in which it exists is, however, a reciprocal one. Not only does the form of the delivery system derive from the values of the society, but the society's values are also conditioned by the form of the system. Thus, the precise form of the system will determine who gets care: whether it is their ability to pay, the urgency of their condition, or some other criterion that determines how and when they get care; it will also determine whether place of residence, social status, or other factors are instrumental in the allocation of health resources among members of the society. In this way the form of the health-care delivery system comes to affect people's perceptions and definitions of such concepts as 'health', 'disease', and 'illness'. It comes to affect what people mean by these and other concepts and, as a result, conditions many of the values people hold.

In this chapter, we examine the British health-care delivery system from this perspective. We regard the British National Health Service as one way of coping with the issues of health-care delivery, and, like any other, a result of circumstances perculiar to that society at given points in time. The National Health Service has strengths and weaknesses within the British context as a device for accomplishing agreed social ends, and has strengths and weaknesses compared to other systems of health-care delivery in terms of the types of output it generates. Our prime intention, however, is to examine the NHS not only in these terms but as a 'social mirror' — in terms of what it reflects about changes in, and the current status of, British society.

For this purpose, the 1974 reorganization of the NHS — the first major reorganization in more than 25 years — strikes us as particularly significant. Indeed, it will serve as the focus for our discussion because it is a provocative datum about social process. It is an instance of planned change in a very large and complex organization, and poses a whole series of questions about organizational growth and development, about adaptability and stability in organizations, and about the forces that promote or inhibit change in our society. The reorganization provides us with data that are relevant to these and other social questions, albeit data that are incomplete and often only suggestive. Taken together with other information about the National Health Service and about British society, though, the reorganization can help us to move toward a deeper understanding not only of questions of health-care delivery, but also of the wider priorities and values of society at large.

Our comments are organized as follows: first, we sketch a brief historical picture of the form and evolution of the NHS since 1948. We then go on to discuss some of the reasons why — by the early 70s — there were significant pressures to reorganize the system. We then say something about the kind of changes that, on the face of it, one might have expected to occur, and proceed to contrast these with the changes that actually did occur. We follow this by explaining why we feel that the changes that occurred are, on the whole, undesirable. Finally, we reflect on what these changes 'mirror' in British society at large and, in particular, what they imply about the idea of 'democracy' in Britain today.

A Brief Review of the British National Health Service

The National Health Service, which is both a health-care delivery system and an instrument for implementing a social insurance principle, came into being in 1948. Its birth was accompanied by great publicity and considerable opposition — including an abortive strike by general practitioner members of the BMA. It was set up by a Labour government as part of an apparently socialist programme including not only the nationalization of health care, but also of the railways, coal, gas, and steel manufacturing. The National Health Service Act established a tripartite organizational structure (i.e. a hospital service, a general practitioner service, and a local authority service) for administering and financing care which appeared as radical departure from earlier methods.

At the risk of over-simplification, it can be said that the over-riding concern of the creators of the NHS was to make good health care available to the whole population without a financial barrier (see Lindsey, 1962 or Murray, 1971). The latter stated the principle as ' ...that the physician should do his work without any reference to the social, financial or racial position of the patient and that the necessary medical attention, preventive or curative, should be given without any question of fees arising' (1971: 1).

There are two essential factors required to meet this objective: the absence of direct charges (or the existence of satisfactory reimbursement procedures), and a reasonable geographical and social distribution of adequate health facilities and services. In these respects, it seems fair to say, that as a result of the NHS the real or perceived financial barriers to general practitioner and hospital care for acute conditions are minimal. Charges are present for drugs and appliances but these appear to cause little obstruction to care, though this conclusion may partly be due to lack of research in this area. In contrast, waiting lists are a barrier to prompt elective surgery in many areas and private medical care is principally marketed for those who can purchase it, as a way of avoiding delay.

Although the NHS has been much criticized in recent years for regional and local inequalities in the distribution of services, in comparison with countries such as Canada or the USA, the geographical spread of services is remarkably good. The extreme kind of local staff shortage that has led North American towns to advertize, 'This town needs a doctor', has not been experienced. Furthermore, the success or otherwise of the NHS in this respect should probably be judged not so much in terms of changes *during* its lifetime, but in terms of the distribution before and after its formation. Indeed, the availability of good surgery, obstetrics, blood transfusion, and anaesthetics, for example, in medium-sized and large towns (including access from remote parts of Wales or Northern Scotland) is rightly regarded as an outstanding success in comparison with the days when specialists were concentrated in London and the biggest cities. Lindsey commented on this point, 'Before the advent of the Health Service, the uneven distribution of specialists and the relatively high fees they charged greatly restricted their usefulness' (Lindsey 1962: 326).

The prevention of illness was another main concern of the creators of the NHS and, although the service is sometimes attacked as being too much a National *Illness* Service, preventive services of a personal and environmental kind, such as immunization and clean air have been developed. A recent, and perhaps the most important addition from an ecological viewpoint, was the development by many local health authorities of family-planning services, in some cases with free supplies, and of domiciliary as well as clinic services.

It is important to remember that there are many health factors that are altogether outside the concern of the NHS. For example, housing conditions and nutrition levels both exert major influences on health, but the NHS has no significant responsibility in these areas. Similarly, working conditions affect the health of millions in such immediate ways as physical safety hazards, noise levels and pollution, and in terms of the psychological and social stresses present in the work situation. These matters are mainly outside the jurisdiction of the NHS as it operates at present. Road accidents are responsible for much suffering and death, but the NHS has no role in specific areas such as vehicle safety design nor in more general areas such as transportation policy. In other words, people's health is determined by a wide variety of factors – the NHS currently deals with some but by no means with all of them.

Thus, although the NHS has largely succeeded in fulfilling many of the aspirations of its founders, its evolution, like that of many large and complex organizations, has mainly been incremental and only partly co-ordinated. As a result, some of its organizational and service features are less good than they might be and certainly the emphasis on illness cure and care, as opposed to prevention and health promotion, are weaknesses it shares with most other Western health-care systems. Yet by the early 1970s the NHS — consuming about 5 per cent of the gross national product and employing nearly a million people — could only be viewed as an important and widely accepted institution in British society.

NHS Performance, Resources, and Trends

How does the NHS perform in comparison to the health services in other countries? The short answer is that in relation to industrialized countries, the health indicators such as specific death rates and life-expectancy are average, whilst the costs expressed as a proportion of GNP or national income are much lower than average. For example, a ranking of sixteen industrialized countries on the basis of four combined death rates (standardized, late foetal, infant, and maternal) put the UK in eighth place jointly with the USA (Ministry of Health, 1967). In 1971 the NHS consumed 5.48 per cent of National Income (£2,369 million) and this had risen from a low of 3.89 per cent in 1954 (Office of Health Economics, 1973). Countries such as Canada, the USA, and Sweden allocate a significantly greater proportion of their national income to health care, respectively, 9.66 per cent, 8.22 per cent, and 7.12 per cent (Office of Health Economics, 1970) (Figures are reversed in order)

In terms of manpower, the general practitioner service has remained at almost the same staffing ratio as at the commencement of the NHS, so that in October 1971 the average number of patients per doctor in England was 2,460 (in 1952 it was 2,436 for England and Wales). In contrast, the staffing ratio of hospital doctors has considerably increased. The number of hospital nurses has also increased substantially since the inception of the NHS, both in absolute terms and as a staffing ratio in relation to the population. For example, between 1959 and 1969, hospital staff as a whole increased by 30 per cent in England and Wales. These staffing changes are reflected in the proportions of the NHS budget that went on hospital and GP services, as is shown in the table.

Most of the capital expenditure of the NHS also goes on hospitals rather than on general practitioners and other community services. Thus in 1970/71 capital expenditure on hospitals in England was £114 million in comparison to £5.1 million for loans for health centres and a further £1.3 million for official loans for other general practice buildings (Department of Health and Social Security, 1972a). It is important to note in passing that the NHS inherited many antiquated hospital buildings so that despite

Table 1 Proportion of NHS budget

	Hospitals	General Medical Services (GPs)
1950	54.9%	11.7%
1970	64.2%	8.3%

Source: Office of Health Economics Information Sheet, March 1973

this proportionately high expenditure on the hospital sector, the typical British hospital is still housed in an old building.

The views of consumers and providers

On the basis of the evidence about the NHS prior to the reorganization in 1974, it is clear that no obvious and widespread dissatisifaction existed. Having said this however, it should be pointed out that broad-based, up-to-date surveys of how the average consumer perceived the NHS were strikingly deficient. Those surveys that did exist, such as the PEP study *Family Needs and the Social Services* (1961), tended to show the NHS as a highly used and much appreciated service. For instance, 82 per cent of the mothers of the families in the PEP survey (families with children under sixteen) thought that the health service had helped their families most in comparison with services such as education, housing and family allowances. Similarly favourable results were obtained in a national survey of 1,331 adults in 1967 (Forsyth, 1967). This low incidence of formal complaints is sometimes used to argue that the NHS is relatively trouble free, but this kind of material must be interpreted cautiously because of the unknown extent to which official procedures inhibit complaints. In relation to general practice, Rose (1972) suggests that such procedures may, in fact, be powerful inhibitors.

In trying to assess the feelings of the providers of care there is always the danger that the selection of correspondence that is published in professional journals and the statements of professional bodies and union leaders will be taken as representative of general views. However, as far as doctors are concerned, the British Medical Association's book *Health Services Financing* (1970) is probably a fair gauge of the attitude of this sector of opinion and influence. The arguments presented in this publication suggest improvements in the workings of the system: 'We believe that it is neither desirable nor practicable to think in terms of dismantling the NHS. It is both more constructive and realistic to suggest how the present inadequate finance might be supplemented...' (1970: xvi). A second index of doctors' perceptions of the NHS at this time was the observation that the net emigration of doctors born in the UK or Eire continued to countries such as the USA and Canada but that by the year 1969/70 it had fallen to 240 doctors (DHSS, personal communication).

Nurses' perceptions can also only be gauged by inference. The professional journals on the whole welcomed the changes in the administration of nursing which preceded and in some ways foreshadowed NHS reorganization (the Salmon and Mayston reforms). What student nurses, staff nurses, and ward sisters thought of the changes and of the NHS in general is much more difficult to assess. Occasional letters from nurses and doctors have suggested that there was an undercurrent of opinion which saw the Salmon reorganization as a means of creating a managerial elite at the expense of the professional and financial status of the working nurse, particularly the ward sister. In addition, the growth in private nursing agencies in recent years implies that — as an employer — the NHS was in some respects falling short. Nurses, although increasingly militant about the poor pay and working conditions within the health service, have however, certainly not pursued policies which would seriously challenge its existence.

So-called ancillary workers within the NHS were also dissatisfied with the NHS as an employer as was evidenced in the unprecedented industrial action during the pay freeze of 1973. At that time unionization of ancillary workers was increasing rapidly, for example, *The Times* (27 July, 1973) reported that the Confederation of Health Service Employees, the largest NHS union and one that recuits mainly ancillary workers, was claiming to be adding 150 new members a day.

In general, up until the proposed reorganization in 1973, the views of the consumers and providers of NHS services — although far from being systematically documented — appear to reflect a positive acceptance of the NHS and a feeling that although efforts should be made to improve it, there could be no question of dismantling or radically altering it.

The Need for Changes in the NHS

In arguing that the NHS was largely successful in achieving the principal objectives of its creators, and in stating that the majority of those providing and consuming its services apparently viewed the NHS favourably, it should not be concluded that its weaknesses were not serious nor that there were few advocates of change. Indeed, by the early '70s a number of drawbacks of the existing NHS structure were openly discussed and it was felt that change was desirable for a number of reasons. These reasons — or pressures — for change fell broadly into five categories.

First, there is a fair amount of indirect evidence to suggest that the 1970 Conservative Government was strongly motivated to contain the rising costs of providing health care within the NHS. Second, the population structure in England and Wales had undergone signficant changes since 1948 and so too had the health care needs of the population. Third, considerable inequalities in local and regional resources existed and were tending to be perpetuated by the prevailing NHS administrative and financial structure. Fourth, a heightened awareness of health 'needs' and a changing philosophy of health care was leading to new demands and priorities often quite incongruous with the existing NHS structure. Fifth, officially the government had committed itself to changing the structure of local government in 1974: some change in the structure of the NHS was therefore inevitable.

The need to contain escalating costs

Although direct evidence of the main determinants of any government policy is extremely difficult to isolate, it is probably fair to say that one concern of the 1970 Conservative Government was to develop methods of containing the cost of NHS services. Indeed, Klein (1974: 4), in commenting on the formulation of government health policy since the late sixties, seems to assume that the escalation in health care costs was a prime determinant of such policy: '...it is possible to see a number of factors pushing for change and helping to explain the form it [change] had taken. First medical care ...is steadily becoming relatively more expensive [and] there is therefore no easy candle-ends way of saving money without changing the system of delivering care.'

Klein's impression that the need to curtail escalating costs increasingly influenced government health policy, is reinforced in an article by Rogaly (1974) in the *Financial Times*: '...health expenditures have been rising faster than GNP, no matter how fast GNP itself has risen. ...Typically, a country that had spent 3.5 per cent of its national product on health in 1950 was spending 6 per cent of a much larger GNP by 1969.' But perhaps the most direct evidence that the NHS would be changed in ways designed to curtail rising costs was the sudden and dramatic increase in the number of Work Study, Operational Research, and other 'efficiency experts' working within the NHS. By 1973 the NHS employed no less than 1,000 such staff at an estimated annual cost of something like £6 million (Draper and Smart, 1974). This was almost certainly a five or sixfold increase in the number of such workers compared with the early '60s. Such observations strongly suggest that the 1970 Conservative Government was intent on achieving 'efficiencies' within the NHS.

The need to take account of a changing population structure

It is easy to forget that before the health service was introduced it was widely felt that preventive services and the much greater availability of health care would lead to a reduction in the burden of sickness. The influential Beveridge Report was quite explicit about this point, '...a health service which will diminish disease by prevention and cure...' (HMSO, 1942: 162). However, the NHS, like health-care systems in other industrialized countries, faced the problem that if acute conditions were prevented or cured, then the population became older and suffered from chronic diseases which, by their very nature, demanded health care over a period of time. It is difficult to demonstrate this increasing burden of chronic illness briefly, but the diabetic treated by insulin throughout adulthood provides an illustration. The growth in the number of old people, both in absolute and proportionate terms is more easily documented. In 1949 the total population of Great Britain was 48.9 millions and there were 5.2 million people aged 65 and over (10.7 per cent). In 1971, for example, the estimated total population was 54.0 million with 7.0 million people aged 65 and over (13.0 per cent).

The growth in the number and proportion of old people in the population, the increasing burden of chronic illness, and the development of technological medicine (largely in hospitals) was accompanied by an increase in the staffing of health services and rising expenditure particularly in the hospital sector. As has been noted earlier (p. 259) the proportion of the health service budget which went to hospital services increased, whereas that for general practitioner services fell.

These changes in the population structure, along with the development in hospital services led sometimes to an appeal for more money and sometimes to cries for a halt. This latter kind of comment is to be found, for example, in a joint report from the Hospital Centre and the Office of Health Economics which stated, 'the working population is now declining as a proportion of the total population, yet the total of hospital and health service staff is still increasing. For how much longer can the health service enjoy this favoured position?' (Hospital Centre and Office of Health Economics, 1971: 25).

The need to reduce local and regional inequalities

During the sixties it also became clear from a number of studies of hospital and community health services that there were wide variations in the scale of provision between different areas. These studies ranged from those of services such as home helps (which were provided by local authorities) to those of the big spenders, hospital services. In the former case different local authorities interpreted permissive legislation to provide services with varying generosity and in the second case, the early years of the NHS were characterized by a small-increment-on-the-previous-year approach to hospital budgeting so that regions that had been well provided for at the beginning of the health service continued to grow at much the same rate as regions that had been under-provided.

Indeed, Klein (1974: 3) argues that DHSS figures for the allocation of funds to different parts of the country suggest: '...(that) the single most important factor in explaining the present allocation of funds is history'. In 1950/51, for example, the South Western (London) Metropolitan Hospital Region (the highest spending region) was allocated twice as much money per head of the population as the Sheffield Region (the lowest spending region). These figures were £6.1 as against £3.0: by 1971/2 these same regions were still respectively the top and bottom spenders, with the more recent figures being £22.1 and £16.6 per head of the population. Over the twenty years, the gap between the highest and lowest region somewhat narrowed — but only somewhat, and mostly toward the very end of the period. Much the same was true for all regions, with those that were 'well-endowed' before 1948 remaining the biggest spenders. A detailed study of the Liverpool hospital region (Logan *et al.*, 1972) noted the shock that was experienced in that region when, in 1962, the then Ministry of Health published its first hospital plan which attempted to rationalize the provision of hospital and specialist services. Liverpool had been a relatively favoured region in this respect and was faced with a substantial reduction in its services.

The discussion of continuing inequalities in the provision of resources to different areas and regions often led to a call for an increase in central control. The underlying idea was that the Department of Health should play a stronger role in setting norms and standards of provision and that it should assume greater responsibility for enforcing these norms. It is relevant to note in passing that the call for an increase in central power was rarely associated with any discussion of the hazards of centralizing power within the NHS, particularly the danger of increasing the bureaucratic characteristics of the system.

The pressures to take account of neglected types of need and an evolving health-care philosophy
Although hospital services had expanded during the lifetime of the NHS, it became apparent, particularly during the '60s, that some sectors of hospital care were suffering relative neglect. Attention focused on the care of the chronic sick including those suffering from mental illness or handicap. Public attention was drawn to these areas of neglect partly by pressure groups such as AEGIS (The Association for the Elderly in Government Institutions). Also significant was Richard Crossman's ministerial decision to make public the disturbing enquiries into gross departures from reasonable standards of care in Ely hospital (Department of Health and Social Security, 1969).

One of the responses to the developing awareness of neglect in these sectors was the creation of a Hospital Advisory Service. However, despite this, many of the problems persisted: as noted in the third report (for 1972) from the Advisory Service (1973), 'most of the comments and observations made in the first and second reports will hold true and the reader is referred to these'. The problems were seen as a combination of relatively low levels of financial support, which affected buildings and equipment as much as staff, and attitudes to patients which led to depersonalization and the associated problems of institutional care.

Parallel to the changing patterns of illness and the changes in the awareness of neglected services, certain changes in the way people felt about health care were also occurring. Of immediate relevance to the major reorganization of the health service was the developing view that the NHS was too divided in its administration and that a unified or integrated service was necessary in order to achieve 'comprehensive care'. Clinical problems, for example, in providing the best care for a patient who needed a smooth transfer from hospital to community services, and a heightening awareness of the high cost of institutional care in relation to domiciliary care, led to increased questioning about the tripartite structure of the NHS. The call for greater integration in the administration of services came from very different quarters; the Porritt report which was published in 1962 on the whole represented the views of the medical establishment. A Fabian group under the editorship of Dr. David Owen, MP produced a book with the title *A Unified Health Service* (1968). Thus, although defenders of the tripartite structure were to be found on both the left and the right, there were strong appeals for an integration of administration that was felt to be necessary for a more comprehensive and more efficient approach to health care.

In addition to the appeal for a simplified administration of the NHS there was also, in some quarters, the emergence of the view that health care needed to become much more sensitive to psycho-social problems. Some writers argued that with a shift from acute to chronic care the psycho-social skills of doctors and particularly general practitioners needed to be developed if only to *maintain* effective relationships with their patients. Others, such as the BMA Planning Unit, which produced the report on Primary Medical Care (1970b), suggested that psychological, sociological, and social skills were now needed to understand the changing presentations of illness and to work constructively with the growing team of providers of health care – what a former editor of the *Lancet* (Fox) called 'the greater medical profession'. Similar views were found in the report of the Royal Commission on Medical Education (HM Government, 1968) which recommended a substantial increase in the teaching of psychology and sociology to medical students and urged the development of social/community medicine.

One aspect of the changing philosophy of health care seems to have had relatively little discussion although it forms the background to a number of specific issues. Conflict about the *goals* of health care was emerging. For example, with the increasing success in preventing death in early childhood (as reflected for instance in falling perinatal mortality rates), it became more of a problem for the paediatrician or obstetrician to know whether his primary objective would be the preservation of life or whether, when faced with a severe congenital and uncorrectable abnormality, he should withhold help. The same dilemma was, of course, experienced at the other end of life and it was one that was perhaps felt most keenly by the junior hospital doctor. An effort to indicate clearly to junior staff whether the objective was cure or simply comfort led one physician to indicate those patients who were 'NTBR' – that is, who were 'NOT TO

BE RESUSCITATED'. Although in this particular instance a public row about these notices led to an ending of the practice, it in no way solved the intrinsic dilemma for the providers of care.

The development of family-planning services and the passing of the Abortion Act in 1967 also brought to the surface underlying problems about the objectives of health care. The plural nature of society was sharply illustrated by the differing views among the public and the providers of care about family planning and abortion.

There was another change in the philosophy of health care which was clearly apparent on the horizon at the time of the reorganization of the NHS but it did not receive public discussion, and not surprisingly it failed to influence the established institutions within health care including the drugs and supplies industries. Essentially, this view was that the drift towards technological medicine was misconceived, that it was based upon a false approach to health problems, which was derived from engineering rather than biology, and that a more ecological approach was necessary. Powles (1973) presented a clear statement of this view and in it he drew together a number of studies that demonstrated the increasing cost of technological medicine in contrast to the diminishing returns (see final chapter).

To sum up, there were a variety of pressures for change in the organization of the National Health Service: pressures resulting from a variety of background forces and emanating from differing groups with different reasons for wanting change. In such circumstances it would not be unduly optimistic to hope for changes that, at least in part, would reflect this diverse and changing background.

The Kind of Change Required

By the early 1970s, then, the NHS exhibited many of the symptoms of any large, complex, and relatively inflexible social system attempting to adapt to an increasingly fluid set of environmental circumstances. Indeed, the background can be summarized as one of change: change in the fiscal orientation of government policy; change in the population structure and patterns of illness; change in the understanding and awareness of the problems of health care; change in the technology of health services; and changes in (and conflicts about) the goals of health care.

In such a dynamic situation, and adopting the language of Burns and Stalker (1961) we would have expected modifications to the structure of the NHS to attempt an organic rather than a mechanistic model of organization.[1] We would have looked, that is, for an organization that fostered the social processes that would enable it to grow and adapt to a changing environment. In contrast to a vast pyramidal structure we would have looked for an organization that would tend to permit a genuine devolution of power – for the decentralization of decisions that were not truly national. Equally, with the changes and conflicts over the goals of health care, we would have sought an organization that would foster the process of participation so that all the providers and consumers of care could share in the determination of goals.

Indeed, by looking carefully at the pressures behind the needs for change, it is possible to see that certain 'open' organizational changes would have been direct and logical responses to these pressures. For example, the local and regional resource inequalities would imply the need for more open discussion of how resource allocation decisions are arrived at; the awareness of the need for greater coordination between policy areas would suggest a looser and less rigid definition of administrative and management roles. Similarly, an awareness of the need for flexibility to respond to changing policies and priorities would have suggested the need to avoid anything smacking of a 'command hierarchy'. These characteristics, in turn, would facilitate the close monitoring of local needs and priorities and the continuous re-definition of goals — two essential conditions for the successful operation of a system as large, complex, and important as the NHS.

In more concrete terms, and dealing with a specific example, such 'open' changes would be designed to result in an organizational structure built around evolving patterns of care, essentially as a support system. Subtle changes have been taking place in the delivery of care over the last twenty-five years or so which are aptly summarized by the concept of a *health-care team*. Examples of such teams would include general practice attachment schemes (for community nurses), mental health, paediatric and geriatric teams (in these cases the patient and the relatives are often full-members of the decision-making group) and teams for complex surgery involving different kinds of doctors, nurses, scientists, and technicians. As with other multi-disciplinary or inter-professional groups, hierarchical or superior-subordinate relationships in many instances seem to be giving way to what Hunter (1971) has described as an 'arena' of skills. Such teams, in fact, operate in a more open manner.

Unhappily, for reasons which are discussed later, the first major reorganization of the NHS was based upon traditional rather than evolving patterns of care and on a mechanistic rather than on an organic model of organization. Consequently, the changes that did occur tended to reinforce rather than modify many of the most rigid and hierarchical characteristics of the system.

The Conditions Under Which Change Occurred

As pointed out at the beginning of this chapter, the values held by a society will, to an extent, be reflected in that society's most important social organizations — in this case the health-care delivery system. It is therefore important, before going on to examine the 1974 reorganization of the NHS, to examine some of the important societal 'conditions' prevailing at the time of the reorganization. In this way, it is possible to understand more fully the relationship between some of the values and priorities of those who were in a position to influence the re-organization and the actual organizational form resulting from the 1973 Act.

In beginning to trace the immediate forces which shaped the formulation of the 1973 Act, it is important first to attempt to understand what the then Secretary of State, Sir Keith Joseph, perceived as a central objective of the Act. In his introduction to the Consultative Document, which was issued in May 1971 and which foreshadowed the White Paper and subsequent Bill, Sir Keith saw the management part of the package as his special contribution, and in describing the proposals said, 'their essence — and their basic difference from earlier proposals — is the emphasis they place on effective management'.

As events later revealed, however, the Secretary of State's definition of the phrase, 'effective management' reflected a preoccupation with what we would regard as a spuriously technical approach to essentially political issues. In particular 'effective management' seemed to consist of a technocratic or managerial definition of needs and priorities; the quantitative expression of these in terms of specific measurements; and the monitoring of these measures to assess progress towards a pre-defined 'goal-state'. It is particularly informative to examine how this idea of 'effective management' came to play such a central role in the formulation of the reorganization proposals.

Technocratic ideas of effective management

The report of an official Committee which considered the role of medical administrators (Department of Health and Social Security, 1972c) was influential in determining one of the primary management roles in the new NHS structure. The strongly technocratic approach which was embodied in the Hunter Report is illustrated by two quotations. The first concerns one of the objectives for managers which is seen as underlying the reorganization of the NHS: 'To define needs locally, regionally and nationally; to set clear objectives and standards for health services and to measure performance against them; relating achievement to the use of resources' (p.13). The second quotation includes a paragraph on 'the question of priorities' which the report considers to be 'at the heart of health services administration at every level'. The community medicine *specialist* is seen as part of administration or management and it is judged that 'he will be qualified to play a major part in the assessment of need, the analysis of existing services and the resolution of problems of choice' (p.13).

Technocratic concepts of need and priorities have largely derived from post-war epidemiology and social medicine. With this history, it is ironic that some of the leading figures in British social medicine have themselves been eloquent spokesmen who have warned against the dangers of technocratic approaches. Thus Morris in his seminal paper 'Tomorrow's Community Physician' (1969: 815) is quite clear that judgements about priorities are not merely technical judgements: '...priorities mean value judgements and politics'. Whilst Logan and his colleagues in their study of the Liverpool hospital region (1972) do not reject a technocratic approach, they state unequivocally in their postscript 'it is essential to adopt a more sophisticated approach to defining need than the original, 1964-vintage model assumed', and their discussion includes a reference to an important paper by Bradshaw (1972) which makes some sociological criticisms of the concept of need.

What seems to have happened is that the epidemiologists' work on death rates led to comparatively high mortality being interpreted as necessarily indicating major 'Health Needs' almost as though they were Platonic absolutes. With more complex problems, such as the conflict between lowering the perinatal mortality rate at the expense of keeping alive children with severe congenital abnormalities (or the *care* rather than the biological aspects of medicine), this definition of need is less useful as an 'objective' criterion for resource allocation.

One of the other major developments from post-war social medicine has been 'health services research'. In Britain this has largely been based on the evaluation of the biological results of health services, derived from the techniques developed for drug trials, particularly the 'double-blind', randomized, controlled trial. For some important purposes, such as the evaluation of surgery or of treatments such as intensive care for patients with heart attacks, this approach affords very substantial gains in knowledge, but this style of health *services* research *reinforces a technocratic and mechanistic view of medicine*. In addressing health services, however, the approach has retained its technocratic nature, it has assumed that the performance of health care providers can be improved through the techniques of 'Scientific Management' (Mouzelis, 1967) and by 'rationalization' of the care delivery system. An example of this approach has been discussed elsewhere (Draper, 1972b). The approach places much emphasis on monitoring the performance of care *providers*. Although Morris, in his paper (quoted above) used the phrase 'monitoring results' he made it clear that he was concerned not with a group of 'outside experts' doing the monitoring, but that instead he wanted a 'routine *self-questioning* of the local medical care system as a whole' (Morris, 1969: 814, our italics).

The question here, however, is not whether statistical and other evaluative skills should be applied to health care at all but *where* those skills should be located in the power structure. That is to say, who should choose the problems for study, who should decide on the research resources for different problems, and to whom should results be reported? Clearly, the people affected by this kind of research and by any decisions which arise from it, are the consumers as well as the providers of care. The point is that 'Scientific Management' typically involves neither self-questioning by workers nor consumer control, nor a combination of these approaches.

The organizational research behind the reorganization

Remarkably little research into organizational and management questions has been carried out within or with respect to the NHS. Thus Cornish (1971), describing research into the management of hospitals which had been sponsored by the Department of Health, rightly characterized the Department's programme as 'exploratory'. This scarcity of empirical research on organizational questions is partly a reflection of a mechanistic frame-of-reference from which health-care delivery questions have been addressed in Britain, and partly a result of the absence of institutions and groups specifically concerned with research into questions of health (and other social services) policy.

Traditionally, organizational problems have been defined as failures in the 'rationality' of the organization, to be corrected by application of the right principle of management. With that point of view, there is little need for research. The purpose of research is to find answers to questions, but from the standpoint of traditional administrative management the answers are known in advance; they are the more rigorous application of the traditional prescriptions about how organizations should be.

This orientation leads to a compounding of the 'single best solution' fallacy (i.e. the idea that there is one best way of doing something if only we were clever enough to find it). Not only is there one optimal way of solving organizational problems, but, because it is a *theoretical* optimum, it is not necessary to check the effects of that solution in practice. The effects are supposedly intuitively obvious and knowable in advance. The orientation also leads to a compounding of practical problems in health-care delivery, because when empirical studies are carried out (Georgopoulos, 1972), the prescriptions of traditional administration are brought into serious question. Indeed, the prescriptions themselves are often responsible for bringing about the problems they attempt to solve.

In addition, the social institutions within Britain for the creation and elaboration of health policies are noticeably deficient (Draper, 1972a). The research staffing of the major political parties is currently quite inadequate to produce detailed proposals for NHS reform. A Royal Commission might have been established to do this work but this choice was made by neither Conservative nor Labour Governments. Furthermore, Britain had no 'think-tank' for the detailed study of health policies at the relevant time. There was no evidence that what was then Lord Rothschild's Central Policy Review Staff had neither the staff or the interest to carry out detailed work on health matters. In any case, the Central Policy Review Staff presents private evidence to the Prime Minister and through him to the Cabinet. It is in no sense a body for the formulation of tentative policies for public discussion. In principle, the Centre for Studies in Social Policy might have performed this role, but it came into being too late and since health policy is only one of its many interests, its efforts would necessarily have been modest. Charities like the Nuffield Provincial Hospitals Trust and the King's Fund have contributed to the development of specific health policies but not in the broader kind of way that would be expected from a think-tank.

A dearth of organizational research was no doubt one of the reasons why management consultants were appointed to advise on the reorganization of the National Health Service and the linked reorganization of the Department of Health and Social Security. The McKinsey Corporation was given these two contracts. It is difficult to judge the contributions that McKinsey made to the reorganization, not least because its advice was not published and because a paper on management in health by Maxwell (1973), Senior Associate of the McKinsey Corporation, explicitly excluded 'a defence of the report on management arrangements'. Two points at least seem clear. First, the McKinsey Corporation has historically been orientated towards American industry rather than to the problems of delivering socialized health care. Second, as Ferris (1966) pointed out in a study of the McKinsey involvement with the Shell Corporation, the McKinsey style is to 'package what its clients want': '...it is also true that McKinsey is always at pains to point out that (at Shell or anywhere else) its consultants see their job as to synthesize existing thoughts rather than to snatch inspiration from the air'. In this situation, if Ferris is right, it is hardly surprising that McKinsey's chief clients – administrators at the top of the Department of Health and Social Security – should produce ideas that were consistent with a form of organization that was essentially a centrally controlled techno-bureaucracy, and that these ideas should be accepted by the consultants. It may also be significant that although the Department purchased management consultancy (the McKinsey Bill alone amounted to at least £220,000), no social survey was commissioned of the ways in which different groups of the public perceived their health-care problems and the NHS.

The reorganization also seems to have been strongly influenced by concepts used in the industrial consulting approach of Jaques (1951). A recent book from the group at Brunel University that has applied the Jaques' approach to hospital organization (Rowbottom *et al.*, 1973) notes on its dust cover that the group '...has been making a substantial contribution to government plans for the unified health service to be introduced in 1974'. A 'building-block' analogy characterizes the approach to health services expressed by the Brunel group, and traditional administrative science assumptions may not have been too distant from its thinking. Professor Kogan, the group's first director, was previously an administrator in central government. There are other problems about the Brunel work, some of which have been discussed elsewhere (Smart and Draper, 1973).

The paucity of available research into the organization of health care, taken along with administrators' resistance to organizational experiment, and a governmental drive to move quickly so that they were not defeated by the Parliamentary timetable (as the previous Labour Government had been), contributed to a situation in which it became impractical to undertake the arduous tasks of formulating specific reorganizational policies for public discussion; of undertaking experiments to test the effectiveness and reaction to these policies; and to consider in depth just what the public interest is in health matters. Instead, the government seemed to accept the idea that more 'effective management' was *a priori* a desirable thing.

The role of the press and media in stimulating public discussion
The treatment of the first major reorganization of the NHS by press, radio, and television affords a revealing illustration of the way in which health policy issues were treated in the UK at this period. Perhaps most striking of all is the neglect of the reorganization by the major medium of communication – television – until government plans and legislation were all but decided. The first BBC television programme on the reorganization was broadcast on July 6th, 1973 – that is *after* the Bill had received Royal Assent! Commercial television was little better because although one of the companies (Granada) had some months earlier produced a series of half-hour programmes on the health service and its reorganization, these were broadcast when the Bill was almost through Parliament and they were screened at highly inconvenient times. In the South they went out at 10.30 on Thursday mornings.

Press coverage of the reorganization was almost as late and tended to be superficial. Although the government issued a 'Consultative Document' on its plans in May 1971, serious discussion largely began in the national press only as late as January 1973 (see for instance the management section of *The Times* January 1, and a half-page article in the *Financial Times*, January 23). Furthermore, a high proportion of the reporting and discussion in the national press was devoted to Clause 4 of the Bill, which concerned family planning – an important topic to be sure, but difficult to justify as the focus of attention.

Work concerning the theoretical basis of the reorganization brought members of the Department of Community Medicine (Guy's Hospital Medical School) into frequent contact with over twenty radio and television producers and research assistants, and with health and welfare correspondents of the national press. It does not seem too harsh a judgement – indeed it was often their own – that with very few exceptions, broadcasting staff were largely ignorant of even the essential features of the reorganization a year after the 'Consultative Document' had appeared and equally ignorant of the major changes taking place in health care, particularly in other relevant countries such as Denmark, Norway, or Sweden. Perhaps because the Government chose to issue its tentative plans (the Consultative Document) to health authorities rather than publish them from the Stationery Office, press comment was not only late but did not deal with fundamental issues until after the civil service, medico-political, and parliamentary battle-lines were drawn up. Quite late in the day a survey of staff in a local health authority (Donaldson, 1973) showed that many staff were strikingly ignorant about the reorganization. It seems reasonable to conclude that public ignorance was profound.

Some strong comments were made in Parliament about the lack of public knowledge of the NHS reorganization. During the second reading of the bill in the Lords, for example, Lord Hayter (House of Lords, 1972a) said 'But the average man or woman in the street knows nothing of what is impending. I believe that it will come as a great shock to many of them.'

It seems relevant to speculate here about the reasons why the mass media neglected this first major reorganization of a key public service. Some of the reasons appear to stem from the internal organization of the national press and the broadcasting media; others seem to reflect more fundamental aspects of contemporary British society. The media appear to view health reporting as primarily concerned with technological medicine, the heady stuff of heroic surgery, 'breakthroughs' in the management of particular diseases, progress in the underlying life sciences. Health correspondents appear to be closer in orientation to their science-reporter colleagues than to social service correspondents. This is consistent with the engineering/technocratic approach to medicine. Some support for this view comes from the fact that when analytical discussion of the reorganization did appear in the national press, it was not provided by the health correspondents. Instead, it came from writers on management and editorial staff, typically in the financial and business sections of the press. These correspondents were understandably skilled in identifying the classical administrative management approach used in the reorganization proposals. Just as understandably, though, they were not conversant with the implications for health care associated with that approach. They did, however, note some of the broader socio-policital aspects of the proposals. (Indeed, Young, writing in *The Sunday Times*, 20 May, 1973, went so far as to suggest a danger to democracy and a shadow of 1984, cast by reorganization.) Their sensitivity to this point may have emerged simply from encountering the same relationship between mechanistic organizational approaches and wider societal issues in the industrial and business setting.

Finally, with very few exceptions, television staff seemed to have little commitment to produce programmes that would promote public involvement in the reorganization process. The very concept seemed alien; the notion that television might be an instrument of participatory democracy, as described for instance in Groombridge's *Television and the People* (1972), was an idea whose time clearly had not come. The drive was to put on programmes when the subject was already 'news' because decisions and action had been taken rather than to produce interesting programmes early enought to foster informed participation.

Thus it is our view that not only was the 1974 reorganization conceived with respect to a particularly narrow and technocratic frame-of-reference, but its paper implementation was largely carried out 'behind the scenes' and with a minimum of public participation – a process impossible to reconcile with the idea of an open and participatory society. Clearly, prevailing influences and events at the time mitigated against an 'open' reorganization. Indeed, the proposals that did emerge and that were then translated into law, were quite different from those that might have been hoped for.

The 1974 Reorganization of the NHS

The *National Health Service Reorganization Act (1973)* applied to England and Wales and transferred the control of the NHS from existing bodies below the Department of Health and Social Security to Regional and Area Health Authorities from April 1, 1974. Very similar changes to those that took place within England and Wales occurred in Scotland, but Scotland had separate legislation which was a year ahead. Changes to the NHS took place within Northern Ireland in advance of the changes in Scotland, England, and Wales but here there are significant differences including a combined administration for health and social services. Apart from the absence of regional authorities in Wales, the changes there were very nearly the same as in England; accordingly, this discussion of the first major reorganization of the NHS concentrates on England and Wales. In effect, the 1974 reorganization was an attempt to achieve two things:
 (i) First, to *integrate the various forms of services and resources under the NHS* primarily by redefining various administrative responsibilities so that, for example, hospital and community services would be better co-ordinated;
(ii) Second, to *introduce a series of 'management' changes* that would give greater central control and, hopefully, greater effectiveness.
In the following section we present a summary of the main features of the reorganization.

Changes meant to integrate services and resources more effectively
The structure of the 1948 NHS was the product of compromise. Because Bevan made a number of crucial concessions both to the medical profession and to the local authority lobby, the health services remained administratively divided (see *Figure 1*). On the hospital side there were regional hospital boards and local hospital management committees. In England, the teaching hospital maintained a special position of their own by keeping their endowments and Boards of Governors. GPs, dentists, and opticians remained as they had been since 1911, that is, independent contractors employed by executive councils. Finally, local authorities kept control over a large number of health functions.

Figure 1   *The pre-1974 NHS*

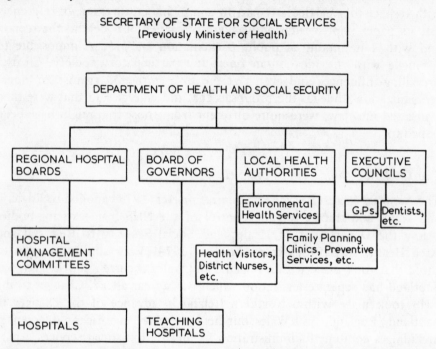

In 1974, in accordance with the idea of better integration, some attempt was made to bring all these services together (see *Figure 2*). The existing fifteen regional hospital boards and 175 local health authorities have disappeared. In their place, in England, there is a hierarchy of fourteen regional health authorities, ninety area health authorities, and 205 districts. The regional health authorities have roughly the same boundaries as their predecessors the hospital boards.

Thus, the teaching hospitals lost their independent Boards of Governors, though for the time being the 1973 Act allows a few postgraduate teaching hospitals to keep theirs. Similarly, local authorities lost nearly all their health services to the NHS including family planning, health centres, health visiting, the ambulance service, and so on. The local authority medical officer of health ceased to exist. His role of keeping an eye on the health of the local population passed to 'community physicians' employed by the NHS.

In principle then, the reorganization goes some way toward producing a unified or integrated administrative chain of command with regional and area bodies that are outside local government. In practice, however, the changes are more accurately thought of as 'partial co-ordination' for at least three reasons. First, in the new structure Executive Councils are preserved in all but name as Family Practitioner Committees which have direct (potentially by-passing) links to the central Department (DHSS) and which will go on administering the contracts of general practitioners, dentists, opticians, and pharmacists. (Although the new Area Health

Figure 2   *The 1974 NHS*

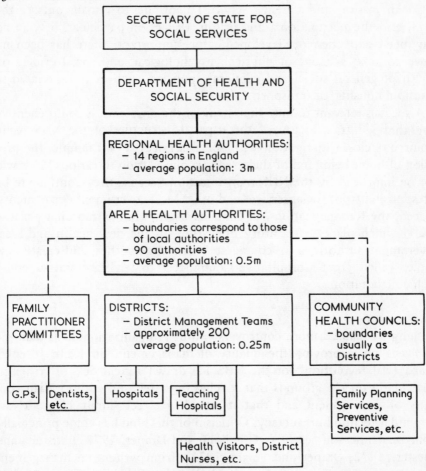

Authorities have responsibilities for the planning of primary medical and related care, it remains to be seen how important this separate administration will turn out in practice.) Second, although the area level of organization was chosen to correspond with the new local government boundaries outside London (of non-metropolitan counties and metropolitan districts, which also came into operation in April 1974), not all local government health services were transferred to the NHS. Environmental health services, involving particularly the work of the public health inspectors, remain within local government so that for the first time the personal and environmental public health services are separated. Third, because the new regions have very similar boundaries to the existing Regional Hospital Boards, most of the existing administrative staff at regional level have been retained, which will inevitably tend to perpetuate their concern with hospitals rather than promoting a comprehensive outlook.

But these changes toward integration should not be confused with the development of comprehensive health care. Some health services (occupational, prison, and defence services) continue to remain outside the NHS, and the occupational and prison services, in particular, have in no way been expanded or developed. More important, there has been no move to take account of physical, psychological, and social effects on health of general social and economic policies, such as those related to taxation, housing, or transport.

Also, it is relevant to note that many of the problems of comprehensive care that led to criticism of the tripartite structure of the NHS really required a closer integration with social services. For example, the provision of home helps and of sheltered accommodation of various kinds will not be improved by the NHS reorganization because they continue to be a responsibility of social services and other local government departments. Indeed, the Reorganization Act contains a somewhat extraordinary clause (10.1) which places a statutory obligation on the new health and local government authorities to 'co-operate' with one another, and create new bodies called Joint Consultative Committees to facilitate and supervise such collaboration.

Management

Nothing has caused more controversy in the reorganization plans than the emphasis on improving the quality of management. Sir Keith Joseph's 'managerial revolution' for the NHS has drawn a great deal of criticism, particularly on the grounds that it relies on dated and authoritarian concepts of management and that it would in effect simply create a vast pyramidal techno-bureaucracy. Criticism of this kind has come principally from academic sources (e.g., Grenholm and Draper, 1972; Batistella and Chester, 1972; Draper and Smart, 1972), from writers on management (e.g., Jones, *The Times*, 1 Jan. 1973; Rogaly, *Financial Times*, 23 Jan. 1973), and from some health service administrators.

In April, 1974, NHS management bodies were put under a single chain of command. The Government's White Paper on reorganization put it this way:

> 'In future, there will be a clear line of responsibility for the whole NHS from the Secretary of State to the RHAs and through them to the AHAs, with corresponding accountability from area to region to centre. The overall responsibility which will rest on the Secretary of State makes it necessary that, in addition to making statutory regulations and issuing guidance, he should be able to give formal directions to RHAs and AHAs...' (DHSS, 1972d).

Thus the new structure is organized in strata with power concentrated at the higher levels, and most of the members of the new authorities being chosen directly or indirectly by the centre. Despite the fact that the government recognizes that these members 'will need ability to give guidance and direction on *policies* to their Chief Officers charged with the management of the service' (italics added), it also stated explicitly that it was more appropriate for members to be appointed after consultation 'for their personal qualities... not elected as representatives' (DHSS, 1972d). In this way, policy control is made a matter for managers and the centre rather than for those directly affected by the policies.

These proposals have led critics to allege that on the whole they will primarily serve to create a vast techno-bureaucracy. First, there is the principle of organization 'that there should be maximum delegation downwards, matched by accountability upwards' (DHSS 1972d, Appendix III). The critics see this principle as being a key feature of a pyramidal organization and they see 'delegation' as being quite different from devolution or decentralization. Second, there is a clearly hierarchical relationship not only between the regional and area authorities but also between the Department of Health and the regions at the top end, and between the areas and District Management Teams at the bottom. Central 'guidelines' or 'norms and standards' are already prolific and powerful. Third, the reorganization has been based upon a definition of a 'manager' which is essentially the kind of definition suitable to an officer of a bureaucracy; '*Manager* is used in the sense of a person who is responsible not only for his own performance but also for that of his subordinates...' (DHSS, 1972b, Appendix III).

Fourth, the membership of the Regional and Area Health Authorities is strongly controlled by central government and explicitly excludes the notion of representatives (House of Lords, 1972b). The Act gives the Secretary of State power not only to appoint all the members of the Regional Health Authorities but also all the chairmen of the Area Health Authorities. In addition, the majority of the members of the AHAs are appointed by the regions. Fifth, the consumer's voice is to be heard only in Community Health Councils which have no executive powers. The Consultative Document (paragraph 20) made it clear that the government saw these bodies essentially as institutions that would 'react to management' rather than be a part of it. The Act leaves a great deal of power in the hands of the Secretary of State to decide the membership of these councils and to decide by regulations their staff, premises, expenses, and rights to call for information from Area Health Authorities.

Sixth, the official documents associated with the Act rely on a technocratic rather than a social or political definition of health needs.[2] Along with this, the role of the medical officer of health is changed from the original nineteenth-century concept of a professional whose job was protected so that he could afford to speak out boldly in the public interest – the highly trained and protected watchdog – to an officer (the 'community physician') who is very much part of the management structure who will assess the health needs of his population by technical means.

Seventh, in the main the reorganization reinforces hierarchical relationships within staff groups such as junior hospital doctors and nurses, in contrast to choosing a professional or organic model of organization. This philosophy led, for example, to the view that consultants could satisfactorily represent the views of junior hospital doctors, and when dealing with District Medical Committees the official management book simply suggested that they 'might also contain representatives of junior doctors' (DHSS, 1972b paragraph 4.15).

It would be inaccurate to characterize all the features of the reorganization as being those of a techno-bureaucracy. Some features, such as the principle of 'clinical autonomy' for doctors, continue an existing and different pattern, that of a professional model of organization (Parsons, 1954) and some features, such as a consensus style of management at some levels (for instance in District Management Teams) reveal a different approach. Furthermore, the elaborate planning processes may not be as centrally controlled as many fear. However, the critics predicted that these exceptions would be unimportant in a structure that centralizes so much power and creates an essentially pyramidal organization. The abrupt and controversial decision in the summer of 1973 to suspend the planning of health centres for example, reinforces the view that central directives would indeed be of profound importance (*British Medical Journal*, 1973). The initial operation of the new structure, such as the central control of manpower and relatively modest capital expenditure, also confirmed the fears of increased central and bureaucratic control.

In essence, then, the reorganization of the NHS was an attempt to solve certain problems in its functioning as a health-care delivery system. The problems were, in many respects, seen as 'administrative' problems requiring a tidying-up of the lines of authority through which the service was run and closer co-ordination between the responsibilities of the different authorities.

The reorganization 'succeeds' in this: the organization chart is somewhat neater than it was before, with the tripartite structure replaced with a single hierarchy; there are more direct lines of 'authority' and 'responsibility' from the top of the pyramid to the base and there is a sharper differentiation between 'health' and 'non-health' activities. Arrangements are more explicit, boundaries more clearly defined, at least in theory, and therefore apparently easier to understand. It is important now to ask just what the real impact of all this will be on the people within and dependent on the NHS.

The Reorganization from a Wider Perspective

In the context of this chapter, the most striking feature of the reorganization is its complete contrast with the sort of open plan sketched in earlier. Instead of an effective devolution of power, a unified and adaptive decision structure, and a less hierarchical administrative plan, we are confronted with the exact opposite. The reorganization effectively increases the centralization of power; in important respects it restricts the opportunity for co-ordinated, and adaptive decision-making, and it certainly reflects a fragmented and mechanistic conception of the objectives of a system of health-care delivery. It is in these principal respects that we feel the reorganization has failed.

Centralization of power

Some argue that the complexity of present-day technological medicine is in itself enough to justify a highly centralized and bureaucratic form of organization. But this assumption is questionable on two accounts. First, students of organizations, such as Donald Schon (1971), have argued that many high-technology organizations are now finding ways of avoiding a pyramidal structure in order to encourage adaption and development. Second, students of the effects of high-technology medicine, such as Powles (1973), are increasingly questioning its efficiency. They point out that much of the effort actually achieves very little and it directs massive resources to the wrong problems. Intensive care for coronary patients is perhaps the best-known example of an extravagant use of people and machines which at best salvage a few survivors from a condition that could often have been prevented or significantly delayed. According to this perspective, the breakthroughs of technological medicine, such as the discovery of penicillin, are the exceptions rather than the rule, and meanwhile we are neglecting the benefits of a more ecological approach to health care. Those who still make the assumption that high technology in itself justifies a massive techno-bureaucracy are therefore increasingly challenged by these kind of doubts cast on the role of advanced technology in health care.

A second argument often put forward by defenders of the policy of centralization is that policy decisions, or 'management' decisions as they prefer to call them, are decisions which only the 'expert' can make and be responsible for. If the views of the 'non-expert' are to be taken into account at all, then this must be on the basis of a limited consultation only. It is argued that only by establishing a hierarchy of control over policy can the NHS become democratically accountable through Parliament.

Doubt is cast on both of these arguments by the recent Royal Commision on the Constitution which investigated whether or not there was a growing demand in the UK for a devolution of power from Westminster, and if so, what should be done about it (HM Government, 1973a). Not only did the Commission find that this demand was substantial, but it recommended ways of devolving power. In particular, concern was expressed about the character of the new health authorities. The minority report of the Commission (HM Government, 1973b: 82) went even further and pointed out that 'the deficiencies from the point of view of democratic control and accountability are obvious'. On the one hand, 'the people in the area most affected by a particular *ad hoc* authority's policies or plans have no satisfactory means of holding its board accountable to them or participating in its decisions' (1973b: 82). On the other, no Minister can be fully accountable for the multitude of decisions made by his civil servants — as is supposed to be the case in the new NHS — and so government by *ad hoc* authorities really means 'government by bureaucrats' (HM Government, 1973b: 83).

Finally, it is also commonly said — though less commonly written — that the increase in central power and the development of a techno-bureaucracy in the 1974 reorganization are justified because they are ways of reducing 'doctor power' or 'syndicalism'. According to this view, some of the major problems of the NHS, such as regional inequalities in the distribution of resources and the continued neglect of sectors of care such as chronic and mental illness services, are attributed to excessive power having been wielded by doctors in what Logan and his colleagues (1972) referred to as 'a syndicalist organization like the NHS'.

Whilst we would agree that a relatively small number of doctors has indeed exercised significant 'braking power' on some issues, we think it dangerously misleading either to characterize this kind of power as syndicalism or to suggest that it has been exerted by *all* or most, doctors. The concept of syndicalism essentially concerns control by workers as a group and not control by a small and privileged minority of workers such as doctors. Power within the NHS has manifestly not been widely distributed among health-care workers. To characterize the present situation as syndicalism seems to us to make it less likely that the potential contributions of wider staff participation in decision-making in the NHS will be examined critically.

Similarly, whilst we recognize the considerable impact of the *sapiential* power of doctors in many situations — an important aspect of 'doctor power' — there seem to be hazards in applying this concept uncritically, particularly to situations involving competition or rivalry amongst doctors. On a number of issues, many groups of doctors (such as junior hospital doctors, geriatricians, psychiatrists, paediatricians, specialists in rehabilitation, and general practitioners), have themselves objected to the influence of an 'inner circle'. Furthermore, it seems doubtful whether the techno-bureaucracy and the civil servants in the Treasury and the Department of Health — the people who will have an increased ability to allocate resources as a result of the reorganization — will prove to be as dedicated protagonists for better geriatric services for example as geriatricians. In the past, geriatricians have clearly not been particularly *effective* as protagonists in battle with traditional specialists, but this is precisely why the concepts of 'doctor-power' or syndicalism are seriously misleading. In the situations to which we have referred, the concept of elitism would seem more appropriate.

Co-ordinated and adaptive decision-making

Many of the pressures for increased co-ordination within the NHS arose at the clinical level, and were expressed as a desire for closer working relationships among personnel and for the wiser use of resources among the three branches of the service (pp. 263–64 above). These pressures did not emerge suddenly; the separation of general practitioners from consultants, for example, and the consequent co-ordination problems in that relationship long outdated the NHS. However, the difficulties presented by that particular feature have increased as the efficacy of some kinds of acute medicine has increased, with far greater numbers of people requiring continued convalescent or maintenance care along with higher levels of social help. The problem was noted by the Guillebaud Committee in the fifties (HMSO, 1956) and by the later Porritt Committee (1962) as well as in the reorganization plans. In both committees and in the reorganization proposals, the issue was whether or not the three existing administrative bureaucracies should be fused into one, partly in the interest of obtaining a higher level of co-ordination within the relatively small groups of health care providers actually involved in caring for a particular patient. That is, the solution to a problem involving the working relationships within small groups of care providers was sought in rearrangements of very large hierarchies not themselves involved in direct patient care. It is possible, of course, that the consolidation of certain administrative support functions and the provision of examples of administrative co-operation might in this respect have an indirectly helpful effect on the providers of care. However, existing impediments to co-operation among care providers seem much more related to the particular identities and prerogatives, to divergent priorities and in fact differing values with respect to the caring-curing process, and to accepted (and acceptable) modes of decision-making among the different providers.[3]

The organizational response contained in the reorganization therefore appears virtually irrelevant to the demand for increased co-ordination among providers. However, this aspect of the co-ordination problem is a severe one, and has led to attempted solutions in some parts of the system. For example, the 'attachment' schemes (p. 266 above) address one aspect of the problem; another is approached in the efforts to bring GPs into hospitals, and consultants out of them (e.g. Barber *et al.*, 1972: 27–32; Illingworth, 1972: 227–31), while a third is attacked in the efforts to implement participative management styles at the ward level in hospitals (e.g. Kean *et al.*). These examples, and they are by no means the only instances of innovations at the direct care level, confront and try to overcome some of the obstacles to more effective co-ordination inherent in the present hierarchical model used by the NHS for health-care delivery. To say the least, it does not seem that such attempts will be encouraged by the new hierarchies that accompany the reorganization.

The changing philosophy of care has been the source of another pressure for greater co-ordination. It is inaccurate to separate this source from the demands arising from direct clinical experience, for we believe that the single most important reason for the change in philosophy has been the experience of health-care providers, followed closely by the experience of health-care recipients. We make the separation nonetheless, because the form of co-ordination implied is somewhat different.

The older philosophy of care is that the biological constituents of a person – his heart, his stomach, his respiratory system – are to be regarded as the appropriate objects of medical intervention, in much the same way that the physical components of a malfunctioning automobile are seen by the car mechanic. The newer philosophy is that health care is a process in which help is made available to a whole person, or, increasingly, to a family or other social group, in short, the philosophical change is from a molecular, fragmented, and essentially mechanistic orientation, to a holistic and organic one.

The change in orientation finds expression in a variety of forms. One important theme concerns the ways in which an individual's component systems affect one another – this is relatively clear in the case of some biological systems (e.g. renal disease leading to cardiovascular abnormalities), but less obvious when biological systems interact with psychological and social ones. However, if research on these interactions continues, and if this information is included in medical education, pressures for more inclusive approaches to care can be expected to increase.

A second theme is the desirability of modifying the 'traditional' doctor-patient relationship, that is, the relationship that evolved as scientific medicine itself developed. In Szasz and Hollender's analysis (1956) the relationship has been likened to that between an adult (the doctor) and a child (the patient); for a number of reasons they suggest that this relationship should rather be one between two adults. One of the more important reasons is that an adult-adult relationship is a more dependable way of ensuring the recipient's participation in, endorsement of, and co-operation with, his clinical management. Brown (1965) has made a similar point for a broadened range of health care providers, with particular emphasis on the depersonalization and dependency resulting from the traditional relationship. As these and related discussions (e.g. Balint, 1957) suggest, it is not merely that degradation of patients should be avoided on ethical grounds, though that is of course true, it is also that overall therapeutic effectiveness increases when care recipients are equal partners in the care-cure processes, and that patient management should help the recipient to attain the highest level of total human functioning of which he is capable. This latter point is emphasized in the World Health Organization definition of health as a positive goal to be pursued – 'a state of complete physical, mental and social well-being, and not merely the absence of disease or infirmity' (WHO, 1965: I).

The co-ordination requirement here is no less than that between the knowledge, skills, and judgement of the care providers with the physical, biological and social-psychological requirements of the recipient. Care is provided to whole people, and to begin to approach maximal effectiveness it must be based on as full and comprehensive a range of resources as is feasible. Care must be flexible and responsive not only to the differences among individuals, but also to the changing requirements of a single person, a family, or other social grouping over time.

The responsiveness and adaptability of providers of care can be encouraged or inhibited by the organizational context in which they work. Bureaucratic organizational forms are designed to promote regularity and standardization of performance; the ideal which they try to attain is that the same job be performed in the same way, time after time after time. (Burns and Stalker (1961) had good reason indeed to call such forms 'mechanistic'!) A mechanistic approach to health-care delivery systems has the effect of inhibiting the adaptive, flexible behaviours needed at the care levels. In this instance, then, the NHS reorganization is not simply irrelevant, as was the case for co-ordination among groups of health-care providers. Instead, it seems likely to exacerbate the problem of adaptability at the level of direct care, and make its solution more difficult.

In any health-care delivery system, the needs for co-ordination, for skilled decision-making, and for flexibility and adaptability are great at the level at which services are provided for people. Identical characteristics are needed by the care delivery system as a whole, if it is to carry out effectively the functions needed for its viability. The manner in which resources are allocated provides one example. As our discussion has suggested, the overall quality of past decisions in this area is open to serious question. They reflect an inability to respond to changed conditions, either through unawareness of the change or, more likely, because of an inability to adapt to those changes despite their being known to individuals and groups within the organization. Thus the relative amount of support allocated to the hospital service has increased at the expense of primary care support, despite substantial shifts in the patterns of health problems and in the structure of the population: support for mental health and geriatric programmes continues at levels appropriate for custodial care, despite the availability of promising new therapeutic approaches. Such perserverance is a characteristic of authoritarian hierarchies.

The NHS's lack of adaptive capacity is underlined by its use of external resources to plan and manage its reorganization (pp. 270–71 above), and by the content of the resulting proposals. Problems of organizational adaptability are relatively common, of course, particularly in organizations that have rapidly changing environments. The NHS is neither the first nor the last to require help from outside to cope with this issue. We stress, though, that adaptability is one of the fundamental problems every organization encounters; inability to deal with it from the organization's own resources is a reflection on that organization's problem solving ability. The ability to solve problems, be they technical or social, is increasingly regarded as the most important property an organizational system should have (see Georgopoulos, 1973).

The substance of the reorganization also indicates the weaknesses of the NHS's adaptive capacities and, more generally, its overall problem-solving abilities. In brief, the reorganization is a 'more-of-the-same' response; it is an increase in the very organizational methods that led to the original problems of co-ordination and adaptability. Such 'positive feedback' or 'vicious circle' phenomena are well known in organizational studies (see e.g. March and Simon, 1958). They illustrate the adaptability problem faced by the NHS all too clearly.

Fragmented and mechanistic objectives

It is one thing for a health-care delivery system to pursue health in the holistic, WHO sense; it is another, yet more daunting enterprise, for a society to pursue an improvement in the quality of life of its members (e.g., Campbell, 1973; Land, 1971). The concept itself is intimidating; after all, is not that what most societies profess to be up to anyway? That may be, but there is a distinction here that we think is useful, and one that is parallel to the distinction between the older and newer philosophies of care. Industrialized societies, of whatever political orientation, have traditionally embraced economic growth as the engine of social progress. They have chosen – unwittingly, but nonetheless determinedly – to evaluate how well they are doing in terms of selected types of societal outputs: in abbreviated form, the Gross National Product. Indices of other societal outputs have not been similarly considered. We compare nations formally, for example, on how much steel they produce, but not on how clean their air and water are; on how many cars, telephones, or refrigerators they have *per capita*, but not on how noisy, stressful, or demeaning their physical and social environments are; on rates of capital growth and on equality or inequality of income distribution, but not on the extent to which their members realize their human potential physically, intellectually, or emotionally; on what manner of politico-economic system is used for distribution of the society's material resources (e.g., 'capitalism' or 'socialism'), but not on the extent to which people effectively participate in making the decisions that affect them. Our societal goals have been fragments of the total experience of living; we have attended to some and ignored others; we have been insensitive to the interplay and interdependencies among them.

The parallel to health care is compelling. In both cases, goals have been defined in segmented, fragmentary, mechanistic ways for objectives that are wholes. As in the changing philosophy of care, arguments for more comprehensive orientations to societal goals are becoming familiar, if not yet commonplace, in some of the more affluent nations (e.g., Reich, 1972;

Ward and Dubos, 1972; Meadows *et al.*, 1972). Even a decade ago the proposition that traditional economic growth could be anything but good was rarely expressed. Today it is rather less than a revolutionary thought.

The phrase 'improving the quality of life' implies not so much setting new priorities, or diverting resources from one societal programme to another, though both these elements are present. Instead, it is a way of expressing a changed frame-of-reference for formal appraisals of societal processes and purpose. It is akin to Kuhn's concept concerning scientific endeavour of the new paradigm that is always needed before progress can occur (Kuhn, 1970). In brief, it points to the systemic integrity of a society, and to the critical interdependence of its component processes. From that perspective, a health-care delivery system like the NHS is itself but one part of an organic whole. Its effectiveness in promoting the quality of life depends on the effectiveness of all the other systems which similarly promote that end, and *vice versa.* 'Health care' and 'social services' interdependency is clear, but both also interact with the educational system; all three affect and are affected by the systems of work and leisure in a society; by transport, by the arts, the production and distribution systems, and by the ways people are involved in their communities and nation. These interdependencies exist now, and always have. The only difference is that we are now beginning to recognize the interdependencies, and develop forms of social organization that correspond to them – e.g., the organic model of Burns and Stalker (1961). The British National Health Service has consistently used a mechanistic model and an organizational model at the other end of the scale from those which address social processes holistically. The NHS in its reorganized form is not compatible with the frame-of-reference needed to pursue improvements in the quality of life.[4]

Conclusion

In attempting to put our assessment of the reorganization into some sort of perspective, we might return to the theme of our introductory comments. From this vantage point, it is only when we view the NHS as an important social system, partly shaping and partly responding to the societal environment with which it interacts, that we can learn something more fundamental about the meaning of the reorganization. Let us return to the question of what the form of the reorganization might express about the wider values of British society.

We have argued that the reorganization reflects a mechanistic and technocratic orientation. Furthermore, we believe that such an orientation does not promote participative democracy. Authoritarian bureaucracies aspire to work from the top down; decisions are made at the top of the bureaucracy and, in the bureaucratic ideal, move progressively down to the working level. People at that level are not expected to make the decisions that determine their work nor the conditions under which the work is carried out. When people at the working level are the recipients of services, as in the NHS, they are even less expected to contribute to the processes of deciding what those services should be. The primary obligation of both providers and recipients is to know their place, and to follow the orders of their betters, that is, the providers, in the case of the patients, and hierarchical superiors in the case of the providers.

Such bureaucratic systems are the antithesis of the democratic ideal, as noted both by analysts of political thought (e.g., Pateman, 1970), and by behavioural scientists concerned with organizational behaviour (e.g., Katz *et al.*, 1966). In such systems, people cannot participate in making the decisions which affect them directly. By virtue of continued exclusion from the decisional processes, and through continued reinforcement of the idea that it is illegitimate as well as ineffective for them to do so, they come to acquiesce to the system, but at a great cost. Part of the cost, and often the most obvious, is that they have no personal stake in the organization, they may do as they are told, but that is all. The goals of the system are not *their* goals. Too often, the goals of their society are not their goals either. Another part of the cost is even more debilitating to the society at large, and is a major way in which the quality of life is degraded. The processes of participation, of mutually determining the course of concerted action, require the development and use of certain interpersonal skills. When these are not developed, the fabric of the society is the weaker, and the lives of the soceity's members are the poorer.

It is our view that this shift away from participative decision processes and toward mechanistic and technocratic processes is equally a shift in what society tends to mean by the term, 'democracy'. Fundamentally, we see the reorganization as an important indicator that our society is moving away from the idea of democracy as *participative* and more toward the idea that democracy is *administered*. A shift we find distressing.

Notes

1. 'Organic systems are adapted to unstable conditions, when problems and requirements for action arise which cannot be broken down and distributed among specialist roles within a clearly defined hierarchy. Individuals have to perform their special tasks in the light of their knowledge of the tasks of the firm as a whole. Jobs lose much of the formal definition in terms of methods, duties, and powers, which have to be redefined continually by interaction with others participating in a task. Interaction runs laterally as much as vertically. Communication between people of different ranks tends to resemble lateral consultation rather than vertical command. Omniscience can no longer be imputed to the head of the concern.' (Burns and Stalker, 1961: 5—6)

'In mechanistic systems the problems and tasks facing the concern as a whole are broken down into specialisms. Each individual pursues his task as something distinct from the real tasks of the concern as a whole, as if it were the subject of a sub-contract. "Somebody at the top" is responsible for seeing to its relevance. The technical methods, duties, and powers attached to each functional role are precisely defined. Interaction within management tends to be vertical, i.e. between superior and subordinate. Operations and working behaviour are governed by instructions issued by superiors. This command hierarchy is maintained by the implicit assumptions that all knowledge about the situation of the firm and its tasks is, or should be, available only to the head of the firm. Management, often visualised as the complex hierarchy familiar in organization charts, operates a simple control system, with information flowing up through a succession of filters, and decisions and instructions, flowing downwards through successions of amplifiers.' (Burns and Stalker 1961: 5)

2 See for example the quotations from the Hunter Report (p. 267) about the role of the community medicine specialist in the assessment of need; see also the Consultative Document (para. 12) which states 'the *Central Department* will determine national objectives, priorities and standards...' (our italics to draw attention to the apparent abrogation of parliamentary rights).

3. See the distinction between organization for work and the performance of work in the previous chapter (p. 233).

4. Since this chapter was first drafted the reorganized NHS has seen an unpredecented series of labour disputes. Whilst part of this turbulence can reasonably be seen primarily as one of the indirect effects of unusually high rates of inflation – staff felt it necessary to force attention to turn to their eroding rates of pay – the disputes can also be seen as a further demonstration of the lack of organizational adaptability of the NHS and the character of the reorganization. It is totally consistent with the narrow mechanistic approach to reorganization that we have described that the key institutions concerned with labour relations – particularly the Whitley Councils – should have been completely left out of what was supposed to be the first major reform of the administrative structure.

References

Balint, M. (1957) *The Doctor, his Patient and the Illness.* London: Tavistock.

Barber, J., Balin, D., Bassett, D., and Haines, A. (1972) General Practitioner Ward in a District General Hospital. *British Medical Journal* 4: 27–32.

Battistella, R.M., and Chester, T.E. (1972) Role of Management in Health Services in Britain and the United States. *Lancet* 1: 626–30.

Bradshaw, J. (1972) A Taxonomy of Social Need. In G. Mclachlan (ed.), *Problems and Progress in Medical Care* (7th ed.). London: Oxford University Press.

British Medical Association (1970a) *Health Services Financing.* London: BMA.

– 1970b. *Planning Unit Report No.4: Report of the working party on primary medical care.* London: BMA.

British Medical Journal (1973) Editorial. Health Centre Funding. 3: 704–5.

Brown, E.L. (1965) *Newer Dimensions of Patient Care.* New York: Russell Sage Foundation.

Burns, T., and Stalker, G. (1961) *The Management of Innovation.* London: Tavistock Publications.

Campbell, A. (1973) Measuring the Quality of Life. *Social Science Research Council Newsletter* **19**: 13—14.

Cornish, J.B. (1971) Research, and the Management of Hospitals. In G. Mclachlan (ed.), *Portfolio for Health: The Role and Programme of the DHSS in Health Services Research. Problems and Progress in Medical Care* (6th ed.). London: Oxford University Press.

Department of Health and Social Security (1969) *Report of the Committee of Enquiry .into Allegations of Ill-treatment of Patients and other Irregularities at the Ely Hospital, Cardiff.* Cmmd. 3975. London: HMSO

— (1971) *National Health Service Reorganization: Consultative Document.* London: HMSO.

— (1972a) *Annual Report* Cmmd. 5019. London: HMSO.

— (1972b) *Management Arrangements for the Reorganised National Health Service.* London: HMSO.

— (1972c) *Report of the Working Party on Medical Administrators* (Hunter Report). London: HMSO.

— (1972d) *National Health Service Reorganization: England.* London: HMSO.

Donaldson, R. (1973) *Staff and Change.* Teeside Health Department.

Draper, P. (1972a) Creating Health Policies in Democracies. *Community Medicine* **128**: 27—9.

— (1972b) Some Technical Considerations in Planning for Health. *Journal of Social Policy* **1**: 149—61.

Draper, P., and Smart, A. (1972) *The Future of our Health Care.* London: Guy's Hospital Medical School.

— (1974) Social Service and Health Policy in the United Kingdom: Some Contributions of the Social Sciences to the Bureaucratization of the National Health Service. *International Journal of Health Services* **4**: 453—70.

Ferris, P. (1966) Shell after McKinsey. *Management Today*, May.

Forsyth, G. (1967) Is the Health Service Doing its Job? *New Society* **10**: 545—50.

Fox, J. (1973) *The Sunday Times Magazine*, 23 March.

Georgopoulos, B. (1972) *Organization Research on Health Institutions.* Ann Arbor, Michigan: Institute for Social Research, University of Michigan.

— (1973) An Open-system Theory Model for Organizational Research. In A. Negandhi (ed.), *Modern Organizational Theory.* Kent, Ohio: Kent State University Press.

Grenholm, G., and Draper, P. (1972) The Consultative Document: Management Assumptions Versus Health Care Objectives. *Community Medicine* **127**: 27—30.

Groombridge, B. (1972) *Television and the People: A Programme for Democratic Participation.* Harmondsworth: Penguin.

H.M. Government (1942) *Social Insurance and Allied Services: Report by Sir. William Beveridge.* Cmnd. 6404 London HMSO.

— (1956) *Report of the Committee of Enquiry into Cost of the National Health Service* (Guillebaud Committee). Cmnd. 9663 London: HMSO.

— (1968) *Royal Commission on Medical Education 1965—68.* Cmmd. 3569 London: HMSO.

— (1973a) *Royal Commission on the Constitution 1969—1973.* Volume I: Report. Cmnd. 5460. London: HMSO.

— (1973b) *Royal Commission on the Constitution 1969—1973.* Volume II: Memorandum of Dissent. Cmnd. 5460—1. London: HMSO.

— (1973c) *National Health Service Reorganisation Act 1973.* London: HMSO.

House of Lords (1972a) *Hansard*. Volume 337, Col. 107 (Lord Hayter). London: HMSO.

— (1972b) *Hansard*. Volume 337, Col. 129. London: HMSO.

Hospital Advisory Service (National Health Service) (1973) *Annual Report of the Hospital Advisory Service for the Year 1972*. London: HMSO.

Hospital Centre and Office of Health Economics (1971) *Do We Spend Enough on Health Care?* London: Hospital Centre.

Hunter, T.D. (1971) Arena or Amoeba: Managing the Health Network. *Hospital* 67: 113–15.

Illingworth, D. (1972) The General Practitioner and the Hospital. *Journal of the Royal College of General Practitioners* 22: 227–31.

Jaques, E. (1951) *The Changing Culture of a Factory*. London: Tavistock.

Jones, R. (1973) *The Times*. 1 January.

Katz, D. and Kahn, R. (1966) *The Social Psychology of Organizations*. New York: Wiley.

Kean, S. *et al*. Unpublished report.

Klein, R. (1974) Policy Making in the National Health Service. *Political Studies* 22(1): 1–14.

Kuhn T.S. (1970) *The Structure of Scientific Revolutions* (2nd edition). Chicago: University of Chicago Press.

Land, K. (1971) On the Definition of Social Indicators. *American Sociologist* 6: 322–25.

Lindsey, A. (1962) *Socialised Medicine in England and Wales*. London: Oxford University Press.

Logan, R.F.L., Ashley, J.S.A., Klein, R.E., and Robson, D.M. (1972) *Dynamics of Medical Care*. London: London School of Hygiene and Tropical Medicine.

March, J., and Simon, H. (1958) *Organisations*. New York: Wiley.

Maxwell, R. (1973) Management for Health. *British Medical Journal* 1: 160–64.

Meadows, D.H., Meadows, D.L., Randels, J., and Behrens, W. (1972) *The Limits to Growth*. New York: Universe Books.

Ministry of Health (1967) *On the State of the Public Health: Annual report of the Chief Medical Officer of the Ministry of Health for the Year 1966*. London: HMSO.

Morris, J.N. (1969) Tomorrow's Community Physician. *Lancet* 2: 811-16.

Mouzelis, N.P. (1967) *Organisation and Bureaucracy*. London: Routledge & Kegan Paul.

Murray, D.S. (1971) *Why a National Health Service?* London: Pemberton Books.

Office of Health Economics (1970) *Information Sheet No.9 (September)*. London: OHE.

— 1973. *Information Sheet No.21 (March)*. London: OHE.

Owen, D. (1968) *A Unified Health Service*. Oxford: Pergamon Press.

Parsons, T. (1954) *Essays in Sociological Theory*. Glencoe, Ill: Free Press.

Pateman, C. (1970) *Participation and Democratic Theory*. Cambridge: Cambridge University Press.

PEP (1961) *Family Needs and the Social Services*. London: Allen and Unwin.

Porritt Committee (1962) *A Review of the Medical Services in Great Britain*. London: Social Assay.

Powles, J. (1973) On the Limitations of Modern Medicine. *Science, Medicine and Man* 1: 1–30.

Reich, C.A. (1972) *The Greening of America*. Harmondsworth: Penguin.

Rogaly, J., (1973) *The Financial Times*, 23 January.

— (1974) *The Financial Times*, 12 July.

Rose, H. (1972) General Practice Complaints — Case for a Patients' Advocate, I and II. *New Law Journal*, 24 and 31 Augjst: 774—6; 786—8.

Rowbottom, R., Balle, J., Cang, S., Dixon, M., Jaques, E., Packwood, T. and Tolliday, H. (1973) *Hospital Organization*. London: Heinemann Educational Books.

Schon, D. (1971) *Beyond the Stable State*. London: Temple Smith.

Smart, A., and Draper, P. (1973) The influence of 'Glacier Think' on 1974. *Community Medicine* 129: 384—5.

Szasz, T., and Hollender, M. (1956) A Contribution to the Philosophy of Medicine — the Basic Models of the Doctor — Patient Relationship. *Archives of Internal Medicine* 97: 585—92.

Young, H. (1973) *The Sunday Times*, 20 May.

Ward, B., and Dubos, R. (1972) *Only one Earth*. Harmondsworth: Penguin.

World Health Organization (1965) *Constitution Basic Documents* (16th edition). Geneva: WHO.

Chapter 9

George W. Brown

Social Causes of Disease

Social Causes

That mice in the laboratory regularly succumb to disease in situations of apparent fear and frustration is not necessarily of relevance to man. In the end, man must be studied where he belongs — in society. This, of course, is a more complex task than running a laboratory experiment; and not surprisingly the greatest difficulty in sociological studies of disease in human populations to date has been methodoligical; because of this it is the dominant theme of the review. The sceptic has little difficulty in presenting alternative plausible interpretations of most published work, and practising doctors on the whole pay little serious attention to the possibility of social influences — at least with regard to the conditions covered by their own speciality. In spite of this I believe that it is reasonably clear that social processes play an important role in the aetiology of both physical and mental disease.

Rather than attempting an exhaustive review of the evidence for the part played by some factors in disease, I have attempted to provide sufficient guide-lines for the reader to assess the case for himself. It is very much a personal statement. My critical tone is a deliberate choice; the field, I believe, needs sympathetic critics rather than uncritical supporters. But this should not be interpreted as unappreciative dismissal of what has been done. Research is difficult; progress is made by the error of others. We avoid mistakes only because others have already made them, and the best that we can hope is that others will find our mistakes interesting enough to be worth correcting.

Much passes for social enquiry and I must make clear what I see as a sociological contribution to the study of disease. At first, the whole notion that society can bring about conditions as serious as cancer or coronary heart disease can appear absurd. Then it may appear obvious: diet, for instance, undoubtedly plays some part in a number of diseases. Large amounts of smoked food are consumed in Ireland and this probably contributes to the high incidence of stomach cancer (Dubos, 1965: 244). There would be no doubt that consumption of smoked mutton is a social fact if action were contemplated to stop production or change eating habits. In most models of disease social factors act as in this example: they either produce the aetiological agent itself or increase the host's chance of contacting such an agent. Dubos has a fascinating account of the way disease has been influenced by social changes. The Manchurian plague at the turn of the century was brought about by the intensive hunting of marmots, which in turn was prompted by increased demand for their fur following changes in women's fashion in Europe; the porphyric person shows disatrous reactions to modern drugs such as barbiturates and so on (Dubos, 1968: 79).

But this is not all. For the sociologist, man is capable of giving meaning to his environment and himself. He plans, anticipates, and reacts to his environment symbolically. The school-child will often take to smoking not because he enjoys the activity as such, but because of its symbolic value in his peer group. Symbolic factors that increase a host's chance of contact with a pathological agent in such a way are of sociological interest. But the sociologist's research role in this kind of problem is likely to be a marginal and uneasy one, much open to misunderstanding by his medical colleagues. He will usually have to await the establishment by others of the causal role of a particular aetiological agent (e.g., cigarette smoke or spirochete). And since there will be hope that the disease can be controlled by preventing contact of agent and host, he is likely to become side-tracked into issues to do with changing individual behaviour — with motivation and even with therapy. His main job when dealing with such aetiological factors is clearly with the meaning of the social activities and any social factors that might influence the relevant behaviour. When he considers, for instance, the complexity of human sexual behaviour or even the social functions of smoking, this is bound, in the first place, to take him some distance from the specific problem of spirochete and tobacco smoke. For example, consideration of what is behind the social behaviour of school children is likely to open up a surprising range of questions about their past and present social milieu.

This model of disease is a very limited one (although of course it may be an effective one). Social factors may influence alcohol consumption, cigarette smoking, and sexual behaviour but thereafter they play no role in the aetiology of liver disease, cancer, or veneral disease — these are brought about by essentially mechanical means. A person's *awareness* of the environment plays no further causal part once contact between that agent and host are made. Enthusiastic gardening may reduce a man's risk of coronary disease; but current theories suggest it will do this whatever his feelings — whether he loves, hates, or is indifferent to the activity (Morris *et al.*, 1972). The symbolic importance of gardening is only significant insofar as it leads a person to do more or less — after this it plays no further part.

In short, the possibility that perceptual and emotional factors as such play a causal role in mediating between environment and disease is not considered. But, put bluntly, can awareness of what is going on in the environment produce disease? It is on this relatively neglected question that I will concentrate. There are in fact two questions: are such perceptual and emotional factors sufficient on their own or do they act in conjunction with a physical agent? For instance, although the most convincing explanation for the dramatic increase in rates of coronary heart disease highlights the consumption of saturated fats (e.g., Epstein, 1966), a substantial intake of such fats is so general in many industrial societies that probably most persons are at an increased risk. Something else must be at work since relatively few in fact develop this disease. There is reason to believe that, at times, social experience plays this role (Jenkins, 1971). One study has shown much higher blood cholesterol levels, which are known to be associated with coronary heart disease, among Benedictine monks than among similarly cloistered Trappist monks (Groen *et al.*, 1962). This almost certainly reflects differences in diet — Trappist monks are completely vegetarian. But in spite of these differences in blood cholesterol level the actual incidence of cardiovascular disease is the same in both groups and much less than among males living outside monasteries. It suggests that some emotional response to the environment interacts with the dietary factor to produce heart disease.

For coronary heart disease to develop physical agents, such as those contained in diet, are undoubtedly important. It is also likely that perceptual and emotional factors on their *own* are sufficient to produce disease. But if such factors have been shown to be implicated and no physical agent isolated, it is, of course, possible that at some later stage a physical agent may be shown to play some part. It seems to me unwise at this stage to worry about whether awareness factors act alone. They probably do — but what is important is to establish whether they play a vital aetiological role irrespective of what may be shown at some later date to be the contribution of some, as yet, unknown physical agent.

I will therefore ask whether something such as enforced rehousing can raise the chance of developing physical or psychiatric illnesses irrespective of whether a physical agent has also been shown to be implicated. I will also want to know when the risk will be greatest. But note, I am not concerned with the fact that as a result of rehousing a housewife may walk further to the shops or see fewer friends, but *how she perceives and reacts emotionally to these changes.* Such symbolic processes are at the heart of sociological enquiry and it is here that the sociologist is most likely to make a distinctive contribution to the study of disease.

There is also self-interest in the choice. The sociologist has never been concerned simply with the workings of society; he has also wanted to know about its impact on the individual. Much of the work I review in this essay is a continuation of the concern of men like Durkheim and Marx with the psychological harm that can come to people in a society dominated by exploitative and contractual relationships. In this sense the study of disease is not a sociological backwater. The term stress can mislead the uninitiated: it may suggest to some that primary concern is with bodily states and with a narrow range of them at that. There must be no ambiguity; our concern is with both, and with the way society affects disease through its influence on a whole range of an individual's emotions such as joy, love, interest, excitement, warmth, anxiety, depression, fear, dissatisfaction, boredom, and the like, as well as on more complex derivates like alienation and anomie — a sense of meaningless — so cherished in the sociological literature.

At this stage of the argument it is essential that aetiological factors, whether physical or symbolic, are not confused with the bodily mechanisms they activate. These are, of course, organic. While some kind of bodily processes must be present whatever is going on, they may not in themselves be abnormal or pathological (Wolff and Goodell, 1968). The activated bodily mechanisms can be protective and only become pathological 'when they are invoked too frequently, or too intensely, or when their action can do little to resolve the particular situation' (Simmons and Wolff, 1954: 118). Of critical importance is the fact that individuals may generalize from physical to social symbols of danger or threat and react with an adaptive pattern that was established earlier in life and only appropriate as a response to physical danger.

One experiment in this tradition was concerned with a person subject to uticaria (hives) (Graham, Kabler, and Graham, 1962). When his arm was struck there were capillary changes in the small blood vessels of his skin (of the kind associated with uticaria) but this also occurred in response to a sham blow. The experimenter then discussed a painful family situation and the forearm responded in a similar way to when the arm was struck. Simmons and Wolff argue that the bodily protective response to a physical blow has been generalized to symbolic blows.

There are other approaches to the study of stress. Selye, for example, has defined stress as all the non-specifically induced changes that occur within a biological system in response to many different agents acting on the organism (see Selye, 1956). He terms it the general adaptation syndrome. Although Selye has emphasized the effect of physical agents, the general adaptation syndrome can certainly be provoked by symbolic factors — such as 'sham blows'. Various responses of the adrenal cortex to long-term stress are involved. One set promotes the production of sugars that provide the body with rapidly mobilized sources of energy. But these also *hamper* the inflammatory processes by which the body combats damage to its tissues and *reduces* resistance to infection (Gray, 1971: ch. 6). This is puzzling. As Gray notes it is an odd way to meet stress and hardly adaptive to the individual. Also (in rats at least) this stage of Selye's general adaptation syndrome suppresses a number of bodily functions to do with sexual and reproductive behaviour. Under prolonged stress there is a shutdown of bodily activities directed towards growth, reproduction, and even resistance to infection, in favour of mechanisms which promote readiness to immediate high-energy action.

Gray seeks to answer the paradox in a theory of population homeostasis. The density of the animal population tends to stay at a fairly stable level which is rarely set by the breeding potential of the population. There must therefore be certain controlling mechanisms which brake the increase in population to which unlimited breeding would otherwise give rise. Gray suggests that Selye's general adaptation syndrome in animals acts as a density-stat (an analogy with thermostat etc.). If it does act in this way to 'overcrowding' we have an explanation in Darwinian terms not only for the suppression of reproductive functions but also for the decreased capacity to cope with tissue damage and infection. It will be adaptive if in such a situation of overcrowding not all survive. Somewhat similar arguments can be developed for the curious susceptibility of human beings to marked and persistent depressive reactions (see Bowlby, 1961; Parkes, 1970).

I have mentioned only some 'stress' reactions. Bodily reactions capable of leading to disease are doubtless many and varied and some responses, such as the general adaptation syndrome, may never have been adaptive for the individual as such. But it is important for sociologists to document the circumstances in which such responses occur *today*. Their origin as evolutionary adaptions is not necessarily of present relevance — other than in the sense that they leave man open to the risk of disease. Nor is detailed knowledge about bodily processes essential. If causal links between social environment and disease are established they must be mediated by some kind of bodily process. Any notion that aetiology can only be said to have been established when underlying bodily processes have been documented would be short-sighted. It is possible to establish important links between social factors and disease and have little or no idea of such mediating processes. Once a link is established it may even be practical to plan preventive work. Indeed, as the daunting complexity of the bodily processes associated with 'stress' becomes apparent, such an independent line by sociological research is not only wise but essential.

I have said nothing about recent criticism of the use of the concept of disease — especially in psychiatry. Much of the criticism stems from the undesirable social and personal consequences that come from labelling a person as having such and such a condition. This is dealt with in another chapter (p. 337 et.seq.), but the day to day use of disease concepts in clinical practice should not be confused with their employment in a research setting. Classification is essential for any enquiry. There is good cause to worry about the built-in assumptions of medical classification and the social consequences of the activity, but to reject the act of classification as the basis of scientific activity because of this, is unwarranted and short-sighted. Placing individuals together because of some apparent common characteristic need not imply acceptance of any aetiological or treatment implications commonly associated with the diagnosis (Zigler and Philips, 1961). Nor does it imply that the symptoms necessarily have an underlying bodily pathology. Having said this, it does not seem to me to matter whether something such as depression is viewed as a disease or a mode of adaptation. It is sufficient that it is almost universally experienced as distressing and that certain 'symptom' syndromes are easily recognized. Of course, it is important for investigators to be pressed to explicate their ideas and not be readily allowed to slip into uncritical acceptance of disease models. But this critical stance should not be confused with the idea that there is nothing to study.

Illustrative Studies

Comments up to now have been general but the research literature is all too specific. One recent review of 'psychological and social precursors of coronary heart disease' lists 162 studies — and this is certainly not comprehensive (Jenkins, 1971). Since this essay must be highly selective I will begin with two studies which I believe are excellent of their kind and which illustrate the two main sociological approaches to disease.

For many infections peaceful co-existence between the infectious agents and the human host is the rule rather than the exception. Meyer and Haggerty (1962) studied streptoccoci in fifteen Boston middle-class families over the course of a year. The families had two or more children and throat cultures were made on all of them every two or three weeks and at times of any obvious throat infection. *Acquisition* was defined as the detection of a new type of streptoccocus, and *illness* by clear clinical signs. Twenty-one per cent of the cultures were positive for the streptoccoci; but only half of the acquisitions were associated with any illness. By means of the regular 3-weekly interviews and diaries kept by the mother, life-events that disrupted family or personal life or caused events and medical measures, particularly when comparing the two weeks before and the two weeks after acquisition of streptoccoci or overt illness were recorded. Streptoccal illness and streptoccal acquisition *without* illness, as well as non-streptoccal respiratory infections were about four times as likely to be preceded as followed by a distressing life-event (see *Table 1*). The level of 'chronic family stress' was also recorded, based on judgments on functioning in seventeen areas such as relation to legal institutions, the relation of the married couple to each other, and adequacy of income. There was a definite association in both acquisition without illness and illness, and a high chronic stress score.

This study is in many ways a landmark, but its shortcomings should be noted. It is not clear, for instance, how many of the events were recorded from questioning of patients *after* the illness had been established. The authors note that: 'Throughout the year parents frequently commented on the relation of acute family crises to the onset of illness'; it is possible that, at times, family members remembered events as stressful in order to explain the illness, and it would be useful to know how far

Table 1   Respiratory infections in families and their relation to acute stress

	episodes of acute stress (nos.)		infections	
	2 weeks before	2 weeks after	total number	associated with stress
strep illness	17	3	56	30%
strep acquisition without illness	12	3	76	16%
non-strep respiratory infection	17	4	201	8%
total	46	10	333	14%

(Amended from Meyer and Haggerty, 1962: 544)

the finding held for events reported to the investigators before the illness occurred. But one advantage of this study is that since acquisitions *without* illness were established independently of any knowledge of life-events, bias for this measure can be ruled out. It is thus difficult to avoid the conclusion that life-events played some causal role in streptoccal infections and illness. The size of the effect is, however, quite modest – something like a third of all beta-strep illness had a stressful event in the two weeks prior to illness or acquisition. But analysis is rudimentary and the importance of social factors could, even from Meyer and Haggerty's data, prove to be greater: for instance, some acquisitions of strep without illness precipitated by a life-event may later have led to overt illness. If this is so, the overall estimate of the role of events will be too low. Moreover, the relationship of life-events and chronic family stress is left unanalyzed; that is, tendency to react to life-events may be greater in the presence of chronic stress. Finally, a difficult but essential step is not attempted: how far are life-events and chronic stress related to extra-familial matters? Can such broader links with societal processes such as unemployment rates explain some instances of family tension? Analysis in the Meyer and Haggerty study is some distance from the broad canvas of epidemiological-like enquiries to which I now turn.

In a study of rheumatoid arthritis King and Cobb (1958) used three questions known to relate reasonably well to the presence of the illness. Two hundred of a sample of 1,323 persons in Pittsburgh were identified as positive on the index, i.e., as having rheumatoid arthritis. They calculated the percentage of rheumatoid arthritis in terms of a number of simple demographic measures (see *Table 2*).

There were differences for men and women. For example, among women 39 per cent who had little education compared with 10 per cent who had more education, had rheumatoid arthritis. For women, four or more children were also highly related to the presence of arthritis. When multiple indices were formed from the separate measures they were even more

Table 2 Percent of persons with certain social characteristics who were classified as having rheumatoid arthritis

	male %	female %
1. Current family income:		
less than $3,000 a year	7.2	7.5
$3,000 − $4,499 a year	3.3	6.2
$4,500 or more a year	0.6	6.8
2. Highest educational level reached:		
less than fifth grade	3.9	39.1
grades 5−8	1.3	8.3
grades 9 or higher	3.5	5.7
3. Marital status:		
single	0.9	7.6
married	2.9	7.4
marriage terminated by death, divorce, or separation	27.3	7.6
4. number of children:		
none, or respondent single	1.1	6.5
1 or 2	7.3	3.3
3	0.4	6.3
4 or more	1.3	25.4
5. Type of leisure activities in the third decade of life:		
no spare time	3.0	9.5
active or inactive	4.2	7.3
6. Judgment of worries compared with others:		
same or less than others	3.3	7.3
more than others	11.7	8.8

(Age-adjusted rates per 100 persons of each sex who are 15 years or older)

(Source: King and Cobb, 1958: 468)

striking differences. For men, for instance, there was a 36-fold difference in prevalence of arthritis between those with an income of less than $3,000, less than fifth-grade education, and the termination of their marriage compared with those who had a higher income, more education, and remained married.

The authors go on to report that for persons with little education increased income is associated with a greater probability of rheumatoid arthritis. But at the other end of the educational scale the rate of rheumatoid arthritis was higher among persons with low incomes. Some interpretive comments are offered by the authors. For example, for women, the crucial factor may be the pressure of work and lack of leisure time that they experience in a society that puts high value on non-work activities (King and Cobb, 1958: 474). One set of commentators reviewing King and Cobb's study have related these paradoxical findings concerning education and income to Durkheim's notion of anomie, namely that under conditions of unanticipated prosperity or economic depression the norms that generally govern behaviour no longer apply, and that 'well-educated persons anticipate and are trained to handle high incomes, while poorly educated persons anticipate and learn to live within low incomes. Deviation from the expected income in either direction tends to produce anomie and anxiety' (Gordon *et al.*, 1968: 51).

The result is certainly intriguing but the status of such interpretations is dispiriting: it is merely speculative. Almost all theoretical activity in this type of study has an *ad hoc* quality. Just why this particular interpretation? The study certainly suggests that there are important sociological factors, but this is all. Something is lacking. Could not the association of low income and divorce with arthritis among men be wholly or partly due to a third factor – the illness? That is, those with chronic arthritis may well have tended subsequently to have experienced a fall in income and to have had a marriage ending in separation. The same could be said of the item about worries. The results for women are more credible, but how far are low education and having four or more children sociological in the sense I have defined it? Both may, for instance, merely be correlated to adverse physical experiences and the correlation with arthritis need not be due in any sense to their symbolic significance. Just what do results mean? Investigators speculate on possible links, but since the associations can usually be interpreted either in terms of the selection of certain kinds of persons into certain kinds of experience or the work of some physical agent, analysis often has the air of unreality.

Some time ago in a discussion of stress and cardiovascular disease, Suchman (1967) noted that in social research:

'nothing is as sterile as demographic group comparisons. Rates analyzed in relation to such categories as sex, age, race, marital status, occupation and geographical region are an essential part of the social book-keeping of modern society. In and of themselves, however, these rates offer little by way of explanation. If one's purpose is to explain the relation between demographic factors and coronary heart disease, one cannot help but get lost in a morass of inconclusive correlations... where does the fault lie? The answer is probably to be found in the essential meaninglessness of gross demographic population categories when viewed as "casual" variables indicative of social processes. These may be convenient, easily studied lables for subdividing populations, but they are not dynamic social ideas and cannot, except in a very limited superficial sense, represent the kind of social phenomena that may cause disease or anything else.' (Suchman, 1967: 109–10)

There is a great need for theoretical definition of measures. Which of the many implications of sex, marriage, age, and education for instance is it that is playing a role in a disease such as arthritis?

But this criticism of the use of demographic-like variables must not be taken too literally. For instance, simple measures of marital status have provided important insights into mortality statistics. Well over a century ago Farr documented for the whole of France how 'if unmarried people suffer from disease in undue proportion, the have-been-married suffer still more'. Probably more well known are the suicide statistics which show that the single and widowed adults of both sexes are in general more vulnerable than the married, and that when the incidence of suicide for the married of either sex is taken as standard, the single and widowed male is relatively more vulnerable than his female counterpart. Durkheim in 1897 in his classic study *Suicide* showed this by using what he called a coefficient of preservation. This is a ratio produced by dividing the suicide rate of the unmarried by the rate for the married *for each sex* separately. Ratios of more than 1.0 indicate a relatively lower rate for the married. The separate ratios for men and women can then be compared. In this way he showed, for example, that in nineteenth-century France while married men with children when compared with unmarried men without children had a coefficient of preservation of 2.9, for married women the same comparison provided a coefficient of only 1.89. The index was 1.50 for married men without children, and for women without children it was 0.67, i.e., married women without children actually had a *higher* suicide rate than single women of the same age (see Durkheim, 1952: 197–98). Gove (1973) has recently extended this method to a range of conditions using US Public Health Statistics. His conclusions are broadly similar to those found by Durkheim for suicide, and he obtains similar results for homicide, motor accident deaths, cirrhosis of the liver, lung cancer, tuberculosis, and diabetes.

Gove argues that the results follow from the fact that men find being married more advantageous than do women, and being single, widowed, or divorced more disadvantageous. Of particular interest is his claim that certain disorders do not fit this pattern. For leukemia and aleukemia (and possible for cancer of the digestive organs) there is little or no relationship between marital status and mortality, and he argues there are understandable reasons for these exceptions. I will not detail his argument, and of course, his particular interpretations can be disputed; indeed, there is no question of any definitive conclusion. The point is that both Durkheim's and Gove's analyses were imaginative. The investigators have developed theoretical notions and use data in a way that much strengthens the argument both theoretically and methodologically. For instance, it has been pointed out that the major reason that the unmarried groups appear to have higher rates of mortality is that the unmarried, particularly the widowed and divorced, are undernumerated in any national census, and further that this undernumeration is greater for males, accounting for the generally larger coefficients of perservation for men (Sheps, 1961). But as Gove points out, this should equally hold for conditions such as leukemia.

When he finds it does not, he concludes that the mortality data he used is likely to have been only marginally affected by undernumeration.

Such imaginative work is exciting and demonstrates what can be done with limited material; but it is hardly a model for fundamental progress in the field. We need to get closer both in theory and measurement to what is actually going on.

Broad Sociological Enquiries

There are two main sociological approaches to the study of disease. One approach, as in the streptoccal infection research, is to start with intensive studies of the individual's milieu, paying detailed attention to the troublesome methodological issues, and slowly to try in a series of studies to relate immediate social factors to broader societal processes. In relating disease to day-to-day happenings in a person's life, such as enforced rehousing or divorce, there is the advantage of some direct sense of what is at work. I will first, however, deal with the alternative approach which, like the study of arthritis discussed earlier, begins with a much broader canvas and hopes that findings can be brought to bear on the individual and his immediate milieu. Psychiatric surveys of whole populations provide interesting examples (Dohrenwend and Dohrenwend, 1969). Two well-known examples, the Midtown Manhattan study in New York and Leighton's work in Stirling County, Canada, are significant milestones.

The Midtown study found that 23 per cent of a sample of 1,660 inhabitants close to the centre of New York were considered psychiatrically *impaired*. In the first report, *Mental Health in the Metropolis*, a series of demographic-like variables are related to the prevalence of psychiatric disorder. They cover age, sex, marital status, parental and own socio-economic status, generation in the US, rural-urban origins, and religious affiliation (Srole *et al.*, 1962). Socio-economic status proved to be much the most important measure. Using parental occupation the proportions rated impaired, from highest to lowest status group, were: 17.5, 16.4, 20.9, 24.5, 29.4, and 32.7 per cent. The use of parental status rules out certain obvious artefacts, the most important being that the association is due to the decline of the individual's occupational level after, rather than before, the onset of the disorder. The second volume, reporting the study, goes further and relates the presence of psychiatric disorder to factors that are part of the biographical experience of the individual (Langner and Michael, 1963). Past influences were parental physical and mental health, childhood health, a broken home, parental quarrelling and disagreement, childhood economic deprivation, and the way the person perceived parental character; and in the present they were work worries, socio-economic worries, the adequacy of interpersonal affiliations, and marital and inter-personal worries. Some of the measures are of somewhat dubious accuracy — the reporting of parental character and even parental health may clearly have been influenced by the psychiatric state of the respondent, the very phenomenon under study.

But leaving measuring problems to one side for the present, the findings in the second volume are intriguing because they show that, although biographical factors relate quite highly to psychiatric disturbance, they do not explain the social class result in the first volume. I will spell this out in detail. Childhood and adult biographical factors are used in a combined stress score and this shows a consistent association with psychiatric impairment. The mere *number* of factors are important rather than any particular combination (Langner and Michael, 1963: 377). The authors conclude that events in the life history seem to 'pile up' bringing with them increasing impairment and that there is no one experience that by itself automatically spells mental disorder for those that experience it.

However, the next set of results is unexpected: these biographical measures are only modestly associated with parental socio-economic status. Lower-class persons do report somewhat more 'adult' stresses, but there is no difference between the classes for stresses reported from childhood (p. 151). The surprising conclusion is that, with the exception of a small group who report none of the ten possible stress factors, those in the low status groups show greater psychiatric impairment regardless of the number of stress factors experienced. In essence, therefore, the mechanism of the association between social class, psychiatric disorder, and stress remains largely unsettled by the Midtown survey. The lower status groups have more psychiatric impairment even when the amount of stress is controlled.

By contrast the Leighton study covers a Canadian rural maritime population and involved a good deal of intensive contact with a number of small communities – and yet the study also, I believe, does not close the gap I have just outlined in the Midtown study. The first volume provided a theoretical background (Leighton, 1959); the second a descriptive account of the communities based on ethnographic studies (Hughes *et al.*, 1960); and the third the results of a psychiatric survey (Leighton *et al.*, 1963). In spite of a mass of descriptive material, much of the third book consists of speculative comment on demographic associations. Nonetheless the study is a good deal more sophisticated than most.

Kunitz (1970) has documented the intellectual roots of the Leighton study in the tradition of functionalist social theory which claims an intimate connection between society and health.

'The point is that functionalist theory, which has come to be equated with equilibrium theory, resting as it does on an organic analogy of society, sees change in terms of disequilibirum, dysfunction, and even at times, pathology. It is in this sense that I would call it conservative. The *gemeinschaft*-like community tends to be static, unchanging, and without history. When it undergoes change, according to this theory, it is likely to disintegrate, and this causes psychiatric problems for its members.' (Kunitz, 1970: 320)

The Leightons, much influenced by this tradition, developed ten indicators of social disintegration. When set forth in negative terms they are economic inadequacy, cultural confusion, widespread secularization, few and weak associations, few and weak leaders, few patterns of recreation, high frequency of crime and delinquency, high frequency of broken homes, high frequency of interpersonal hostility, and a weak and fragmented network of communications (Leighton *et al.*, 1963: 26). It is then argued that the development of psychiatric disorder results from the interference of social disintegration with the possibility of achieving, what they argue are, the ten basic human strivings – physical security, sexual satisfaction, the expression of love, the expression of hostility, the securing of love, the securing of recognition, the expression of spontaneity, knowing one's place in society, membership of definite human groups, and the sense of belonging to a moral order (Leighton, 1959: 148).

The trouble is, as Kunitz (1970) points out, that on the face of it the ten basic strivings are essentially the same as the indicators of social disintegration and there is, in fact, no independent assessment made of them. One of the measures of disintegration is marital instability and by asking about someone's marital history one has an indicator of the interference both of a community's level of disintegration, and an indicator of the interference with the expression of love and sexual satisfaction (one of the basic strivings). Hence there is an inevitable tautological element in much of the analysis. How far the onset of disorder is associated with 'alterations in numerous habits and patterns of interpersonal relationships' is not documented because the data have not been collected; alteration has simply been assumed. Because of this the basic contribution of the study has been to examine the prevalence of psychiatric disorder in various communities, a number of which were especially selected because of certain obvious indications of disintegration.

For the crucial test of the social disintegration hypothesis two communities were picked out (by key informants) as outstandingly high on integration (Lavellee and Fairhaven), and three as outstandingly disintegrated. Results are in the expected direction, but there is one anomaly. Fairhaven, one of the integrated communities, is much nearer results for the less integrated areas, and it turns out this is largely due to the extent of psychiatric disorder among women. The proportions in the most severely psychiatrically impaired category are shown in *Table 3*.

The authors note that they had previously shown that mothers in Lavallee are comparatively high on self-esteem, while the opposite is true of those in Fairhaven. They also comment that the difference may be a matter of situation rather than culture *per se*. 'One is tempted at first to think that there is something about being the wife of a fisherman with its storms and fears that precipitated psychoneurotic and psychophysiological symptoms' (Leighton *et al.*: 341).

They are fully aware that the most parsimonious interpretation of

Table 3 Per cent of persons placed in the 'Almost certainly psychiatric disorder' category by sex and type of community

	men %	women %	(N) %
integrated — Lavallee	13	23 ⎫	
integrated — Fairhaven	23	52 ⎭	(82)
three non-integrated areas	55	57	(69)
county as a whole	21	42	(1,010)

(The percentages are approximate and calculated from Leighton *et al.*, 1963: 331, Figure 19)

these results is that the differences are due to long-term selective processes. The disintegrated villages had been economically depressed for a long period (it is likely that relatively more 'disintegrated personalities' failed to move elsewhere). However, it is unlikely to be the sole explanation. For example, a further paper has been published dealing specifically with the effects of improving social and economic conditions (Leighton, 1965). Leighton describes one of the disintegrated and very depressed villages that after 1950 gradually reached a state of comparative independence and self-sufficiency. At the turn of the century it suffered a major loss of economic support, and, although some inhabitants moved, enough remained to perpetuate the communities. At the time of the first survey there was severe poverty. Literacy was rare and the families showed a high rate of broken marriage, parental quarrelling, and child neglect. In spite of the smallness of the village there was a surprising degree of isolation between families. It so happened that after the initial survey some steps were made to improve conditions. Adult education classes were begun and the older children were sent by bus to a school out of the village. There was also an upswing in employment opportunities. Electricity came to the settlement and television appears to have influenced 'dress, speech and manners'. There was undoubtedly considerable change over a fifteen-year period both in behaviour and general attitudes. Correlated with this, Leighton reports that there was an overall reduction in psychiatric disorder so that by the second survey the community's mean rate was the same as the county as a whole. Material on the *same* individuals is not reported, but it seems likely that there had been a real change in the amount of psychiatric disorder. It also suggests that in spite of the possible selection of constitutionally predisposed individuals, environmental factors are of dominant importance.

My overall reactions to the study, given the years of effort that went into it, is some sense of disappointment. Measurement of psychiatric disorder leaves much to be desired, social factors are poorly specified, and the disintegrated communities so grossly underprivileged that the generality of the findings are of somewhat doubtful status. It is surely reasonable to hope for something more.

At this stage the reader may ask how much work such as the Leightons' squares with the general notion that the 'stress of modern life' have contributed to increased psychiatric (if not physical) illness. The term 'modern life' is, of course, vague. Most work has dealt with the results of rapid urbanization and social change rather than modern life as such (however this is interpreted). It is clear that urbanization and industrialization may serve to increase certain disease rates and to decrease others, and the overall rate may be the result of such negative and positive trends. It does appear, however, that change can lead to appreciably raised rates of disease. There is some suggestion, for instance, that rates of coronary heart disease are greater in populations experiencing rapid social change and that migrants from disparate cultures also have a greater rate, particularly if there has been some failure in adaptation (e.g., Bruhn *et al.*, 1968). Gorden (1957; 1967) has dealt with the very large differences in coronary heart disease between Japan and the US (see Scott Matsumato, 1971: 123). Japan has one of the lowest rates of coronary heart disease in the world and the US one of the highest. A genetically determined difference in tendency toward heart disease is discounted by the fact that Japanese in the US exhibit American coronary rates. Gorden notes one intriguing finding that the rates for Japanese in Hawaii is intermediate between that for Japan itself and the mainland United States. To make progress we must establish what it is about these places that is different.

Tyroler and Cassel (1964) looked at the effects of industrialization on deaths from coronary heart disease in the essentially rural state of North Carolina. The units of study were counties which were placed in one of four categories according to the size of their largest town. *Within* each county rates for rural and urban residents were calculated. The death rates of rural residents increased according to the degree of urbanization of the county, and also increased between 1952 and 1960 in each of the four types of county. Trends for urban dwellers on the whole showed few differences and, unlike the rural rates, did not increase with time. The authors suggest that whatever deleterious influences accompany urbanization they had reached a plateau for the urban dwellers by 1952 but continued to exert their influence on less adapted rural residents. While much work remains to be done, a *prima facie* case has been made for the harmful influence on health of rapid industrialization. Just what is at work still remains unclear. Is it simply change or something more specific to industrial society? There are interesting clues. One study, for instance, suggests that rates of coronary heart disease are *not* associated with prestige or status levels of occupations but with the overall reported level of dissatisfaction with work for a particular occupational group (Sales and House, 1971). More settled conditions following rapid change will almost certainly have a differential effect according to socio-economic class. To spell out more clearly what is going on we must, I believe, turn to the more intensive study of the living conditions of particular individuals.

Intensive Studies

The work on rheumatoid arthritis has already been mentioned and is particularly interesting here as it includes more than a broad analysis of the demographic variables already reviewed. A further study by Cobb and his colleagues gives hope that we can push beyond very general notions of stress and disease to explore the relationship of specific social factors to particular conditions (Cobb *et al.*, 1969a). Exploratory work had suggested that rheumatoid arthritis in adults is related to early punitive parental behaviour that led to a long history of resentment or inhibited anger in the child which in adulthood promotes, precipitates, or exacerbates the disease. Hostile feeling tends to recur in situations felt to be injurious but beyond control and are chiefly aroused in relation to figures of authority. The theory therefore suggested that adults with rheumatoid arthritis would tend to recall parental authority as being arbitrary and their childhood response as being one of resentment, of hostile feelings that must not be expressed. The recent work has relied on retrospective accounts, but it is backed up by independent reports from adult siblings. The agreement between the accounts of family life derived from the two sources was reasonably high — for example, the correlation (r) for the same-sex siblings recalling mother's authority is 0.55. The study itself is based on the comparison of patients and a sample from the general population with and without rheumatoid arthritis.

Results could be predicted from the theory. Although memories about father's behaviour showed no association with rheumatoid arthritis, women with rheumatoid arthritis reported much more often than women without arthritis, a combination of arbitrary authority in their mother combined with resentment on their own part (63 per cent and 21 per cent respectively). Men, who suffer much less often from rheumatoid arthritis, recalled no consistent pattern of authority (Harburg *et al.*, 1969).

The authors go on to relate these core findings concerning family life to background social factors and to details of the respondent's current marriage. For example, women with rheumatoid arthritis were found to be much more likely to come from families where the mother's educational level was discrepant with the educational or occupational level of the father; or where the father's occupation was either of higher or lower status than would be expected from his education. Sociologists call this *status incongruity* and there are various ways of measuring it (see Dodge and Martin, 1970; Shekelle, Ostfield, and Oglesby, 1969). The basic idea behind most work is that such status incongruities result in conflicting expectations about the behaviour of others and uncertainty about the appropriateness of one's own behaviour (King and Cobb, 1969). Sixty-eight per cent of the daughters of parental marriages with high incongruity had rheumatoid arthritis, 40 per cent of the intermediate group and 20 per cent of the low. Men, however, did not conform to this pattern. It is noticeable that the respondent's *own* status incongruity does not relate to rheumatoid arthritis but it did to low self-esteem. The authors suggest that their findings would fit a general theoretical framework which postulates the following process: status incongruity among parents → conflicting expectations and uncertainty about appropriate behaviour as parent and spouse → unsatisfactory relations between parents and higher experience of frustration → arbitrary authority in treatment of same-sex offspring → child's poor identification with parents and feelings of rejection → unstable and inadequate self-image and low self-evaluation of child and adult → symptoms of poor physical and mental health (Kasl and Cobb, 1969).

This recent work of Cobb and his colleagues has I believe advanced knowledge a great deal further because the measures of status incongruity have a quite different standing from that in the earlier study (see p. 297–99). The measures are conceptualized in terms of a theory about the aetiology of rheumatoid arthritis. The theory suggests that it is understandable that the respondent's *own* status incongruity be related to low self-esteem but not to rheumatoid arthritis. In Suchman's sense the theory ensures the measures have meaning.

The authors have developed a coherent theory about a particular disease and manage to relate their core findings regarding early childhood experience to known aspects of the American social structure (for example, it has long been known that divorce rates are higher among spouses who come from different social backgrounds), and to research on personality and the dynamics of particular marriages. The interpretations based on results of the first demographic-like enquiry we discussed earlier gained little support, nor did social class emerge as an important factor.

Loss and Meaning

An equally rewarding way to begin intensive work has been to look at the role of more recent life-events in causing illness — particularly events associated with important changes in life-style. In a paper published in 1944, Lindemann described a syndrome of symptoms found in acute grief and Bowlby (1961) and Parkes (1970) at the Tavistock Institute, have since done much to support and develop his basic scheme. All agree that although there is a common pattern of response to bereavement which is called grief, it may be delayed, exaggerated, or apparently absent. There has been a good deal of exploration of the causes and consequences of these 'distorted' reactions.

There is now good evidence that bereavement leads to increased risk of physical and psychiatric illness. Most work is based on medical or census records (e.g., Parkes, 1964; Stein and Susser, 1969). It is also known that there is an increase in mortality among widowers in the first year of bereavement (Young, Benjamin, and Wallis, 1963; Rees and Lutkin, 1967) and that health may well be affected for as long as two years. The increased mortality (at least in British widowers over fifty-five) seems particularly due to mortality from coronary thrombosis and arteriosclerotic heart disease (Parkes, Benjamin, and Fitzgerald, 1969). Two studies have shown deterioration in self-reported health in a considerable proportion of recently widowed women (Marris, 1958; Parkes, 1970); and in England, at least, there is a rise in the number of consultations with general practitioners following bereavement (Parkes, 1964). However, all these investigations lack comparison ('control') groups: that is a socially comparable group who have *not* been widowed. Nonetheless, a recent study done in Boston had one and confirmed these general results, although only a third of the widows and widowers selected co-operated (Parkes and Brown, 1972).

In a study based on the analysis of death certificates, widowers in England and Wales showed a 40 per cent greater mortality rate in the first six months of bereavement compared with married men of the same age (Young, Benjamin, and Wallis, 1963). Rees and Lutkin (1967) in a survey of the relatives of 903 patients in a semi-rural part of Wales showed that 4.8 per cent of the close relatives of the dead person died within a year of bereavement compared with 0.7 per cent of the relatives of a comparison group of non-bereaved persons. (The latter rate is, however, somewhat low by general population standards.) The greatest increase was in widows and widowers. After the first year mortality rates fell off sharply. The mean age of those dying was somewhat lower than in the population as a whole (69.75 and 73.35 respectively). The authors conclude that there is a group of relatively young persons (with an average of sixty-five years) that appears to be particularly at risk in the first year of bereavement. While the main effect is over within a year there is a possibility of an influence over an even longer period. In a study of suicide, for instance, Bunch (1972) found a greater than expected number of suicide deaths among those bereaved for one to five years; and there is plenty of evidence that early loss of parent has a perceptible influence on subsequent rates of psychiatric disorder (Bowlby, 1961; Birchinell, 1972; Granville-Grossman, 1968).

The events I have considered so far concern bereavement. Marris (1974) has related such grief reactions to a much broader range of social changes such as enforced rehousing, and the rise of educational elites in East Africa. He describes a characteristic paradox in all his examples of change. There is a need to deny the change and also a need to accept that a change has occurred; what has happened has to be accepted and some meaningful continuity accepted between past, present, and future relationships. Adjustment to a major loss is therefore likely to be both painful and erratic: 'caught between the impulse to deny change and refute the need for any radical reinterpretation of life, and the search for a new sense of continuity that can assimilate change.' Marris argues that whenever people suffer loss their reaction reflects a conflict that is essentially similar to that seen in the grief processes experienced when an individual loses someone close to him.

The theory Marris had in mind is reasonably clear. We depend on the fact that for most of the time our day-to-day lives are predictable. But this is not only derived from continuous routine activities; we also need some continuity of meaning. Indeed major changes in routine may be welcomed as long as there is continuity of purpose. Loss of someone close can strike at this sense of purpose or meaning since it commonly involves not only a lost *object,* but a lost *role* (Averill, 1968). Szasz (1962) has emphasized the loss of a 'game' — a series of rules and norms for significant action. Such games dissolve when the person around whom anothers' identity has been fabricated and sustained no longer exists, and subsequently the performance that was constructed around that person ceases to have meaning (Becker, 1962). Intensity of grief is therefore related not only to degree of love but to the breadth of activities and plans involved in the lost relationship. Grief can be great in a run of the mill marriage or a downright unhappy one. The importance of a sense of meaning is most poignantly seen in the loss of meanings that are attached to activities that are *past.* Bergman, in his film *The Lie* shows a man struggling with the knowledge that his marriage, spanning many years, has been sustained from the start by his wife's affair with a lover she knew before her marriage. He faces not only the loss of his wife and his role as a husband but his whole conception of his life over many years. Meaning in such circumstances can be lost, although everyday life can carry on in essentially the same way as it has always done. (It would not in this sense help if the man's wife had been willing to stay and change her ways.)

In delayed or inhibited grief there is apparent calm acceptance and little expression of sorrow. Marris describes a sense of hollowness as if concern for all but the most superficial of day-to-day activities had been suppressed. By contrast chronic grief is the indefinite prolongation of the initial state of yearning and despair. Ordinarily, in grief, there is an impulse to return to the past and also to reach forward to the future where the past is forgotten. Each impulse is checked by the pain it arouses and there is continual weaving back and forth — until in time there is some measure of resolution. When this is absent as in delayed and chronic grief there is evidence that there is an even higher rate of psychiatric and physical illness (e.g. Parkes, 1964; Engel, 1967).

If we take Marris's point that all change involves loss we can generalize this model to other contexts: we can look for such reactions whenever a familiar pattern of life is disrupted. For example, because we can hold unrealized plans and aspirations it is indeed possible to experience a sense of lose for something never or only fleetingly experienced. It is still part of oneself. For the same reason there can be risk in experiencing things that are difficult to repeat (Parducci, 1968). A particularly intriguing notion of Marris's is that changes that occur in situations such as courtship can be seen as the process of mourning in reverse. Courtship is a gradual commitment to wishes for a home and children with a particular person. Like mourning, plans and marriage have to be grounded in new circumstances and at times too much of oneself and possible alternative courses of action may have to be abandoned to make the final step of marriage. Durkheim in *Suicide* argues along similar lines: for instance, he interpreted the correlation between suicide and economic booms as due to a break down in the established normative framework and therefore leading to a potential increase in meaninglessness. In his words a person may become lost in the 'infinity of desire' and 'passion, no longer recognizing any bonds, no longer has any aim'. The same sort of thing can happen when someone is inordinately successful. Success even when it has become avidly sought may be dangerous.

Parkes (1971: 113) uses the term psychosocial transitions for any change that has large effects on the conceptions a person makes about the world. 'Frightening situations or transient illness which, although they may threaten life or cause extreme pain, give rise to no lasting effects on the assumptive world are not psychosocial transitions. Neither are life-long states of deprivation, deformity or stigma (though they could, and have, been considered as stressful).' Parkes makes an important distinction here. But it should be emphasized that psychosocial transitions can differ greatly in the amount of change they necessitate in everyday assumptions; as a result, they vary in how far they are welcomed, how much anxiety they provoke, and so on. Moreover 'loss' events are not the only type of life-events of importance in the aetiology of disease. I will discuss later how 'a frightening transient illness' is capable of provoking a major schizophrenic illness, but apparently not a depressive illness. Nor must we forget that events can lead to new kinds of adaptation and growth. One way they do this is through their link with the past. Events may not only pose a problem in the present; they may trigger off partly resolved conflicts from the past (Rapaport, 1962); and a crisis situation may be used as an opportunity to resolve these unresolved conflicts.

If we are to develop our understanding of the effects of life-crisis there are two immediate tasks. We must develop theory about particular diseases (schizophrenia as distinct from depression, and rheumatoid arthritis as distinct from heart disease) and also establish whether different kinds of life-event play a role in different diseases. Special situations may be studied, such as enforced rehousing (Fried, 1965), parenthood, (Dyer, 1965; Le Masters, 1957), premature birth (Kaplan and Mason, 1960; Rapaport, 1962), and fatal illness in children (Freidman, Mason, and Hamburg, 1963). Alternatively we can look at the total *range* of possible life-events. The latter approach not only presents the greatest challenge, but it is most easily linked to the sociologist's concern with 'whole societies'.

Once these tasks have gone some way the challenge is two-fold: to spell out the role of current and past experience in determining vulnerability to events; and to relate both life-events and vulnerability factors to the broader social structure. Both are crucial, but I would particularly draw your attention to the issue of vulnerability, for it is here, I believe, that exciting theoretical and practical issues reside. We have already touched on the issue of vulnerability at several points — for example, in the Midtown study lower-class men and women appeared to be more likely to develop psychiatric disorders even when past 'stresses' were controlled. Such differences in vulnerability are by no means to be equated with genetic or somatic differences. However, progress in developing theory about such issues has been bedevilled by methodological problems, particularly to do with whether life-events play any causal role at all in onset of disease; and it is to these methodological problems that I now turn.

Life-events and Measurement

Most of the problems and doubts that arise in studying the relationship between life-events and the onset of disease revolve around some issue to do with measurement. I have discussed three of these at length elsewhere (Brown, 1974) and here I briefly outline each in turn.

1. Direct contamination

Reporting of a life-event can be influenced by knowledge of the illness itself. This means that the measurement of life-events may be contaminated by the very thing to be explained. This may occur because whether or not the way a particular event is reported reflects one way of coming to terms with the illness. A man may exaggerate his wife's attachment to her dog killed months before the onset of a severe depressive illness as a means of trying to make sense of the catastrophe that has occurred. Events are not something in the real world that simply require description. They have meaning and emotion attached to them and it is this that makes them objects for sociological study but at the same time it also makes them open to change after the event itself is over. In this sense no life-event can be said to have its meaning finally settled: where such change occurs before the onset of disease it may, of course, be of some causal importance but when it occurs after onset it can only be a source of possible contamination.

The research process itself can easily get caught up in such processes of changing meaning. In the streptoccal throat infection study (Meyer and Haggerty, 1962) the regular questioning by visiting researchers about symptoms and events may have suggested to some parents that there can be a causal link between the two. This notion may then have influenced reporting, once the child was ill, of the stressfulness of things that had occurred. There need be no fabrication − simply a tendency under some circumstances but not others for a more complete recall of events.

In order to make certain that the respondent's interpretations of what has occurred are consistent with the investigators', it is necessary to try to bring under control the symbolic significance of events; but this is the very element, from the sociologist's view, that is of importance if life-events really have a causal link with disease. One obvious method of tackling the problem would be to collect information about all events *before* the occurrence of illness. It is a costly and dramatic remedy and unfortunately one that will not solve the problem. In order to argue causally it is also necessary to demonstrate that any association between life-events and disease is not the result of a common factor influencing them both. This is the well recognized issue of spurious relationships. It is not solved by a longitudinal research design and it brings us to the two remaining problems of measurement.

2. Spuriousness involving measurement error

It is possible for a correlation between life-events and disease to be due not to a direct causal link but to the presence of a factor prior in time influencing them both:

Diagram A

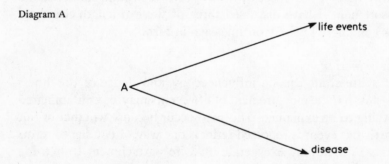

'A' influences the chance of a life-event and also the chance of disease: a change in 'A' that increases the chance of a life-event will tend also to bring about (or make less likely) the disease. There will be a correlation between life-events and disease but no causal link. If 'A' were in some way prevented from bringing about life-events there would be *no* reduction in the rate of disease. Certain forms of measurement error exemplify such a spurious link between life-events and disease. For example, some may *report* events as more stressful than they really were because of a high level of anxiety (i.e. 'A'). It is also possible that such high anxiety may lead quite independently to a greater rate of disease. In this case there would be no causal link between the stressful events and the disease; the correlation would simply reflect the effect of a high level of anxiety on the persons reporting the events. Some kind of unbiased measurement procedure would solve the problem, but spuriousness may yet take another and even more difficult form.

3. Spuriousness without measurement error

Accurate measurement is not necessarily enough to deal with the issue of spuriousness. Completely accurate descriptions of the stressfulness of a life-event would not avoid false conclusions if, for example, a third and prior factor influenced the subject's *experience* and not merely his report of the stressfulness of the event as well as the illness itself. For example, a personality trait such as high anxiety ('A') may lead to *both* a greater chance of illness *and* a greater tendency to *experience* life-events as stressful. Again the correlation between life-events and illness does not represent a causal link; it is simply produced by 'A'.[1] Since this kind of spurious link may occur *even if the measures are completely accurate*, the reduction of invalidity is not merely a matter of avoiding measurement error.

The three measurement problems I have outlined are not just academic quibbles; they affect the confidence that can be placed in a good deal of research. For example, the Schedule of Recent Life Experience (SRE) developed by Holmes and Rahe (1967) has been widely used and even found its way into television and Sunday Colour Supplements' discussions of illness and stress. In prospective research it has successfully predicted substantially higher rates of illness for those with higher scores on the SRE schedule (Rahe, 1969). And yet the research does not provide convincing evidence for a causal link between life-events and disease. The questions about life-events are so general that it is completely open for the respondent to report what he wishes. Forty-two possible life-events are given pre-arranged scores (established earlier from common-sense judgments of the degree of social readjustment required by the event). These weights range from 100 for death of spouse, through 50 for marriage, to 11 for minor violations of the law. One item, for instance, asks about 'change in health in a family member'; but it is left open just how it is to be interpreted. Just *what* is a change in health and *who* is a family member? There is bound to be variability in interpretation by respondents; but the same score is given to anyone ticking the item. There is no elucidation by the investigators of why this item has been ticked. Although the study was designed to avoid the use of personal meaning it has in fact very little control over the way meaning influences the final life-change scores. Because of this open-endedness there is considerable risk that the illness, or factors related to it, will influence the filling up of the questionnaire by raising or lowering the threshold of either i) what is considered worthwhile to report or ii) the range of persons subsumed under an item that has been ticked on the questionnaire. For example, in response to the question about change in health a respondent under certain circumstances may be more likely to report a quite trivial condition; or, leaving aside severity, be more likely to report illnesses occurring to a wider range of kin than he would usually consider in answering such a question. It can be shown that the method is in fact open to all three sources of invalidity I have just outlined (Brown, 1974).

At the heart of these difficulties is the issue of meaning. Although a matter of considerable complexity, I believe for the purposes of this type of research the problem reduces itself to how far it is possible to take account of the full social circumstances surrounding an event and yet avoid the contamination inherent in any use of the respondent's account of what he has found stressful. I will discuss ways of dealing with the problem with illustrations from two London studies carried out with my colleagues. The first deals with schizophrenia and is complete (Brown and Birley, 1968; Birley and Brown, 1970); the second, dealing with depression, is in progress (see Brown *et al.*, 1973; Brown, Harris and Peto, 1973; Brown, 1974; Brown, Bhrolchain and Harris, 1975 for preliminary accounts).

Psychiatric Disorder in London

A solution to the measurement of life-events that was developed in the study of acute schizophrenic conditions consisted of completely ignoring the respondent's definition of what had been stressful. Pre-determined life-events were recorded, if they had occurred, without use of the respondent's account of his reactions to the event. This method of approach controls contamination by both the respondent *and* the interviewer and in this way combats all three sources of invalidity discussed above.

We avoided using the respondents' reports of the stressfulness of events by restricting our questions to classes of events which, on the basis of our experience, are most likely to produce marked emotional arousal. We defined before any of the main interviews were carried out i) the classes of event that were to be counted and ii) the persons to be covered who might be involved in them. Other investigators might have wished to include additional events but this does not matter — if we had chosen the wrong ones, it would only have *reduced* the positive relationship we found. Only standard questions about the occurrence of the event were asked and questions about *reactions* to, or *feelings* about, the events avoided. In essence it was not up to the individual respondent to decide *what* event or *what* person to include; and possible bias from the investigator was controlled by detailed instructions established before the collection of data. This obviously helped to control contamination in the reporting of the event due to knowledge of the illness; and since reaction to the event was ignored we can hope to rule out the possibility that some unknown factor is influencing both onset and the reporting of experience of events. A comparison group of individuals not suffering from schizophrenia was interviewed to establish the rate of life-events in the general population. The survey supported the hypothesis that life-events are of causal import- ance in the onset of schizophrenia (see Brown and Birley, 1968).

However there was a cost to this solution. A wide range of events are treated alike and given equal weight in the analysis. This would be ex- pected to reduce greatly the efficacy of our measure of life-events. In work on depression begun in 1967, therefore, we have attempted to do more and to include some notion of personal meaning. But, within the framework we adopted, we were still able to recognize and control sep- arately meanings and distinguish them from the events themselves. In this way we can, hopefully, still know how to interpret our results.

We asked about and recorded life-events in the same way as in the schizophrenic study. However, once events were effectively recorded the interviewer covered in as free flowing way as possible a lengthy list of enquiries about the circumstances surrounding each event. She asked in detail about what led up to and what followed the event, and the feelings and attitudes surrounding the event and the associated circumstances. The idea was to obtain a full description of the subject's situation at the time of the event. We were interested not only in what happened but in the meaning of what happened for the subject — in the sense of the social implications and the thoughts and feelings she had before the event, at the time, and since. The interview was tape-recorded and using this additional material the interviewer completed many scales dealing with *each* event.

The scales are designed to take account of relevant aspects of the cur- rent situation as well as past experience and plans caught up in the event. The most important measure which was rated was that of long-term *contextual* threat. This was measured on a four-point scale marking the degree of threat implied by the event about one week after its occurrence. The top two points on the scale represented severe threat; the bottom two much less severe. The rating was made by the interviewer reading to other members of the research team an account of the event and its surrounding circumstances but leaving out any mention of the person's reaction. The description was then rated independently by all the members of the research team present in terms of how threatening the event would be to most people in the subject's situation. Thus, events such as desertion by one's husband, or death of parent, would be rated 'marked' threat, irres- pective of the reported reaction; while for a married woman with children at home a son's engagement to what the interviewer and other investigators judged an unexceptional girl (and most girls would be considered so) would be rated 'none' even if the mother said she had found it very distressing and could not bear the thought of his leaving home. A moderate rating would be given to a mother whose son, seen daily, announced he was going to Canada. In this way meaning was brought back into the measures but *under the investigator's control.*

To summarize, the contextual measure of threat was made in three stages: first, the event was obtained by a method that ignores the respondent's judgment of its impact on her; second, the interviewer went on to collect extensive background material; third, a rating of threat was made by persons not involved in the interview, taking into account circumstances surrounding the event but without information about the subject's actual reported reaction. The rating was based on how members of the team thought most people would be expected to react in the circumstances. Since self-reports and definition of threat and unpleasantness are controlled both at the stage of establishing the occurrence of the event itself and also at the stage of rating the threat, we believe we have reduced both the risk of contamination and of arriving at invalid conclusions because of the effect of unknown third factors related to the experience of stressfulness of events (i.e. the issue of spuriousness). In short, we have attempted to meet all three sources of invalidity we discussed earlier. One way of viewing the approach would be to say that 'error' deliberately introduced by the investigator may enable him to arrive at valid conclusions about the causal role of life-events in disease. In this paradoxical sense, error must often be introduced by the investigator in order to deal with possible uncontrolled bias. I believe it is a mistake to think that science depends on error-free measurement. The measures used in the schizophrenic and depression research, although imperfect, are quite capable of allowing us to arrive at our goal: *minimum* estimates of the causal role of life-events.

This measure of contextual threat suggests that certain kinds of life-event are of importance in the onset of depression. A random sample of women from the same local population as the patients provided comparative data about the rate of events. Twenty-one per cent of the 'normal' women in the general population had had at least one severe long-term threat in a nine-month period before the interview, contrasted with 61 per cent of the patients in the same period before onset. We estimate that at least half of the patients had had a severely threatening event of aetiological importance.[2] The long-term contextual threat rating coincided closely with experience of loss, using this term in a broad sense.[3] Seventy-seven per cent of patients with a severe event had had at least one involving loss.

Let me sum up my argument about methodology so far. The issues of bias are critical and to deal with them we are faced in the measurement of life-events with controlling meaning — something that is an essential component of the phenomena we wish to measure. The crude first step taken in the London schizophrenic study controlled meaning, but at the cost of treating all events as alike. I have discussed the general outline of the solution developed in the London depressive study; it is present, at least by implication, in much sociological writing, for instance in Weber's discussion of motivational understanding (*Erklarendes Verstehen*). It lies essentially in the convention of dealing with events in commonsense terms.

Given knowledge of behaviour, experience, and circumstances, how would it be reasonable to expect an individual to react? In this way we developed contextual measures of threat based on wide knowledge of everything surrounding the event as such but excluding any knowledge of the person's account of his feelings and reactions to it. Interpretation and classification can only approximate to what actually happens, and will often be in error. But is is a certain kind of error. First, it avoids the risk of invalidity that must be present when personal meaning is allowed full play. Second, as I have said, the resulting estimates of the role of life-events are bound to be conservative since events that proved 'stressful' for idiosyncratic reasons will be missed.

I believe that in the end justification for the approach can only come from forging links between analysis and theory. We have found, for example, that there is no association between depression and severe events with a short-term threat (judged by the situation on the day it occurred) once long-term threat is controlled. The result is quite clear-cut and makes sense in terms of theoretical notions about the nature of depression. Most important, it is difficult to argue that the association between long-term threat and onset is due to some artefact or unknown intervening factor. If this were so, why should results differ so dramatically when the simple distinction is made between perspective on the day of the event and that one week later? Why should bias be restricted to just one of the two measures? Of course, the plausibility of our findings rests on far more than this particular point. The argument can continue. For example, for schizophrenia the results are quite different. When events were rated on the threat scales short *and* long-term threatening events of all degrees of severity were shown to be capable of provoking schizophrenic reactions and this conforms to the theory that sees schizophrenic patients as particularly vulnerable to too much stimulation of any kind (see Brown and Birley, 1968; Wing and Brown, 1970; and Brown, Birley, and Wing, 1972).

I have, in fact, not attempted to support my case for the use of contextual meaning with much more than a general argument, but we have already a good deal of evidence in its favour. For example, events associated with pregnancy or birth are related to onset of depression within the year, only if they are also defined as severely threatening. There were 4.4 births per 100 patients that were rated non-severe on long-term threat, and the 'normal' women had had 4.9 per 100; but there were 5.6 births rated severe per 100 patients compared with none among the 'normal' women. [4] It is apparently only when pregnancy and child care are directly associated with a major social problem that depression is likely to ensue. Leaving aside the substantive issue, such a result indicates how much would be lost if events were not considered in terms of the particular biographical context in which they occurred.

The Causal Link between Life-event and Diseases

However, establishing a causal relationship is not the end of scientific enquiry: it is then necessary to ask exactly what is going on. Many people are likely to agree that life-events seem to play a role in onset, but at the same time argue that events merely aggravate a pre-existing condition, or assert that genetic, constitutional, or other bodily influences must be critical because so many people experience life-events without breaking down (Davis, 1970). At present I can see no way of ruling out genetic, constitutional, and predispositional factors in most psychiatric disorders. It is still possible to argue, for instance, that there is a greater amount of psychiatric disorder among working-class women since, because of selective processes occurring over many generations they are more likely to be genetically predisposed to such disorders (see Dohrenwend and Dohrenwend, 1969). Individuals with genetic predisposition will tend to decline in terms of social class so that over a number of generations the lower social classes will contain a greater proportion of individuals with genetic predisposition. Although a direct attack on the heredity and constitutional issue cannot be made with our data, my colleagues and I have argued that the nature of the causal link between life-events and illness need not be left to the play of opinion and prejudice (Brown, Harris, and Peto, 1973).

There are two positions that can be taken: the first emphasized the importance of bodily predispositional factors and plays down the role of life-events. In this view events are seen at most as triggering an illness that would have occurred before long for other reasons. According to such a *triggering* theory an event at most brings onset forward by a short period of time. The second, opposing, view is that events play an important *formative* role and onset is either substantially advanced in time or brought about by it.

If a choice can be made between a triggering or formative effect it would have crucial bearing on the genetic-environment issue; a formative effect would point to critical environmental influences whatever the role of genetic factors. We therefore wish to evaluate the importance of social influences while not ruling out the influence of constitutional or other factors. In fact we do not see these influences as at all incompatible. A person predisposed for somatic reasons may *also* have some chance of developing the disorder following certain social experiences. We think it misleading to conceive of individuals as divided into two clear-cut groups, the one vulnerable and the other immune to life-events. We therefore reject the whole notion behind disease labels such as 'reactive' and 'endogenous' – at least on present knowledge. Nonetheless, I think it important that some environmental factors have been effectively linked to disease and further links seem likely. This needs to be said now since the social environment can usually be more easily manipulated than many 'endogenous' processes. The range of environmental factors that can be influenced to man's advantage has certainly not yet been exhaustively documented.

The causal model of disease that we have followed is a general one in which each individual has at any point in time a probability that he will suffer onset of the particular disease during a short period of time — say, the following month. We call this probability the *onset rate.* Although this probability may be very great it might not be manifest in any way that is observable before the occurrence of a breakdown. When a life-event occurs this onset rate may be influenced, perhaps for a limited period, perhaps forever. For example, the onset rate for one person may gradually increase throughout childhood but be markedly elevated by the death of a mother at the age of ten and never return to its original level although over the next fifteen years grow gradually less. The failure of his marriage at twenty-five may raise it markedly again and one year later he may actually suffer a breakdown. We have referred to the component of the onset rate that is *not* brought about by events under study as *spontaneous* — even though in practice the onset might have been the result of an observed event or other social factors and long-term problems such as loneliness. An onset in which the spontaneous component is relatively small compared with the size of the total onset rate is probably (but not certainly) provoked by a life-event.

While the argument is too complex to present here, it is possible to calculate a conservative estimate of the spontaneous component for a group of individuals who have broken down following a life-event. This is important as it allows an estimate of the average time after an onset *provoked* by an event when a spontaneous onset would have occurred if the onset had not been brought about by the event. We call this *brought forward time*, and it allows us to choose in a particular study between the triggering and the formative hypotheses. We have already noted that all persons whose onset was provoked by an event may have been on the verge of a spontaneous onset anyway; and in such instances the event would merely have triggered the illness and brought onset forward by a short time. However, if the brought forward time is long it makes the idea of a triggering effect very unlikely and enables us to argue for a formative effect. The brought forward time formula in fact gives a grossly conservative estimate and we have therefore arbitrarily taken twelve months as the critical length of time. We are confident about claiming the existence of a formative effect if this period is exceeded; although others when they have followed our detailed argument might want to settle for shorter or longer periods.

In fact for the depressed patient the brought forward time is over two years and a formative effect is clearly indicated. We believe that for half of the depressed patients the attack would not have occurred for a long time, if at all, without the severely threatening event and the set of circumstances surrounding it which occurred in the nine months before onset. Therefore, without taking any direct account of constitutional or genetic factors life-events have been shown in the study to be of critical causal importance in the onset of depression. This case will hold whatever subsequent research establishes about the role of constitutional factors.

In the same study 16 per cent of a random population sample of women were considered to be suffering from a clear affective disorder. Like the Midtown study there is a clear social class gradient: 5 per cent in the high status group, 20 per cent in the intermediate, and 29 per cent in the low status group were disturbed. The low and intermediate groups can be combined into a lower-class group of whom 24 per cent were disturbed compared with 5 per cent in the high class. Life-events played the same role in onset of depressive symptoms among those in the community, as they do with patients, and preliminary analysis does not suggest that the brought forward time is less than twelve months for any status group. We can therefore also make a case that life-events are of formative importance in *all* social class groups, irrespective of any part that genetic or constitutional factors may play in the vulnerability of the low class women.

Disease and the Broader Social System

There remains the issue of how far much immediate social experience can be linked to broader societal processes. In addition to life-events we have shown that marked long-term difficulties, not the result of events in the year of study, also play a role in the onset of depression, although the strength of the effect is only about half that for events. However, although severely threatening events and marked difficulties are more common in the lower status group, analysis shows that life-events and difficulties do little to explain the class difference in psychiatric disorder that we have also found. This is illustrated by the finding that while 6 per cent of the high-class women broke down following a severe life-event or marked difficulty in the twelve months before interview, as many as 30 per cent of the lower-class women did so. Although life-events and difficulties are therefore of obvious importance in bringing about psychiatric disorder, other environmental factors are still needed to explain the fact that in the general population survey low-class women are more likely to be disturbed. This is reminiscent of certain of the Midtown Manhattan results, and like others we have to bridge the gap between social class and the experiences in day-to-day life that are influencing rates of illness.

There is widespread agreement that primary groups such as the family are likely to be critical. Durkheim, for example, stressed the protectiveness of the family against suicide, in arguing that it was proportional to its degree of integration (e.g. 1952: 201–2). (He saw integration as a function of the size of the social unit.) Durkheim discusses many possible social causes or 'currents of suicide' but he was

'in effect, seeking to specify all those social factors which can impair the psychological health of the individual by rendering social bonds inadequately or excessively effective (thereby reducing his immunity to suicide). He was, in other words, by implication proposing a social-psychological theory about the social conditions for individual psychological health — a fact partially concealed by his use of the language of "forces" and "currents" ... This aggressively sociologistic language, implying that individuals merely responded differentially to external collective forces, was at odds with the central socio-psychological theory advanced in *Suicide* — namely that only in certain social conditions, where social bonds are neither too lax nor oppressive, that is socially given goals and rules are neither too ineffective nor too demanding, can the individual achieve psychological or moral health and equilibrium' (Lukes, 1973: 215—16)

This comment by Lukes makes good sense. Indeed it is dispiriting how little we have added to Durkheim's broad interpretations. The weakness of his analysis resides in its vagueness about the nature of the link he discusses. This is masked by his confident discussion of agents such as suicidogenic currents that he saw permeating society. He argues, for instance, that there will be a low rate of suicide in societies where there is high integration in the individual family unit. But it is possible to conceive of societies in which the immediate family is highly integrated but has a high rate of psychiatric disorder because the individual family member is inadequately protected from the consequences of its dissolution. This indeed may be the greatest where the marriage has been highly integrated and emotionally successful. Durkheim's analysis is inadequate because it is too static. (This was, of course, understandable given the source of his data.) He paid insufficient attention to the great variability in social context that is possible when considered from the perspective of the individual on which society impinges.

It seems to me that further analysis of data such as ours on depression can go in two directions. It can expand the time dimension, particularly for 'negative' experiences. We know from our work that loss of a mother before the age of eleven increases the risk for women of developing depression after a major life-event. (This, of course, has long been anticipated in the literature, e.g. Bowlby, 1961.) Perhaps lower-class women experience more major threatening experiences earlier in their lives and in this sense are more at risk for depression (i.e. have a higher *onset rate*). This might explain, for instance, the apparent tendency for social class differences in rate of disorder to narrow with increasing age. This problem will certainly turn out to be a more complicated one. For example, it may well prove to be coping skills, developed around crises in early life, that are critical. Alternatively, we may radically alter the focus of study and look at pleasant rather than unpleasant experiences. Perhaps a higher-class woman tends to be more protected because of greater variety in her life and a greater input of 'positive' experiences. She can more often travel, visit friends, buy a hat; she has perhaps greater confidence and skills in seeking out pleasurable experiences; and also there may be more articulated goals to which she can reasonably expect to achieve. But if this possibility is pursued it will inevitably involve more profound study of family life. For instance, in our present work, the difference in rate of disturbance between the low-class and high-class women is greatest when the youngest child at home is less than six years old – see *Figure 1*. (The proportion psychiatrically disturbed in this life-stage is surprisingly and disturbingly high.) As I have already mentioned the differences occur largely because low-class women are more likely to break down following a severe event.

Figure 1   *Percentage of married women with definite psychiatric disturbance, by life-stage and social class*

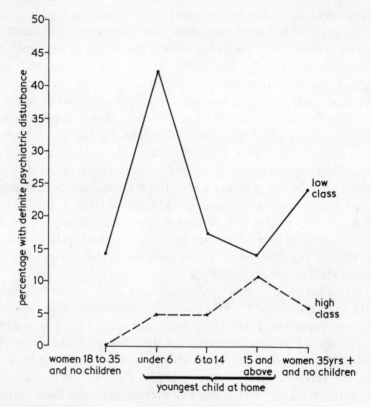

One factor of importance is the existence of an intimate tie with a husband or boyfriend. (We rated as intimate any relationship in which the woman reported that the two of them could talk over things that were important to either.) Women with a severe event are much less likely to develop a psychiatric disorder in the year of study if they have such an intimate tie; and there is a spectacular drop in intimacy among lower-class couples with a child under six – see *Figure 2*. Such a link with life-stage also indicates that intimacy is in part a sociological variable: the implication is that this is the most difficult time for a low-status marriage and there-after things steadily improve. But low intimacy is *not in itself* causally related to a greater risk of psychiatric disorder: it is that women without such an intimate relationship are much more likely to break down when a severe life-event occurs. (Seventeen of our twenty-one cases had 'low intimacy' and a live-event or major difficulty [5]). This is why we view it as a vulner-ability factor and not a causal factor as such. There are several other such factors. Another one which clearly protects women is whether they go out to work: women *with* a child at home, who are at risk because they had an event or difficulty, and are without an intimate relationship with their husband, stand much less chance of developing depression if they go out to full- or part-time work. Although results are preliminary (and we await the results of a recently completed replication) we believe that our four vulnerability factors, together with events and difficulties, explain the majority of the depressive eposides we studied in women with children at home. For example, whereas over half the women with a child at home who had at least two of the vulnerability factors (three children of fourteen or less, not working, low intimacy with husband, and loss of mother by the age of eleven) broke down if they had had a severe event or marked difficulty in the period before onset, none of these women who did not have an event or difficulty broke down. The vulnerability factors also largely explain the social class differences (Brown, Bhrolchain and Harris, 1975). The picture is rather more complicated than that which I have outlined, and the results need to be replicated; but the examples are enough to illustrate the kind of complex inter-relation-ships that further detailed research can be expected to show between 'social' variables and disease.

We have to specify more clearly what we mean by concepts such as support and integration – both in the sense of spelling out the relevance of the total context in which they operate, contingent social factors that may be important, and their relevance for different diseases. For instance, Fried (1965) has shown that, in Boston, working-class women who were most integrated into the activities and life of the local commun-ity were most likely to be suffering from depression two years after enforced re-housing. As a further example, it is clear that family inte-gration has a quite different significance for schizophrenic and depress-ive patients (see Brown, Carstairs, and Topping, 1958: table 5; and Brown, Birley, and Wing, 1972); and is probably different again for conditions such as rheumatoid arthritis (e.g. Cobb *et al.*, 1969 a and b). I believe that only when these small-scale theories have been developed for particular medical conditions are we likely to be able successfully to push back analysis into the broader social structure. Potential influences are so many that it is easy to become lost without the guidance of ideas that firmly link the disease with the immediate social context, past and present.

But at some stage we must examine the role of the encompassing social

Figure 2   *Percentage of married women rated high ('a') on intimacy with husband, by life-stage and social class*

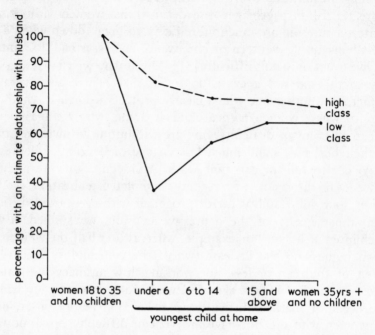

system. Modern sociology has been predominantly concerned with the description of the structure of society as an ongoing and persistent phenomenon: the individual being seen very much as at the mercy of social forces. I find it helpful to remember another tradition. Georg Simmel in a series of brilliant essays deals with the life of small intimate groups. He emphasizes that society is composed of various forms of social tie centering round the individual and that these must be understood for themselves and not merely as ingredients of an inclusive social system. He makes clear the changes that are possible and the way that the forms of social tie originate in interaction.

To quote a recent commentator:

'Forms develop in interaction. And this means not only that a form originates in the process of interaction and subsequently restrains and restructures the actor's behaviour, but also that the actors "add" elements to, or "subtract" elements from established forms. For Simmel the actors never lose this spontaneity, this influence on forms. The forms thus have a dual character, at once superior to the actors and subject to them.' (Tenbruck, 1965: 92)

Simmel emphasizes choice, struggle, growth, and decay. Life-events, of course, will often bring major changes to such small-scale structures. These and idiosyncratic modes of adaptation probably produce a very wide range of forms of social tie in a city like London. Simmel's analysis promises something else. For him the forms he discussed were assumed to transcend a particular culture. It is a somewhat obscure notion, but not absurd in relation to the aetiology of disease.

Why should it not be possible to identify cross-cultural situations that, say, give rise to different kinds of psychiatric disorder? Such an enterprise makes sense, for instance, in considering the role of primary relationships in the onset and course of schizophrenic disorders. In London the tension level in the living group is a critical factor in bringing about episodes of acute schizophrenia and this in turn is influenced by the family unit's wider social links with relatives and friends, and also by the patient's ability to 'withdraw' from too instrusive emotional contact in the home. Among the most important of Simmel's ideas is that separation is an integral part of relating to people. Closeness implies also degrees of distance. This essential dualism is poignantly seen in the dilemma of the schizophrenic patient. He is highly vulnerable to the baleful effect of close emotional ties but at the same time is greatly at risk of relapse if he withdraws too far from social intercourse (Wing and Brown, 1970; Brown, Birley, and Wing, 1972). But, of course, cultural values cannot be ignored and will often produce important variations on such a basic principle. Roger and Hollingshead in a study of schizophrenia and the family in a slum in Puerto Rico describe the behaviour that surrounds the notion of *machismo* in Latin America, a pattern of masculine virility, independence, and dominance. In their slum a married man typically spent a considerable portion of his time and money on drink, gambling, and other women. His wife was resigned and accepting. In London the patient tends to disengage himself from social intercourse; but in Puerto Rico the pattern for husband and wife is different. The schizophrenic male withdraws *into* the family and his wife usually reacts positively to this in spite of his odd behaviour. Roles tend to be reversed and tension relieved. She may take on outside work and will nurse and protect him at home (this is much less likely in London). The husband of a disturbed woman will merely tend to move further *away*.

There is no doubt about the importance of such cultural norms: unfortunately in a place like London they are a great deal more difficult to recognize and handle in analysis. In her classic study of family norms in London, Elizabeth Bott notes how often the twenty married couples she studied in London muddled what were essentially personal norms with what she calls 'norms of consent'. She emphasizes the ability of individuals, particularly when living in dispersed networks of friends and relatives, to choose between many norms and select a congenial version to make their own. But it is a matter of degree; there is no doubt that societal values (and changes in them) are an important way in which society impinges on the life of the individual. Perhaps the most obvious impact of the wider system is the structure of constraints and opportunities that are unequally distributed throughout the class structure. The ways in which this happens are many. In the London study of depression many important life-events and difficulties were associated with housing. Women who broke down during pregnancy or birth often lived in miserable, if not appalling conditions. Opportunities are part of the wider economic and political system. In London the housing situation has in many ways taken an ominous turn for the worse (Eversley and Donnison, 1973); and there is a widely recognised 'crisis in low-income housing'. Property developers, for instance, have amassed fortunes, particularly by office development in central London, and this has been a factor contributing to the general spiralling of the price of land and houses.

There are of course many other factors. There is increasing obsolescence of large tracts of housing built toward the end of the nineteen century, and the situation has been aggravated by a recent move of industry from the inner London boroughs. The picture is extraordinarily intricate involving the interplay of local and national factors. In this it is probably typical of broader social processes and to push back causal links between more immediate social factors and illness is to risk becoming emeshed in highly complex issues.

At the same time there is temptation to become engrossed in radical criticism of the current political system. The study of disease will inevitably tend to highlight sensitive issues to do with power and privilege. To take one instance: only a little more than half the women in Camberwell with a psychiatric disorder were seeing any kind of doctor for the disorder — and scarcely any a psychiatrist. This clearly cries out for more information about the way in which women are treated by the medical profession — and further raises somewhat awkward questions about the role of psychiatry in the total pattern of care. A whole series of issues opens up at this interface between individual experience and the broader social structure — a mixture of practical, moral, and political themes that run from down to earth administrative matters to questions concerning the economic and political system as a whole. Some will understandably wish to become involved in doing something about the situation — or at least gear their research to this end. But there is some danger that too early and too close a concern with action may inhibit the development of theory about the effect of *particular* social contexts on *particular* diseases. Not all that happens in the current social system will be harmful; and many experiences are probably common to a wide range of political and cultural systems. Moreover the effect of most social circumstances on health is still unclear. Where does one place, for example, avid television watching that takes up so much of the time of the typical citizen today?

I do not suggest withdrawal from wider concerns. Indeed I believe that research on disease must be directly informed by moral and political issues. In any case, as research programmes develop withdrawal will become increasingly difficult: that so many working-class women in Camberwell are psychiatrically disturbed is hardly a neutral fact. The issue at present seems to me less fundamental and to do with the best division of scarce intellectual and research resources. There is a danger if problems are too broadly stated that little worthwhile knowledge will be forthcoming. I have no doubt that at present the major research focus of the sociologist concerned with disease must be with the effect of the immediate social context on the individual and his living unit and how those caught up in the situation try to influence and to change this context. But I have also argued that links with broader societal processes cannot be ignored. Some of these will be obvious, and as with housing and depression a further, more detailed, study will often perhaps best be left to specialists in the particular substantive area. A major danger is that we will often settle too soon for resounding conclusions about the effect of the broader structure and underestimate the tremendous scope of idiosyncratic adjustment in modern society. We can certainly go ahead in the hope that we can tease out common patterns that are important to the genesis of disease in all this variety; but isolating persuasive reasons for particular patterns of adjustment is another matter.

But this is no invitation to retreat to the rather vacuous generalizations that have been so common in this field — often not so much more sophisticated than the pace-of-modern-life explanation. There is no general solution. We will have to go ahead with a somewhat uneasy division of labour. Both individual-orientated and society-orientated studies will continue to go their ways; I should add that both are part of the sociological enterprise. Indeed, each provides a good deal of justification for the other. What would have been the point, for example, of Marx's analysis of capitalist society without his abiding concern with the role of the immediate social context on the health and well-being of the individual? There is flexibility and much confusion — but this is one of the charms of social analysis.

The confusion, however, must not be overstated. Methodological issues no longer seem so impenetrable; and the effect of the immediate context in terms of factors such as life-events and the quality of relationships in the home are clearly of importance. Research, I believe, will come more to deal with three major issues. First, what are the social factors in a person's past and present that render him vulnerable to or protect him from potentially adverse factors in his current environment? What is the quality of people's lives and what meaning do their day-to-day lives hold for them? Here is probably the most promising source of insights into differential vulnerability.

Second, how far do different patterns of social factors affect different diseases and how far can different diseases be grouped together as responding to the same social factors? Conditions such as schizophrenia, rheumatoid arthritis, and depression respond to different factors in the social environment. At the same time, however, it is probable that many diseases will also share in their aetiology the same social factors. Streptoccal infections of the throat for instance, apparently respond to much the same patterns of factors as schizophrenia. There is evidence that diabetes, hypertension, and myocardial infarction as well as peptic (and presumably duodenal) ulcers are unduly common among those having close responsibility for the lives of other people, for example, anaesthetists and air traffic controllers (e.g. Cobb and Rose, 1973). Such work will also, of course, tell us more about 'adverse' social factors and this in turn will stimulate moves to change the quality of people's lives — or, at least, the societal structure that adversely affects life-chances.

The third issue is ameliorative and will prove the greatest challenge. It is easy enough to argue that environmental hazards such as polluted water should be changed: but man's symbolic environment will not always be so easily dealt with. His symbolic environment is also circumscribed by social *values*. Practices valued by one group may not be by another. But the would-be practitioner need not despair. Old enemies such as poverty are clearly implicated and there can be little dispute over their undesirability. The issue then becomes *how* to bring about change and at this point we return to politics (hopefully aided by rational enquiry). The study of society and disease is no more a political backwater than it is a theoretical one.

Notes

1. It is, however, possible for anxiety to lead to greater experienced life stress and for this *in turn* to lead to disease: $A \rightarrow X \rightarrow Y$. In this case the link between X and Y is not spurious. The investigator, however, must establish this in his analysis by ruling out the possibility of spuriousness (see Blalock (1964) for a discussion of the problem). This possibility need not bother us here.
2. This is a corrected percentage allowing for chance association of a severe event and onset; see Brown, Harris and Peto (1973) for the correction formula.
3. We include i) separation or threat of it, such as death of a parent or a husband saying he is going to leave home; ii) an unpleasant revelation about someone close forcing a major reassessment of the person and the relationship, such as finding out about a husband's unfaithfulness; iii) life-threatening illness to someone close; iv) major material loss or disappointment or threat of this, such as a couple living in poor housing learning that their chances of being rehoused are minimal; v) an enforced change of residence or threat of it; and finally vi) a miscellaneous group of crises involving some element of loss, such as being made redundant in a job held for some time or obtaining a legal separation.
4. The differences are statistically significant: $p < .05$.
5. These are women who developed psychiatric disorders in the year before interview; a further 14 women had been disturbed for longer than one year.

References

Averill, J.R. (1968) Grief: Its Nature and Significance. *Psychological Bulletin* **70**:

721—48.

A comprehensive review which makes the important distinction between mourning (conventional behaviour determined by the custom of society) and grief (a set of psychological and physiological reactions which have originated in evolutionary processes).

Beck, A.T., Sethi, B.B. and Tuthill, R.W. (1963) Childhood Bereavement and Adult Depression. *Archives of General Psychiatry* 9: 295—302.

Becker, E. (1962) Towards a Comprehensive Theory of Depression. *Journal of Nervous and Mental Diseases* 135: 26—35.

Birchinell, J. (1972) Early Parent Death and Psychiatric Diagnosis. *Social Psychiatry* 7: 202—20.

Bowlby, J. (1960) Separation Anxiety. *International Journal of Psycho-Analysis* 41 (Parts 1 and 2): 1—24.

— (1961a) Childhood Mourning and Its Implications for Psychiatry. *American Journal of Psychiatry* 118: 481—98.

— (1961b) Processes of Mourning. *International Journal of Psycho-Analysis* 42 (Parts 4 and 5): 317—40.

These are early but still important statements by a well-known researcher.

Birley, J.L.T. and Brown, G.W. (1970) Crises and Life Changes Preceding Onset of Schizophrenia. *British Journal of Psychiatry* 116: 327—33.

Blalock, H.M. (1964) Controlling for Background Factors. Spuriousness Versus Developmental Sequences. *Social Inquiry* 34: 28—40.

Brown, G.W. (1974) Meaning, Measurement and Stress of Life Events. In B.S. Dohrenwend and B.P. Dohrenwend (eds.). Stressful Life Events: Their Nature and Effects. New York: John Wiley.

Brown, G.W. and Birley, J.L.T. (1968) Crises and Life Changes and the Onset of Schizophrenia. *Journal of Health and Social Behaviour* 9: 203—14.

Brown, G.W., Birley, J.L.T., and Wing, J.K. (1972) The Influence of Family Life on the Course of Schizophrenic Illness. *British Journal of Psychiatry* 121: 241—58.

Brown, G.W. Carstairs, G.M., and Topping, G.G. (1958) The Post-hospital Adjustment of Chronic Mental Patients. *The Lancet* i: 685.

Brown, G.W. Brolchain, M. N., and Harris, T. (1975) Social Class and Psychiatric Disturbance among Women in an Urban Population. *Sociology* 9 (May).

Brown, G.W., Ni Bhrolcháin, M.N., and Harris, T. (1975) Social Class and Psychiatric Disturbance among Women in an Urban Population. *Sociology* 9: 225—54.

Brown, G.W., Sklair, F., Harris, T.O., and Birley, J.L.T. (1973) Life Events and Psychiatric Disorder: 1. Some Methodological Issues. *Psychological Medicine* 3: 74—87.

Bruhn, J.G., Stewart, W., Lynn, T.N., Bird, H.B., and Chandler, B. (1968) Social Aspects of Coronary Heart Disease in a Pennsylvania German Community. *Social Science and Medicine* 2: 202—12.

Bunch, J. (1972) Recent Bereavement in Relation to Suicide. *Journal of Psychosomatic Research* 16: 361—66.

Cobb, S., Kasl, S.L., Tabor, J., and Norstebo, G. (1969b) The Intrafamilial Transmission of Rheumatoid Arthritis — 7. *Journal of Chronic Diseases* 22: 279—95.

Cobb, S. and Rose, R.M. (1973) Hypertension/Peptic Ulcer and Diabetes in Air Traffic Controllers. *Journal of the American Medical Association* 224: 489—92.

Cobb, S., Schull, W.J., Harburg, E., and Kasl, S.V. (1969a) Prologue — The Intrafamilial Transmission of Rheumatoid Arthritis: An Unusual Study. *Journal of Chronic Diseases* 22: 193—94.

Davis, D.R. (1970) Depression as Adaption to Crisis. *British Journal of Medical Psychology* 43: 109—16.

Dodge, D.L. and Martin, W.T. (1970) *Social Stress and Chronic Illness.* London: University of Notre Dame Press.

An attempt to apply measures of 'status integration' using published national statistics. The main problem is that of possible ecological fallacies: i.e. the fact that correlations between group data can exist with no correlation between the same measures when they are used on individuals making up the group data.

Dohrenwend, B.S. and Dohrenwend, B.P. (1969) *Social Status and Psychological Disorder: A Causal Inquiry.* New York: Wiley.

A very useful review of community studies with results summarized in conventional tables. Considers the genetic vs environmental explanation for social class differences but fails to reach a conclusion.

Dubos, R. (1965) *Man Adapting.* New Haven, Conn.: Yale University Press.

These are stimulating introductory arguments from an ecological perspective by a distinguished microbiologist.

— (1968) *Man, Medicine and the Environment.* London: Pall Mall Press.

Durkheim, E. (1952) *Suicide.* London: Routledge & Kegan Paul.

Dyer, E. 1965 Parenthood as Crisis: A Restudy. In H. Parad (ed.), *Crisis Intervention: Selected Readings.* New York: Family Service Association of America.

Engel, G.L. (1967) A Psychological Setting of Somatic Disease: The Giving-Up — Given-Up Complex. *Proceedings of the Royal Society of Medicine* 60: 553—55.

Engel, G.L. and Ader, R. (1967) Psychological Factors in Organic Disease. In *Mental Health Program Reports No. 1568.* National Institute of Mental Health, Bethesda, Washington DC.

Epstein, F.H. (1966) Epidemiological Approaches to the Study of Coronary Heart Disease. *Medical Times* 94: 735—74.

Eversley, D. and Donnison, D. (1973) *London: Urban Patterns, Problems and Politics.* London: Heinemann.

A recent statement by a variety of specialists about 'housing problems' and other issues in contemporary London.

Farr, W. (1859) *Influence of Marriage on the Mortality of the French People.* London: Savill and Edwards.

Fried, M. 1965. Transitional Functions of Working Class Communities: Implications of Forced Relocation. In Kantar, M. (ed.), *Mobility and Mental Health.* Springfield Illinois. C.C. Thomas.

Friedman, S.B., Mason, J.W., and Hamburg, D.A. (1963) Urinary 17-Hydroxy-Corticosteroid levels in Parents of Children with Neoplastic Disease. *Psychosomatic Medicine* 25: 364—76.

A successful attempt to relate external conditions to measurable psychological responses. Confirms the importance of 'anticipatory grief'.

Gordon, R. (1957) Mortality Experience among the Japanese in the United States, Hawaii and Japan. *Public Health Reports* 72: 550.

— (1967) Further Mortality Experience among Japanese Americans. *Public Health Reports* 82: 973—4.

Gordon, G., Anderson, O.W., Brehm, H.P., and Marquis, S. (1968) *Disease, the Individual and Society.* New Haven: College and University Press.

Gove, W.R. (1973) Sex, Marital Status and Mortality. *American Journal of Sociology* 79: 45—67.

Graham, D.T. Kabler, J.D., and Graham, F.K. (1962) Physiological Response to the Suggestion of Attitudes Specific for Hives and Hypertension. *Psychosomatic Medicine* 24: 159.

Graham, S.T. and Stevenson, I. (1963) Diseases as Response to Life Stress In H.I. Lief (ed). *The Psychological Basis of Medical Practice* New York: Harper & Row, An early but still important review.

Granville-Grossman, K.L. (1968) The Early Environment of Affective Disorder. In A. Coppen and A. Walk (eds.), *Recent Development in Affective Disorders.* London: Headley Brothers.

Gray, J. (1971) *The Psychology of Fear and Stress.* London: Weidenfeld.

Groen, J.J., Tijong, K.B., Koster, M., Willebrands, A.F., Verdonck, G., and Pierloot, M. (1962) The Influence of Nutrition and Ways of Life on Blood Cholesterol and the Prevalence of Hypertension and Coronary Heart Disease among Trappist and Benedictine Monks. *American Journal of Clinical Nutrition* 10: 456–70.

Harburg, E., Kasl, S.L., Tabor, J., and Cobb, S. (1969) The Intra-familial Transmission of Rheumatoid Arthritis – 4. Recalled Parent-Child Relations by Rheumatoid Arthritics. *Journal of Chronic Diseases* 22: 223–38.

Holmes, T.H. and Rahe, R.H. (1967) The Social Readjustment Rating Scale. *Journal of Psychosomatic Research* 11: 213–18.

Hughes, C.C., Tremblay, M.A., Rapoport, R.N., and Leighton, A.H. (1960) *People of Cove and Woodlot.* New York: Basic Books.

Jenkins, C.D., (1971) Psychologic and Social Precursers of Coronary Disease Parts 1 and 2. *New England Journal of Medicine* 284: and 285: 6.
An excellent recent review of the state of research into coronary heart disease.

Kaplan, D.M. and Mason, F.A. (1960) Maternal Reactions to Premature Birth Viewed as an Acute Emotional Disorder. In H. Parad (ed.), *Crisis Intervention: Selected Readings.* New York: Family Service Association of America.

Kasl, S.L. and Cobb, S. (1969) The Intrafamilial Transmission of Rheumatoid Arthritis – 6. Association of Rheumatoid Arthritis with several forms of status inconsistency. *Journal of Chronic Diseases* 22: 259–78.

King, S. and Cobb, S. (1958) Psychosocial Factors in the Epidemiology of Rheumatoid Arthritis. *Journal of Chronic Diseases* 7: 466–75.

Kunitz, S. (1970) Equilibrium Theory in Social Psychiatry: the Work of the Leightons. *Psychiatry* 33: 312–328.

Langner, T.S. and Michael, S.T. (1963) Life Stress and Mental Health. London: Collier-Macmillan.

Leighton, A.H. (1959) *My Name is Legion.* New York: Basic Books.

– (1965) Poverty and Social Change. *Scientific American* 212: 21–7.
This paper is probably the simplest introduction to the work of the Leightons and their collaborators.

Leighton, D.C., Harding, J.S., Macklin, D.B., MacMillan, A.M., and Leighton, A.H. (1963) *The Character of Danger.* New York: Basic Books.

Le Masters, E.E. (1957) Parenthood as Crisis. In H.J. Parad (ed.), *Crisis Intervention: Selected Readings.* New York: Family Service Association of America.

Lindemann, E. (1944). Symptomatology and Management of Acute Grief. *American Journal of Psychiatry* 101: 141–48.

Lukes, S. (1973) *Emile Durkheim and His Work.* London: Allen Lane.

Marris, P. (1958) *Widows and Their Families.* London: Routledge & Kegan Paul.

– (1974) *Loss and Change.* London: Routledge & Kegan Paul.

Matsumato, S. (1971) Social Stress and Coronary Heart Disease in Japan. In H. Dreitzel (ed.), *The Social Organisation of Health*. New York: Macmillan & Co.

Meyer, R.J. and Haggerty, R.J. (1962) Streptoccocal Infections in Families. *Pediatrics* 29: 539–49.

Morris, J.N., Chave, S.P.W., Adam, M.B., Sirey, C., Epstein, L., and Sheeham, D.J. (1973) Vigorous Exercise in Leisure Time and the Incidence of Coronary Heart Disease. *The Lancet* i: 333–39.

Parducci, A. (1968) The Relativism of Absolute Judgments, *Scientific American* 219: 84–9.

Parkes, C.M. (1964) Recent Bereavement as a Cause of Mental Illness. *British Journal of Psychiatry* 110: 198–204.

— (1970) 'Seeking' and 'Finding' a Lost Object: Evidence from Recent Studies on the Reaction to Bereavement. *Social Science and Medicine* 4: 187–201.

— (1971) Psycho-social Transitions: A Field for Study. *Social Science and Medicine* 5: 101–15.

Parkes, C.M., Benjamin, B., and Fitzgerald, R.G. (1969) Broken Heart: A Statistical Survey of Increased Mortality among Widowers. *British Medical Journal* 1: 740–43.

Parkes, C.M. and Brown, R.J. (1972) Health after Bereavement. *Psychosomatic Medicine* 24: 449–61.

Rahe, R.H. (1969) Life Crisis and Health Change. In P.R.A. May and J.R. Winterborn (eds.), *Psychotropic Drug Response: Advances in Prediction*. Springfield, Illinois: C.C. Thomas.

Rapaport, L. (1962). The State of Crisis: Some Theoretical Considerations. *Social Science Review* 36. Reprinted in H.J. Parad (ed)., *Crisis Intervention: Selected Readings*. New York Family Service Association of America.

Rees, W.D. and Lutkin, S.G. (1967) Mortality of Bereavement. *British Medical Journal* 4: 1–11.

Rogler, L.H. and Hollingshead, A.B. (1965) *Trapped: Families and Schizophrenia*. New York: John Wiley.

Sales, S.M. and House, J. (1971) Job Dissatisfaction as a Possible Risk Factor in Coronary Heart Disease. *Journal of Chronic Diseases* 23: 861–73.

Selye, H. (1956) *The Stress of Life*. London: Longmans, Green & Co.

Sheps, M. (1961) Marriage and Mortality. *American Journal of Public Health* 51: 547–55.

Simmons, L.W. and Wolff, H.G. (1954) *Social Science in Medicine*. New York: Russel Sage Foundation.
An early but still important general introduction.

Shekelle, R.B., Ostfeld, A.M., Oglesby, P. (1969) Social Status and the Incidence of Coronary Heart Disease. *Journal of Chronic Diseases* 22: 381–94.

Srole, L., Langer, T.S., Michael, S.T., Opler, M.K., and Rennie, T.A.C. (1962) *Mental Health in the Metropolis*. New York: McGraw-Hill.
This is the first report of the Midtown study.

Stein, S. and Susser, M. (1969) Widowhood and Mental Illness. *British Journal of Preventive Social Medicine* 23: 106.

Suchman, E. (1967) Appraisal and Implications for Theoretical Development, In S.L. Syme, and L.G. Reeder, (eds.), *Social Stress and Cardiovascular Disease*. *Milbank Memorial Fund Quarterly* 45(2) Part 2.

Szasz, T.S. (1962) *The Myth of Mental Illness* London: Secker and Warburg.

Tenbruck, F.H. (1965) Formal Sociology. In L.A. Coser (ed.), *George Simmel*. Englewood Cliffs N.J.: Prentice Hall.

Tyroller, H.A. and Cassel, J. (1964) Health Consequences of Culture Change — II. *Journal of Chronic Diseases* **17**: 167—77.

Wing, J.K. and Brown, G.W. (1970) *Institutionalism and Schizophrenia: A Comparative Study of Three Mental Hospitals 1960—8.* Cambridge: Cambridge U.P.

Wolff, H.S. and Goodell, H. (1968) *Stress and Disease* (2nd edition). Springfield, Illinois: C.C. Thomas.

Young, M., Benjamin, L., and Wallis, C. (1963) The Mortality of Widowers. *Lancet* **ii**: 454—56.

Zigler, E. and Philips, L. (1961) Psychiatric Diagnosis: A Critique. *Journal of Abnormal and Social Psychology* **63**: 607—18.

Chapter 10

David Field*

The Social Definition of Illness

In this chapter I shall be concerned with the ways in which illness is defined. In particular I shall be concerned with the consequences of calling a person 'sick', or 'ill' and the elements involved in such labelling.

Disease and Illness

At the outset I should indicate the way in which two crucial terms will be used. 'Disease', as throughout this book, refers to a medical conception of pathological abnormality which is indicated by a set of signs and symptoms. 'Illness' on the other hand refers primarily to a person's subjective experience of 'ill health' and is indicated by the person's *feelings* of pain, discomfort, and the like. It is possible, of course, both to feel ill without having a disease or to have a disease without feeling ill (see *Figure 1*).

Figure 1   *Possible relationships between disease and illness*

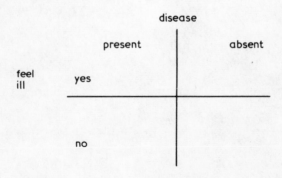

* The original version of this chapter was written while I was on leave of absence from Leicester University as Visiting Lecturer in Sociology and Community Health at Brown University, USA.

The distinction I am making between disease and illness can be illustrated by a consideration of the way these words are normally used. Disease is invariably used in a fairly limited and scientific sense as the Oxford dictionary definition illustrates: 'a condition of the body, or of some part or organ of the body, in which its functions are disturbed or deranged; a morbid physical condition.' Illness on the other hand is defined much more loosely as 'the quality or condition of being ill (in various senses)'. These senses are listed as '1. Bad moral quality, condition or character... 2. Unpleasantness, disagreeableness; troublesomeness; hurtfulness, noxiousness, badness. 3. Bad or unhealthy condition of the body; the condition of being ill; disease, ailment, sickness, malady.' From these definitions we can see that with disease the focus is objective, and is seen in terms of the specific impaired state; whereas with illness the focus is more on the subjective and diffuse consequences of the disease process. To say that a person is ill implies that the consequences of such a state transcend the merely biological and physical consequences of organic malfunction and affect his whole social life in important ways. To be ill is not simply to be in a biologically altered state, but also to be in a socially altered state which is seen as both deviant and (normally) undesirable. Illness, then, refers to an altered set of feelings manifested in terms of what doctors call symptoms, but experienced by the ill persons as real, diffuse, and often unspecifiable subjective states. People respond to illness (not disease) and develop systematic categorizations whereby they define such conditions, and thence gain some sort of control over them. The language of disease, with its physiological and clinical emphasis, is used by medical personnel to interpret and to treat the subjectively experienced 'illnesses' that people bring to them.

The training of doctors in Britain, as in other Western European nations is firmly based on a disease theory of illness. That is, it is based on the assumption that a sound knowledge of the biological, chemical, and physical processes of health and disease, together with the ability to correctly identify the various biological, chemical, and physical signs and symptoms of disease provide a sound basis for the practice of medicine. Duff and Hollingshead summarize this view as follows:-

'From the perspective of theoretical medicine, the best patient care is derived from the classic model which ties diagnosis and treatment into a sequential relationship. Ideally, the processes of diagnosis and treatment should be appropriate and specific to each patient. This model assumes, first, that optimal care of the patient will follow the most accurate diagnosis... second, that the physician responsible for the patient's care will prescribe and administer the appropriate treatment for the diagnosis.' (1968:6)

However, as they discovered in their study of patient care, this model is too simple to explain the realities of illness behaviour and leads to serious problems in patient care. The aim of this chapter is to consider some of the important factors that affect the *social* definition of illness and hence its treatment by physicians and ill people. In this context I shall look at some of the unanticipated consequences of medical practice. This is not to imply that disease theory has no utility, but rather to suggest that an awareness of social and psychological factors is also important for the practice of medicine. In particular it is suggested that physicians should be aware of how their clients define their illness. It is important to be clear about the distinction that is being made between disease and illness. I am *not* saying that they are two separate and unrelated sets of phenomena. What I am saying is that they relate to different levels of experience: the organic and the psycho-social, and that the relationship between them is not a simple one-to-one relationship but is complex and depends on both the nature and severity of the disease and a multitude of social and psychological factors.

I have already indicated that it is possible to have a disease and yet not to feel ill. It is also the case that people who notice symptoms of disease and/or feel ill may or may not seek medical aid. As was noted in Chapter 5, more than three-quarters of the adult population will experience at least one 'disease episode' in any month, and less than a third of these people will see a doctor in connection with that episode. Entry into medical treatment, then, is *not* an inevitable consequence of having a disease. This is not simply a case of people failing to recognize that they are 'ill' but is also due to the fact that a great amount of illness is regarded as 'minor' and 'normal'. That is, people may feel that they are 'ill', and accept the need to take some sort of action, e.g. an early night or self-medication, but not define themselves as sufficiently ill to require specialist help. I suggest that most episodes of illness begin in this way. That is, initially illness is seen as 'minor' and amenable to non professional care and only after some time is professional care sought and the ill person formally enters into what Parsons (1951) has called the 'sick role'[1].

In terms of the figure on page 162 of this book we can distinguish a number of relationships between disease and 'illness'. In the outer circle, those people who report no symptoms, are the people who are well. In the next circle are people who are diseased, but who have taken no action at all. In the next circle inwards are those people who have defined themselves as 'ill' and are taking some 'non-medical' action with regard to their illness. Finally, the remaining groups in the diagram, those visiting their GPs, those in hospitals, and those who are out-patients, are all people who have in some way or another defined themselves or been defined by others as so ill that they cannot engage in the full range of their normal activities and have had this confirmed by a doctor, i.e. they have entered the 'sick role'. In this chapter I shall primarily be concerned with this latter group.

The significance of the distinction between 'disease' and 'illness' may become clear if we consider Lemert's distinction between 'primary' and 'secondary' deviance (1964). Lemert distinguishes between those departures from the normal state of affairs that, although present, are dealt with as part of normal social activity (primary deviance), and those variations that result in a new definition of social activity, and that take note of and incorporate the primary deviations as reasons for such alterations of conduct (secondary deviance). In the case we are considering here, disease episodes that are ignored represent primary deviance; disease episodes that lead to changes in normal behaviour and are interpreted in terms of 'illness' represent secondary deviance.

The importance of Lemert's distinction is that it focuses on and clarifies the crucial part played by the *reactions* of individuals to the initial variation or difference. If it is seen by both the individual manifesting it and by others who may notice it as merely a slight and acceptable modification of normal behaviour, then it will not lead to any substantial redefinition of the individual, nor, in the case of disease, will it lead to entry into the 'sick role'. Such 'normalizing' of primary deviance is a common and frequent part of our daily life, and it may continue even in the face of very extreme departures from the normal and expected. The studies by Davis (1963) and Yarrow (1955) referred to in an earlier chapter (pp. 79—83, 175—6) provide excellent accounts of this tendency to 'normalize' unusual behaviour. However, as both studies also show, when a person's behaviour persistently fails to meet the expectations of others, such 'normalization' will break down; and a search for an explanation of the unusual behaviour will be initiated. Obviously we react differently towards people whose behaviour we define as resulting from illness than we do towards those who are defined as 'swinging the lead'. The label we use in interpreting unusual or different behaviour is, then, crucial; for it is pivotal to the way in which such differences are responded to. What, then, can we say about the consequences of calling somebody ill?

Types of Illness

A number of general features associated with illness should be noted. Unlike many events in a person's life illness is characterized by its unscheduled nature, and is normally an involuntary and undesirable condition. In all cases it involves some loss of control by the ill person over their normal social activities, although the extent of this varies markedly between different types of illness. In the initial stages of illness uncertainty, anxiety, and ambiguity are present to a greater or lesser extent, and are resolved (or at least mitigated) by the attachment of a diagnostic label. This label serves a number of functions, the most important of which are to legitimate the status of the sick person as ill thereby releasing them from their normal obligations, and to structure behaviour with regard to the illness by directing the attention of the ill person and others with whom he interacts as to what are the appropriate attitudes and actions to take with regard to the illness.

While these general features seem to characterize all types of illness there are clearly important dimensions along which illnesses vary, and which affect the responses made to illness by those who are ill and the people they interact with. Fabrega and Manning (1972) identify four important dimensions: the *duration* of the disease episode; the extent and possibility of cure, i.e. *prognosis;* the degree of discomfort, incapacity, and disability; and 'the potential for self-degradation' or *stigmatization.* On the basis of the ways in which these dimensions vary and inter-relate four main types of illness may be analytically distinguished, which I will refer to as: (1) short-term acute illness; (2) long-term non-stigmatized illness, e.g. diabetes; (3) long-term stigmatized illness, e.g. multiple sclerosis; (4) mental illness.[2] The nature and type of professional intervention will clearly vary between these four types of illness as will the extent and effectiveness of lay intervention (see *Table 1*). The 'disease theory' of illness seems most clearly and easily applicable to diseases of the first type, and the physician's actions and responsibility most clearly defined here.

When most people talk of illness, it seems that they have in mind illness of a short-term and definite character, that is, illness that can be characterized as 'short-term acute'. Such illness is easily recognized since not only are the symptoms clear and unambiguous, but they are also normally accompanied by discomfort and the subjective feeling that one is physically other than normal. When the disease leading to such feelings is, as is most usually the case in our society, one of the infectious diseases, lay knowledge of the symptoms and of the likely course and treatment of the illness are often well known. This is particularly the case with regard to what are now considered to be the common illnesses of childhood: measles, chicken pox, mumps, etc. Indeed, in such cases the role of the doctor may be seen as scarcely more than confirming the lay diagnosis and treatment — usually in terms of isolation of the ill child (although in multiple children families it is often the practice to keep both ill and well children together so that all children become ill at the same time). At the

Table 1   Four types of illness

	type I: short term acute	type II: long term non stigmatized illness	type III: long term stigmatized illness	type IV: mental illness illness (see text)
onset and course of disease	rapid onset. short, predictable course.	onset may be rapid but is more often slow and insidious. Within limits the course is predictable.	as for Type II.	onset can be rapid or slow and insidious. Course is often largely unpredictable.

Table 1   Four types of illness *(continued)*

	type I: short term acute	type II: long term non stig- matized illness	type III: long term stigmatized illness	type IV: mental illness (see text)
clarity of symptoms	clear and un- ambiguous to both lay pub- lic and phys- ician.	usually unclear to lay public and to phys- ician until a number of sophisticated diagnostic tests have been made	often clear to lay public, although they may be unable to inter- pret them. Clear to physician once diagnostic aids used.	varies widely. Usually ambiguous for both public and physician.
medical diagnosis	highly certain and reliable as the under- lying bio- logical pro- cesses are well understood.	usually certain and reliable. The unfolding of the bio- logical course of the disease fairly well established.	as for Type II	uncertain and unreliable as the processes are not well understood.
medical treatment	effective and curative. Ill- ness is revers- ible.	effective to moderately effective but not curative. The disease process may be halted or controlled, but not reversed.	as for Type II	no unequivocally effective treatment. Although it is sometimes reversible it often is not.
physician's Role	a) to identify the disease. b) to legitimate temporary re- lease from social obli- gations. c) to certify the short term impact of the disease.	a) as type I b) to legitimate indefinite re- lease from social obli- gations. c) to aid in the definition of the long term impact of the disease.	a) as type I b) to legitimate permanent re- lease from social obli- gations. c) as type II, especially with regard to the rehabilitative process.	a) to certify the indi- vidual as different. b) to legitimate *others'* definition of the indi- vidual as being incapable of fulfilling social obligations. c) to construct a social identity and ways of acting acceptable to others.
impact on self- conception	minimal as the label is tem- porary even though it may be all-pervasive at the time.	variable, depending on the degree to which the illness is internalized. However, there is always some effect since the label persists.	Considerable and unavoidable. The illness often becomes the central organ- izing aspect of identity for both the individual and others.	variable, ranging from slight to severe. The extent to which the label 'mentally ill' becomes central for the individual and others varies widely.

Table 1   Four types of illness *(continued)*

	type I: short term acute	type II: long term non stig- matized illness	type III: long term stigmatized illness	type IV: mental illness (see text)
social consequences	in short run the individual is released from a wide range of social obligations while retain- ing most of his rights. Minimal long run con- sequences.	short run consequences are as for type I. Long run consequences are variable and to some extent under the individual's control.	Severe. Due to the visibility of the physical con- sequences, the individual cannot exert much control over placement into a 'spoiled' or stigmatized category. Illness inevitably be- comes disability.	vary widely. At best may be short run and minimal, at worst an all pervasive and permanent discrediting of the individual as a competent and normal actor.

time of the illness the label of illness is often all-encompassing and becomes the central organizing feature in the life of the ill person and often
of his family. However, it is understood that this is only for a temporary
period and that complete recovery will follow. During the period of the
illness the ill person is largely released from a wide range of social obligations, and receives special rights and attention because of his illness.
This is, however, also understood to be temporary and it is expected that
the ill person will resume his normal activities immediately on the
cessation of the illness. This resumption is usually, but not always,
marked by the pronouncement of the physician that the person is recovered.

Although many illnesses of this type are cared for in the home, in some
cases admission to a hospital as an in-patient is required. This is obviously
the case where the cause of the illness is a diseased organ which requires
surgical removal, but there are also cases where intensive care is required
due to the severity of the illness. Where admission to hospital is required
the course of the illness is likely to be much more clearly defined than
where illness is cared for in the context of the home. However, in both
instances the course of the illness is relatively clear cut, especially when
compared to the other types of illness. One important consequence of
hospitalization, especially when children are hospitalized, is that the
isolation of the ill person from their family may lead to problems of
readjustment to normal life when they are released (Robertson, 1958;
Stacey, 1970; Duff and Hollingshead, 1968). This problem is clearly more
salient for illnesses requiring long term hospitalization.

When one turns from the consideration of illness that is of a short run,
self-limiting character to the chronic illnesses which are not so clearly
defined in terms of onset, duration, and termination, a number of important differences appear, and the interactions between the biological nature

of the disease episode and the social definition of illness become less direct and clear. With conditions such as multiple sclerosis, cancer, diabetes, and the early stages of coronary disease, the physical and behavioural symptoms are often so slow in developing that they are hardly noticed. Medical diagnosis, when it is sought, may be initially uncertain and depend upon the use and analysis of a number of sophisticated diagnostic tests. Further, the duration and effect of the disease may not be predictable in anything but fairly gross terms for a considerable period of time, mainly because the disease processes which are characteristic of chronic illnesses are not reversible. Thus, there are often large areas of uncertainty on the part of both the physician and the ill person and his family as to the length, severity, and social consequences of these illnesses. Whereas with short-term, acute illnesses the 'boundary' of the illness is fairly clearly defined, and the illness usually has little impact beyond the episode itself, in the chronic illnesses this is not the case. Indeed, with the latter the most problematic aspects of 'treatment' are often those concerned with the long-term effects of the illness, and recovery and rehabilitation are problematic areas of concern for both patients and physicians.

As Fabrega and Manning suggest, chronic illnesses may be analytically divided into two types on the basis of the social consequences stemming from the labelling of the illness by the 'lay public' as stigmatizing or non-stigmatizing. It must be stressed that the consequences of such labelling are most powerful during the recovery and rehabilitation stages. With both types, although the biological nature and course of the disease may be well known and understood, available treatment is usually restricted to control rather than to cure. Also, the disease is in a sense always present, if only in latent form, even after treatment has finished, and has an impact on future life. Clinically, emotionally, and socially the consequences of these types of illness are long term and persistent; and the illness leads, to a greater or a lesser extent, to modification of the person's conduct and character as perceived by both himself and others. To reiterate the point, the differences between the two types are directly consequential of the fundamental difference in attitude towards the illness. In one, illness is not perceived as stigmatizing the individual where in the other it is. Diseases leading to non-stigmatized long-term illnesses are those in which the physical impairments or functional incapacities which result from them are either minimal and/or not readily apparent. Diseases leading to stigmatized long-term illness by contrast are those where the physical impairments or functional handicaps are immediately obvious and further are socially unacceptable. The consequences of this differential labelling are that, although in both cases the character and conduct of the ill person is redefined in the light of the perceived consequences of the illness, in the first case the ill person has some genuine control over the impact of the disease episode on his identity and way of life whereas in the latter he has much less control due to the coerced and stigmatizing identity attributed to him.

A good example of a non-stigmatizing long-term illness is that of heart attack. Heart disease is the commonest cause of death in the most 'advanced' nations, and considerable research has focused upon it. I will not be concerned with the onset of the attack but with its consequences. Persons who suffer from a recognized heart attack are in a very real sense different from what they were prior to the attack both in the way they regard themselves and in the way they are regarded by others. In a very real sense they continue to be affected by their attack even if they return to work; the possesssion of a 'heart condition' has inevitable and significant consequences for their way of life. Yet, the extent to which the attack affects the person is to some degree influenced by the patient and depends on a variety of factors other than the underlying biological nature of the disease episode. A study by Monteiro (1970; 1973), for example, brings out clearly the complex relationship between the 'primary' physiological aspects of the attack, and 'secondary' social and psychological elements involved in the reaction to it. (See also Croog, Levine, and Sifre, 1968; Weinblatt *et al.,* 1966).

Monteiro's study is based on interviews with 115 male residents of Rhode Island, USA who had sustained a heart attack during the period October 1, 1966 to March 30, 1968. This data is supplemented by reports from the physicians who treated these men and by a large representative sample survey of households in the state. It is clear from the study that while the severity of the attack and the degree of impairment resulting from it set limits on the extent to which normal activities could be resumed, recovery was also determined by the sometimes complex inter-relationships between a number of social and psychological elements. The most important of these seemed to be the type of occupation of the men; their commitment to work; the level of threat which the attack was perceived to hold for each person; and the expectations of others, especially the immediate family.

Monteiro found that the type of occupation the men pursued was significantly related to whether or not they resumed work. As with other studies (see Weinblatt's review, 1966) she found that those men in white-collar (non-manual) jobs were more likely to return to work than those in blue-collar (manual) jobs. While 61 per cent of the former resumed work, only 39 per cent of the latter did so. It has been suggested that such differences in the return to work are related to the type of work and especially to the degree of activity required, with the implication that return to work is greatest in the least taxing, white-collar jobs. However, after a careful analysis, Monteiro concludes that for her sample there were no significant differences with respect to activity levels and levels of tension associated with work.

The inter-relationship between commitment to work, perceived level of threat, and expectations of others are conceptualized in *Table 2.* The persons who returned to work, in contrast to those who did not, had significantly higher levels of commitment to their work and experienced their heart attack as much less threatening. They also expected to be able to perform at higher levels of activity and felt better physically.

Table 2 Some factors affecting outcomes of heart attacks

commitment to work	threat level	third party expectations	outcome
high	high	activity	work
		inactivity	no work
high	low	activity	work
		inactivity	work
low	high	activity	no work (cardiac invalid)
		inactivity	no work (cardiac invalid)
low	low	activity	work
		inactivity	no work

Source: Monteiro, 1970: 43

With regard to the expectations held by others, Monteiro reports that

'the respondents almost unanimously agreed that as a result of their heart attack, other people, mainly family and friends, expected them to be passive and "take life easy". Ninety per cent of the cardiacs studied, including men who had returned to work as well as men who were permanently disabled, said that people did not expect them to be active, and that furthermore others believed that activity might precipitate another attack.' (1973: 555)

If the ways in which people view illness are important for the way they act towards it, then we would expect that these men would be influenced in their behaviour by the views of those they closely associated with. This does seem to be the case with men in blue-collar occupations. Seventy four per cent of the blue-collar respondents who did not return to work said that they did not do so mainly because of family expectations that they should not. However, such expectations do not seem to have been influential in determining whether or not men in white-collar occupations returned to work. This different impact of family expectations *may* account for the previously mentioned differences in the return to work rates between the two groups, although it is clearly not the only reason. When Monteiro investigated the impact of family expectations on leisure activities she found that both white-collar and blue-collar respondents were influenced by their families expectations that they should be inactive. Her conclusion was that their activity levels were suppressed, and that 'in general the post infarction group tend to relaxed inactivity, for even in the working group the largest proportion spent their evenings inactively' (1970: 104).

Within the category of persons who did not return to work, two sub-groups can be found. The first comprises those men who are seen by their physicians as being unable to perform some or most of their normal activities, but who are performing at, or even above, the activity level that they were thought to be capable of. The other group were regarded as 'cardiac invalids', i.e., they were judged by their physicians to have the physiological capacity for activity, but believed themselves to be disabled and so restricted their activity to levels below those which they were thought to be capable of.[3] It would seem probable that for this group the perceived expectations of others that they be inactive is most influential. Yet this is not entirely so, for they are well aware that their physicians expect more of them and view them as being 'not really ill'. One striking difference between these two groups of non-workers is in their respective attitudes to pain. While 73 per cent of the non-workers reported experiencing chest pains (as compared to 48 per cent of the workers), the cardiac invalids emphasized their pain, and used it as a reason for avoiding further activity more than the 'legitimate' invalids. This latter group tended to de-emphasize their pain. While both groups of non-workers restricted their activity Monteiro reports that

> 'It is clear that the cardiac invalids who by definitions should have the potential for more activity in fact are even less active than the other respondents (who don't work). This is a situation in which the individual's definition of himself as incapable of activity has led to real behaviour in which he over-demonstrates his incapacity.' (1970: 101)

Klein's (1965) clinical experience of twenty male 'cardiac invalids' led him to a very similar conclusion. He concluded that such people hold 'strong cultural beliefs that the heart remains in a fragile state and that physical activity is always potentially harmful to the post-infarction patient' (143).

We can see from Monteiro's study that the 'objective nature' of the disease episode with regard to its severity and residual incapacity is not, in itself, sufficient to explain the cardiac patients recovery behaviour. Rather, the patient has to construct a new way of life, which although 'caused' by the attack, is shaped much more by a complex set of social and psychological elements. It is also clear that, to a greater or lesser extent, the patients determine the impact of the attack on their life. Finally, it is clear that neither the cardiacs nor their family or friends see the attack as something of which to be ashamed or as something which somehow 'spoils' the person's character, and I suggest that it is this absence of stigmatization that allows the patient such latitude in his adaptation to his heart attack.

Where the disease causing long-term illness results in a readily apparent physical handicap or functional capacity the consequences are greatly different to those cases where it does not do so. It is worth reiterating that, as Fabrega and Manning put it, 'the physiologically determined symptoms, the general subjective experience that one is "physically ill", and the experienced disability may be identical for diseases (of these two types)' (1972: 107). It is in the definition of the disease as *stigmatizing* that the difference lies. The physical deformity, such as the withered limb of the polio sufferer, or the hard to conceal functional incapacity, such as paralysis caused by a stroke, serves to set the individual apart from the normal round of life in a way which is somehow threatening and disquieting. Goffman (1963), neatly sums up some of the consequences of the stigmatizing label:

'An individual who might have been received easily into ordinary social intercourse possesses a trait that can obtrude itself upon attention and turn those of us whom he meets away from him, breaking the claim that his other attributes have on us. He possesses a stigma, an undesired differentness from what we had anticipated ... we believe the person with a stigma is not quite human. On this assumption we exercise varieties of discrimination, through which we effectively, if often unthinkingly, reduce his life chances. We construct a stigma-theory, an ideology to explain his inferiority ... We tend to impute a wide range of imperfections on the basis of the original one ... Further, we may perceive his defensive response to his situation as a direct expression of his defect ...' (1963: 5—6)

Perhaps one reason why so few disease episodes are referred to a doctor and thus become defined as illnesses is that illness is always seen as threatening to our everyday world, and especially liable to spoil our social identities. (I shall return to this point later.)

Illnesses of the type we are considering here (and some mental illnesses, see below, pages 349—54) are characterized by the greatest 'spoiling'. The *physically based* blemish or incapacity resulting from the illness is so obvious that it overrides other attributes and becomes central in restructuring the victim's identity. The new identity is incorporated in and structured by the reactions of the person and others interacting with them towards the stigma. What results is the development of a new set of stable definitions of the person's conduct and character. (By contrast, although the stigma of some mental illness is also all-encompassing, it has no apparent physical location. It is the person *as a whole* who is spoiled.)

One study of the effect of such stigmatization is Macgregor's study of facial deformities (1951). Such deformities, (which may be inherited) are interesting because in one sense they are irrelevant to social interaction in that they do not, of themselves, directly hinder or interfere with the capacity to interact. Yet, *in fact,* they provide the basis for the imputation of identities (or characteristics of the person) that do lead to 'spoilage' of interaction. As Macgregor puts it:

'Except when the disfigurement is accompanied by a functional impairment such as a harelip with cleft palate, these facially deformed individuals do not necessarily suffer from organic or functional inability to perform the normal activities of daily living. Nevertheless they are handicapped because of the way they look. The twisted mouth, the conspicuous port-wine stain or the peculiarly shaped nose may well be a barrier to the privileges and opportunities available to the non-handicapped. Such an affliction, therefore, is more of a social handicap than a physical one for the individual's suffering results from the visibility of the defect and what it means to others as well as to himself.'

(1951: 629–30)

It is clear that it is not the physical impairment *per se* that is important, but the socially imputed meanings based upon it. Such people as Macgregor's respondents are construed by others — and often by themselves — as somehow not 'proper people'; they are somehow seen as lacking social competence or moral character because of their physical blemish. Macgregor found her respondents suffered overwhelmingly from a range of psychic disorders, often of a very serious kind. Although the facial deformity did not of itself inevitably impair the *capacity* for normal social interaction, it in fact did so because of the imputation of negative moral characteristics to the individual on the basis of their appearance. 'Indeed the (clinical) severity of the disfigurement had no direct proportional relationship to the degree of psychic distress it engendered nor the kinds of adjustments made to it' (1951: 632).

Where the physical blemish is newly acquired as a result of an accident or disease episode a new dimension is added to the problems of recovery and rehabilitation. Not only does the person have to adjust to the physical consequences of the impairment, he has also to cope with the social and psychological consequences of the resulting 'spoiled identity'. Unlike the person with an inherited deformity there is not a gradually developing awareness of differentness built up over time and 'managed' by parents, but an 'immediate' and often traumatic acquisition of a spoiled identity which is both undesired and, to a large extent, unknown as to its consequences. Davis poses the problems facing such persons very clearly:

'Unless he has been impaired from birth or early childhood, so that his primary identity is that of a handicapped person, it is more than likely that he will share, initially at least, many of the prejudiced and squeamish attitudes that are commonly shown toward the handicapped. He will tend, openly or secretly, to place a high value on many activities and pursuits that are closed to him because of his impairment. His attempts, if any, to be accepted by "normals" as "normal" are doomed to failure and frustration: not only do most "normals" find it difficult to include the handicapped person fully in their own category of being, but he himself, in that he shares the "normal" standards of personal evaluation, will in a sense support their rejection of him. For the fact remains that, try as he may to hide or overlook it, he is at a distinct disadvantage with respect to several important values emphasized in our society: e.g., physical attractiveness; wholeness and symmetry of body parts; athletic prowess; and various physiognomic attributes felt to be prerequisite for a pleasant and engaging personality.' (1963: 138)

In a very real and important sense the stigmatizing illness spoils the person's conception of himself, and he has somehow to come to grips with the idea that he is now an 'incomplete' person in the eyes of others, and that he cannot hide his defect from their view. It is hardly surprising, then, that one of the major problems confronting persons who become physically incapacitated or deformed, and their families, is the emotional adjustment they must make to their deformity. Not only are the clinical consequences of such illnesses serious and hard to manage, but the social and emotional consequences are also difficult and often intractable.

Regardless of the source or nature of the stigma there are a number of common elements in the ways in which people come to grips with the problems it poses. These have been identified by Goffman in his general analysis of the problem, and documented by studies of the reactions of people to a number of stigmatizing illnesses. The problems posed can be divided into three roughly sequential issues that must be resolved by the disabled, and also by those regularly associating with them.[4] The first is to somehow or other come to grips with the question of 'Why me?' and to accept the inevitable changes that the illness creates. Next is the problem of assessing the extent of the interference with normal life, which is often accompanied by serious frustrations and emotional setbacks. Finally, there is the often massive problem of constructing a new way of life around a new set of attitudes and a new set of social relationships and activities. All this is not easy and is not addressed alone. One important source of aid is that of medical and other professionals. Their part in the reconstruction of the person's world is often central to the shape of the resulting solution to the basic questions of 'Who am I now?' and 'What can I do?'.[5] It is therefore important that they understand something of the important social and psychological problems confronting such people.

Analytically, four approaches to handling disability may be distinguished, although in practice these approaches are combined to varying degrees. The first is the clinical: that is, the attempt to treat the impariment clinically so as to remove it or to minimize its impact. While this is the obvious first step, it is also clear that in many cases purely clinical treatment of the individual's disability is insufficient. This is true for both stigmatized and non-stigmatized cases (cf. Montiero, 1970; Duff and Hollingshead, 1968), but is more evident for the former where the stigma associated with the physical or functional disability may be sufficient to exclude the patient from normal social intercourse, and create serious difficulties of adjustment. The second strategy is in many ways no more than an extension of the first. This is to adjust the person to their disability by the provision of technical aids (e.g. prostheses) and/or psychological help. Again, this rarely is sufficient in itself, for the disabled are frequently assumed by their social contacts to be incapable of activities that they can in fact perform. Thus, it is insufficient merely to train them to be technically competent, and to cope with *their* psychological problems. In a further approach alternative systems for obtaining their various needs can be provided for the disabled, for example with respect to income via disability pensions and the like, or to housing via institutional care.[6] While this type of approach clearly goes beyond the previous two, and may well avoid the problems raised in relation to them, it has its own problems. The most central of these is the exclusion of the disabled from normal life. The fourth approach is to adjust the situations the disabled find themselves in, rather than to adjust them to such situations or to exclude them from them. This is obviously easier said than done, for it may require the redefinition of work tasks, the altering of architectural features, and a host of other changes aimed at making the physical environment easier for the disabled (themselves a very diverse group) to cope with. Even harder are the attitudinal changes required to alter the social and psychological environment in a similar way. This need to expand the scope of rehabilitative and supportive services for the disabled beyond treatment of the specific disability to the wider social milieu within which the disabled operate has been stated before and, at least as far as altering the physical environment, advances have been made. Little, however, has been achieved with regard to the social aspects of the problem, and it is clear that this aspect, and particularly the problem of stigmatization needs to be addressed directly if the position of a great number of the disabled is to be improved. It is, however, exceedingly difficult to specify how to make an impact effectively in this area.[7]

The common consequences of stigmatizing illness can be summed up under the consideration of how they relate to activity and to attitudes. In the area of activity, the physiological or functional incapacity will lead to some restriction and restructuring of activity. However, there will also be a contraction in areas of social activity which is not directly attributable to the severity of the impairment but rather to the social construction of stigma. This curtailment results from the reluctance of others to interact with the individual, and also from the individual withdrawing from situations in which he might be rebuffed. In extreme cases the stigmatizing illness may result in the almost complete social isolation of the individual. The attitudes which result are more variable in strength and impact. On one side there are the attitudes towards oneself as somehow 'spoiled' and inferior. These are often coupled with feelings of uncertainty and inadequacy. I suggest that to some extent these negative attitudes are held by most, if not all, stigmatized people in the period immediately following their illness and that for some they never disappear. However, a set of off-setting attitudes usually develop around such ideas as that the illness has somehow 'been a blessing in disguise' because it has led to the discovery of 'true values', 'real friends', 'hidden sources of strength' and the like

(Voysey, 1975). Finally, there is a redefinition of the previously accepted world of normality as somehow deficient and so not as great a loss as originally had been thought. The common element in all these reactions is the attempt to minimize the sense of loss and to support a definition of the stigmatized person as, despite his stigma, a worthy person.

One further important point to be made is that physical disability has effects on people other than those who are disabled. The physical handicap disables not only its possessor but also, to a greater or lesser degree, those with whom he interacts. By virtue of his differentness and his incapacities for some actions the disabled individual challenges our world of the taken for granted. His presence limits normal interaction in a whole host of ways. Kleck (1968: 24–6), for example, has shown how, in a controlled experiment individuals faced with interactions with a visibly disabled person (a leg amputee) are more likely to agree with him, keep greater physical distance, and avoid particular topics of conversation. This 'disabling the normal' (Hilbourne, 1973) also seriously effects the families of the disabled both by restricting the range and flexibility of their activities due to the demands for help made by the presence of the disabled, and by their acquisition of what Goffman has called 'courtesy stigma'. That is, by virtue of their close association with the disabled their families may also become stigmatized. This is particularly the case for parents with disabled children, especially if the disability is present from birth (Voysey, 1972a; 1975). It is therefore important that physicians be able to recognize the problems of these people also, for they too are faced with restructuring their previously taken for granted world to accommodate to the new and 'non-normal' state of affairs.

The Special Case of Mental Illness

The research and debate concerning mental illness presents a confusing array of evidence and interpretation which makes it difficult to systematize and to arrive at an accurate and precise depiction of this type of illness. Indeed, there is debate as to whether 'illness' is the appropriate label to apply (Begelman, 1971; Davis, 1970; Gove, 1970; Sarbin, 1967; Scheff, 1966, 1974; Wing, 1973). What does seem clear is that in comparison to other types of illness, mental illness presents the greatest problems of interpretation and action for both physicians and the lay public. This is the type of illness that is least firmly known to be influenced by the underlying biological disease process (when there is one), and where the social factors, especially those associated with the labelling of a person as mentally ill, are certainly influential.

One reason for the confusion and difficulties is the failure of many of the participants in the debate to take sufficient account of the wide range of conditions that are covered by the term 'mental illness'. Such conditions include severe psychotic illness (such as 'schizophrenic' breakdown), psychosomatic states, mild anxiety, and depressive and neurotic states. These latter types, although severely inconveniencing, are obviously quite different from psychotic conditions. Indeed, the bulk of 'mental illness' is of the less dramatic non-psychotic type where the patient complains of definite symptoms (e.g. crying, tiredness, being frightened to leave the house, unsatisfactory sexual relationships, irritability) much in the same way as in the case of other types of illness. The main difference is that in 'mental illness' the cause of the illness is attributed to emotional difficulties rather than to a specific physiological pathology, perhaps because such a pathology has been ruled out. Much mental illness can therefore be understood as non-stigmatizing, long-term illness, or even as acute short-term illness. However, it is often the case that 'minor' mental illnesses are sometimes viewed as akin to the more extreme psychotic conditions, and so carry some stigma with them. It does seem, however, that the stigmatizing of these conditions is decreasing.

Due to these considerations, in this discussion I will concern myself primarily with the more severe psychotic forms of mental illness. These forms typify the general social processes involved in the social definition of mental illness. Further, it seems that it is these forms of mental illness that most people think of when they use or hear the term 'mental illness' (or its colloquial equivalents), and that the stigmatization of non-psychotic forms is mainly the result of their confusion with and 'contamination' by the more severe psychotic forms. In mental illness the attachment of a label is often a result of a breakdown in social expectations. The sick person consistently fails to fulfil the expectations of others with regard to what is 'proper' and 'normal' behaviour. This is also an important element leading to definitions of someone as being physically ill. However, there is a fundamental difference involved. With regard to physical illness the problem focuses around the person's incapacity to meet expectations although both he and others realize that he would otherwise fulfil them. With mental illness the problem focuses around the apparent inability of the 'ill' person to understand that he is in fact failing to meet social expectations, although it must be recognized that in many cases he is all too aware of this inadequacy. Not only does he fail to meet expectations, but he *acts* inappropriately. Whereas in physical illness expectations are just not met, in mental illness expectations are actively violated. There is, consequently, a strong element of moral judgement involved in assessing the conduct and character of the mentally ill. Since they engage in 'wrong' conduct, the temptation is to infer that this is the result of a 'wrong' or defective character. In the early stages of interpretation especially, behaviour, which later becomes accounted for as resulting from mental illness, is often attributed to personal defects such as 'maliciousness' (Yarrow, 1955).

It is not just that the mentally ill fail to meet our expectations in a different way from the physically ill. The types of expectation they violate are more basic and fundamental. As Scheff puts it:

'There are innumerable norms over which consensus is so complete that the members of a group appear to take them for granted ... A person who regularly violated these expectations probably would not be thought of a merely ill-bred, but as strange, bizarre, and frightening, because his behaviour violated the assumptive world of the group, the world that is construed to be the only one that is natural, decent, and possible.' (1966: 32)

According to Scheff, the label of mental illness may be applied to make sense of the behaviour of people who *consistently* violate such common and taken for granted expectations. (He terms such behaviour 'residual rule breaking'.) It is important to stress that it is not the intrinsic nature of the conduct itself that leads to the definition of mental illness, but its situational inappropriateness and impropriety. For example, while it is perfectly acceptable and expected that a male lover will caress and fondle his female partner's breasts in private, it is entirely unexpected and disapproved of that he should attempt to do the same to a stranger in a public place.

Scheff argues that the attachment of the label of mental illness does not inevitably follow from what would clinically be regarded as evidence of mental disorder. For example, there have been many epidemiological studies that come to the conclusion that, as is the case with physically grounded disease episodes, there were more 'active cases' than were being treated for mental illness.[8] On the basis of such studies, Scheff suggests that 'most residual rule breaking is unrecognized or rationalized away' (1966: 51).

Perhaps the major factor in the denial or 'normalization' of the behaviour of the mentally disordered is the stigma attached to calling someone mentally ill, for to define someone as mentally ill is seen as a desperate and final resort. This interpretation would go some way to explaining the findings of Goldberg and his colleagues (1970) that general practitioners consistently fail to diagnose or treat large numbers of emotionally disturbed patients, and the similar findings of Duff and Hollingshead (1968). This fear of mental illness seems to derive from the existence of a generally shared negative stereotype of mental illness which is, Scheff suggests, learned in early childhood and continually re-affirmed by the mass media and via anecdotes, jokes, etc., in everyday social activities.[9] The main elements of this stereotype appear to be conceptions of the mentally ill as incurable, 'dangerous', and engaging in extreme forms of bizarre behaviour. It may also be felt that mentally ill people not only act differently but look different.[10] Scheff also makes the point that such stereotypes have an impact on the shaping of the behaviour of the person once he is defined as mentally ill. He sums up his argument as to the importance of the stereotype of mental illness in this way:

'The discussion here suggests that *everyone* in a society learns the symptoms of mental disorder vicariously, through the imagery that is conveyed, unintentionally, in everyday life. This imagery tends to be tied to the vernacular of each language and culture; this association may be one reason why there are considerable variations in the symptoms of mental disorder that occur in different cultures. If ... this imagery is available to the rule-breaker to structure and thus to "understand" his own experience, the quality of the societal reaction becomes extremely important in determining the duration and outcome of the initially amorphous and unstructured residual rule-breaking.' (1966: 80)

I suggest that there are similar stereotypes, which function in the same way, with regard to other illnesses such as cancer, and heart attack. [11]

If the stereotype of mental illness is so negative, what are the consequences of its application? Scheff suggests that one important consequence is to stabilize behaviour and lead to the production of symptoms. In this context Scott's observations (1969, 1970) about the power of the professionals' conceptions to influence their clients behaviour is relevant, for such conceptions may provide a very important basis for the reconstruction of the character of the mental patient and the patterning of his behaviour. (See the discussion by Siegler and Osmond (1966) on this). A recurring theme is that the mental patient must first accept that he is sick — with the implication that such acceptance also involves conforming with the professional's notion of *how* he should be sick — before recovery can begin. Another important consequence closely related to the first is that the label of mental illness implies a great loss of the person's creditability as a person. Of all types of illness, mental illness is most global in its scope for the attachment of the label applies to all areas of social activity and directly brings into question the character of the person. [12] All conduct becomes questioned in the search for the causes of the illness. A third consequence of being labelled as mentally ill is that it is very hard to entirely lose the label. Just as a cardiac patient is seen as always having a 'heart condition', so is the ex-mental patient seen as having 'mental illness' in a latent form ready to be 'reactivated'. Just as the physically deformed are permanently discredited and suspect, so too is the known ex-mental patient. However, there is a difference — the mental patient can to a large extent disguise his former status and so avoid such discredit whereas the deformed cannot. It must be stressed that these consequences are variable in their strength and impact.

There are, of course, positive consequences associated with the labelling of illness and with the gains resulting from the resolution of anxiety and the help given to the ill person in dealing with his illness. These positive aspects are also evident in the case of mental illness. First, the labelling of 'non-social' behaviour as illness is, of itself, important in removing, or at least alleviating previous interpretations of the person's conduct and character in morally negative terms. Second, the mentally ill person is indeed facing problems, and the labelling of his problems in illness terms at least entitles him to ask for and receive aid in resolving them. These are important offsetting consequences to the negative ones indicated above.

As I have, mentioned (p. 349), there is a controversy as to whether the label of 'illness', together with its implied focus on disease in the individual, is appropriate. It has been cogently argued by a whole range of scholars that mental illness is a social product (Laing, 1966; Szasz, 1961) and that although there are admittedly physiologically based mental illnesses, the most important causes of mental illness are interactions with others and the social stresses of social life. A 'disease theory' of mental illness is therefore, it is argued, inappropriate since what are referred to as 'mental illnesses' are essentially problems in living; the result of the way we define and organize our world. In support of this view they point to the fact that the psychotic and other 'mentally ill' persons come to be defined as 'ill' because they do not conform to the demands and expectations of social life.

As the genesis of 'mental illness' is in the problems of living which people experience then, they argue, their solution requires addressing the social and inter-actional bases that generated them. The value of regarding such problems as *illness,* despite the sometimes very real advantages for the way in which the affected person is regarded, is therefore seriously questioned; for it restricts the way in which these problems are addressed and deflects attention away from other potentially more productive ways of addressing the problem.

The opposing view is clearly stated by Wing who argues that:

'the great advantage of the disease theory lies in the usefulness of its predictions. Although very little can be said about necessary or sufficient causes, there is ample evidence that a diagnosis based upon the more characteristic symptoms leads to a number of useful predictions as to pharmacological and social treatments, rehabilitation and prognosis.' (1973: 156)

Wing has two telling arguments against 'labelling theory', at least in so far as it applies to schizophrenia. The first is that proponents of this approach are themselves unclear about the nature of illness. They confuse different types of abnormality and deviance, and fail to distinguish between primary and secondary impairments (see also Begelman, 1971). Second, how do labelling theorists account for the development of symptoms such as thought disorder out of normal social action? The weight of the argument against labelling theory seems to be that they have an insufficiently clear notion of disease theory, and confuse metaphor with reality (Begelman, 1971). However, while labelling theory may be unable to account for the *genesis* of mental illness, it does seem to point up some of the important 'secondary impairments' that may result from the application of the definition of a person as mentally ill.

At this point it must be made clear that the problems experienced by the mentally ill and their families are very real, even if their origin is less easy to uncover and treat than is the case with other types of illness. Invariably the patients complain about the undesirability of their conditions, with the exception of some psychotics. Whereas with a stroke patient or a person suffering from the 'flu' there is a clear and understood reason for his condition, with mental illness this is not the case. A complex set of social and interpersonal factors, often of uncertain impact, are more likely to be seen as causing the illness. It is in the area of psychotic 'mental illness' that both the potential advantages of the illness label (in terms of legitimating failure to meet obligations and of structuring anxiety producing situations in terms of potential solutions) and the limitations stemming from its restricted focus of attention towards 'primary' biological conditions and the inadequate evidence that this is helpful seem to be in greatest opposition. However, as I have attempted to indicate in the discussion of the other types of illness, these gains and losses of the 'vocabulary of disease' are present to a greater or lesser extent in all types of illness.

Medical and Social Definitions of Illness

To this point the discussion has focused almost exclusively on the ways in which illness is variously interpreted and acted towards by ill people and the lay public in general. I now turn to consider the part played by the physician in the social definition of illness. The physician plays a crucial role in legitimating the validity of a person's illness. In a very real sense the physician, as Freidson has stressed (1970), plays a crucial moral role: without his 'stamp of approval' that the person is genuinely ill, the person will be viewed as somehow morally suspect — as a malingerer or hypochondriac. This 'moral' role of the doctor in legitimating illness, and hence legitimating absence from such central activities as school and work, is most clearly seen in countries such as the Soviet Union where medicine is under the direct control of the state, and the doctor is accountable to the state rather than to his peers (Field, 1953). However, it is clearly an important aspect to the role of the physician in our society also.

A second important point to note is the pervasiveness of the medical view of illness. This pervasiveness is apparent in both the way we habitually react to what we consider illness, and in the expansion of the 'medical model' to account for a whole range of phenomena that are not unambiguously caused by underlying disease processes, e.g. mental retardation. [13] This trend, which Zola (1972) calls the 'medicalizing' of society, dates back at least as far as the early and successful public health measures of the nineteenth century. Since that time modern medicine has been involved in what Zola terms 'the expansion of what in life is deemed relevant to the good practice of medicine'. The force of this movement derives in part from the laudable concern to maximize health, and in part from the dramatic and significant success of some forms of modern medical intervention. The pervasiveness of this process and its impact on our daily life is readily apparent, as leisure activities such as smoking or eating (to 'excess') come to be defined as bad because they are hazardous to health. This is not the place to pursue this aspect of the impact of medicine on our lives any further, although it does raise an important and fundamental issue which Zola succinctly states:

'By locating the source and the treatment of problems in an individual, other levels of intervention are effectively closed. By the very acceptance of a specific behaviour as an "illness" and the definition of illness as an undesirable state, the issue becomes not whether to deal with a particular problem, but *how* and *when.* Thus the debate over homosexuality, drugs, or abortion becomes focussed on the degree of sickness ... or the extent of the health risk involved. And the more principled, more perplexing, or even moral issue, of *what* freedom should an individual have over his or her own body is shunted aside.' (1972: 500, emphases in the original)

The pervasiveness of modern medicine is, as we noted, also evident in the way we react towards illness, for most, if not all, of us use a medically based notion of 'disease' to systematize and make sense of illness. That is, we look for a set of 'objective' symptoms which will define our illness as a particular instance of a general category of disease with known causes, progressions, and treatments.[14] One of the crucial points in defining illness for both physician and patient is the attachment of the diagnostic label, for the label often serves to relieve one kind of anxiety by objectifying the situation. Also it serves to structure the situation by pointing towards the expected prognosis and treatment. However, despite the commonly shared general acceptance of the 'disease model' of illness, there is unlikely to be complete consensus between patient and physician with regard to illness. There is always the potential for disagreement and conflict between the medical definition of the situation based on a seemingly precise and objective language of disease and its associated biological imagery emphasizing bodily functioning, and the more general lay views which are primarily concerned with the consequences of illness for social functioning. While patients always see themselves as ill, the physician tries to translate this subjectively felt condition into the appropriate 'objective' category of disease. In this process he may well lose sight of the patient's subjective sense of being ill. This is almost inevitable, and yet these subjective elements are always present, and crucially affect the course of the illness, the effectiveness of the treatment, and the rate and even the extent of recovery. By applying his medical vocabulary of disease, with its main emphasis on bodily functioning, the physician may well lose sight of the fact that illness affects social ways of acting, and that for the ill person the degree to which his social functioning and way of life are affected is his main immediate concern. The implication is that the physician's language of disease is insufficient, *in itself,* for it 'mistranslates' cf   Rosenheim + Gravard.

and loses sight of the very important subjective sense of being ill.

A study by Duff and Hollingshead (1968) at a prestigious university teaching and community hospital in the USA bears directly upon the problem of the gap between the diagnosis and treatment of the disease on the one hand, and the care the patient receives for his illness on the other. Their study utilized detailed observations at the hospital; interviews with patients and their families, with physicians, and other hospital personnel; the use of medical records; and visits to the patients' homes. In this review of their work I focus only on that part of the study concerning patient–physician relations, and the inadequacy of the 'disease model' of illness. In this context three inter-related observations can be made. The first is that the narrow focus on disease and the consequent neglect of social and psychological features of illness can result in serious negative consequences for the treatment of the illness. Second, all physical illness involved a change of mental status which may be relatively mild and short-lived, but is significant and sometimes persists well beyond the 'physical cure' of the illness. Third, there is often a failure in communication between physician and patient with regard to the social and emotional aspects of illness.

One of the more startling findings of the Duff and Hollingshead study is the extent to which the emotional aspects of illness were overlooked. According to them 'the mental status of only 11 per cent of the patients was perceived accurately by their physicians' (Duff and Hollingshead, 1968: 213). It is clear that serious deficiencies in patient care resulted from this unawareness of the patients' emotional status and the failure by the physicians to appreciate the fears and problems in living that their illness produced for most, if not all, patients. All of the 161 patients interviewed expressed feelings of apprehension, anxiety, and fear with regard to their feelings about entering the hospital, with over half (52 per cent) being fearful. Anxiety and fear of entering the hospital were linked to the more generic anxieties and fears stemming from the threat of illness to their normal activities and life itself. Yet, despite these anxieties and fears the patients themselves not only for the most part accepted the inattention of the physicians to these elements of their illness, but actively co-operated with the physicians in downplaying the 'subjective' side to being ill. Duff and Hollingshead sum up the two sides to the doctor–patient relationship thus:

> 'The patient was confused about his symptoms and fearful about his illness. He frequently delayed reporting his symptoms because he feared not only illness but the physicians whom he saw. He suspected that they might fail to understand him, keep the truth from him, tell him unpleasant truths, or discover embarrassing things about him. The patient often informed the physician selectively, describing his physical symptoms but not his emotional state, since it was acceptable, though unpleasant, to be physically ill but not acceptable to be mentally ill.

Thus, the patient presented a limited history of his problem, yet he and his physician believed that this history was adequate for diagnostic and treatment purposes. In many instances it was not adequate.

'The physician focused his interest on physical disease; he was usually not concerned with personal and social influences in relation to the disease. He altered his communications with patients to meet their expectations and, at times, to protect himself from patient and family reactions. Between them, the patient and the physician defined the patient's problem and determined what information was important in the diagnosis and treatment of his disease. This definition, however, rarely took into account the presence of emotional or family disturbances and the extent to which they influenced the patient's symptoms. Psychiatric diagnoses were rarely applied; psychiatrists were infrequently consulted. Instead, the problems of the patient were viewed in a physiologic or 'mechanistic' context.' (1968: 368–9)

The neglect of emotional problems, with the accompanying negative consequences for patient care, is thus the result of two factors. It results partly from the physician's way of viewing illness mainly in terms of disease, and partly from the patients' acceptance of such a model as appropriate and their denial of emotional problems for as long as possible due to their fear of mental illness. As patients so clearly accept medical expertise it is up to the physicians rather than to the patients to define emotional problems as the appropriate province of treatment and care, and to recognize the limitations of the 'disease theory' of illness.

Let us briefly consider another aspect of the physician's activity — the process of diagnosis. Once a person has been tentatively identified as ill by himself or others, he may seek out a physician in order to obtain a diagnosis of what is wrong with him, for diagnosis is seen as the first step to recovery. The diagnosis received is, as we have seen, of crucial importance to how the person views his illness. There is another less obvious aspect to diagnosis. Because the consequences of 'missing' illness are seen as more disastrous than that of incorrectly defining a state of health as 'illness', and because of pressure from their patients to receive a diagnosis of disease, what Scheff (1966) has referred to as a basic 'decision rule' is evident in much medical diagnosis. This rule can be succinctly stated as: 'If in doubt, presume illness.' (Although as we have just seen, this is not the case when 'mental illness' is concerned where the opposite tendency seems to apply.) Scheff cites two striking examples to support his argument. The first was a study of physicians' judgements on the advisability of tonsillectomy for school children. The thousand children were screened by one group of physicians and about 60 per cent of them had their tonsils removed. The remaining children were then examined by a second group of physicians and nearly half of them were recommended for the operation. Finally, this last 'healthy' group were examined by yet another group of physicians and again nearly half of them were recommended to be operated on. In the second, a study of 14,867 films screening for tuberculosis signs, 'there were 1,216 positive readings which turned out to be negative and only 24 negative readings which turned out to be clinically active!'. This is startling even though such tests are known to be provisional and not definitive.

According to Scheff there is 'a considerable body of evidence in the medical literature concerning the process in which the physician unnecessarily causes the patient to enter the sick role' (1966: 106). As he notes, most people if they have disease signs and are told by the physician they are ill 'obligingly come up with the right symptoms' (1966: 107). Further, this may occur even if the diagnosis is kept from the patient for, 'By the way he is handled, the patient can usually infer the nature of the diagnosis, since in his uncertainty he is extremely sensitive to subtleties in the physician's behaviour' (1966: 107). An important consequence of this decision rule is that people may be unnecessarily labelled 'ill'. Contrary to the assumption that this mistaken labelling will not have serious consequences, Scheff argues that in a significant number of cases it does so. The weight of the medical label is such that it can fundamentally change a person's life style. For example, to define someone as 'ill' because they have high blood pressure may fundamentally alter their way of life. Yet, there is no conclusive evidence that high blood pressure inevitably leads to clinical malfunctioning (Scheff 1966: 115). It must be stressed that 'over-diagnosis' is a natural consequence of the medical decision-rule to 'find illness', and that this rule is itself based on the attempt by the medical profession to prevent harm resulting from their activities. There is another important influence which also leads to such behaviour − the patients themselves. As Friedson puts it 'the fact seems to be that the everyday practitioner feels impelled to do something if only to satisfy patients who urge him to do something when they are in distress' (Friedson, 1970: 258).

This leads me to another aspect of diagnosis. The core of diagnosis is the attempt to resolve uncertainty by patient and physician as to the nature of the illness, and hence to its appropriate treatment and expected consequences. As I have suggested there are varying degrees of certainty in these areas. Davis (1960) distinguishes two types of uncertainty: 'clinical' and 'functional'. The former is when geniune uncertainty exists as to the diagnosis and prognosis. The latter term refers to a situation where the physician knows the diagnosis and prognosis, but keeps the patient and family in a situation of uncertainty. He may, as Davis suggests, do this because he is reluctant to break 'bad news', and uses 'uncertainty' as a way to avoid doing so. However, it may well be that such a strategy is functional for *both* the physician and his clients. By delaying in the breaking of bad news a certain amount of 'preparation time' is allowed for the patient and family to become resigned to it. Sudnow (1967), for example, reports the case where a patient being operated on for a gunshot wound died unexpectedly. The family were gradually led to the acceptance of his death via a series of progressively worse 'progress reports' from the operating theatre when the patient had in fact been dead all the time (65–6)! Glaser and Strauss (1965) in their study of dying see uncertainty of death and the handling of it as central to the whole management of the patient and his family. Similarly Roth's (1963) study of the treatment of TB patients places uncertainty at the heart of the conflict between patients and physicians as to the speed of their recovery, and suggests that other than purely clinical factors are at work. Other examples could be provided, but the point is clear; diagnosis and treatment involve much more than is included in a 'disease theory' of illness.

Summary and Conclusion

Freidson (1970) and Zola (1972) have both argued that the practice of medicine is a moral enterprise – that is, that it cannot be regarded as the neutral practice and application of a corpus of knowledge and techniques referring to disease. Despite the supposed excusal from responsibility involved in calling somebody ill (Parsons, 1951) in fact some moral evaluation is always involved in the definition of illness. (We get a cold because we failed to wear warm clothes, we relapse because we go back to work too soon, etc. These are clearly moral and not clinical evaluations.) As Zola puts it, '… at every level, from getting sick to recovering, a moral battle raged' (492). As I suggested earlier, illness is always a threat to our everyday world and involves a change in our conduct and character.

It has been argued in this chapter that one of the key variables in the social construction of illness is the degree to which the illness 'spoils' or 'stigmatizes' the ill person.[15] There seem to be two main dimensions affecting this; the loss of self-reliance and the degree of 'differentness' from normal resulting from the illness. Both of these factors crucially affect the degree to which the person can conceal his 'spoilage'. If we consider illness in this way it suggests that one reason why people delay going to see a physician may be because to do so effectively prevents such concealment. From this view the decision to seek help is seen to involve both gains and losses. What is gained is the resolution of uncertainty and the receiving of professional help in 'handling' the illness. What is lost is the definition of oneself as a normal person (even if this is only temporary) and a possible loss of involvement in normal activities. (There are of course other gains and losses involved too, e.g. economic.)

In my discussion of the four analytically distinguishable types of illness I suggested that the degree of 'spoilage' resulting from an illness was an important dimension affecting the social definitions of illness. Of necessity the picture presented was somewhat general and abstract since empirically there is much variation, as both the nature of the disease and the nature of treatment affect the extent to which such spoilage or stigmatization can be concealed. Let me give an example. Diabetes may be both a non-stigmatizing *and* a stigmatizing illness depending on the success of the treatment and the course of the disease. It is possible to gain some control over the progress of the disease by the use of insulin injections. However, one of the side effects of the insulin treatment is that it sometimes leads to an unexpected loss of consciousness – which may be very stigmatizing for the diabetic. Also, the course of the disease is not arrested, but merely slowed down, and eventually may lead to gangrene of the lower limbs. This in turn may require surgical treatment, e.g. amputation of toes, leading to a visible physical handicap which may become a source of stigma. The successful treatment of illness entails an awareness by the physician of these non-clinical aspects to the illness.

I therefore looked at the way physicians defined illness and tried to indicate some of the important consequences of this for the structuring of illness and for patient care. Although it was suggested that the disease-oriented model of modern medicine was in itself inadequate for the treatment of illness (as distinct from disease) it must be stressed that I do not intend to imply there is no utility to the 'medical model'. Rather, I have assumed that the very real merits and achievements of modern medicine are so well known that they did not require elaboration. I felt it more important to explore some of the unanticipated consequences of the medical model and their implications for the treatment of illness.

To conclude, I suggest that *'illness'* must be seen as problematic and socially defined, for the ways in which patients and physicians define and act towards illness are only partly determined and shaped by the 'primary' underlying disease process by which illness is produced. If the physician is, as Freidson (1970) so cogently argues, a 'moral entrepreneur', then he must be aware of this fact, and of the social consequences of his practice of medicine.

Notes

1. Unfortunately there is little evidence bearing directly on this hypothesis. Apart from the studies of Davis (1963) and Yarrow (1956) the work of Freidson (1970), McKinlay (1972), Robinson (1971) and Zola (1973) seem to support the suggestion.

2. It must be stressed that the four types represent an attempt to typify the main ways in which people view illness. The types are meant to be suggestive, not exhaustive, and to be used as a way to identify elements that while common to all illness vary along certain important dimensions with respect to one type of illness as compared to another.

3. It should be noted that Monteiro found a low level of consensus between *all* types of patients (i.e. workers, 'legitimate' invalids, and 'cardiac invalids') and their physicians regarding the severity of the attack. Patients saw their attack as more severe than their physicians, and both estimates of severity were higher than 'objective' estimates based on extracts from the medical record. This is reported more fully in Monteiro 1974.

4. There are a large number of studies bearing on the problems of rehabilitation of the physically handicapped, and what follows is an attempt to summarize in a very general way some of the main points that have been made. For discussion of many of the social and other implications see Sussman (1966). See also Barker, Wright, and Gonik (1953), Davis (1963), Goffman (1963), and Voysey (1972a, 1972b, and 1975).

5. For example Scott (1969, 1970) has shown how the attitudes of workers with the blind influence the adaptation made by blind people to their blindness. He found that in different societies there were differing conceptions of what blindness involved. In Sweden blindness is seen as a technical handicap, and emphasis is placed largely on teaching the newly blind mastery of the technical aids that will restore them to 'normal life'. In the United States of America most conceptions are psychologically based, and focus on helping the blind person to come to grips with his psychological problems, to accept his condition, and to learn to live with it. In England attention focuses on psychological factors, and there is little technical instruction in such things as unaided mobility. Rather, it seems that the emphasis is on generating cheerfulness in the face of adversity. Such differences in professional outlook obviously have a direct impact on the restructuring of life, for to receive help and aid from such professionals involves an acceptance of their definition of the situation. Scott concludes that: 'Gradually, over time, the behaviour of blind men comes to correspond with the asumptions and beliefs that blindness workers hold about blindness' (1969: 119 and 1970: 285). That is, blindness *per se* is not sufficient to account for the behaviour and attitudes of blind people.

6. One example of this type of approach with which I am familiar is the Highland Heights project in Fall River, Mass., USA. Mainly as a result of frustration at the lack of supportive services, architectural barriers, community disinterest, etc., Dr Greer initiated a programme focusing around such issues and based on a large apartment house complex for the partially disabled where such people could live independently. The innovative aspect of the program is that the apartment complex is on the same site as a medical facility which provides supportive services as required. The development of this project has served as a catalyst in the community for the provision of a range of services for the disabled which were previously absent. An initial report on the program can be found in Sherwood *et al.* (1973). I am grateful to Dr Greer for the opportunity to visit the project on a number of occasions when I spent time with both staff and patients. I am also grateful to him for his comments on an earlier version of this chapter.

7. In this respect the difficulties encountered by 'mental health education' projects is instructive (Cummings and Cummings, 1957).

8. For example Leighton (1963), Srole (1962), Brown, Bhrolcháin, and Harris (1975). The first two studies use a very wide definition of mental illness, and the majority of the cases are found in the 'mild' and 'moderate' categories. The Brown study is concerned only with depressive disorders in women.

9. Unfortunately, the evidence as to the existence of a commonly shared stereotype of mental illness is more suggestive than firm. A recent unpublished study by Cook of Leicester schoolchildren (1972) found some evidence to support Scheff's argument.

10. This may be another problem confronting the physically deformed: the assumption that they are also 'mentally deformed'.

11. Again there is a paucity of evidence. But see Jenkins and Zyzanski (1968); Monteiro (1973); Pratt (1956); and Titley (1969).

12. It has been suggested that the label of 'aged' or 'old' has similar consequences and that 'old' and 'sick' are often equated. This is not the place to discuss this problem at any length. However, given the relatively large proportion of our population who become 'old' at 65 by virtue of forced retirement this is clearly an important issue, which has implications for medical practice.

13. The term 'mental retardation' covers a wide range of conditions and there are over a hundred known 'causes'. It applies to the seriously disabled and intellectually feeble who literally cannot do anything for themselves, through Down's syndrome (mongolism) to those who have not noticeable physical defect and variably adequate intellectual capacities. As Edgerton (1967) points out for the latter 'it is only rarely possible to specify the cause of their relatively lesser intellectual abilities' (2–3). Further most of the mentally retarded fall into this category of the 'mildly retarded'. Mercer (1973) in her examination and comparison of the assumptions and implications of medical, statistical, and 'social-system' definitions of normality and abnormality and the differing strengths and weaknesses of these approaches to the understanding of the problem of mild mental retardation concludes that the respective 'definitions of abnormality' are likely to converge when the behaviours being examined are extreme and when they involve visible biological irregularities. However, 'when there are no biological signs and deviance is predominantly behavioural', the social model is 'likely to reflect the social reality more accurately' and prove most useful for understanding such behaviour (85). (See also Edgerton: 209–15.)

14. In other societies different vocabularies are used in the same way. For example, many 'primitive societies' had a magic-based explanation of what we call 'illness', and treatment therefore involved a complex (but internally logically coherent) set of procedures to determine the source of the magical invasion and how to magically defeat or appease the appropriate powers. This procedure was usually accompanied by other and, in our view, more appropriate procedures. However, without the former the latter would not work. For two examples see Devereux (1961) and Hallowell (1955).

15. I am grateful to David Tuckett for his useful comments on a previous version of this chapter. I have used a number of his suggestions and comments in this conclusion. I should emphasize the speculative nature of the following discussion.

References

Barker, R.G., Wright, B.A., and Gonik, M.R. (1953) *Adjustment to Physical Handicap and Illness.* New York: Social Science Research Council.

Begelman, D.A. (1971) Misnaming, Metaphors, the Medical Model, and some Muddles. *Psychiatry* 34: 38–58.
    An attack on the critics of the disease theory model of mental illness, and in particular of Szasz (1961) and Sarbin (1967).

Brown, G.W., Bhrolcháin, M.N., and Harris, T. (1975) Social Class and Psychiatric Disturbance among women in an Urban Population. *Sociology* 9(2): 225–55.

Cook, A.P. (1972) *Exploration of Children's Stereotypes of Mental Illness.* M. Phil. thesis, University of Leicester.

Croog, S.H., Levine, S., Zifre, L. (1968) The Heart Patient and the Recovery Process: A Review of the Directions of Research on Social and Psychological Factors. *Social Science and Medicine* 2: 111–64.

Cumming, E., Cumming, J. (1957) *Closed Ranks.* Cambridge, Mass: Harvard University Press.

Davis, F. (1960) Uncertainty in Medical Prognosis — Clinical and Functional. *American Journal of Sociology* 66: 41–7.

Davis, F. (1963) *Passage Through Crisis: Polio Victims and their Families.* Indianapolis: Bobbs-Merrill.

Davis, D.R. (1970) Depression as Adaptation to Crisis. *British Journal Medical Phychology* 43: 109–16.

Devereux, G. (1961) *Mohave Ethnopsychiatry: The Psychic Disturbances of an Indian Tribe.* Washington: Smithsonian Institution Press (reprinted 1969).

Duff, R.S., Hollingshead, A.B. (1968) *Sickness and Society.* New York: Evanston, and London: Harper and Row.

Edgerton, R.B. (1967) *The Cloak of Competence: Stigma in the Lives of the Mentally Retarded.* Berkeley and Los Angeles: University of California Press.

A participant-observation study of the lives of 48 former patients at an institution for the mentally retarded. Edgerton concludes that the training and treatment of the ex-patients fails to prepare them adequately for their lives in the community. The ex-patients were all very aware of the stigma of being mentally retarded, and saw their main problem as being that of demonstrating 'competence' and so avoiding the label of mentally retarded. However, they were usually unable to do this in any but passing encounters. Their lives are lived under a guise of competence as 'normals' participate in a 'benevolent conspiracy' to maintain its appearance.

Fabrega, H. and Manning, P.K. (1972) Disease, Illness, and Deviant Careers. In R.A. Scott, and J.D. Douglas (eds.), *Theoretical Perspectives on Deviance.* New York: Basic Books.

A thought provoking review of the key concepts and logical structure of labelling theory as it relates to illness.

Field, M.G. (1953) Structured Strain in the Role of the Soviet Physician. *American Journal of Sociology* 58: 493–502.

Freidson, E. (1970) The Social Construction of Illness. Part III of his *Profession of Medicine: A Study of the Sociology of Applied Knowledge.* New York: Dodd, Mead & Co.

An excellent, thorough, and insightful analysis of the topic. The book as a whole is a critical analysis of the medical profession in terms of its organization and belief system, and the consequences of these for the ways in which illness is dealt with.

Glaser, B.G., Strauss, A.L. (1965) *Awareness of Dying.* Chicago: Aldine Publishing Company.

An excellent study of the ways physicians, nurses, patients, and families cope with dying in hospital.

Goffman, E. (1963) *Stigma: Notes on the Management of Spoiled Identity.* Englewood Cliffs, N.J.: Prentice-Hall Inc.

Five essays exploring the various ways in which both stigmatized people and 'normals' handle the problems of stigma. A very influential work.

Goldberg, D., Blackwell, B. (1970) Psychiatric Illness in General Practice: A detailed

Study using a New Method of Case Identification. *British Medical Journal* 2: 439—43.

Gove, W. (1970) Societal Reaction as an Explanation of Mental Illness: an Evaluation. *American Sociological Review* 35: 873—84.
A critique of Scheff.

Hallowell, A.I. (1955) The Social Function of Anxiety in a Primitive Society. In his *Culture and Experience.* London: Oxford University Press.

Hilbourne, J. (1973) On Disabling the Normal: The Implications of Physical Disability for Other People. *British Journal Social Work* 3: 497—504.

Jenkins, C.D., Zyzanski, S.J. (1968) Dimensions of Belief and Feeling Concerning Three Diseases, Poliomyelitis, Cancer, and Mental Illness: A Factor Analytic Study. *Behavioural Science* 13: 372—81.

Kleck, R. (1968) Physical Stigma and Non-Verbal Cues Emitted in Face-to-Face Interaction. *Human Relations* 21: 19—28.

Klein, R.F., Dean, A., Willson, L.M., and Bogdonoff, M.D. (1965) The Physician and Postmyocardial Infarction Invalidism. *Journal of the American Medical Association* 194: 143—48.

Laing, R.D. (1966) *The Politics of Experience.* Harmondsworth: Penguin.

Leighton, D.C., Harding, J.S., Macklin, D.B., MacMillan, A.M., Leighton, A.H., (1963) *The Character of Danger.* New York: Basic Books.

Lemert, E.M. (1964) Social Structure, Social Control and Deviation In M.B. Clinard (ed.), *Anomie and Deviant Behavior.* New York: Free Press.
This is probably the best statement of Lemert's analysis of societal reactions to deviance.

Macgregor, F.C. (1951) Some Psycho-social Problems Associated with Facial Deformities. *American Sociological Review* 16: 629—38.

McKinlay, J. (1972) Some Approaches and Problems in the Study of the Use of Services — An Overview. *Journal of Health and Social Behavior,* 13: 115—52.

Mercer, J.R. (1973) Who is Normal? Two Persepctives on Mild Mental Retardation. In E.G. Jaco (ed.), *Patients, Physicians, and Illness* (2nd ed.). New York: Free Press.

Monteiro, L.A. (1970) *Social Factors Influencing the Outcome of Heart Attacks.* Ph.D. Dissertation, Brown University.

— (1973) After Heart Attack: Behavioral Expectations for the Cardiac. *Social Science and Medicine* 7: 555—65.

— (1974) *The Eye of the Beholder: Differential Perceptions of a Medical Condition.* Paper presented to the Annual Meeting of the American Sociological Association, Montreal, August 1974.

Parsons, T. (1951) Social Structure and Dynamic Process: The Case of Modern Medical Practice. In his *The Social System.* New York: Free Press.

Pratt, L. (1956) How do Patients learn about Disease? *Social Problems* 4: 29—40.

Robinson, D. (1971) *The Process of Becoming Ill.* London: Routledge & Kegan Paul.

Robertson, J. (1958) *Young Children in Hospital.* London: Tavistock Publications.

Roth, J.A. (1963) *Timetables: Structuring the Passage of Time in Hospital Treatment and Other Careers.* Indianapolis: Bobbs-Merrill.
This study focuses around Roth's observations of the ways in which TB is defined and structured by physicians and patients. Roth himself was hospitalized for TB in two different hospitals, so in a very real sense the study is based on the method of participant observation.

Sarbin, T.R. (1967) On the Futility of the Proposition that Some People be Labelled 'Mentally Ill'. *Journal Consulting Psychology* **41**: 447–53.

Scheff, T.J. (1966) *Being Mentally Ill: A Sociological Theory*. London: Weidenfeld and Nicholson.

Scheff explores the nature of the label of mental illness, and the consequences of attaching it to individuals. A thought provoking and influential work.

– (1974) The Labelling Theory of Mental Illness. *American Sociological Review* **39**: 444–52.

A response to critiques of 'Labelling Theory'.

Scott, R.A. (1969) *The Making of Blind Men*. New York: Russell Sage Foundation.

A compelling look at the way in which the people working with the blind in the United States impose their definition of what blindness 'is' on their clients.

– (1970) The Construction of Conceptions of Stigma by Professional Experts. In J.D. Douglas (ed.), *Deviance and Respectability*. New York: Basic Books.

An interesting exploration of professional workers' conceptions of the stigma they are handling.

Sherwood, S., Greer, D., Morris, J.H., and Sherwood, C.C. (1973) *The Highland Heights Experiment*. Government Printing Office, Washington D.C.: Department of Housing and Urban Development.

Siegler, M., Osmond, H. (1966) Models of Maddness. *British Journal of Psychiatry* **112**: 1193–2103.

A systematic comparison of professional 'models of madness' in terms of their implications for diagnosis, treatment strategies, definitions of causation, and their interpretation of the character and conduct of patients and families. Although somewhat uneven in its assessment of the various models, the article points up clearly the important practical consequences flowing from the way in which schizophrenia is defined.

Srole, L., Langer, T.S., Michael, S.T., Opler, M.T., and Rennie, T.A.C. (1962) *Mental Health in the Metropolis*. New York: McGraw Hill.

Stacey, M. (ed.) (1970) *Hospitals, Children and Their Families: The Report of a Pilot Study*. London: Routledge & Kegan Paul.

Sudnow, D. (1967) *Passing on: The Social Organization of Dying*. Englewood Cliffs, N.J.: Prentice-Hall Inc.

An excellent compact ethnographic analysis of how the inevitable yet feared and problematic business of dying is handled in two dissimilar hospital settings in the USA based on Sudnow's field observations. Sudnow's acute observation and analysis clearly beings out that dying is not simply a physiologically defined matter, but that it is essentially a socially constructed affair.

Sussman, M.B. (ed.) (1966) *Sociology and Rehabilitation*. American Sociological Association.

Szasz, T.S. (1961) *The Myth of Mental Illness*. New York: Free Press.

One of the most significant attempts to analyze 'mental illness' in terms of conceptualizing it as 'problems of living' rather than as 'illness'.

Titley, R.W. (1969) Imaginations about the Disabled. *Social Science and Medicine*. **3**: 29–3.

Voysey, M. (1972a) Impression Management by Parents with Disabled Children. *Journal of Health and Social Behaviour* **13**: 80–89.

– (1972b) Official Agents and the Legitimation of Suffering. *Sociological Review* (new series) **20**: 533–52.

– (1975) *A Constant Burden: The Reconstitution of Family Life*. London: Routledge & Kegan Paul.

Routledge & Kegan Paul.

Weinblatt, E., Shapiro, S., Frank, C.W., Sager, R.V. (1966) Return to Work and Work Status Following First Myocardial Infarction. *Americal Journal of Public Health* **56**: 169–85.

A review of studies.

Wing, J.K. (1973) Social and Familial Factors in the Causation and Treatment of Schizophrenia. In L.L. Iversen, and J.P.R. Rose (eds.), *Biochemistry and Mental Illness.* London: The Biochemical Society.

Yarrow, M.R., Schwartz, C.G., Murphy, H.S., and Deasy, L.C. (1955) The Psychological Meaning of Mental Illness in the Family. *Journal of Social Issues* **9**: 40–47.

Zola, I.K. (1972) Medicine as an Institution of Social Control. *Sociological Review* (new series), **20**: 487–504.

A stimulating look at some of the unanticipated and unnoticed consequences of attaching the label 'illness' to an increasing range of activity. This is speculative sociology at its best.

— (1973) Pathways to the Doctor — From Person to Patient. *Social Science and Medicine* **7**: 677–89.

Part IV

Conclusion

Chapter II

David Tuckett

- 5 1

Doctors and Society

Changes in Medicine

Mckeown (1971a: 6–7) has identified six aspects of the traditional medical task: the diagnosis or identification of disease, the pathology or understanding of disease, the prevention of disease, the cure of disease, the estimation of the prognosis or anticipation of the probable results of disease, and the palliation or alleviation of the effects of disease. Considering these aspects historically he points out that although several diseases were recognized more or less precisely at an earlier date, the reliable identification of disease really began in the nineteenth century. Second, in spite of earlier advances in related sciences such as anatomy and physiology, an accurate understanding of disease processes was also delayed until the nineteenth century. This later understanding, of course, owed much to the recognition of the bacteriological origins of infections. Third, although some reforms were anticipated earlier, effective preventive measures did not begin until the control of the environment and its effects promoted by individuals such as Edwin Chadwick and Sir John Simon in the middle of the nineteenth century. Such measures were not related to prevention *vis-à-vis* the individual and, with the single exception of vaccination against smallpox, this latter type of effort was not possible until after 1900. Effective treatment and cure was also delayed until the twentieth century. Indeed, although some useful drugs were introduced much earlier (for example, mercury, iron, quinine, and digitalis) the circumstances and manner of their use, and the limited grasp of their mode of action suggest that they must have been relatively ineffective. On the surgical side, before the discovery of anaesthesia, operations were mainly for cataracts, amputations, incisions for abscesses, lithotomy, and trephining of the skull. Even after the introduction of anaesthesia results were poor until aseptic techniques became widely used. With regard to prognosis Mckeown suggests that predictions even today remain largely a matter of clinical impression usually not submitted to scrutiny. The systematic calculation of prognosis, based on medical evidence, is still a science in its infancy. Finally, if relief of both physical and mental suffering are included under palliation, Mckeown argues that this is certainly the oldest and was, at least until the development of other aspects, the most important medical task.

It is of considerable interest to assess how far the development of doctors' ability to carry out each of these tasks has contributed to the well-being of the recipient of medical services. In this connection I am going to disregard improvements in diagnosis and the understanding of pathology because, to the patient, both tasks are of minor significance unless they improve the doctor's ability to prevent, cure, predict and alleviate.[1]

First and Second Stages in the Development of Medicine

In order to analyse the contribution made by developments in doctors' ability to carry out these tasks I am going to consider the history of morbidity and mortality (in the industrialized countries where changes have been broadly similar) in three stages. These are drawn onto *Figure 1* which presents changes in crude and age-adjusted death rates for the USA. The first stage comprises the period until 1937; the second, 1937–54; and the third, 1954 onwards. Comparative British data, but on infant mortality (which accounted for most of the changes in death rates and life expectation) is shown in *Figure 2*.

Figure 1   *Stages in the history of medical effort*

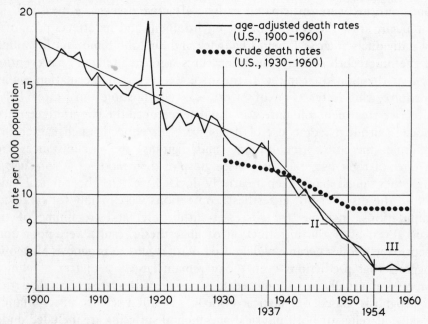

Source: McDermott (1969: 15)

Mckeown has argued that the dramatic changes in mortality that occurred in the first phase (and are shown in both figures) were not

Figure 2   *Deaths of children under 15 years attributed to scarlet fever, diptheria, whooping cough, and measles (England and Wales)*

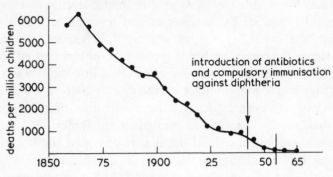

Sorce: Porter (1972: 95)

the result of the developing medical technology in cure, prevention, or prediction. This is not surprising. In the curative field there was little technology until the second phase. In the area of preventive medicine the one effective innovation, immunization for smallpox (Razzell, 1965) is not thought by Mckeown to have contributed much to reductions in total mortality. He suggests that the most convincing explanation for the reduction is that it resulted from improved food supplies (the result of agricultural and industrial development) which had the effect of tipping the balance in favour of host individuals rather than the parasitic micro-organisms that caused infectious disease (by far the most significant category of disease in this first phase). Fertility control, which kept population growth below increased productivity in agriculture, and public health engineering, were also important (Mckeown, 1971b: 32–6). Mckeown's view is supported by McDermott for US data (McDermott, 1969: 10–12).

By the time effective medical technology (for example sulphonamides and antibiotics) were available in stage two (*Figure 1*) a very large amount of the total improvement that has taken place throughout history had already happened (*Figure 2*). Nonetheless, the arrival of medical ability to intervene and cure caused a further decline which is illustrated by McDermott's age-adjusted data (see *Figure 1*). McDermott (1969: 14–15) suggests that by 1937 most of the improvement that could be accomplished in reducing infant deaths (particularly the large number from diarrhoea) by altering living conditions inside and outside the home had already occurred. In the period 1937–54 major progress was made, of a different kind to that achieved before, so that there was a major extension of life and a change in the disease pattern for early life. Maintained by the continued use of anti-microbial drugs this achievement of second stage medicine continues to the present day. Most childhood and early adult disease could now be cured. For example, in the USA the death rate from TB (one of the five leading causes of death in 1937) declined by 70 per cent in seven years from 1946—53. Similarly pneumonococcal pneumonia, miningococcal meningitis, bacterial endocarditis, syphillitic heart disease, and rheumatic heart disease showed a dramatic decline. Many diseases could be readily treated by antibiotics and leave little disability — the dreaded childbed fever, erysipelas, quinsy sore throat, typhoid fever, gonorrhea, adult dysentry, anthrax, syphilis, staphlycoccal osteomyelitis, and so on. Both in specific and non-specific (unintended) ways the anti-microbial drugs had a huge impact on the disease pattern — some diseases disappeared without even being specifically treated, presumably because individuals had received antibiotic treatment for something else. In large measures it is these antimicrobial drugs that provided the key element in the technological infrastructure on which the future development of medicine was based in the post-war period. But it should be noted that their main application was and is to the infectious disease of early life.

The Third Stage

After these great successes, the second quarter of the twentieth century saw further major changes in the medical effort. There was an increased understanding of pathology, increased ability to make accurate diagnoses (aided by special tests and investigations), the further development of preventive techniques, and a vast new array of drugs and surgical skills and procedures. What may be termed scientific medicine, or as Mckeown (1971b: 31) terms it the 'engineering approach' to biology and medicine (with its origins in the seventeenth century) became dominant.

'Nature was conceived in mechanistic terms, which led in biology to the idea that a living organism could be regarded as a machine which might be taken apart and reassembled if its structure and function were fully understood. In medicine the same concept led further to the belief that an understanding of disease processes and of the body's response to them would make it possible to intervene therapeutically, mainly by physical (surgical), chemical or electrical methods.
The consequences of the engineering approach are even more conspicuous in medicine today than they were in the seventeenth century largely because the resources of the physical and chemical sciences are so much greater. Medical education begins with the study of the structure and function of the body, continues with examination of disease processes, and ends with clinical instruction on selected sick people; medical service is dominated by the image of the acute hospital where the technological resources are concentrated; and medical science reflects the mechanistic concept, for example in the attention given to the chemical basis of inheritance and the immunological response to transplanted organs. These researches are strictly in accord with the physical model, the first being thought to lead ultimately to control of ·

gene structure and the second to replacement of diseased organs by normal ones.' (Mckeown, 1971b: 29—30)

Figure 3   *NHS (current) expenditure 1951—72 (at 1970 prices)*

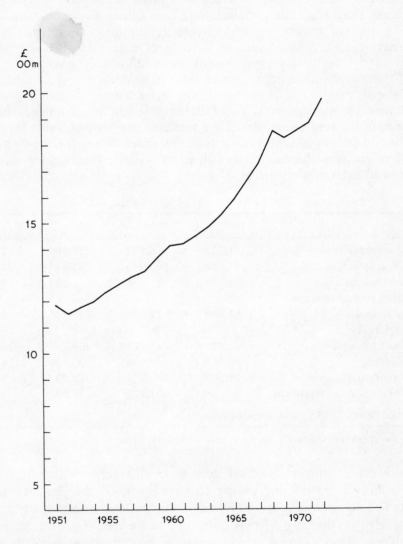

Source: Central Statistical Office, 1973: 16—17

The emphasis on scientific curative skills in the third stage, based on the concept of the body as a machine, is reflected in the high proportion of NHS expenditure allocated to hospital care (commented on in an earlier chapter pp. 258—9) and in the rapid increase in various aspects of the 'input' into the service. The increases are illustrated in *Table 1* and the escalation in health service expenditure that resulted is shown in *Figure 3*. National health expenditure at constant prices (i.e. after allowing for inflation in costs) rose 60 per cent (at about the same rate as GNP) in the period 1951—72. Health expenditure in the UK now accounts for

4.6 per cent of GNP but this is low compared to many other industrial countries. The emphasis on high cost sophisticated technology and scientifically based procedures reflected a major emphasis on the priority attached to the curative aspect of the medical task (as compared to the preventive and the palliative) which took place in this phase. As we moved into the third stage the popular image of medicine became dominated by the notion of miraculous technologically complex cures. The dramatic life-saving ability of doctors, as a result of extensive publicity, became part of the day-to-day experience of most individuals. Even if they have not themselves taken advantage of the developments the mass media have informed them − as in the television series *Your Life in Their Hands*. Doctors are modern gods and folk-heroes and, for example, when Dr Christian Barnard visited Brazil, he was able to fill a vast football stadium (twice in one day) with ardent fans desperate to see the man who was able to exchange human hearts (Illich, 1974: 54). Third stage medicine is above all 'scientific' medicine.

Table 1   Rising imput into the NHS − 1949−73 (England and Wales)

	1949	1959	1969	1973
hospital medical staff	11,735	16,033	22,001	25,337
hospital nursing staff	137,636	190,946	262,644	310,760
general practitioners	−	22,091	21,505	22,686
hospital professional and technical staff	13,940	21,878	33,245	40,858
prescriptions:				
number (thousands)	202,011	214,029	264,172	284,128
cost (£000)	30,331	72,968	163,226	245,943
pathology requests	11,500	17,279	38,792	51,319*
radiology units of treatment	−	21,127	33,882	39,508

* 1972 figure. 1973 figures are not comparable.

Sources: DHSS, 1974b: 30, 68, 99; Welsh Office, 1974: 19, 47, 66.

However, although medical activity proliferated in the third stage its achievements do not appear to have matched the dramatic results obtained by second stage innovations. As McDermott and many authors have argued, the very success of second stage medicine created its own problems. The first and second stages of medical effort took place in a situation where perhaps half of the population under consideration was less than fifteen years old. In these circumstances most of the health problems of the society centred around the infectious diseases of the first years of life. Once these were solved by improved environmental conditions and the new antimicrobial technology, the population began to live on, in large numbers, to middle and old age. For these age groups the medical problems were quite different from those encountered with infectious disease and could not be solved by the antimicrobial strategy. They required further developments and it was to these that most of the medical effort was directed in the third stage. The great rise in expenditure in the post-war period would not have been necessary if the infectious diseases of early life had still been the major target. How much has this third stage expenditure contributed?

Whether we adopt a crude approach to mortality by looking at changes in the expectation of life in the third stage, or are more specific and look at standardized mortality ratios (defined above p. 110) for individual diseases, the picture for the post-war period is a depressing one — particularly for males where improvements (as with tuberculosis) are offset by deterioration (as with carcinoma of the lung and ischaemic heart disease). As I mentioned in an earlier chapter (above pp. 110–11) the situation for males from the lower socio-economic classes is actually worsening. In the UK age-specific death-rates for unskilled manual workers aged fifty and over were probably higher in 1959–63 than they were in 1930–32 during the depression (Registrar-General, 1969: 18–29).[2] Men of any social class are twice as likely as women to die in middle-age in England and Wales — the vast majority from heart-disease, lung-cancer, and bronchitis (Central Statistical Office, 1974 : 137). Indeed Powles (1973: 3) has actually argued that death rates for men of middle age may be rising and it is certain that in Britain and the USA they have failed to decline (US Department of Health, Education and Welfare, 1971; Haas, 1968).

Cochrane (1972: 15–16), Powles (1973), and Morris (1964: 8) have also tried to estimate the changes in the morbidity experience of individuals that may be credited to medical effort. The indicator they use is that of certified spells of sickness absence. This is, of course, not a measure of sickness but of illness behaviour (see pp. 159–89). Quite literally, it reflects the extent to which individuals go to doctors and successfully obtain a sickness certificate. Sickness absence rates therefore presumably reflect the illnesses individuals have, the propensity of patients to take these to doctors, and the propensity of doctors to define illnesses as worthy of time off work.

A less contaminated measure of changes in morbidity would require a longitudinal survey of randomly selected individuals' illness experiences over relevant periods of time. However such studies are expensive as well as being methodologically complex and have not yet been adequately completed. In their absence there are studies, such as those referred to in an earlier chapter, that deal with the morbidity experience of populations at one point in time. Since the various studies have been carried out over the last forty years we can compare their results. Although such analysis gives little cause for confidence (methods and definitions varied, etc.) it can be concluded that there is no prima facie case for an improvement in morbidity. Whether we take the earliest Peckham study (Pearse and Crocker, 1944) or the most recent in Bermondsey and Southwark (Epson, 1969; Wadsworth, Butterfield, and Blaney, 1971) or the others in between (for example, Stocks, 1949) the picture is very much the same.

Sickness absence rates — and whether they are considered as indicators of illness or illness behaviour they presumably say something about how far individuals feel they are 'healthy' — have probably worsened over the period. Morris (1964: 8), reviewing the period from the 1920s to the early 1960s concluded that 'Sickness absence rates in men show no improvement'. Examining the trends in the 1950s the same author showed an 'appreciable rise of chronic sickness among men in their late forties, and a very substantial one, amounting to 30% in men in their early sixties' (1964: 11). More recent trends support this conclusion (DHSS, 1973a: 37–43), and Cochrane (1972: 15–16) and the Office of Health Economics (1971a) have pointed out how sickness absence rates, even after making allowances for their different effects, make days lost through strikes look rather insignificant. In 1968 about 328 million man working days were lost due to sickness compared to five million from strikes. Of course a strike, involving total shutdown for a short period may have a rather more severe effect on the economy than the simple days lost suggest. Nonetheless the lost productivity from sickness is so much greater that it must be regarded as far more serious.

As Cochrane (1972: 14–19) has pointed out, although the evidence on changes in the expectation of life, standardized mortality ratios for particular diseases, and on sickness absence rates together provide tentative estimates of the rather limited impact that the increased expenditures on scientific medicine have had in the last twenty years, such data are not in themselves sufficient. (For example, even had there been great improvements it would be necessary to isolate other possible causal factors (environmental influences for instance) before concluding that medical effort was responsible.) One way this more precise kind of relationship between input and output can be examined is through the direct study of the effectiveness of the particular drugs or procedures that make up 'third stage' medicine.

Cochrane himself examined some of the most common procedures that are part of today's approach to medicine. He argues that a great many procedures, most of which are often routinely applied, do not show any beneficial effect when submitted, in conditions of the best medical practice, to randomized controlled trials (RCTs). An RCT involves the random (and blind) allocation of individuals with a given condition to two groups. One group is given the procedure and another is treated in an alternative way — for example, not treated at all, given a placebo, kept at home rather than being sent to hospital, etc. Two examples of RCT procedure have already been mentioned in earlier chapters (pp. 25–6 and pp. 52).

Randomized controlled trials are always controversial and invariably create ethical difficulties. Against an RCT one may argue in terms of the death or disability that results to any patient from whom the experimental drug or procedure is withheld. On the other hand the absence of an RCT can result in many patients being subjected to useless but dangerous drugs, uncomfortable and worthless procedures, longer than necessary stays in hospital, and so on. Furthermore without an RCT a useless procedure will continue to command resources that might otherwise be used to influence death and disability elsewhere. Many RCTs conducted have shown how treatments with severe dangers attached to them have little value and to my way of thinking any remaining drugs and procedures over which there is doubt should be tested and all procedures and drugs to be introduced in the future should *have* to undergo an RCT. If we believe in new treatments we should be willing to subject them to testing.

Examining various RCTs relating to several common drugs and procedures Cochrane builds up a convincing case for the relative inefficiency of many current techniques. There is, in his view, for example, no good evidence to suggest that the controversial coronary care units are beneficial when compared to treatment at home; there are even some indications they may be harmful (1972: 51). Yet such intensive care units cost £21.9 million in 1969 alone (Office of Health Economics, 1971b) and in the United States take up 10 per cent of all available nurses (Holland, 1971).

Similarly there is no demonstrable benefit to be derived from the use of insulin or of tolbutamide and pheniform (the latter two may actually be dangerous) in mature diabetes (in contradistinction to their use in juvenile diabetes) (Cochrane, 1972: 55). Yet most mature diabetics are still treated in this way. Cochrane also argues that there is little to be gained from the treatment of diabetes in (relatively more expensive) outpatient departments rather than in general practice (1972: 56–7).

Neither is there evidence that the prescription of iron to non-pregnant women with low haemoglobin levels is effective in curing the classical symptoms of anaemia. Nor is there substance to the widespread belief in the value of argotamine tartrate in the treatment of newly diagnosed cases of migraine (Cochrane 1972: 29). To take a further example, complex surgical procedures can be applied which cost a great deal and do not achieve very much. The Medical Research Council, for example, found that individuals who received surgery for oat-celled carcinoma of the bronchus had a rather poorer survival rate than a matched group from whom surgery was withheld (MRC, 1966).

To take another example Cochrane argues there is little evidence to support the practice of concentrating more and more births in hospitals (1972: 63–6). In Holland, where confinement rates are about one third of those in this country (29 per cent of births taking place in hospital compared to more than 80 per cent in the UK), there is also one of the lowest perinatal mortality rates in the world. Despite this and other facts women in the UK are often encouraged, and no doubt have come to expect, to have their babies in hospital. This is very expensive (maternity beds taking up 9 per cent of all non-psychiatric beds as we saw earlier

p. 6) and may also cause disruption to the women, their families, and to the psychological well-being of the newborn. Similarly there is little justification for the long stays in hospital practised on many patients in connection with hernia repair (Morris, Ward, and Handyside, 1968), coronary heart disease (Harpur, 1971), or tuberculosis (Dawson, 1960). For hernia the RCT showed that discharge after one day would be as satisfactory as discharge after seven days. Yet the average length of stay for this condition in Great Britain is nine days.

The various results Cochrane and others report, therefore, do not create great optimism about the effects of modern medical care and it has to be pointed out, as Cochrane does, that these results are obtained for those therapies, usually administered in optimum conditions, that individuals have been brave enough to test. Many other aspects of treatment we simply have no evidence about. Yet the results from almost all RCTs warn that it is 'dangerous to assume that well-established therapies which have not been tested are always effective' (Cochrane, 1972: 29). Cochrane is equally critical of the value of much individually oriented preventive medicine — for example, cervical smear tests.

Cochrane concludes his review of present medical practice in a definite manner:

'An investigation into the working of the clinical sector of the NHS strongly suggests that the simplest explanation of the findings is that this sector is subject to a severe inflation with the output rising much less than would be expected from the input. The evidence is based on a historical survey, crude input and output measurements, and measurements of effectiveness and efficiency in the diagnosis and treatment of common diseases.' (1972: 86)

He suggests:

'There are facts from history: the desire to treat on the one hand; and the desire to be treated on the other. There is a strong suggestion that the increase in input since the start of the NHS has not been matched by any marked increase in output in the "cure" section... there were strong suggestions of inefficient use of effective therapies and considerable use of ineffective ones... two sectors of the community take the rest for an inflationary ride...' (1972: 67)

Returning to Mckeown's six aspects of the medical task, it would seem that the emphasis on cure that achieved priority in the third stage development of medicine has not really paid off. This is Mckeown's own assessment:

'Since the time of Kapler and Harvey, medical thought has been dominated by the belief that improvements in health must rely largely on an engineering approach, based on an understanding of the structure and function of the body, and of the disease processes which affect it

In fact man's health offers only limited scope for this approach.' (Mckeown, 1971b: 49)

Caring

'Past improvement has been due mainly to modification of behaviour and changes in the environment and it is to these same influences that we must look particularly for further advance. This interpretation does not overlook what is sometimes referred to as the pastoral role of the doctor; on the contrary, it underlines its significance, *for since most major diseases and disabilities are either preventible or intractible, care rather than cure should be our concept of the main focus of personal medical attention.*' (Mckeown, 1971b: 49; italics added)

As I suggested in discussing the second phase this statement of Mckeown's could be disputed for that period. But, for the third stage, it appears that, despite the technical achievements of the twentieth century which have produced some astonishingly impressive results (for example 'the pill') and the modifying of some hitherto 'incurable' diseases, the results of what Mckeown has referred to as the engineering approach have not, overall, been very encouraging.

At the same time it is also being recognized that the view of the body as a machine, and as a number of mechanical parts, has had serious disadvantages in underemphasizing the part that can be played by aspects of the medical task other than curing. The palliative/ameliorative aspects of medicine tended to get lost as a 'whole' person was split into a number of body-systems each with a specialist to deal with them. 'Caring' although accorded a role in lip-service usually has a low priority when doctors are allocating time and resources — sometimes with quite unacceptable results. This is illustrated if we consider the differential sums allocated to in-patient hospital care in different parts of the health service. In *Table 2* (based on Cochrane) where this has been done, we see

Table 2 Cost (£'s) per 'in-patient week' for various services in NHS hospitals during the year ended 31 March, 1973 (England)

	acute (over 100)	long-stay	convalescent	maternity	mental illness	handicap
medical staff	5.32	1.42	0.58	3.47	1.42	0.73
nursing staff	24.72	15.98	11.94	39.85	11.3	10.14
domestic staff	4.27	2.47	2.47	6.17	1.24	1.41
catering	8.18	4.54	5.51	8.52	3.77	3.58
laundry	1.57	1.00	0.33	2.71	0.64	0.75
power, light, heat	2.61	1.64	1.46	3.08	1.34	1.18
building, engineering, maintenance	3.39	2.02	1.58	3.47	2.10	1.85
general cleaning	0.87	0.59	1.21	1.58	0.35	0.32
net total cost	91.54	40.25	32.27	95.26	30.34	28.02

Source: DHSS, 1973c.

that not only have we allocated more money to patients suffering from acute diseases so that they have more medical and nursing staff to look after them, but we have also determined that some patients do not deserve the same standards of material comfort. Mental patients, for example, seem to need cheaper food. In few better ways than in such differences in the allocation of funds, at least in my view, can the dominant priorities of scientific medicine be demonstrated.

However, the emphasis on scientific medicine (and the consequent inflation of demand for expensive and sophisticated inputs) has not only led to inequality in the allocation of resources to different sectors of health care, it has also led to a lowering of the priorities placed upon 'caring' in other ways. Many appointment systems and systems of hospital care are organized so that the experience of being a patient, particularly in hospital, is unnecessarily unpleasant and doctors and nurses often do not seem to perceive as a priority a relationship with more than a particular organ of the patient's body. The 'whole person' has got lost. In one study Barnes illustrated what can happen by reporting the experience that the husband of one patient described when he accompanied his wife on admission to hospital. It was not untypical in the sample studied and it is so important in the context of the argument so far that I quote it in full:

' "The other day my wife telephoned me to say she had fallen down and probably broken her wrist. Would I come and take her to hospital? On arrival, my wife sat down and waited while I queued at the emergency admission office. When my turn came, the woman took my name and address and other relevant information and then asked for the name of the patient. This was the first reference to who it was needing attention. I explained we had called our family doctor and he advised my wife to come to hospital for X-ray. I returned to my wife. Her name was called five or ten minutes later.

While she was being interviewed by the doctor, I telephoned home to tell our two children we would be a bit late getting home. By this time, my wife had been put into a wheel-chair and I was asked to take her to the X-ray department. We waited for a few minutes until a technician came out and started to wheel my wife away into another room. I asked how long it would take. She didn't know. I pressed for an answer indicating my concern for our children. She then said it would take about ten or fifteen minutes. Within ten minutes my wife returned. The technician told us to go back to the admission department. How long would it be before the results would be known? She couldn't say. We were to go back to the admission department. This we did, and surprisingly enough — to us — the X-ray results were made known in a very short time.

While waiting, I telephoned home again to let the children know that mother was all right but perhaps they should go ahead and get themselves some supper. My little girl was quite put out to know that her mother was in hospital.

At this point a nurse appeared and said our family doctor was on the telephone. My wife spoke to him and he said she should be admitted to have the bone set. He would arrange that this be done by whichever specialist we liked. A nurse started wheeling my wife away, and I followed. I asked where we might be going and the nurse said we were going to 'admit' my wife. Would we be coming back? Oh no, she would go directly to bed. I suggested perhaps I should have brought along her things. Yes, that would be a good idea. So I went back to fetch them.

When I returned, there seemed to be a little annoyance because I had not been there to give information for filling up the forms. I apologised, saying where I had been. While the forms were being completed, the girl taking information was interrupted three times by calls from doctors and twice by calls from other nurses. When the forms were completed another girl came up with another form and asked my wife to sign it. I jokingly asked my wife if she knew what she had signed. She didn't. I asked the nurse and she said it was to get permission for my wife to be admitted and attended to.

I asked if I should take my wife's clothes home or leave them there. They suggested I take them home. I asked if she would be remaining in hospital overnight. They didn't know. Could I bring the children to see her after they had had supper? They didn't know this either. But the doctor would be down later in the evening. I left and returned home."

Several points concerning the expectations of the patient and her husband and the hospital's answer to them are elaborated in this cameo of hospital life. Nothing went wrong as far as the hospital was concerned. The patient's medical and personal information was recorded correctly, the doctor saw her, an X-ray was taken, the hospital obtained permission to treat her, she was admitted and put to bed. The hospital got on with its job of providing her with a medical service she could not get outside. It gave efficient attention to her broken wrist. Any other consideration which might have interfered with the hospital's job was excluded. Because she was a patient, she was expected to behave like one; to go to the ward in a wheel-chair, be undressed, and put to bed. Until the husband started asking questions and thus looked as if he might hold up the hospital's job, it was not considered necessary to give any information at any point about what was happening. No-one was interested in the two children left at home. No-one was interested in the patient's personal belongings; these only held up the form-filling when the husband was not there at the time the hospital needed him. The husband later observed:

"It struck me that the procedure was somehow like a factory assembly-line. The pressures were such that individual attention and concern for the patient's feelings just could not be taken into account. Things just kept happening to us. We had to ask all the questions. When we asked, an explanation was given, as briefly as possible, but *we* had to ask." ' (Barnes, 1961: 9—12)

A great deal of the evidence in Chapter 6 suggests that doctors often fail to take account of many of what patients consider their needs and, in Chapter 5, I discussed how it might be useful to take the patients' perspective seriously. I pointed out the dangers of a 'rational perspective' where what seem, to the doctor, apparently insignificant complaints are regarded as 'trivial' and a waste of the doctor's time. Chapter 7 analysed some aspects of hospital organization that can contribute to the deprived social and emotional experience of patients in hospital. Being a patient is too often an experience involving submission to arbitrary authority, and to dehumanization, depersonalization, and isolation.

Of course, in suggesting that the very great emphasis we have placed on scientific cure has been at the cost of care and humanity I have no wish to create a false antithesis. It seems to me that any implication that the highly 'scientific' doctor is less likely to be humane than the one whose techniques are traditional would be false. Used properly, technology, such as a blood urea estimation, can be a valuable extension of physical examination and can help to identify the cause of obscure and serious ill-health entirely resistant to ordinary methods of physical examination. Similarly, the prescription of certain drugs (for example of the anti-allergy and pain and anxiety relieving type) can play an important part in alleviating a patient's problem and there is no intrinsic reason why these cannot be part of a humane approach to caring as well as curing. The problem is that in practice the technical side often predominates at the expense of the human.

The Ecological View

The engineering approach to science and to medicine has produced great leaps forward in our knowledge. By conceiving of human beings as objects it has been possible to describe the complex anatomical and physiological relationships that exist. We now know a great deal about the functioning and purpose of different organs of the body. As we have seen, however, it has proved a lot more difficult (with the exception of infectious diseases) to use this knowledge to permit effective intervention. Thus although the pay-off in terms of knowledge has been tremendous, in terms of the cure of disease and suffering (at least in the third stage) it has been much less.

On the other hand the concentration of energy on the engineering approach has had serious drawbacks. As in other areas of science and philosophy the ability to conceive of ourselves as objects, made possible by the Cartesian division of mind and body, has created difficulties. Reductive mechanistic thinking has allowed us to conceive of disease without seeing people, to apply drugs to alter the functioning of one organ without thinking about the effects on others and so on. In the previous section I have suggested that this has led to a failure in medical performance by reducing the emphasis on the human side of practice – what I have termed 'caring'.

It is in this kind of context that what may be termed an ecological approach to science and to medicine has been evolved, and in the process, old discarded holistic notions revived. The knowledge of organ functioning gained by the engineering strategy can be subsumed into an approach that considers discordant organs against a background of the total environment in which we live – the other organs of the body, the patient's feelings and experience, and the social, psychological, and physical environment. Disease is seen as a misbalance and as a breakdown in the complex and ongoing relations that exist between human beings and their environment. Disease is firmly placed back in a whole person living and dying in a complex environment.

To take one example of this approach the American microbiologist Dubos, suggests that the historical rise and fall in the incidence of tuberculosis was the result of minute biochemical changes in the human body. These changes altered the usual relationship of bacillus to the human body and were, in turn, related to stress and other factors resulting from alterations in the environment associated with industrialization (1965: 163–195). This is also the kind of argument that Mckeown used in emphasizing the historical significance of our increased standard of living and improved food supplies in reducing mortality in the nineteenth century, and is similar to the view of Powles, who, concluding his discussion of the causes of the decline of infectious disease, writes:

'This rather schematic account of the changing impact of infectious disease throughout the three main phases of human history – hunter-gathering, agricultural, and industrial – has demonstrated the major importance for health, of man's interactions with his environment – that is his ecology. The provision of food, sanitary control and the regulation of births have been the three central factors.

This is not to underrate the recently acquired capacity to intervene in individuals by means of immunisation and antibiotics. But it does put that capacity into perspective! (Powles, 1973: 6)

Authors like Powles, Dubos, and McKeown argue that in considering the relative impact of curative medicine on disease (in the second phase) as opposed to the role of environmental changes (in the first stage), medical strategy should pay more attention to the latter. Thus, for example, although a micro-organism often has to be present to cause an infectious disease it is not a sufficient condition. What has always been recognized in principle needs emphasis: the disease condition results from a particular interaction of host, bacterial agent, and social and environment situations. Successful antibiotic treatment may often depend on some of these other factors. Also, there is the possibility that influencing environmental factors in order to facilitate peaceful co-existence between host and agent might be an alternative, or at least complimentary strategy, to that of relying only on biochemical agents. As Dubos states it:

'It is clear, in conclusion, that the type of relationship existing at any given time between hosts and their parasites is the outcome of many different factors, including past racial experience, evolutionary adaptation through genetic changes and immunologic processes, and transient disturbances in the internal and external environments. In the classical infections of exogenous origin, the determining etiological event of the disease is exposure to the infective micro-organism. In endogenous microbial disease, the immediate cause is the environmental factor that upsets the biological equilibrium normally existing between the host and the microbial agents (persisters). ...

So far, the main goal of medical microbiology has been to prevent infection from taking place or, if it occurs, to treat disease once it has become established. The techniques designed to this end aim at attacking the microbial agents. It might be worth considering now whether useful practices of disease control can be derived from the fact that peaceful co-existence with pathogens often occurs in nature. This approach will require that the determinants of infection be separated conceptually from the determinants of disease; its objective will be to understand and control the processes responsible for converting infection into overt disease.' (Dubos, 1965: 194–5).

Societal Causes

It is within the context of this much more complex, ideological view of disease that the findings discussed in Chapter 9 become important. In the UK the major diseases, measured by the criteria of their contribution to lost working days[3] certified by a general practitioner, are cardiovascular disorders (accounting for 14 per cent of days lost for men and 9 per cent for women; respiratory disease (28 per cent and 19 per cent); accidents (7 per cent and 4 per cent); mental and nervous disease (13 per cent and 18 per cent); and muscular-skeletal diseases (12 per cent and 11 per cent) (DHSS, 1973a: 42–3)). Now, as we saw in Chapter 4 and Chapter 9, it is precisely for these diseases that there is growing evidence for a major aetiological contribution from social factors.

A high proportion of the conditions classified under three of these headings (mental and nervous, respiratory and accidents) for example, are known to have a very strong social class gradient (at least insofar as they cause death pp. 110–11) suggesting that aspects of societal organization a the distribution of power and advantage in society are major causes. Furthermore, cardiovascular disease, which also has a class gradient – but one which is not yet particularly strong[4] — is believed to be significantly related to smoking (as are many respiratory diseases which form another major category) as well as other socio-behavioural characteristics. Finally, there is growing evidence for the view that muscular-skeletal diseases, such as rheumatoid arthritis, have a complex socio-psychological aetiology (pp. 306—7).

In view of the earlier discussion of the success of present medical techniques a case can certainly be made for the view that alterations in the aspects of society that lead to these major conditions would do a lot more to influence a reduction in suffering than any amount of pharmaceutically or surgically based medical techniques — unless, that is, there is some major revolution in the latter's effectiveness. Smoking, for example, is a habit that has an important role in society, not least by creating a great deal of money for government and cigarette manufacturers and their employees. Yet, virtually *no* non-smoker will die from lung cancer (Doll and Hill, 1964). The Royal College of Physicians (1971: 27) estimated that there were 31,000 more deaths in Britain among men aged thirty-five to sixty-four than would have occured if they had all been non-smokers. Twenty thousand of these deaths were directly, and eleven thousand indirectly, attributable to smoking. Indeed 'if cigarette smoking were to cease there might in twenty years time be no more than 5,000 annual deaths from cancer of the lung'. At present, there are 35,000 deaths (CSO, 1974: 138). If present smoking habits continue, there will be 50,000 in twenty years time (Royal College of Physicians, 1971: 64). It seems likely that few medical or other actions would have anything like the effect on a disease that a successful ban on smoking would.

In various ways then our societal organization — the social structure and culture that distributes and perpetuates power and usual ways of doing things — is a major threat to health. Nowhere is this better illustrated than in the field of industrial accidents which, research suggests, are directly related to the hazards that we *create* in work situations. Manual workers in industry can expect to have at least one injury during their lifetime that will keep them off work for more than three days. Those in the building industry can expect three or four such accidents in their lifetime and one in fifty can expect to die in such an accident (Kinnersly, 1973: 94—211). A recent study by the National Institute of Industrial Psychology is interesting because it raised doubts about the extent to which these deaths and injuries can really be called 'accidents'. To reach their conclusions observers studied what happened on the shop-floor by working normal factory hours over a period of forty-two months. Among their conclusions they say:

'The three factors we found to be of over-riding influence on the accidents in this study were:
(a) that risks were so much an integral part of work systems as at

present arranged, that the more work was done, the more accidents occurred;

(b) that the risks which accompanied each task were specific and could be changed by changing details of the task;

(c) that people reduced their accident rate by gaining experience, i.e., they learned to avoid risks. But this experience was also highly specific and became blurred after time spent on other tasks. (Powell *et al.*, 1971: 36–7)

The investigators suggest that the 'two main lines of accident prevention policy must be a method of *design and layout*, which will eliminate hazards currently being built into systems of work, and *training*, to reduce the effects of inexperience' (Powell *et al.*, 1971: 37; italics in original).

They point out that one of the main problems is that 'much that is known about accident prevention is not applied' (1971: 36). The existing system of industrial organization does not motivate management to make strenuous efforts to prevent accidents. 'The true cost of injuring people is hardly noted by an industrial firm in its accounts' (1971: 46). The way things are organized safety measures are likely only to interfere with production and, by costing money or labour or time, reduce profits. As a more militant writer (Kinnersly, 1973) has put it, there is an inherent contradiction, in our system of industrial organization, between profits and the welfare of workers.

Medical Care Resources and Political Interests

The research findings I have reviewed in this chapter suggest that many currently applied medical techniques are of little intrinsic value. The vast majority of diseases which now contribute to death or days lost through sickness are medically neither preventible nor curable. Such findings suggest that certain aspects of the medical task outlined by Mckeown, notably the notion that a doctor can and should intervene physically and biochemically to cure disease, have wrongly attained higher priority than other aspects of the task such as alleviation and palliation – what I have been calling 'caring'.

I have also reviewed other evidence suggesting that the cause of many diseases that now constitute the disease burden of our society can be found in a complex chain of interaction between 'whole' humans and their physical and social environment – including the symbolic or cultural environment that gives individuals identity and meaning. Furthermore I have suggested in an earlier chapter that the reasons why many people choose to consult doctors are inextricably bound up with their social and emotional experience and cannot simply be seen in narrow 'medical' terms. As a result, therefore, of our increased knowledge of the kinds of conditions brought to doctors, of the effectiveness of most medical intervention, of the causes of many diseases, and of the way people use doctors, it is not difficult to make specific recommendations for changes in the role of doctors, in medical values, and in the distribution of resources allocated to improve health and alleviate disease.

At least two responses to this situation are possible — not necessarily mutually exclusive. One set of views advocates changes in the way doctors think of their role, suggesting either that they develop caring skills and broaden their area of operation to deal with the social and emotional problems that are part of much illness or that they scale down their area of operation and concentrate only on those conditions and those treatments where medical techniques are of proven efficacy. In this latter view the 'non-medical' aspects of the present task would be handed over to other members of a health team — social workers, nurses, health educators, rehabilitative workers, etc.

A second set of views, based on the evidence for a major societal element in aetiology, would support a redistribution of funds away from present health-care activities towards concentration on societal problems — housing, job satisfaction, poverty, the provision of play groups, changes in value systems, etc. In this view any 'medicalization' of problems that are really social in origin is reactionary because it obfuscates the relationship of society and disease and perpetuates a disease-provoking society. This view does not exclude the possibility of the medical alleviation and palliation of disease but suggests that this should not be done in such a way as to mystify the real cause of the problem. Disease in this view must be recognized as an inherent part of a particular form of social structure and culture and not an uncontrollable external event.

In the space available it is not my intention to add to the discussion of these possibilities any further. Rather I want to say something about the relationship of particular types of medical care strategy to the political and social structure and to attempt some explanation why, despite its manifest inappropriateness to the needs of many consumers of medical care, the present emphasis in medicine is likely to be perpetuated for a considerable time.

The first point to reiterate is the one made by Draper, Grenholm, and Best (p. 269) in an earlier chapter, namely that there is a great danger of falling into the 'single-best solution' fallacy. Both among the providers and consumers of care there is conflict and division of interest. On the side of providers there are many medical professionals, particularly those who are most influential in medical schools and the Royal Colleges of Physicians and Surgeons, who generally advocate further development in medicine along the scientific-technological-engineering road. A comparison with American medical care (for example an analysis of the hardware in use or of the specialties that have proliferated) shows that British medicine still has a considerable way to travel down that road. On the other hand there are other providers, such as many psychiatrists, geriatricians, and general practitioners — who together make up a very sizeable proportion of all doctors in the UK — who often support a broadening of the medical role and a much greater emphasis on palliation and alleviation. This latter viewpoint has been influential in reforms to the medical curriculum and in planning for future general practice (H.M. Government, 1968; BMA, 1970). The suggested reforms, however, have not yet obtained any sizeable backing in terms of resources.

On the side of consumers there are also divisions and conflicts. One excellent example of this is provided in a paper by Albee on the debate over the future direction of effort in the field of subnormality in the USA. Albee argues that there are, in terms of their medical care and medical research needs, two groups of patients. There are the majority — 'those who are normally slow, not victims of inherited or acquired diseases ... people who are born retarded simply because intelligence is distributed normally throughout the entire population' — and a sizeable minority — 'those who are retarded because of organic reasons, like injuries, trauma, infections and biochemical imbalances' (Albee, 1970: 27 and 29). The majority group require 'not medical treatment, but rehabilitative training — so that they can use their maximum potential'. Such individuals can, according to a special panel set up by President Kennedy, 'with specific training and assistance, acquire limited job skills and achieve a high measure of independence; they represent 85 per cent of the retarded group' (President's Panel, 1962). In the case of the minority group, however, research may show how intervention can prevent retardation by bio-chemical or other means. It is in this direction that most medical care and research is heavily biased — to the extent that very few resources are diverted to training and care for the majority. According to Albee what has happened is that a combination of factors has enabled the minority group of patients to benefit at the expense of the majority — although how much they will benefit from the research remains an open question. Because of various forms of gene linkage majority type retardation is somewhat less common in high IQ families than in low IQ families and therefore occurs most commonly in lower-class families (which have a smaller proportion of high IQ individuals). The various charities involved in funding research are of course dominated by middle-class parents who have tended to see the problem in terms of the minority. Biochemical studies of the urine, blood, and tissues of retarded patients have been undertaken and research on defects or absences of necessary metabolic enzymes have been supported. Albee argues that this direction of effort is further accentuated by the failure of middle-class society to accept and recognize that some people are 'naturally slow' just as others are 'naturally geniuses' and that the former do not fit in with the kinds of life-style available. Finally, the allocation of research money to complex (and esoteric) biochemical relationships is compatible with the high status enjoyed by scientific and engineering medicine reflecting a lack of concern with the more simple, caring aspects of medicine.

This example, and there are many more, makes it clear that decisions about medical care provision, which are invariably decisions about priorities to be given to one group rather than another, are influenced by, and influence, wider political and social questions. Discussions about the allocation of resources to health care as opposed to other social or environmental services are of the same kind.

It follows from this discussion that it is likely that the existing distribution of medical care effort, and the fate of any attempt to alter it, are significantly influenced by those who gain from it — particular patients, particular doctors, the medical equipment supply industry, drug companies, and so on. To continue with the earlier example, an alteration of spending patterns on mental subnormality in the USA, would reduce the funds allocated to specific research institutions and redistribute resources from one group of patients to another. It could also reduce the demand for drugs. Many individuals and organizations benefit from the current allocation of medical care effort. In addition, the present allocation is supported by a set of beliefs and values that are continuously propagated and reinforced — like those of any other ideology.

In Chapter 10, David Field drew attention to what has been termed the increased 'medicalization' of society — the use of a particular version of the medical model to account for a whole range of phenomena not unambiguously caused by underlying disease processes. Some recent work on drug company advertising illustrates the way a particular medical version of day-to-day problems is promoted by drug companies anxious to increase their profit margin.

'On the inside front cover of a professional journal (Journal of the American College Health Association, 1969) an advertisement states: "A whole new world ... of anxiety ... To help free her of excessive anxiety ... adjunctive Librium." Accompanying the bold print is a full-page picture of an attractive, worried-looking woman, standing with an armful of books. In captions surrounding her, the potential problems of a new college student are foretold: "Exposure to new friends and other influences may force her to reevaluate herself and her goals. ... Her newly stimulated intellectual curiosity may make her more sensitive to and apprehensive about unstable national and world conditions." The text suggests that Librium (chlordiazepoxide HCL), together with counseling and reassurance, "can help the anxious student to handle the primary problem and to 'get her back on her feet.'" Thus, the normal problems and conflicts associated with the status change and personal growth that accompany the college experience are relabeled as medical-psychiatric problems and as such are subject to amelioration through Librium.

In another journal (American Journal of Diseases of Childhood, 1969) an advertisement advises a physician how he can help deal with such everyday anxieties of childhood as school and dental visits. It portrays a tearful little girl, and in large type appear the words: "School, the dark, separation, dental visits, 'monsters'." On the subsequent page the physician is told in bold print that "the everyday anxieties of childhood sometimes get out of hand." In small print below he reads that "a child can usually deal with his anxieties. But sometimes the anxieties over-power the child. Then, he needs your help ... Your help may include Vistaril (hydroxyzine pamoate)." ' (Lennard, 1971: 20–1)

American advertising may be more extreme but the same tendency can also be observed in the UK where one can find:

'C.I.B.A. Pharmaceutical Company's man with the megaphone head which they used to suggest to doctors the use of their habit-forming drug Ritalin for "environmental depression" caused by "NOISE: a new social problem"; Merke, Sharp and Dohme's picture of a heavily made-up woman with "Lady, your anxiety is showing" written across her face for whom they enjoin the use of Triavil, their mixture of an anti-depressant and major tranquillizer, to deal with her depression and anxiety; U.S.V. Pharmaceutical Corporation's picture of a gorgeous young woman with a "swimsuit by Jantzen and a body by 'Dexaspan' ", which is their strongly habit-forming mixture of amphetamine and barbiturate; Geigy Corporation's picture of a man with a 100-pound weight instead of a head on top of his shoulders, with which they advertise the use of their anti-depressant drug, Tofranil, for "when depression comes to mind"; Sandos Pharmaceuticals' advertisements with which they suggest the use of their major tranquilizer, Mellaril, for the doctor's "little patients"; "Dennis the Menace", with whom "a quiet moment is unknown", "and here's Sulky Sue, what shall we do". Mellaril will presumably quieten Dennis the Menace, and according to Sandos, it will make Sue more amenable; Eli Lilly and Company's photograph of the man who "tries to hide fear behind bravado" for whom they recommend their anti-depressant, Aventyl, and finally their picture of a Tuinal Capsule, their expensive mixture of barbiturates, to wish you "good night".' (Malleson, 1973: 68–9)

Such advertising attempts to exert a powerful influence on public opinion and professional advice and contrasts with Cochrane's evaluation of the effectiveness of psychotropic drugs:

'Present-day psychiatry is therefore in my view basically inefficient in that it encourages the use of therapies, many of which are of unknown effectiveness and which may possibly be dangerous ... I would ban the prescription of amphetamines and put a large number of other psycho-tropic drugs on a list which could only be prescribed by psychiatric consultants ... [since] there are fewer consultants than GPs it will make the prescriptions more difficult to get.' (1972: 59–60)

He advocates urgent action to rectify the lack of adequate RCTs.

In 1971 the pharmaceutical industry spent over £15 million advertising its products to sell to the National Health Service. In the same year 24,668 general practitioners wrote 294,389,000 prescriptions – 11,934 each (DHSS, 1974b: 28, 85). One English general practitioner reported that he was receiving, on average, fourteen pounds of drug advertising through his front door every month (Wilson and Hooper, 1966). As we have seen earlier in the chapter a large number of the products advertised are of unproven value.

The weight of all this drug company activity, presumably regarded as efficacious by them, is not effectively countered by any alternative view of the solution to medical problems. Although governments attempt to monitor drugs for safety there is no compulsion in the UK to prove effectiveness – if there was, many drugs would disappear without trace. The effect of drug advertising, together with the way the media present health issues (pp. 271–3), make it easy for individuals to equate recovery from complaints with medication. It seems not unnatural to believe that future advances in medicine will be in the field of pharmaceutical or surgical 'miracles' although the facts, as we have seen, provide no such optimism.

As well as the powerful interests of drug companies, medical supply industries and the like, the existing distribution of health care effort is also reinforced by the existing distribution of power and prestige within the medical profession and the medical schools. No director of research demonstrating the ineffectiveness of medical techniques by means of randomized controlled trials has received the Nobel prize. Medical salaries, via the existing merit awards are biased in favour of those making engineering type innovations – at the expense of the consultants trying to help the old and the mentally ill. [5] Staffing arrangements in medical schools continue to promote scientific-engineering perspectives: at a recently established medical school three new professors in physiology have taken precedence over any in family medicine. Similarly, when the health service was re-organized, despite the tremendous importance attached to role definition, career structure, and responsibility to those working in the new service (pp. 276–8), there was one notable absence – health education – an area of activity involving intervention quite different to that implied in the engineering model. Furthermore, the budget allocated to health education, remained rather less than that allocated to Librium alone.

The present direction of health-care effort, therefore, is supported by powerful vested interests and if the direction is to be altered equally powerful mobilization will be required to support it. The employers of medical care, patients, many of whose interests are patently not served by the present distribution of care resources, provide one possibility of alternative power. The 'problem' with patients as a pressure group, if that is how one sees it, it analogous to sociological discussions of power and mobilization introduced by authors like Marx (1963), Truman (1951), Smelser (1962) and Lockwood (1958) – to take but a few examples. In such approaches one distinction often made is that between manifest and latent interests. The distinction rests on the fact that although an analytic perspective may indicate shared (latent) interests within one group of people that are opposed to those of another (the classic Marxian example is that of proletariat and capitalists) this is not necessarily the way the individuals themselves see it and it is quite possible that some individuals with the same latent interests will oppose each other – tendentiously termed 'false consciousness'. In studies of trade-union growth the isolation of individuals with similar latent interests, the lack of information and feedback about the relationship of each person's relationship to others (patients think it is only they, or their relatives who are not cured by one or other form of treatment), individual apathy, and the difficulty of communicating, increase the possibility of false consciousness and make it difficult for them to act as a coherent group – thus making it impossible to act as a political force. Patients, who do not come together in the way factory workers do, are necessarily isolated, and it is for this reason that they are particularly vulnerable to the picture painted by the mass media, which by mystifying the reality of medicine, gives them the impression that it is successful with most other patients: if they, or their relatives, were not cured it must have been bad luck. The provision of consumer information to patients (in my view a form of health education) and the presentation of research findings (by medical sociologists and others) to the public are therefore important if patient power is to become realized. It is possible that, if they develop their own systems of information collection and dissemination, the new community health councils set up in 1974 (p. 277) will perform an important function. Producer groups, such as ancillary workers in hospitals, who are less tied to the existing distribution of resources and who are also a large potential patient group, may also have a similar (potential) role.

Certainly, at the present time, there is an effective alliance between, on the one hand, the most influential doctors, the drug companies, and some patients and a lack of effective counter-action on the part of other patients. While this situation persists it is difficult to see how those individual doctors, and others, who want to change the direction of care will be successful.

The Doctor's Dilemma

Nonetheless, I think it would be quite wrong to suggest that the only reasons for the domination of the present approach to medicine (despite its lack of effectiveness) are entirely the result of power and politics. Even if consumers were well organized, not apathetic, and able to exert their authority as employers of health services there would still be another fundamental problem which I mentioned in an earlier chapter and which derives from the essentially individualistic nature of clinical practice. I should like to end this chapter by pursuing this a little further.

The nature of the clinical contact between the typical doctor and his patient is an individual one. The patient comes to the doctor with a problem and, whatever it is, he wants the doctor to do something about it. Now, as I have suggested elsewhere in this chapter, it is very unlikely that the doctor will be able to do as the patient wants. Just as he often does not have the appropriate technology to cure most symptoms so he cannot give all his patients council houses or good jobs. It is highly probable that, regardless of the doctor's intervention, the patient's disease, though perhaps alleviated somewhat, will continue to disable him or sooner or later kill him. In the case of a 'non-medical' symptom the problem will also probably continue to persist. I have elsewhere described this situation as the fifth conflict in the doctor's role (p. 196), and it is a situation that I believe to be *by far the most common in medical practice.* Faced with it the doctor has to be content with trying to alleviate the patient's suffering or, in the case of the 'non-medical' problem, help the patient to embark on a course of action, perhaps with the doctor's and others' help, that may change his situation in the long run. Either course involves the doctor in a caring human relationship and involves the doctor admitting to himself, and perhaps also to the patient, that he has no wonder cure. This difficulty will be intensified by the fact that the patient, relatives, and the doctor are likely to be emotionally upset at the patient's suffering and by the fact that, as we have been discussing, the popular view of medicine is one of a highly potent form of intervention.

The role I have outlined, and the role I considered in much more detail in Chapter 6, is not an easy one. It involves coming to terms with the limits of reality and demands considerable personal maturity. It is also unlikely, at least with some patients, to be a popular role. The honest doctor who recognizes he can rarely offer a cure will find his role distinctly unrewarding — particularly if he entered the profession with the popular stereotype of its efficacy. The satisfaction that this doctor derives from his work will have to come not from the production of wonder cures but from his ability to help patients cope with their suffering and make the best of their situation. The importance of medical education and social and professional support is to allow doctors to reward themselves by this kind of activity — as I discussed in Chapter 7.

In practice (see Chapter 6) the acceptance of the doctor's limited role in helping his patients is frequently avoided and is one reason why RCTs, and similar controlled studies (which in any case require a certain degree of sophisticated understanding of notions of probability and an ability to think in population rather than individual terms), are too threatening to be considered by most clinicians. There can always be exceptions to any scientific generalization and it is natural to hope (particularly if a patient is going to die) that with any luck one will turn up 'this' time. Furthermore the cost in terms of alternate use of resources is more difficult to conceptualize than the cost of his disease to a suffering patient. The escalating number of prescriptions and the increased volume of tests, operations, and out-patient referrals can be interpreted as the product of a failure to face up to the facts. Many medical actions are magical placebos designed to convince doctor and patient that something is being done, that the situation is under control. As Cochrane put it, two sections of the community (doctor and patient) take the rest for 'an inflationary ride'. The underlying problem and ways of handling it remain as a result largely unconfronted – when financial constraints are reached then we all blame the Department of Health or the Treasury for not devoting enough money to health care.

There is a further related difficulty which may be still more fundamental: in compensation for the tremendous negative rewards to be derived from admitting failure there are few positive ones. If operations fail then at least doctor and relatives can say they have tried. If operations (that have little chance of succeeding) are not done, patients and relatives are likely to complain and those who benefit as a result – for example the people who do not get ill as a result of a diversion of medical resources to improve housing conditions or to provide day care centres – are unlikely to thank the doctors and relatives. There are few thanks from present generations who never got polio or dyphtheria or smallpox as a result of preventive measures. They don't know what they've missed. It seems that by their very essence preventive measures are much less likely to be rewarded than curative ones (which fail!).

In short, although it is easy for economists, sociologists, or community medicine specialists to talk about the cost-benefit relationships of medical procedures that have low effectiveness, it is a different matter for the clinician in the field, or the politician on the husting, who take the blame. My argument is that medical problems that have group causes are presented individually. Only if we can develop a way of rewarding the allocation of resources to groups and still keep individuals happy, perhaps by much greater public debate and increased honesty about the issues, are we likely to succeed in shifting resources out of curative medicine towards (often non-health service) preventive action. In this view the present elitist structure of the health service and the increased central control discussed in Chapter 8 are likely to constitute retrograde steps. Much of our health care is likely to continue to emphasize impossible cures and thus to inhibit health and promote suffering. It is fortunate that none of these arguments apply to alleviation or palliation which can produce an immediate response from patients, and hence a reward for doctors.

Notes

1. The significance of diagnosis in labelling the problem was discussed in the last chapter (pp. 354–9).
2. There are numerous difficulties in comparing rates over time because of changes in

classification procedures and so on. However, taking account of these difficulties the Registrar-General estimates that the conclusion reported, that there is no evidence of an improvement in the relative standing of unskilled workers, and some evidence of a decline, seems plausible (Registrar-General, 1969: 18–29).

3. I give women's figures, but since statistics for days lost through sickness for women are very unreliable (because they often do not bother to get a certificate) they should be regarded as highly tentative.

4. 'Yet' seems appropriate in view of the dramatic changes in the trend over the last three sets of figures.

5. This can be seen by looking at the distribution of awards in the Annual Report of the DHSS. Cardiology (68% of consultants having awards); neurology (58%); neurosurgery (69.1%); plastic surgery (52.8%) and thoracic surgery (79.8%) have the highest rates and represent the prestige part of the profession. Those working in mental health (23.7%) and geriatrics (21.2%) are at the bottom. As we have seen, without denigrating the achievements of the former group, there is no good evidence to suggest this is the priority the society needs. (DHSS, 1973b: 182–3)

References

Albee, G.W. (1970) A Revolution in Caring for the Retarded. In Strauss, A. (ed.), *Where Medicine Fails.* Chicago: Aldine.

Barnes, E. (1961) *People in Hospital.* London: Macmillan and Co.
A report of a study group looking at psychological problems of general hospitals. It contains many provocative findings and much good quality ancedotal material.

BMA Planning Unit (1970) *Primary Medical Care.* London: BMA.
A report of a working party on the future of general practice.

Central Statistical Office (1973) *National Income and Expenditure 1973.* London: HMSO.

Cochrane, A.L. (1972) *Effectiveness and Efficiency: Random Reflections on the Health Service.* The Rock Carding Lecture 1971. London: The Nuffield Provincial Hospitals Trust.
A concise monograph publicizing and evaluating evidence relating to the effectiveness of current medical treatments. Professor Cochrane is director of the MRC Epidemiology Unit in Cardiff.

Dawson, J.L.Y., Devadatta, S., Fox, W., Radharkrisna, S., Ramakrishnan, C.V., Somasundarah, P.R., Stott, H., Tripathy, S.P., and Velu, S. (1966) Tuberculosis Chemotherapy Centre, Madras. A five-year study of patients with pulmonary tuberculosis – a current comparison of home and sanatorium treatment for 1 year with isoniazed plus P.A.S. *Bulletin of the World Health Organization* **34**: 533–51.

Department of Health and Social Security (1973a) *The State of the Public Health, The Annual Report of the Chief Medical Officer for the Year 1972.* London: HMSO.

– (1973b) *Annual Report 1972.* London: HMSO.

– (1974a) *Hospital Costing Returns.* London: HMSO.

– (1974b) *Health and Personal Social Service Statistics for England 1974.* London: HMSO.

Doll, R. and Hill, A. (1964) Mortality in Relation to Smoking: Ten Years Observations of British Doctors. *British Medical Journal* **1**: 1399, 1460.

Central Statistical Office (1974) *Social Trends 1973.* London: HMSO.

The famous prospective study of cancer and smoking among British doctors.

Dubos, R. (1965) *Man Adapting.* New Haven: Yale University Press. This is a fascinating account of the kinds of relationships that exist between microbes and humans.

Epson, J.E. (1969) *The Mobile Health Clinic.* An Interim Report on a preliminary analysis of the first 1,000 patients to attend. London: London Borouth of Southwark Health Department (mimeo). See chapter 5.

General Register Office (1969) *The Registrar General's Quarterly Return for England and Wales, quarter ended 30 June, 1969.* London: HMSO.

Haas, J.H. (1968) Geographical Pathology of the Major Killing Disorders, Cancer and Cardiovascular Disease. In G. Wolsenholme and H. O'Connor (eds.), *Health of Mankind,* CIBA Foundation 100th symposium. London: Churchill.

Harpur, J.E., Kellett, R.J., Conner, W.T., Galbraith, H.-J.B., Hamilton, M., Murray, J.J., Swallow, J.H., and Rose, G.A. (1971) Controlled Study of Early Mobilisation and Discharge from Hospital in Uncomplicated Myocardial Infarction. *The Lancet* ii: 1331—4.

H.M. Government (1968) *Royal Commission on Medical Education. Report* (Todd Report). London: HMSO.

Holland, W. (1971) Clinicians and the Use of Medical Resources. *The Hospital (London)* 67: 236—9, July.

Illich, I. (1974) *Medical Nemesis: The Expropriation of Health.* London: Calder & Boyars.

A provocative and stimulating, but highly polemical and controversial, attack on the current direction of health care, written from a theological point of view. For Illich pain and suffering are significant human experiences and medical effort, especially when much of it is piatrogenic, takes these away from people. Individuals have forgotten how to care for themselves and others and the 'medical establishment has become a major threat to health'. It is necessary to recover self reliance urgently.

Kinnersley, P. (1973) *The Hazards of Work and How to Fight Them.* London: Pluto Press.

This is a polemical but useful book which graphically draws attention to the serious disadvantages of manual workers in terms of health. The data is based largely on official statistics.

Lennard, H., Epstein, L.J., Bernstein, A., and Ransan, D.C. (1971) *Mystification and Drug Misuse, Hazards in Using Psychoactive Drugs.* New York: Perennial Library.

A polemical but very readable account of the relationships of doctors, patients, and society to drugs of both a medical and illegal kind.

Lockwood, D. (1958) *The Black-Coated Worker.* London: Routledge & Kegan Paul.

Malleson, A. (1973) *Need Your Doctor be So Useless?* London: George Allen and Unwin.

A polemical attack by a psychiatrist on the traditional therapeutic model particularly in psychiatry.

Marx, K. (1963) *Early Writings.* Trans. T.B. Bottomore. London: Watts & Co.

McDermott, W. (1969) Demography, Culture, and Economics and the Evolutionary Stages of Medicine. In E.D. Kilbourne and W.G. Smillie (eds.), *Human Ecology and Public Health* (4th edition). London: Collier-Macmillan.

A neat and insightful analysis of the effectiveness of medicine in different times and places. The idea of three stages is taken from here.

Mckeown, T. (1971a) A Sociological Approach to the History of Medicine. In G.

McLachlan and T. Mckeown (eds.), *Medical History and Medical Care*. Oxford: Oxford University for the Nuffield Provincial Hospitals Trust.

— (1971b) A Historical Appraisal of the Medical Task. In G. McLachlan and T. Mckeown (eds.), *Medical History and Medical Care*.

Medical Research Council (1966) Comparative Trial of Surgery and Radiotherapy for The Primary Treatment of Small-celled or Oat-celled Carcinoma of the Bronchus. *The Lancet* ii: 979--86.

Morris, D., Ward, A., and Handyside, A.J. (1968) Early Discharge After Hernia Repair. *Lancet* i: 681—85.

Morris, J. (1964) *Uses of Epidemiology* (2nd edition). Edinburgh: Livingstone.
An excellent introduction to epidemiology.

Office of Health Economics (1971a) *Off Sick*. London: Office of Health Economics.

— (1971b) *Hypertension, A Suitable Case for Treatment*. London: Office of Health Economics.

Pearse, I. and Crocker, L. (1944) *The Peckham Experiment*. London: George Allen and Unwin.

Porter, H. (1972) The Contribution of the Biological and Medical Sciences to Human Welfare. Presidential Address of the British Association for the Advancement of Science. Swansea Meeting, 1971.

Powell, P.I., Hale, M., Morton, J., and Simon, M. (1971) *2000 Accidents: A Shop Floor Study of Their Causes*. Report No. 21. London: National Institute for Industrial Psychology.

Powles, J. (1973) On the Limitations of Modern Medicine. *Science Medicine and Man* 1: 31—48.
This paper raises many of the issues discussed in this chapter and has been quite heavily drawn on.

Presidents Panel on Mental Retardation (1962) *A Proposed Program for National Action to Combat Mental Retardation*. US Public Health Service, Washington D.C.: US Government Printing Office.

Razzell, P.E. (1965) Population Change in Eighteenth-century England. A Re-interpretation. *Economic History Review*, selected series, 18: 312—32.

Registrar-General (1969) *Decennial Supplement, 1961: Occupational Mortality Tables, England and Wales*. London: HMSO.

Royal College of Physicians of London (1971) *Smoking and Health Now*. London: Pitman Medical.
A well argued and accessible documentation of the facts about smoking and health.

Smelser, N.J. (1962) *The Theory of Collective Behaviour*. London: Routledge & Kegan Paul.

Stocks, P. (1949) *Sickness in the Population of England and Wales*. Studies on Medical and Population Subjects, No.2 London: HMSO.

Truman, D. (1951) *The Governmental Process*. New York: A.A. Knopf.

US Department of Health, Education and Welfare (1971) *Leading Components of Upturn Mortality in Men, United States, 1952—67*. Vital and Health Statistics, Series 20, No. 11. Washington D.C.: US Government Printing Office.

Wadsworth, M., Butterfield, W.J.H., and Blaney, R. (1971) *Health and Sickness: The Choice of Treatment*. London: Tavistock.

Welsh Office (1974) *Health and Personal Social Services Statistics for Wales No. 1. 1974*. Cardiff: HMSO.

Wilson, A.T. and Hooper, G. (1966) One Year's Advertisements. *British Medical Journal* 1: 542.

Name Index

Subject Index